Houghton Mifflin Company Editorial Adviser in Education

HEROLD C. HUNT

CHARLES WILLIAM ELIOT PROFESSOR OF EDUCATION

HARVARD UNIVERSITY

HOUGHTON MIFFLIN COMPANY · BOSTON

THE CHANGING

SOVIET SCHOOL

The Comparative Education Society
Field Study in the U.S.S.R.

EDITED BY

GEORGE Z. F. BEREDAY

WILLIAM W. BRICKMAN

GERALD H. READ

WITH THE ASSISTANCE OF

INA SCHLESINGER

THE RIVERSIDE PRESS · CAMBRIDGE

CONTENTS

v

PART THREE

FOREWORD

"A n enigma inside a riddle
wrapped in a mystery" — this was the description Winston Churchill
applied to the Soviet Union during World War II. Later he referred to
it as the "iron curtain" country.

The continuance of these impressions, world-wide, probably influenced
Soviet leaders to approve, early in 1958, an agreement between the
United States of America and the Union of Soviet Socialist Republics
permitting an exchange of missions in cultural, technical, and educational
fields. Implementation of this agreement has made possible many visits
between the two nations.

One such visit this volume, *The Changing Soviet School*, describes.
Made under the auspices of the Comparative Education Society, it
involved the participation of more than seventy of its members who
spent a month late in the summer of 1958 in an intensive tour of the
U.S.S.R., visiting schools, colleges, universities, collective farms, and
industrial plants, and, in general, seeking to learn about Soviet life and
culture.

Subsequently the collaborative efforts of the participants were organized into a book by George Bereday, William Brickman, Gerald
Read, and their associates, and this has resulted in the most intensive
reporting of any organized tour to date.

Certain to complement the literature in an area of significant and
continuing interest, *The Changing Soviet School* is presented not only as
an authoritative analysis of Soviet educational practices at the time of
observation but against a carefully authenticated background of historical
reference antedating the 1917 Revolution. Changes in educational
policy occurring since the visit, already operative or contemplated, are
likewise treated.

Inherent in *The Changing Soviet School* is the obvious challenge confronting American education today. Practices which the study reports reflect the close relationships among government, industry, society, and education. Education in the U.S.S.R., it is clear, is used as a tool to further the realization of Soviet goals, whatever they may be. "Without teaching," Lenin once observed, "there is no knowledge; without knowledge there is no communism."

Education in a free society does not operate in the Soviet manner. We must, therefore, meet the challenge in our own way. Education in the Soviet Union is apparently serving effectively the needs of that country, but its spirit and purpose are so contrary to the objectives our people and nation have for their schools and colleges as to make comparisons with the educational process in the United States difficult if not meaningless. Our emphasis, since the origin of the first school here, on freedom and individual initiative, resourcefulness and responsibility, makes it impossible to assess the respective merits of the two systems of education, so different are their basic concepts. Understanding of this difference is essential, however, and it is to this understanding that *The Changing Soviet School* contributes.

Here, in essence, is the value of this volume. It is to be hoped that wide reading and study will complement the efforts, individual and collective, which it represents. The Comparative Education Society is to be warmly commended for its professional contribution.

HEROLD C. HUNT

INTRODUCTION

Since the day when, some 150 years ago, a Frenchman, Jullien de Paris, put out the first pamphlet on comparative education, a handful of scholars have worked toward the acceptance of a simple principle. They believed that knowledge of foreign education helps in understanding one's own schools and in devising sound educational policy. This principle is now generally recognized. In particular, it is now plain that our lack of knowledge of Soviet education has had an important bearing upon our own educational successes and failures.

The need for accumulating pertinent facts and analyzing them in terms of broad social considerations has not been lessened now that our initial indifference to the work of the Soviet schools has been replaced by a flood of reports, some competent, some naïve. Are the Soviet schools really a mortal challenge, a military operation organized for a breakthrough? Or are they, rather, like all other educational systems, a blend of old beliefs and new ambitions, hopeful of their potential but not too certain of their methods? There is an obvious reason for continuing serious research. Brick by brick, the edifice of sound knowledge and mature scholarship has to be built. The number of Americans deeply familiar with and attuned to the rhythm of Soviet culture must continue to grow. In particular, we must work to overcome our painful deficiency in following the written sources and to add to our scanty capital of direct observation.

The present book engages in some exploration of the primary and secondary materials on Soviet Education. The core of the book, however, and its claim to strength, is the record of the observations made by some seventy American educators who spent one month in the Soviet Union in August and September of 1958. Half of their time was spent in conferences with educational officials in Moscow, Leningrad, Kiev, and Tashkent. The other half was used to visit the schools. The recorded notes of the participants were absorbed into the main part of this book. We hope that these eyewitness accounts, in spite of their obvious limitations, will add to the store of information about the Soviet system and complement the few existing studies based on research in published Soviet sources.

The emphasis of this book is on the *changing* Soviet school. The newly enacted reforms in Soviet education bear witness to the interdependence of the Soviet school and the evolving Soviet society. Since the school is an important index of the continuities and changes to which that society is subject, we shall not have a good picture of the total span of the evolution which Soviet institutions are undergoing without a record of the schools for each relevant period.

The book is written according to the following plan:

Part One is a summary of the philosophical, social, and historical antecedents of the present-day school. It is concerned with the spectrum of cultural forces — the traditional Russian nationalism and Western ambitions, the Communist reformist zeal, and the prerevolutionary respect for classicism and science — that affect the Soviet school. The convergence of psychological, political, economic, and social factors determines current pedagogical direction. An understanding of the contemporary Soviet educational scene depends upon a familiarity with these introductory materials.

Part Two describes the Soviet school in its formal organization. It reports on the educational theory and practice at preschool, primary, secondary, and higher-education levels. The major emphasis is on secondary education. The three chapters devoted to this subject explore its general characteristics, its old methods of instruction, and its new move toward polytechnization. Since the major policy decisions now being worked out in the Soviet Union deal with the secondary-school level, it is a focal point in our discussion. At the same time, for the sake of continuity and completeness, this crucial level has to be placed in its context. Hence it is preceded by a study of preschool and primary education and followed by a description of the universities and institutes and agencies for teacher training, and of teacher activities.

Part Three surveys selected issues in Soviet education. Many vital problems could be fruitfully isolated for study both because of their importance for the U.S.S.R. and because of the lessons they afford for other countries. Because the Soviet school is universal in its reach, what it does with its marginal groups, the talented and the handicapped, is of interest and relevance. Because it plans for an organized absorption of children into the framework of its *Weltanschauung,* a survey of its out-of-school provisions and of its philosophy of moral education is to the point.

An advanced comparative analysis cannot take place without abundant descriptive data. A picture of the Soviet school as free as possible from the biases of its admirers and its critics should aid our understanding of the coming educational revolution.

Our purpose is, first of all, to supply a photograph of the Soviet school system as it was on a significant watershed. During the school year beginning in September, 1958, the reform movement for the poly-technization of Soviet schools, revived in 1952, received national sanction in legislative form. Henceforth, over a period of five to seven years, an attempt will be made to rebuild the system and to channel a signifi-cant proportion of youth of the university-entrance age directly into pro-duction. A record of school practices taken in September, 1958, therefore, catches the system at a significant moment. We may speculate whether the monopoly of the traditional emphasis dominant in the last twenty-five years of Soviet practice is to be broken or whether, in spite of the projected program of drastic changes, much of this traditionalism will persist. From talks with Soviet educators, and from the as yet feeble attempts at practical implementation of the reforms, one can get the initial sense of the nature of such change as is likely to take place.

A second reason for this book is that a close observation of any phase of Russian reforms refines our feeling for the dynamics of the Soviet system. The postwar economic recovery of the country shows that as a static system it is capable of survival and self-preservation. But it is as a dynamic system, a system whose potential for development can give us comfort or cause anxiety, that we need to know it. Obviously the dynamics of change in schools are not the same as the dynamics of change in other, more spectacular areas of Soviet economy. We need to know more clearly the potential effectiveness of a school program upon the economic and social areas. But the dynamics of the Soviet schools give us some idea, however small, about the over-all potential of the system, the energy or apathy of its people, their conviction or cynicism, their self-centeredness or altruism. When observed in the schools, these factors give an insight into the wider issues.

Our third purpose is to demonstrate the similarity of the American and Soviet system inherent in their mass character. In spite of the great difference in philosophy and politics, there are areas of resemblance that only recently have become apparent. For instance, most people pressing for education of the gifted in this country seem to assume that the Russians have it and frequently point to the Russian system as an example.

In actual fact, the pressure for education of the gifted within the formal system appeared in Russia about the same time as it appeared here, and the omission of such proposals from the recent legislation indicates clearly that there are groups strongly opposing them. The pressure for concentration on high ability is an inevitable corollary of the diffusion of attention necessary to run a system of education for all. Polytechnization, too, is a mass-education phenomenon. How to bring specific groups of students to the university-entrance level and under the same roof train the remainder (and a majority) in immediately practical skills has been one of the major problems of mass education. Above all, how to prevent each of these groups from discouraging the other, while maintaining a close contact between them in the interest of social fraternity and harmony, is a question paramount in educational thinking today. Soviet education must be watched closely for any answers it may be able to supply us in what is essentially our common dilemma.

There is merit in having persons who are thoroughly at home in various branches of pedagogy in their own country scrutinize the relevant areas in another. The size of our group, larger than any other group of American educators ever to visit the Soviet Union, enabled us to plan a thorough program of visits. Divided into committees concentrating on aspects of education on which the participants work in the United States, the members were able to apportion the labors of the study and each person's responsibility was limited to the area of relevant competence. Our professor of geography studied nothing but the teaching of geography, our professors of childhood education devoted themselves to the kindergarten, and so on. The fact that this was not an official project, but that the group were guests of the Trade Union of Educational, Cultural, and Scientific Research Workers, insured not only greater informality but also better opportunity to linger around the schools and to prepare each visit ahead of time with the teachers involved.

With this book in mind, we also briefed the participants before their departure and exhorted them throughout the preceding year to acquire a smattering of the Russian language. In the latter insistence we were far from successful. But the group did contain twelve people who had a sufficient command of Russian to follow the proceedings with some understanding. The three leaders of the group, Dr. William W. Brickman, Dr. Gerald Read, and Dr. William H. E. Johnson (as well as Dr. George Bereday, Editor of the Society's *Comparative Education Review*, who did not participate in the field study but who assumed general editorial responsibility for this volume), had all previously been to the Soviet Union, one for a period of two years. Two had spent two weeks in Moscow the preceding winter specifically preparing the study with their Soviet colleagues. Two had spent a month in the summer of the same year as members of the Seminar on Soviet Education at the Institute for the Study of the U.S.S.R. in Munich, Germany. No one can claim that our results have been achieved by watertight research. But we did take as many precautions as were feasible under the circumstances.

We tried to spread those members of the group who had taught or written on Soviet affairs so as to insure the presence of a specialist in places and at times crucial to our purpose. Each morning meetings were held at which the findings of the preceding day were analyzed by the team as a whole and summarized for further inquiry. The visits to schools were preceded, as is the Soviet custom, by conferences with the director of each establishment. The team also tried to follow up its work by personal interviews with key people. Much of the interviewing had, of course, to be done with the help of Russian interpreters, but the presence in our group of people who understood Russian insured some system of double check on their work. As a consequence, we avoided such common misunderstandings as putting the American interpretation on the Russian word for *school* or confusing the adjective *Russian* with the word *Soviet*. The need for careful interpreting in intercultural encounters cannot be too strongly emphasized. It can serve as an example of the difficulties attendant upon and the care that has to be exercised in undertaking enterprises of this kind.

In future years we plan to organize several further studies in the Soviet Union and thus to follow up our findings. For the time being, we present them, with all their limitations, as a record of the team's observations. For this reason we also include a good many verbatim quotations by Soviet educators themselves. One never knows what and how much in these statements is pious hope, what is descriptive of actual practice, and what is a summary of achievements. But there is an advantage in knowing just how professional workers in the Soviet Union rationalize to themselves the system under which they are forced to live. We are responsible only for the accuracy of these quotations, although, of course, our interpretations are our own.

Our gratitude goes to Ivan I. Grivkow, President of the Trade Union of Educational, Cultural, and Research Workers, who generously acted as host throughout the visit. Our thanks are especially due to the Fund for the Advancement of Education of the Ford Foundation, for a grant that made the preparation of this volume possible. We also wish to acknowledge our debt to Dr. William H. E. Johnson and to Mr. R. V. Rapacz for their help in some phases of the editorial work. Mr. Nicholas DeWitt of the Russian Research Center of Harvard University read the entire manuscript and deserves credit for his many comments, without which this book would have been considerably weaker. Miss Sharon Kiyama has our thanks as an invaluable chief typist and commentator. Mrs. Ina Schlesinger acted as research assistant in the project. Her patient effort is evident and acknowledged through every page of this work.

G. Z. F. B.
W. W. B.
G. H. R.

PARTICIPANTS

The following members of The Comparative Education Society participated in the Soviet Field Study, 1958:

Annie Elizabeth Adams, Surrey County Council, Kingston-upon-Thames, England
Juul Altena, Wagner College
Wilma M. Barnett, Muskingum College
Alan E. Beeman, University of Wisconsin
Ellen Y. Beeman, University of Wisconsin
William F. Benjamin, George Peabody College for Teachers
Clarence Bergeson, University of Maine
Edna A. Bottorf, Lock Haven State Teachers College, Pennsylvania
William W. Brickman, New York University
Robert S. Brown, Marion Public Schools, Ohio
E. E. Church, Potomac State College of West Virginia University
Ruth M. Clark, University of Denver
Pauline Collins, Manhassett, New York
Raymond L. Collins, Manhassett Public Schools, New York
Helen Dobro-Shulak, Queens College, New York
Viola Ruth Dunbar, *Chicago Sun-Times*
Edward Dyer, Hiram College
Marion Edman, Wayne State University
Urban H. Fleege, De Paul University
Lorene K. Fox, Queens College, New York
Gertrude Zemon Gass, Merrill-Palmer School, Detroit, Michigan
H. Harvey Gass, Wayne State University
Glen T. Goodwill, Santa Monica Public Schools, California
Florence Anna Heisler, Brooklyn College
Carl Hood, Eastern Michigan College
Ellen Hood, Ypsilanti Public Schools, Michigan
Frances L. Horler, University of Rochester

Clifton Blair Huff, Kansas State Teachers College
J. Franklin Hunt, Hamilton College
Annette Fox Johnson, University of Pittsburgh
William H. E. Johnson, University of Pittsburgh
Walter V. Kaulfers, University of Illinois
Victor R. Kelley, University of Arizona
Mae Elizabeth Kelly, Roger Ludlowe High School, Fairfield, Connecticut
Emily Klinkhart, American Foundation for the Blind, New York
Frederick Kring, Grove City College
Arthur E. Lean, Southern Illinois University
Lucile Lindberg, Queens College, New York
Rosella Linskie, Memphis State University
Alberta Lowe, University of Tennessee
Gaither McConnell, Newcomb College, Tulane University
Stella Marquez, Salinas Public Schools, Puerto Rico
Murray Lincoln Miller, Illinois State Normal University
L. Warren Nelson, Miami University, Ohio
Dora Pages, Catholic University of Puerto Rico
Deborah Partridge, Queens College, New York
Lincoln Pettit, Michigan State University
Cary Potter, National Council of Independent Schools
Harold Pryor, Austin Peay State College
Gerald H. Read, Kent State University
George A. Roeper, City and Country School of Bloomfield Hills, Michigan
Antone Romney, Brigham Young University
Julian Roth, Los Angeles State College
Herbert C. Rudman, Michigan State University
Seymour St. John, The Choate School
Freyda Sanders, Akron, Ohio
Gabe Sanders, University of Akron
Albert Schatz, National Agricultural College, Pennsylvania
Ina Schlesinger, Columbia University
John W. Shirley, North Carolina State College
C. W. Sorensen, Illinois State Normal University
Alma Stegall, Virginia State College
Blair Stewart, Oberlin College
Byron D. Stuart, Upsala College
J. Harold Tarbell, Lafayette College
John W. Tenny, Wayne State University

Katherine Vickery, Alabama College
Chester S. Williams, University of Oklahoma
H. E. Williams, Southern College, Arkansas
Fremont Wirth, George Peabody College for Teachers

PART
ONE

1

GENERAL CHARACTERISTICS
OF SOVIET EDUCATION

Autumn of 1958 was an unusual period for Soviet education. It was then that the world which had come to expect and accept reports of the excellence of the Soviet schools was startled by the news of planned reforms, in both organization and curriculum. From an ambitious design of a universal, academically oriented secondary education, the Soviet system seemed to swing toward a concept of an extended and practical primary school followed by various forms of vocational apprenticeships or professional training. From emphasis — indeed, pride — in theoretical groundwork, official thought seemed to veer toward insistence on "applied" learning. Strange pronouncements, such as the call for sewing classes, driver education, and "workshops," began to fall upon unbelieving Western ears.

To students of comparative education, long sensitive to the complexity of the forces that move the wheels of educational progress in all countries, the proposed changes occasioned no great surprise.[1] They were, in fact, the logical consequences of the theoretical assumptions and actual practices under which the Soviet system was and is operating. The nature of Communist education stems

3

from its two basic characteristics: it is a *planned* system and it is a *mass* system. Its frictions and difficulties are direct results of the inflexibility of a predetermined educational program, admirable perhaps in its own right but seldom capable of providing sound universal education. In an over-all perspective the Soviet system of education, like all other systems, reveals itself to be a kaleidoscope of strengths and weaknesses. It is the purpose of this chapter to characterize the major outlines of this vast and changing panorama.

Soviet Philosophy of Educational Planning

Of all past and present philosophies of education, the Soviet is most uniquely the product of "pure reason." It is not intended, at least in its original Marxist design, to reflect the fortuitous convergence of historical forces.[2] It does not represent, as, say, the English system does, a careful but piecemeal structure built over many centuries of trial and error.[3] Rather, like the French system, it is a neat blueprint in which regularity of outline and orderliness of procedure outweigh the uncertainties of the historical ebb and flow. Unlike the French system, however, the Soviet design is distinguished by the boldness of its reach. It is second only to that irregular but gargantuan product of human optimism, the American system of education, in its ambition to include the entire population in its operation. The Soviet system is a methodical plan for the education of all citizens. It stems from the confidence, which can be traced back through Marx and Rousseau to Francis Bacon, that man, by the use of reason, can provide by legislation for all present and future social emergencies. Not only do the Communists believe that their Party should have the power to legislate for social change; they also claim that it has the wisdom to determine what that change should be. Consequently, Soviet leaders claim to know what is good for everyone by way of education. By thus solving their philosophical problems they can concentrate on devising the best means to teach all Soviet citizens whatever they have decided to teach them.

It goes without saying that such assumptions are open to grave moral and practical objections. Throughout man's known history there have been men who proclaimed their faith in the unlimited power of human reason to organize social life. Others have been less convinced that life can ever be purely an affair of the mind. They felt and still feel that education, particularly as preparation for life, is a matter of emotion as well as of reason, of the heart as well as of the head. Even if one could succeed in establishing the doctrine that claims the power to change man (if need be, by force) to make him capable of creating and reaping future benefits, one would still question whether the fulfillment of such future promise, at a price that denies man's essential freedom at present, would justify the procedure. It is in its failure to reconcile social reformist zeal with respect for individual right to ethical self-determination that we find firm ground for censuring the Communist experiment.

Practical no less than theoretical considerations prompt one to query the wisdom of attempting to determine man's fate by exclusive reliance on a preconceived *plan*. To say that human beings generally behave in predictable ways under given stimuli is to say no more than that they might also behave in unpredictable ways. Obviously, the same people may behave in different ways, even in identical circumstances. Any experienced wartime commander will attest that under the same conditions the same men are capable of great bravery or great cowardice, depending upon their state of mind at the time. There is thus enough uncertainty about human behavior to suggest that even the most detailed blueprints should be used only as guides to initial understanding, not as specific directions for action. Any inflexible attempt to regulate all human conditions is likely to run into snags that may nullify the investment made in erecting the machinery of persuasion.

Evidence all over the world seems to indicate that centralized educational planning usually ends in the disappointment of the planners. Attempts to legislate educational change result in no more than series of schemes, each rapidly superseding the other, each equally limited in its application.[4] The course of prerevolutionary as well as of Soviet educational history was weakened precisely by such spasmodic legislation. In contrast to the American practice (uneven as it is), in which educational change follows the evolvement of social change in the thousands of diverse local communities, the Soviet educational system throughout its recent history has had to face social change already accomplished and was forced to adapt itself to it by hasty legislation. There is ground to believe, to use a recent instance, that the reform enacted in December, 1958, can be considered a poorly thought out, *ad hoc* piece of legislation that is going to disappoint everyone concerned. It will neither bring about a greater dedication to manual labor nor prevent the deterioration of preparation for university training.[5] The social and economic changes that the Soviet society is now undergoing, in some ways so similar to past American experience, require something better than periodic review and organization. Rigid educational planning cannot in the end provide for the many unpredictable situations brought about by rapid progress. The enormous successes of the American educational experiment in the past and the impressive way in which it is now rapidly renovating itself are one tangible proof of the value of a free-wheeling, individual-oriented system. It is this record of success — even when set against the record of our failures — that strengthens the belief that the Soviet system of rigidly fixed educational goals is not a suitable alternative.

Growth of a Mass System

Although the Communists have chosen to ignore these ethical and practical considerations, there remains the fact that they have advanced, with fanatical courage and conviction, a bold plan for the mass amelioration of the human condition. The Soviet system sets itself the task of organizing the nation for economic and social advancement. It holds that the defeat of old abuses is more important than the loss of old roots. It postulates education geared not to the present but to the future. It claims not only that out of present privation will come future abundance but, more paradoxically, that out of present restrictions will come ultimate liberty, out of the hatred of adversaries will arise an era of universal fraternity.

Insofar as it has gone, the application of this philosophy has coincided with an impressive growth of educational facilities. Soviet leaders never tire of pointing to the great contrast between their achievements and the meager educational provisions before the Revolution. In actual fact, however, the Soviet Union inherited from tsarist Russia not only a vigorous intellectual tradition but also a history of attempts to universalize education. These early attempts, symbolized best by the years 1863 and 1905, are significant today chiefly because they demonstrate the exaggeration of subsequent claims made by the Communist Party. But even given the good quality of prerevolutionary education, the Soviet achievements are spectacular. The high priority assigned to education and culture in national policy has led to tireless and dogged efforts. As a result, the Soviet school system is today a vast network binding together the enormous expanse of territory and the diverse peoples that inhabit it. Since all economic and social activities are regulated by the state, the provision for educational facilities is almost automatic. Behind each yellow block of Moscow apartments there blossoms as if by magic an appropriate red brick schoolhouse.

Somebody has said that if you have seen one Soviet school you have seen them all. There is some justice even in such a flippant dismissal of the issue. The uniformity of practice is remarkable. An almost intangible supervision on the part of the Central Committee of the Communist Party, guided by the educational research done by the R.S.F.S.R. Academy of Pedagogical Sciences, is all that seems to be required to insure uniform textbooks, priority for buildings, and an orderly flow of new school directors and teachers. This steel girding of the Soviet school is only superficially concealed by the outward decentralization.

The least that can be said about government financing of education is that it is generous. One cannot accurately assess the respective expenditures on education in the United States and the U.S.S.R., if only because in the former the percentage spent on education refers to a budget covering only a small proportion of total public and private services, while in the latter the percentage spent on education refers to the total budget for all the manifold activities for which the state is responsible. (An almond is 10 per cent of ten almonds, but it is not 10 per cent of an almond cake garnished by ten almonds.) The actual disbursement of money for education in the Soviet Union is made through local government agencies, but financial provisions in the national budget insure ample maintenance. The various arrangements by which the fifteen republics and the union government parcel out the responsibility do nothing to conceal the unity of organization that has hitherto been the main source of support, financial and administrative, of the Soviet school system.

Structure of the System.   On the eve of reform there were in the Soviet Union approximately 110,000 elementary four-year schools, 60,000 seven-year schools, and 25,000 ten-year schools, a total of nearly 200,000 regular schools of general education. There are, in addition, some 7000 auxiliary special and part-time schools, 3750 technikums and professional schools, 730 institutes of higher education, and 39 universities. The countryside is dotted by 150,000 libraries, 850 museums, 500 theaters, 2700 Pioneer palaces, 500 stations for young technicians and naturalists, 240,000 movie theaters, and 70 circuses. A task force of 1,625,000 teachers and other personnel mans this extensive enterprise.[6]

The general outline of the system, both before and after reforms, is presented in the diagrams on pages 10–11. The preparatory institutions include both nurseries (six months through three years of age) and kindergartens (ages three through seven). The primary school, the only level serving the total age group, takes the first four grades (ages seven through eleven). Until 1959 an overwhelming majority of children continued their education to age fourteen in incomplete secondary schools (grades five through seven). The current reform, apart from raising the age of universal compulsory education to fifteen and thus creating the eight-year school, begins at the next level.

Hitherto, a select though increasingly large group of pupils fourteen through seventeen years of age went through the complete ten-year school. Now, they and eventually all or a majority of other youngsters of their age are to be assigned at age fifteen to one of three major kinds of schools — technikums, schools for rural and urban youth, and the new polytechnical schools of general education — to pursue separate paths of further education. So far, labor reserve courses, a form of on-the-job training, are continuing to claim some youngsters. In addition, a minor group is funneled off at varying ages to special schools, including boarding schools, military schools, experimental schools, art, music, and ballet schools, and schools for the handicapped. These schools do not seem to have been affected by the current reforms.

At present only a minority of ten-year-school graduates enter the universities and institutes, which accept seventeen-year-old students but supposedly reserve 80 per cent of the available places for older candidates who have completed military service or two years of experience in production. The current reorganization of this level means that after graduation from the secondary level those with the requisite scholastic and political credentials will be able to enter these institutions at eighteen or after military service. At this level a network of correspondence courses and evening classes supplements the full-time residential offerings, and there is to be some enforcement of an obligation for all students to spend a period in part-time work. The four or five years of higher education are followed by postgraduate study for a mere handful of diploma holders. In addition to the institutions of higher education, various research institutes and centers also offer postgraduate study.

The Soviet system, like the American, is a remarkable mass enterprise. The intensive educational campaign conducted in the late twenties and early thirties rendered substantially the whole population literate or at least semiliterate. The new goal of eight-year universal compulsory education by 1965 is a retreat in terms of the previous goal of ten-year education for all by 1960 but an advance in terms of the status quo. The number of university students has more than doubled since the war. The fervor of adult educational activities and the dissemination of culture have been remarkable; nowhere else does one notice so many waitresses or cab drivers reading serious literature.

Population and school-attendance figures substantiate the ambitions of the Soviet educational plan to reach all the people. The figures now available estimate the situation as follows: 2500 out of each 10,000 people were in some type of school in 1955–1956; 814 of these were in grades five to ten of the general secondary school, 100 were in professional secondary schools, and 93 were in institutions of higher learning.[7] These figures, which account for one-fourth of the total population, expand as we single out for consideration only the present younger generation. Approximately 10 per cent of the appropriate age group attend institutions of higher education, second largest proportion in the world after the United States, with 33 per cent of its youth in colleges. About 30 per cent of the appropriate age group complete secondary education, a close second after the United States, with 45 per cent. At the age of fourteen 80 per cent of the age group are still in school, in the United States some 90 per cent.

There are, of course, substantial gaps in the structure. Taking

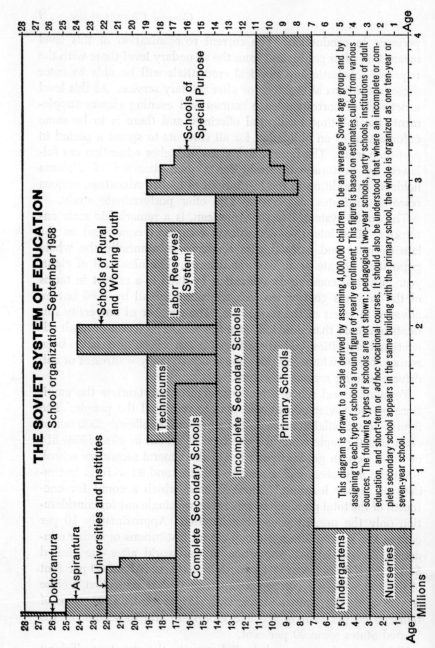

THE SOVIET SYSTEM OF EDUCATION

School organization—September 1958

This diagram is drawn to a scale derived by assuming 4,000,000 children to be an average Soviet age group and by assigning to each type of schools a round figure of yearly enrollment. This figure is based on estimates culled from various sources. The following types of schools are not shown: pedagogical two-year schools, party schools, institutions of adult education, and short-term or *ad hoc* vocational courses. It should also be understood that where an incomplete or complete secondary school appears in the same building with the primary school, the whole is organized as one ten-year or seven-year school.

Age — 28, 27, 26, 25, 24, 23, 22, 21, 20, 19, 18, 17, 16, 15, 14, 13, 12, 11, 10, 9, 8, 7, 6, 5, 4, 3, 2, 1 — **Age**

Doktorantura
Aspirantura
Universities and Institutes
Schools of Special Purpose
Schools of Rural and Working Youth
Labor Reserves System
Technicums
Complete Secondary Schools
Incomplete Secondary Schools
Primary Schools
Kindergartens
Nurseries

Millions — 1, 2, 3, 4

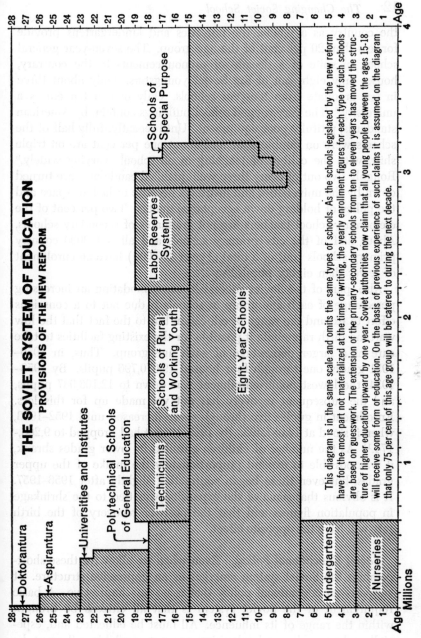

THE SOVIET SYSTEM OF EDUCATION
PROVISIONS OF THE NEW REFORM

This diagram is in the same scale and omits the same types of schools. As the schools legislated by the new reform have for the most part not materialized at the time of writing, the yearly enrollment figures for each type of such schools are based on guesswork. The extension of the primary-secondary schools from ten to eleven years has moved the structure of higher education upward by one year. Soviet authorities now claim that all young people between the ages 15-18 will receive some form of education. On the basis of previous experience of such claims it is assumed on the diagram that only 75 per cent of this age group will be catered to during the next decade.

the country as a whole, the nurseries and kindergartens provide for less than 20 per cent of the age group. The seven-year general school, in spite of a decade of pronouncements to the contrary, houses only eight out of ten Soviet youngsters. Only about three in ten graduate from ten-year schools. Only one in ten enters a university.[8] The very rugged school buildings contain, by American standards, pitifully poor equipment. Until recently, fully half of the schools were on double shift and about one per cent are on triple shift, with the caliber of teaching in all schools varying widely.[9] Roughly two out of every three well-qualified candidates are turned down by the universities and institutes because of lack of space and the policy of holding down acceptance quotas. Two per cent of the elementary-school teachers are not graduates of secondary schools. About half of the city primary schools and all but 2000 country primary schools (out of a total of over 100,000) have an enrollment of fewer than eighty pupils.[10]

Also, part of the Soviet success in accommodating an increasing percentage of each age group in schools is due not to a conscious effort to expand the range of education but to the fact that the low wartime birth rate made it possible for the existing facilities to take care of a larger percentage of each age group. Thus, in 1950–1951 grades one through four housed 19,670,796 pupils. By 1953–1954, the lowest point, enrollment was down to 12,106,037 pupils, and the subsequent recovery has not yet made up for this loss. Enrollment in grades five through seven increased until 1952–1953, when it stood at 14,087,403. By 1955–1956 it had dropped to 9,268,-174.[11] As the number of children enrolled in lower grades shrank, it was possible to expand proportionately the intake of the upper grades, but even these began contracting slightly after 1956–1957. It is obvious that some of the expansion was tied to the shrinkage in population figures and that the postwar recovery of the birth rate will have the opposite effect.

Soviet Educational Policy.   Even when we allow for these short-comings the Soviet system emerges as an impressive structure. It supports an educational policy that is no less impressive. A basic requirement of the Soviet system is that all citizens be brought within the range of its influence. All must be educated and, especially where radio and television are not available, all must be taught to read. Having thus set the stage by postulating universal literacy, Soviet leadership faces a threefold task: first, to bring all men to share and believe in the Communist ideal — hence the monopoly of moral and political views openly acknowledged as indoctrination; second, to cement the bonds among the different groups of the new society by establishing a common culture — hence the insistence on common subjects and a uniform system of grades and examinations; third, to further the cause of socialism by teaching all citizens vocational skills appropriate to the fulfillment of the state's economic ambitions — hence the emphasis on production tasks to be undertaken and the scientific and technical training necessary to complete them. These three purposes — political, cultural, and vocational — provide the foundations of Soviet education.

In fulfillment of the political goals, the schools have had considerable success in evoking commitment to communism. Many groups in the West underestimate the people's enthusiasm for their own system. Not only are Soviet citizens as loyal to their government as are serious citizens everywhere, but Soviet propaganda has convinced them that the government is *their* government. However little sense it makes politically, there are millions of people in the Soviet Union who feel that the Revolution was *their* Revolution. Now that the terror has receded and political indoctrination in the schools has become less blatant, while at the same time the first fruits of enforced industrialization have been made available, one senses much more spontaneity and attachment, if not to communism as a social system, at least to communism as the Russian way of doing things. The occasional reports of cynicism or apathy toward the regime tell only half the story; the "right" values are quite effectively instilled in a substantial proportion if not in a majority of the pupils in school.

Enthusiasm for culture is a second prominent feature of Soviet education. It is a mistake to regard this solely as the result of the official commitment to learning, though the efforts of the state are unprecedented in their scope. The Russian people have a strong tradition of veneration for culture. To this is added now the excitement of seeing a new society rise around them and the realization that education provides the best means of social betterment in this society. The ideal of a literate and enlightened citizenry accords with the premises of the original Marxist doctrine, but it is the channeling of careers through schools that has produced the present passion for schooling. By drawing the people together and creating an opportunity for them to share common experiences, the schools have helped to reinforce the quality of cultural life, which has received a further boost from the destruction of distance through industrialization and from the opportunities furnished by the rising wealth of the economy.

Finally, the Soviet schools channel youth through the common course of study in such a way as not to lose sight of individual occupational talents. This book devotes little space to vocational education, not because of lack of interest in this area but because vocational schools are not under the ministries of education and did not lend themselves easily to direct observation by the Comparative Education Society. The growing field of after-school and postschool specialization has extended what was formerly essentially a university concern to the field of senior secondary education. The December, 1958, reform has made several explicit provisions for further diversifying vocational opportunities. The unified eight-year school, which is to succeed the present seven-year school, will present more practical subject matter. The three types of schools designed to take over the task of the senior secondary classes — the technikums, the schools for urban and rural youth, and the new polytechnical schools of general education — are to offer programs substantially more vocational in character. Practice in industry and vocational courses are also to be expanded.

Planning for Mass Education

The Soviet achievements are a result of grand ambitions carried out with considerable planning. But the current reforms raise the question as to whether continued success can depend on planning. It is one thing to plan for a breakthrough, for planning then is essentially an emergency operation. It is another thing to plan after a measure of success has been achieved. The tools developed for a society of want may not be suitable for a society of abundance. The very successes of the Soviet Union may now lead to a defeat of the methods by which they were attained.

It must be remembered that any institution develops in terms of "more" or "less" success. In the face of grievous educational shortages of all kinds the world over, no one can depreciate the Soviet effort, which has created an imposing and effective educational enterprise. But there is a difference between making an *initial* effort and running the complicated machinery of a network of institutions already established. When a project is just getting under way all additions are spectacular. In a village without any school, building one is an epoch-making event; building a second one still doubles the rate of progress. All later expansion, however, is in diminishing proportion. And with new problems of maintenance and administration arising as the scope of education widens, the excitement generated by fast progress is submerged in the day-to-day concerns of school life.

Soviet education has so far been in the first stage of development. It is only beginning to face the difficulties of the second and subsequent stages. Expansion has not only dominated the scene but also served as a convenient rationalization for all difficulties that might have inhibited the project otherwise. As the Minister of Education of the R.S.F.S.R. put it,

> We know that American education has very fine buildings, excellent school equipment, and amenities. We should like to have them and we know that we have a long way to go in this respect. But we are only beginning to lift our country upwards. And our immediate problem is to *put* every child *into* a school. That is why we have to content ourselves with very modest buildings and school furnishings.[12]

So far the successes have greatly overshadowed the failures. It is only now that the problems of efficient management are moving to the front of the stage.

Every success in the implementation of educational ambitions brings new problems for the Soviet planners. The sheer pressure of numbers creates strains difficult to foresee and to deal with successfully. First, the greater the number of people included in the schools, the more divergent the tastes, abilities, and inclinations that must be considered. These diverse demands are stronger than the master plan of unified administration that the Soviet authorities now enforce. Under their impact, the old *pro forma* decentralization is beginning to assume a new, more meaningful, and more effective character. Second, the extension of education to those destined for manual occupations has brought new pressures to bear as the rank and file of common men acquire larger social and educational ambitions. The unified curriculum as well as central administration is likely to be attacked. Flexibility in both administration and programming must be maintained to meet a barrage of unfamiliar problems. This impact of mass education is nothing new. It is a phenomenon long wrestled with in the American educational system.

The symptoms of the Soviet malaise could be suspected from the moment the administration moved toward greater decentralization. In the field of education, of course, outright organizational centralization has never been admitted to be the official rule. In spite of the obvious fact that curricula, political content, and teachers' pay were identical everywhere and thus centrally controlled, Soviet educators insisted that the central government proved its intention to give some responsibility to the local level by placing administration in the hands of the republics and by allowing leeway in the matter of school buildings and minor curriculum divergencies, best exemplified in the teaching of foreign languages. Indeed, from the beginning of the Soviet rule local soviets and parent groups have performed a carefully assigned role. That qualification notwithstanding, there is no doubt that the general design of the authorities was to keep school operation centralized, in purpose and in actual practice.

As the numbers to be educated increase, however, it becomes more and more difficult to provide for all contingencies by central administrative decisions. The large volume of published discussion that preceded the school reform, the new compulsory vocational programs, whose character will depend on regional needs and decisions, and the weakening of the powers of the Union Ministry of Higher Education — these may be forerunners of increased pressure for more local self-determination. This much can be deduced from the avid interest displayed by the Soviet educators when told about local government of American schools.

The impact of mass education is even greater in curriculum than in administration. Here the principle of centralization and unity has always been explicitly defended. Soviet educators still regard an identical basic curriculum for all students as vital. That everyone should be forced to learn the same things seems to them to satisfy the old principles of "sound" pedagogy. They stubbornly insist that even the special-purpose schools, such as military schools or schools of ballet and music, teach the entire curriculum of the general schools as well as their specialty.

Yet the new law sanctions what amounts to a serious undermining of the old unity. In the new design, the eight-year school, though standard in its academic program, will gear its polytechnical program to the needs of local industries. Further, the senior cycle of secondary schools is to be more completely diversified in character. The technikums have always concentrated on distinct vocational specialties. Now the schools of rural and urban youth are to have their curricula adapted along industrial or agricultural lines.[13] The third type of senior secondary school, the "secondary general education and polytechnical school with industrial training," is to be dependent on the facilities available in adjacent industries. [14] Thus, the regional economic councils can be expected to influence the formation of what is now regarded as the most important part of the curriculum; and with different vocational preparation the old interchange of students between different regions will be no longer automatic.

It is significant that Soviet educational planners in their discussions with American visitors exhibited more interest in the English tripartite system, which divides eleven-year-olds into academic (grammar), technical, and modern (general) "streams," than in the American comprehensive school, which postpones specialization until fifteen and insists on its taking place under a common roof. Obviously, under the necessity of accommodating mass ambitions and serving mass talents, the Soviet thinkers, though unable to hold to the notion of one curriculum for all, prefer alternative rigid curriculum schemes to a system of electives that approaches much more closely the ideal of tailor-made, individual instruction. Although several lower-level educators have exhibited a lively interest in the elective system, Soviet policy-makers who visited American schools were more ambivalent in their comments and only their adverse reactions have been published. The necessity of an elective system in schools serving all types of occupations is not likely to be recognized soon in the U.S.S.R., even for senior adolescents. Instead of radical recasting in either administration or curriculum, the Soviet theory and practice go through more or less helpless flipflops under the steadily expanding mass-education ambitions.

The new reform is thus, in a sense, an attempt to regain control over this rising tide. That the promise of the Revolution must be fulfilled and that the Soviet masses, like masses all over the world, must be given access to the whole range of education, no one is now inclined to deny. The obligation of the Soviet schools to teach all comers cannot be altered or avoided. Their problem is, therefore, how to adapt the tradition of rigid planning to the inexorable force of social changes now plainly appearing.

This problem Soviet educators are at present incapable of solving satisfactorily. Their faith in planning will not be easily dislocated. They are unable to grasp, let alone solicit, the spontaneity of an unplanned world, which alone measures up to the multiple aspirations of a mass society. Instead, they keep adopting new plans, more diversified perhaps, but nonetheless rigid.

But no plan will now do. In view of the emerging social stratification, the question in Soviet education is whether mass pressures can at all be handled by planning, whether more or less centralized. In the United States we are wont to equate decentralization with increased equality of educational opportunity, because here decentralization means wider unplanned participation of the people in decision-making. In the Soviet Union, however, decentralization under planning brings more power not to the people but to the lower echelons of party and government organs. Even if decentralization materializes, the interests of the people may be no better safeguarded than when their fate rested squarely in the hands of a central hierarchy.

The top Communist Party leaders, so far in complete control of the state, have acquired all the outward characteristics of an elite. But at least they appear to be championing the cause of educational equality by opposing intellectual snobbishness. It is immaterial whether they are motivated by Communist ideals, whether they seek popular support as a hedge against political instability, or whether, having finally established themselves as a top class, they want to prevent the formation of a middle class between themselves and the people. The fact that the Party leadership champions the cause of mass education against the hereditary ambitions of the middle-level bourgeoisie [15] might lead one to believe that continued centralization would be more consistent with Communist aspirations.

Yet, mass pressure has weakened Soviet belief in centralization. And decentralization, even if it put decision-making in the hands of local officials, would at least enable the people to exercise better their sometimes inarticulate but always relentless influence.[16] Thus the loss of strength by the center and the gain in independence in the provinces is a move in the direction of the people's ultimate achievement of mastery over their own fate. Through the development of democratic freedom as we now know it or through fulfillment of the Communist promise that the state will "wither away," the future augurs the end of monolithic planning. What does seem clear at this point is that the Soviet system, like all systems, must restore flexibility to its central place in education. Instead of tinkering with administrative provisions, it must concentrate on keeping open the doors to universal enlightenment, through which alone men will finally discover that their best interests lie in individual self-determination nourished by fraternity.

Restatement of the Problem

The Soviet system has two major characteristics: it is a planned system and it is a mass system. The essence of a plan is that it attempts to plot the course of progress. The essence of mass pressure is that it defies such restriction. On the one side, the expansion of the Soviet school system creates new day-to-day problems and contingencies. On the other side, the plan establishes overriding uniformities; it fastens upon one chosen educational principle as an inflexible premise around which to build a system. These two characteristics are plainly incompatible. It was virtually certain that a concentration on exclusive academic study would throw out of balance an orderly supply of highly trained manual workers, just as it is certain that the present planned trend toward training for manual work will endanger traditional academic standards. When the dynamics of an expanding system require flexibility, planned national (and hence bureaucratized) policy will be looked to in vain as a remedy.

But now that the Soviet educational policy has revealed weaknesses it would be senseless to swing from excessive praise to excessive condemnation. All educational systems combine positive and negative features — of good learning and of snobbery masquerading as good learning; of arrogant ignorance and of ignorance that tries to hide under a thin veneer of sophistication. The Soviet system is no exception. It carries the ballast of rigid traditions and the bonds of axiomatic philosophy, yet it contains some inspiring notions and tries some courageous solutions. It provides its pupils with a program that, no matter in which direction it swerves, carries the stamp of authoritarian restrictions, but still it is the first to unearth and serve the millions of humble folk in a forgotten continent.

The efforts of the Soviet people to erect a giant educational machinery deserve impartial treatment. In the Soviet educational fabric introduced in this chapter and presented at length in this book the weak thread of planning and the strong thread of mass scale belong together. It is the purpose of these pages to survey in detail this credit and debit balance.

2

THE DEVELOPMENT OF
EDUCATION IN TSARIST
RUSSIA

Americaninterest in the Soviet
school system soared with the first Sputnik. The man in the street
began to demand information about Soviet education. Even the
intellectuals and professionals seemed to realize for the first time
that they had been unaware of something important. In point
of actual fact, however, there never was any dearth of information about education in the Soviet Union or, for that matter,
about education under the tsars. In its first issue (1855) Henry
Barnard's *American Journal of Education* carried an article on
Russian education. The publications of the United States Bureau of
Education carried information on Russia's educational system
periodically during the nineteenth and twentieth centuries; and
less than two years after the Revolution, the Bureau issued its
first bulletin on the Soviet schools — *Educational Changes in Russia,*
by Theresa Bach. During the pre-Sputnik period Americans had
many opportunities to become acquainted with the new schools.
John Dewey, Samuel N. Harper, Thomas Woody, and I. L. Kandel,
among others, wrote about them, on the basis of either observations
or documents or both. Perhaps the one person who stands out in

terms of continuous research and thinking about education in the Soviet Union is George S. Counts, whose books on the subject reach back to 1931. It was unfortunate that American educators and others did not take seriously enough the results of Counts' research and his analyses,[1] although most of what Counts prophesied has still not come true.

The Beginnings of Education in Russia

An understanding of the Soviet school system as it is today depends in large measure on our awareness of its history, including the history of the development of education in imperial Russia. Some historians begin the account with Tsar Peter I, the Great (1689–1725), who introduced Western ideas to the Slavic people. Although there can be little doubt that the first basic changes in Russian culture and education were made during Peter's reign, it is necessary to keep in mind that a scholastic substratum had existed for at least a century prior to Peter. In fact, the growth of education in Russia can be best comprehended through an analysis of the evolution of religion after the official introduction of Greek Orthodox Christianity in 988 A.D., during the reign of Vladimir I of Kiev. In succeeding centuries, the major educational effort was connected with teaching religious doctrine, on both ecclesiastical and parochial levels.

The historical source materials of several centuries seldom mention the existence of schools, and probably few were in operation until about the sixteenth century. Nevertheless, we do find reference to educational work, such as that of Prince Yaroslav the Wise (1019–1054), who fostered art, architecture, and music, ordered the translation of Greek literature, brought about the original codification of Russian law (*Russkaia Pravda*), and opened libraries and schools where even Greek and Latin were taught.

Another early ruler who thought in educational terms was Vladimir II Monomakh (1113–1125), the "King Alfred of Russian history." His *Charge to My Children*, written in 1096, contained many educational maxims and advice on how to improve one's educational status. Vladimir was also conspicuous for his social reforms, including the liberalization of the *Russkaia Pravda*.

The period of the Mongol or Tatar conquest (1273–1480) was

marked by the borrowing of cultural features from the Orient. The tolerance of the Tatars led to the rise of the Orthodox Church, and after the removal of the metropolitan see to Moscow that city became important as a center of Russian life.

Up to about the end of this period there seems to have been very little progress in establishing schools. Whatever culture and literacy existed was mainly confined to the monasteries, many of which had well-filled libraries. Instruction was generally on an individual or at most on a limited group basis. There was a great deal of oral explanation and memorization, but some books were available for instruction.

The 1946 edition of Yesipov and Goncharov's well-known *Pedagogika,* which contains a historical chapter lacking in later editions, maintains that culture and literature were more highly regarded in Russia between the tenth and thirteenth centuries than they were in contemporary western Europe.[2] However, there is little evidence to substantiate this claim. Soviet educators have glorified the Russian Kievan period, with its modest literature, and have overlooked the society that produced a Chrétien de Troyes, a Walther von der Vogelweide, and a Saxo Grammaticus.

From Ivan the Great to the Romanovs

A new era commenced with the victory over the Tatars and the reign of Ivan III, the Great, as Grand Duke of Muscovy (1462–1505). Ivan appropriated the royal title of tsar (from Caesar) after the capture of Constantinople by the Turks and the consequent disappearance of the Eastern Roman Empire. It was in his reign that the institution of serfdom was inaugurated, at the very time when it was on its way out in western Europe.

At the same time, Ivan was aware of the extent of cultural and industrial retardation in his country. In 1472 his second wife, Sophia Palaiologos, niece of the last emperor of Byzantium and a refugee in Rome, brought with her to Moscow a retinue of Byzantine Greeks and Italians who possessed cultural and technical skills. Italian influence soon began to be felt in the Russian diplomatic service, architecture, art, handicraft, and engineering. The outstanding constructions during Ivan's reign were the Uspensky Cathedral, built by Alberto Fioraventi and Pietro Antonio, and the

Kremlin Wall. In addition, Italian and German craftsmen taught the Russians numerous practical skills.

The reign of Tsar Ivan Grozny — the Terrible — (1533–1584), first ruler to be designated Tsar of All the Russians at the coronation, brought further importation of engineers, physicians, and skilled craftsmen, this time mainly from England. An attack was made on the corruption, ignorance, and illiteracy of the clergy at the Church Council of 1551, which adopted the *Stoglav* (*Book of One Hundred Chapters*), a work containing decrees on the religious and secular education of children who were to be trained as priests. The *Stoglav* also directed that schools be established, but no substantial change seems to have occurred in education.

If schools were rare, there was at least an attempt to teach through the home. The *Domostroi* (*House Orderer*), a book on moral conduct attributed to Daniel Silvester, confessor to Ivan IV, included the principles and procedures of educating children. This volume, according to Yesipov and Goncharov,[3] is typical of the educational methods prevailing in Russia from the fifteenth to the seventeenth century. The *Stepennaia Kniga* (*Book of Degrees*), apparently compiled under the direction of Metropolitan Macarius of Moscow in 1563,[4] expressed views sympathetic to humanistic pedagogical ideas.[5] A third work of educational significance was the *Azbukovnik* (*ABC of Knowledge*), an encyclopedic dictionary of useful knowledge.[6] Also during this time, in 1563, the establishment in Moscow of the first Russian printing press made possible the publication of several literary and didactic writings.

All these efforts did not yield much fruit. A British observer, Dr. Giles Fletcher, who visited Russia in 1588–1589, only four years after the death of Ivan the Terrible, reported widespread ignorance in the country. In his account, *Of the Russe Common Wealth*, published in 1591 in London, Fletcher stated that the imperial tyranny stifled the Russians' natural aptitudes for learning and the arts and prevented them from traveling, "that they may learne nothing, nor see the fashions of other countries abroad."[7] As far as the priests were concerned,

They are men utterly unlearned, which is no marviele, forasmuch as their makers, the bishops themselves . . . are cleare of that qualitie,

and make no farther use at all of any kind of learning, no not of the
scriptures themselves, save to read and sing them.[8]

The Early Romanovs

The revolutionary process by which Russia became modernized
started rather slowly during the reign of Ivan IV. Called the Time
of Troubles, it accelerated after the death of Ivan's successor, Fedor
I, in 1598, the final year of the Rurik Dynasty. Four monarchs
ruled prior to the accession of the first tsar of the new dynasty,
Michael Romanov, in 1613. During this interregnum there appeared several primers for the learning of reading and writing and
a work on grammar. Tsar Boris Godunov (1598–1602) had some
grandiose cultural and educational plans for his country, including a
university, very few of which he was able to put into operation;
however, he did succeed in sending a large number of young persons to France, England, and Germany and in obtaining the services of foreign scholars and scientists, whom he rewarded hand-
somely.

Michael Romanov and the West. Tsar Michael Romanov (1613–
1645) further developed intellectual and technical contacts with
the West. He engaged foreign military officers and men, particularly from Scotland, to train a regular Russian army and to
help establish military manufactures. As the Russians became
convinced that Western military science and technology were
superior to their own, they became more amenable to further
foreign influences. The foreign colony in Moscow, named the
Nemetskaya Sloboda (German Quarter), probably because most
of its dwellers were from Germany, was "the natural intermediary
between Russia and Western Civilization." [9] This colony was
formed as early as the time of Ivan IV, but it grew considerably under Michael.[10] The first foreign influences were on Russian
everyday life but in time extended to the cultural arts, especially
under Michael's successor.

Several young Russians were sent by Tsar Michael to study
in England, as is evident from his correspondence with King James
I. On June 17, 1621, Michael wrote to the English monarch as
follows:

Whereas about 18 years past, in the time of the Emperor and greate Duke Burris Pheodorowich of all Russia there was wnt into your Majesties Dominiones fower young gentlmen of our Kingdome by name Mekepher Alphery, Soffone Kosuchove with others, to trayned upp in the English and Lattin tongs and soe to be retorned againe and delivered to the Lordes of our Counsell.[11]

He requested the return of the four, who according to information, not only had been

. . . deteyned and kept in England against their wills, but one of them, Mekepher Alphery, by reason of his younger yeares hath forsaken our trew and undoughted religione and is become a preist, whether urged thereto against his will or willingly is to us unknowen.[12]

On January 4, 1622, Ambassador Isaak Samoilovich Pogozhevo delivered a scroll to the Privy Council with a repetition of the complaint:

Abowt the yeare 1604 in the tyme of the Emperor there weare sent into England certein yong russe gentlmen to be trayned upp in the Lattin and English tounge, namely Mekepher Alpherovsin Greogroy, Saffon Cossickoves, Fedra Semonove, and Cazaren, but by reason of the long troubles in our Country of Russia they have here remayned to this tyme.[13]

Mikepher Alphery, now a graduate of Cambridge, did meet with the Russian ambassador on February 10, 1622, but he refused to return to Russia, since he had become an Anglican priest and had married an Englishwoman.[14]

Sir John Merrick, the English ambassador to Moscow, summed up the case in a memorandum to the Privy Council in 1622:

Mekepher Alphery who only of the four was in England (the rest, two of them are dead in the East Indya, another is remayning in Ireland) was delivered to the Emperors last Ambassadors to use the best meanes they could to persuade his retorne into Russia, but he humbly besought the Kinges Majestie that he might not (against the law of Nationes) be forced out of the land.[15]

There is further evidence of study abroad during the reign of Michael. An exchange of correspondence with King Charles I of

England in 1628–1631 reveals that Ivan Almanezov, the son of a Moscow interpreter, studied medicine and other fields at Cambridge University. Michael requested special privileges for this young man, so that he could pursue his studies without inconvenience, for future service under the tsar. Almanezov obtained the M.A. in 1632 and the M.D. in 1638 at Cambridge and did not return to Russia until 1642 or 1643. It is entirely possible that he spent as many as twenty-six years in England.[16]

The missionary work of the Jesuits, which had been so successful in many parts of central and eastern Europe, aroused the anxiety of the Russian Orthodox Church. The Orthodox Fraternity School of Kiev, founded in 1615, aimed to combat Catholicism through the study of Catholic literature. Metropolitan Peter Mogila's College, opened in 1631 in Kiev, transformed the Fraternity School along the lines of a Jesuit school and carried on the struggle against the Jesuit influence. Renamed the Academy of Kiev in 1701, this institution stressed the study of philosophy and theology in the Latin language, and "the use of even a single word of the vernacular language was severely punished." [17] The Academy was very successful, from both educational and literary standpoints. Mogila, it should be noted, had studied at the Sorbonne and was conversant with western European culture.

Also of interest to the development of education at this time was the formulation, in 1624, of the Rules of the School of the Lutsk Brotherhood in Kiev. These regulations describe the proper qualifications of teachers, as well as the character and curriculum of other schools organized by the Brotherhood.[18]

The Ecclesiastical Problems. Educational activity seemed to gather momentum during the reign of Alexis (1645–1676). His adviser Fedor Rtishchev, who devoted his life to scholarship and education, founded a monastic school in 1648–1649 near Moscow, in which the classical and the Slavic languages, theology, philosophy, and rhetoric were taught with considerable success. In addition to instruction, the monks at Rtishchev's theological school were required to translate various foreign works of learning into Russian.

Another of Rtishchev's educational achievements was to commission a monk, Epiphani Slavinetski, to prepare a Greek-Russian dictionary for use in the theological school. Later Slavinetski and two other monks, Arsenius Satanovski and Damaskin Ptitski, were engaged by the Muscovite hierarchy to translate the Greek Bible into Russian. These monks also translated a variety of volumes, such as geographical, medical and scientific, and educational treatises, which were exceptionally well received by all who were able to read. In addition, to Slavinetski is attributed a pedagogical work, *The Book of Children's Manners*, dealing with the behavior of children toward older persons, in church, in school, and at home.

The role of religion and religious functionaries in Russian life was evident in the controversies that arose in the middle of the seventeenth century. The reforms of Patriarch Nikon (1652–1658) evoked sharp differences of opinion from those who wished to retain the old religion. These Old Believers, at one time under the leadership of one Avvakum, were persecuted by the Orthodox Church, but in spite of the burning of Avvakum, their ideas did not die. The Church Council of 1660–1667, which removed Nikon, also laid a ban on the Old Believer movement in an effort to crush it, but without success. Kluchevsky regards this religious schism as rendering a direct service to Western influences by breaking down "the attitude of suspicious hostility to the West which was so widely diffused throughout the Russian community." [19] The religious controversy weakened the blind reverence for antiquity and raised serious questions about the policies of both church and state. The road was now properly paved for the future Westernizing influences, particularly those to be initiated by Peter the Great.

A secondary outcome of the religious schism was the founding of a new theological school, in 1666, with Simeon Polotski, tutor of Tsar Alexis' two elder sons, as director. The curriculum of this school, which was located in a monastery in Moscow, stressed grammar and Latin and embraced other liberal subjects. Although the school lasted only two years — 1666–1668 — and had only four students, it was "important as the official recognition of the necessity of higher education"; [20] and its classical emphasis was a reply to the Old Believers, who had condemned Western learning. Polotski, it should be added, was the author of two school dramas and two works with pedagogical content. Moreover, his pupil, Silvester Medvedev, organized a school in Moscow in 1682 on the model of the Kiev Academy, emphasizing Latin studies.

The cultural-educational situation toward the end of Alexis' reign has been well described by Kluchevsky:

> Moscow came to feel the necessity of assimilating, firstly, European arts and comforts, and, in later days, European scientific erudition. Beginning with foreign officers and German artillerymen, it ended with German ballets and the Latin Grammar.[21]

But it appeared that the cultural development overbalanced the educational. In 1673, Johann-Gottfried Grigori, a Lutheran pastor in the German quarter, instructed twenty-six young men in dramatic art; "in other words, though Moscow had not yet compassed elementary schools for the teaching of letters, she had succeeded in organizing an academy of drama!"[22]

By the end of the rule of Fedor II (1676–1682), a battle seems to have shaped up between the advocates of Latin and of Greek. A new Moscow school, opened in 1681, offered two courses, one in the Greek language and one in the Slavonic language. From thirty pupils at the time of its origin, the school enrolled no less than 233 pupils by 1686. The school with the Latin course, founded in 1682 by Medvedev, was merged with the Greek school in 1687 to form the Slavic-Greek-Latin Academy, "which became not only the center of higher learning but also the all-powerful arbiter in educational and religious matters."[23] This academy, directed by two Greek-born and Padua-taught scholars, the brothers Ioanniky and Sophrony Likhudy, was granted monopolistic privileges in teaching foreign languages, approving foreign-language teachers, admitting foreign scholars to Russia, enforcing religious orthodoxy, and rooting out all forms of heresy. Indeed, to the great Russian historian S. M. Soloviev, this academy "was not a school at all but a fearful inquisition."[24]

The general status of education in 1683, shortly after the accession of co-Tsars Peter I and Ivan V, was characterized by a translator of the Psalter who was painfully aware of the pressing need to reorganize by educational means the prevailing ecclesiastical system: "Our Russian people are gross and unlearned. Not only plain men, but also men of the clergy, do seek not the verities, or understanding of the Holy Writ, but do slander those who be learned, and call them heretics."[25] This complaint is an echo of the judgment of Dr. Giles Fletcher, made almost a century earlier.

Although it has much justification — only the theological academies of Kiev and Moscow and several church schools with few students being then in existence — it would be an exaggeration to assert that the Russians made no advance at all in education and culture prior to the end of the seventeenth century. The long isolation from Western culture no doubt contributed to Russia's backwardness in education, and its achievements in this respect could not even be mentioned in the same sentence with those of Holland, Poland, Switzerland, and other countries. But the various attempts at education, including the tsars' connections with foreign countries, formed the basis for the efforts of Peter the Great and later for those of Catherine the Great.

From Peter the Great to the Great Reforms

Peter I, the Great (co-tsar, 1682–1689; tsar, 1689–1725), dedicated himself to the aggrandizement of Russia along political, economic, social, military, cultural, and educational lines. He not only turned his eyes toward the West for inspiration but actually lived there and learned the Western technology and culture at first hand.

The Establishment of Schools. His reign was marked by the founding of radically new types of schools, such as the School of Mathematics and Navigation in Moscow (1701), doubtless "an offshoot" [26] of the Royal Mathematical School of Christ's Hospital, an institution visited by Peter during his sojourn in England. This was the first secular school in Russia, and all but one of its instructors were British. The Engineering and Artillery School (1712) and the Naval Academy (1715) further indicated Peter's intense efforts at modernizing the technology and education of his realm. In the field of elementary education, he issued a ukase establishing cypher (arithmetic) schools, two in each province, with the later provision of compulsory attendance for children between the ages of ten and fifteen. These schools, however, never really established themselves because of a later ukase (1721) ordering bishops to set up schools in their eparchies (dioceses). The eparchal schools, which paralleled the cypher schools without duplicating their range of mathematical offerings, but surpassed them in religious content, proved to meet more closely the needs of the Russian people at the time, with the result that the cypher schools were weakened.

Sometime around 1715 Peter the Great initiated correspondence with Christian Wolff, the professor of philosophy at the University of Halle, who had pioneered in the use of German instead of Latin in his lectures, relative to the organization of an academy of sciences. He also solicited the views, by letter and in person, of the German philosopher Gottfried Wilhelm Leibniz, founder of the Berlin Academy of Sciences (1700). In 1724, Peter issued a ukase creating an Academy of Sciences at St. Petersburg, the city he had built. According to his original plan, this academy was to consist of seventeen professorships (a university, in other words) and a Gymnasium, which would prepare students for higher education. The ukase, however, did not include provisions for the secondary school, nor did the academy itself, established in 1725 after the death of Peter, pay any attention to education below the university level. Because subsequent scholastic developments discouraged the seventeen professors, who had been imported from Germany, from fulfilling their functions as university lecturers, the academy turned out to be at first an institution where the professors lectured to each other and later a research institute. The establishment of a real university in Russia was, thus, still a matter of future realization.

In 1716 John Perry, an English engineer who had been in Peter's service from 1698 to 1712, wrote an appraisal of the culture and education of Russia in the era of Peter. Although he appreciated the tsar's efforts and his success in sending nearly a hundred students to England, Holland, and Italy, he deplored the depth of the ignorance of the Russian clergy.[27]

The St. Peterburg Academy of Sciences was opened in 1725, when Catherine I was already tsarina. In the last year of her reign, 1727, another institution of importance was opened — the Kharkov Collegium, a higher theological academy that later developed into the University of Kharkov. Interestingly enough, Empress Catherine I, who rose from a peasant girlhood in Lithuania, never became adept at the arts of reading and writing.

From Peter the Great to Tsarina Elizabeth there was a letdown in the pace of educational progress. During this time three monarchs were in power, but apart from the *Kadetskii Korpus,* organized in 1731 in St. Petersburg in the reign of Empress Anne (1730–1740), very little was done of an original nature. The *Kadetskii Korpus* provided training not only for the nobility as cadets for the military service but also for the civil service.

Of particular importance to the educational development of this period was the appearance in 1733 of Vasili Tatishchev's *Dialogue on the Benefits of Science and the School.* Tatishchev was a historian who had worked closely with Peter the Great on educational matters. In his book he took up, in question-and-answer form, the problems of scientific research and teaching. He favored the exercise of freedom in both areas. Among his ideas was the recommendation that the teacher not only know his subject matter but also possess the ability to teach.

The rule of Empress Elizabeth (1741–1762) produced Russia's first real institution of advanced learning, the University of Moscow, which opened its doors in 1755. The intellectual father of this institution was the renowned poet and scientist Michael V. Lomonosov, who is credited with having reformed the Russian literary language. Lomonosov, who had been a student of chemistry in Germany, exhibited French influences in his literary writings. It was through the University of Moscow and the St. Petersburg Academy of Sciences that the ideas of Leibniz, Wolff, Kant, and other German philosophers entered the stream of Russian thought in the eighteenth and nineteenth centuries. The philosophers of the Enlightenment were later followed by the philosophers of idealism, particularly Fichte, Schelling, and Hegel, and these pointed the way to Feuerbach, Marx, and Engels. This chain of intellectual events determined to an appreciable extent the interest of Russian thinkers in Marxian philosophy.

The Rule of Catherine II. The high point of Russian educational development in the second half of the eighteenth century occurred during the reign of Catherine II, the Great (1762–1796), "the first Russian ruler who could read and write [and] the first who was really educated." [28] Catherine contributed to the growth of the Russian Empire by the acquisition of much territory and by numerous social reforms. As an admirer of French literature and thought, she did a great deal to elevate the cultural level of

Russia, at least as far as the nobility was concerned. Catherine's attachment to French culture was also evident in the Smolny Institute, founded in 1764 in St. Petersburg. This school, which consisted of one department for girls of the noble class and one for girls of the middle class, offered a common curriculum of general courses (Russian, geography, history, arithmetic, foreign languages) as well as courses in domestic science for the middle-class girls and polite studies for the noble-class pupils. The language of instruction in this institution, which was possibly the first European secondary school for girls under state auspices, remained French until 1783, when French was replaced by Russian.

France was also the chief source of educational theory for Catherine. Although in *The Instructions to the Commissioners for Composing a New Code of Laws* (1767) [29] she drew heavily upon John Locke's *Some Thoughts Concerning Education*, her main educational mentors were Montaigne and Rousseau. When it came to a practical plan for the establishment of a system of schools in Russia, she first turned to Denis Diderot, the great French philosopher and editor of the *Encyclopédie*. In 1770 Diderot presented to her his *Plan d'une Université pour la Russie*.[30] Since this plan was more appropriate for an advanced rather than for an educationally underdeveloped country, however, Catherine had to look elsewhere for guidance.

Catherine tried to get some form of compulsory public education under way. In 1775 she issued a decree creating a Board of Public Welfare in each province (*guberniia*), which would build and maintain schools in every town and larger village. Her intentions were never realized, mainly because of insufficient funds, but she did not give up. She kept in touch with the leading intellects of Europe and constantly sought practical information about education. Her invitation to the widely known German-French Baron Friedrich Melchior Grimm to direct education in Russia was refused, but Grimm did send, in 1777, an educational plan.

Finally, in 1782, Catherine took definite steps to improve the educational situation in Russia. In this year she set up a Commission for the Establishment of Schools, charged with the duty of organizing a public-school system. The Commission recommended opening elementary, secondary, and higher institutions, and in 1786 its plan was incorporated in the Statute of Public Schools in the Russian

Empire.[31] Upon the suggestion of Emperor Joseph II of Austria, Catherine appointed Fedor Jankovitch de Mirievo, a Serb-Croat educator who had achieved success in educational administration and reform in both Austria and Hungary, as special adviser to the Commission. Jankovitch de Mirievo, who professed the Greek Orthodox faith and knew the Russian language, performed a variety of tasks. He helped draft the Law of 1786, supervised the translation and adaptation of Austrian textbooks, and introduced other Austrian school practices, most of which had been derived from Prussia. The Commission's activities also included the founding, in 1783, of a Major School (*Glavnoe Uchilishche*) in St. Petersburg for the training of teachers and the drafting of an ordinance, in 1784, placing private schools under government supervision.

Although the educational reform initiated by Catherine was very important, it had serious shortcomings and never attained the goals she had in mind.[32] The schools were for both boys and girls and were free and not subject to church control. On the other hand, there were no schools for peasants in the country districts, insufficient facilities for the training of teachers, too few schools, lack of financial resources for maintaining the schools, and little cooperation by parents. After some initial success, the schools founded in Catherine's reign began to decline both in quality and in quantity.

During this era the new movement in education that was flourishing in Germany became felt in Russia through Johann Georg Schwarz, a German Freemason who became a professor at the University of Moscow. Schwarz very strongly influenced Nikolai I. Novikov, a journalist-publisher who was interested in education and in the dissemination of the best literature, native and foreign. This energetic Russian became director of the printing press of the University of Moscow, published several journals, and performed many deeds of philanthropic service. Among his activities was the opening and maintaining of free primary schools for underprivileged children.[33] The outcome of his varied enterprises was the arousal of suspicion on the part of Catherine, the discouragement of his work by the government, and finally, in 1792, a sentence of imprisonment for fifteen years.

Novikov received a pardon at the hands of Tsar Paul I (1796–1801), the son of Catherine; but, broken in body and spirit, he had lost his usefulness to Russian culture and education.[34] The treatment of Novikov was similar to that meted out by Catherine to the liberal critic Alexander N. Radishchev, author of *A Journey from St. Petersburg to Moscow* (1790), a sociopolitical work showing English, French, German, and American influences.

Catherine's impact on Russian culture and education has been variously assessed by historians. Quite a number take great pains to exhibit appreciation for her achievements in these fields. Try as one may to be as generous as possible to her, it is difficult not to take most seriously the judgment of Alexander N. Rypin, a nineteenth-century Russian historian, that "in the closing years of her reign Catherine was destroying with her own hands the tender growths of culture that she had once endeavored to implant." [35]

Reform and Reaction. Catherine's successor, Paul, was by no means a liberal tsar; nor was he especially interested in culture and education. His educational background was above that of the average Russian sovereign — he was fluent in French and German, knew Church Slavonic, and was at home in literature, geography, history, and mathematics. In 1797 he founded two new ecclesiastical academies in St. Petersburg and Kazan; and in 1798 he ordered the establishment of a university in Dorpat and issued several other ukases affecting education. In the main, however, Paul's activities "left no important traces in Russian education." [36] He prohibited the importation of foreign books, discouraged and censored the publication of domestic literature, and banned all liberal and foreign ideas and customs. "Russian students were recalled from foreign countries, and it became almost impossible for foreigners to enter the country." [37] These repressive measures, added to the closing down of the printing presses by Catherine, "put Russia intellectually in a strait jacket." [38] It would not be too difficult to correlate the growing despotism of Catherine and Paul with their reaction to the extremist tendencies of the French Revolution.

The assassination of Paul in 1801 and the succession by his son, Alexander I (1801–1825), gave promise of a new era in Russian life and education. Alexander was educated under the influence of his grandmother, Catherine the Great, and a Swiss revolutionary thinker who had been profoundly influenced by the eighteenth-century French Enlightenment, Frédéric César de la Harpe. Until 1812 he showed distinct liberal tendencies in cultural and educational affairs. Turning his back on his father's policies, he reinstated the privileges of publishing, the importation of foreign literature, the admission of foreigners, and the practice of foreign study. More positively, in 1801 he empowered a Secret Council (Comité Secret) of his personal friends, including Prince Adam Czartoryski, to take up matters of educational policy. The deliberations of this group, which breathed the spirit of the French Revolution, resulted in 1802 in the establishment of a Ministry of Public Culture, Youth Education, and Dissemination of Science.[39] The first minister was Count Peter V. Zavudovskii, who had served as chairman of Catherine's Commission for the Establishment of Schools from 1782 to 1799. The significant functions of the Ministry, however, were under the direction of the tsar's former tutor, Michael N. Muraviev, and included the supervision of all types of cultural and educational institutions except the military and naval schools, the Cadet Corpus, the Holy Synod academies, and the girls' schools under imperial protection. The organization of the country's educational system then followed with the adoption of the Preliminary Regulations for Public Education (1803) and the Statute of Schools Subordinate to Universities (1804). The new system, which showed many resemblances to Condorcet's plan for public education in France (1792), involved the creation of six districts, with the university in each district in charge of secondary education.[40] To the existing and recently revived Universities of Moscow, Vilna, and Dorpat were added the new Universities of Kharkov and Kazan (1805) and the Pedagogical Institute in 1816, incorporated in the newly founded University of St. Petersburg in 1819, discontinued in 1827, reorganized in 1828, and finally abolished in 1858.[41] Some educational work in the early part of Alexander's regime was carried on by private individuals in, for example, the Richelieu Lycée (1817), which developed into the University of Odessa, the Yaroslavl Lycée, and the Lazarev Institute of Oriental Languages in Moscow (1815). The tendency of the nobles to educate their children in private schools was combated by the government with the establishment of a *lycée* at Tsarskoe Selo (1811) and similar institutions elsewhere. The Tsarskoe Selo *lycée* may have been set up under the influence of the brilliant administrator Michael Speransky.[42]

The growing religious mysticism of Alexander following the defeat of Napoleon resulted in an increase of the influence of the church over schools. The third Minister of Education, Prince Alexander N. Golitsyn (1816–1824), was charged with putting the spiritual element back into education. To help this process, in 1817 the tsar issued a Manifesto Concerning the Establishment of the Ministry of Spiritual Affairs and Public Education, which brought about a union of the Ministry of Education and the Holy Synod. In 1819 Golitsyn formulated the degree requirements for the universities, ordered the teaching of the catechism and Bible reading in the secondary schools, and sent his assistant, Michael Magnitsky, to clear the University of Kazan of all liberal tendencies. Two other lieutenants of Golitsyn, Runich and Karneyev, were responsible for purging the University of St. Petersburg and the University of Kharkov, respectively. "Thus, in the name of public peace and order, higher education had largely been throttled by the end of the reign of Alexander." [43]

The eventful year 1819 was also marked by the founding of the University of St. Petersburg and by the beginning of Count Michael Speransky's service as Governor General of Siberia, where, until he returned to St. Petersburg in 1821, he was able to open "many Lancaster schools of mutual instruction right away without waiting for the full development of a regular school system." [44]

Alexander I died November 19, 1825, before the secret societies that had plotted against his autocratic regime had found a chance to act. "With all his good intentions he accomplished nothing for Russia and did nothing to civilize her people." [45] The situation seemed ripe for revolutionary action, particularly when confusion arose as to which of the dead tsar's two brothers, Constantine or Nicholas, would succeed him. Constantine, the elder of the two, renounced the throne and Nicholas became tsar in time to crush the Decembrist Revolt (December 14, 1825).

The Repressive Policies of Nicholas I. Nicholas I (1825–1855), who neither forgave nor forgot the uprising, looked at once to the schools, since he attributed the unrest to their teachings. Even before his coronation in 1826 he created a Committee for the Organization of Schools, under the direction of Admiral A. S. Shishkov, who had been appointed Minister of Education in 1824 by Tsar Alexander I. Shishkov was convinced that "to teach the whole nation to write and read would do more harm than good." [46] He and his colleagues undertook to fulfill the tsar's desires to undo the educational reforms of Alexander. Their work was made easier by a decree by Nicholas, in 1827, making it impossible for serfs to enter secondary schools and universities. The following year saw the issuance of a statute that allocated the higher educational institutions to the middle and upper classes and consigned the children of the lower classes, including the serfs, to the parish schools. This new statute, based on one enacted by King Frederick the Great of Prussia, stated that "the general aim of all schools is to give a moral education and to furnish the young with the means of the acquisition of the knowledge that each most needed according to his status." [47] Another feature of this law was to render impossible graduation from the primary school into the secondary school, and thus to insure that no one from an unauthorized social class would have an opportunity to rise.

Shishkov resigned in protest after his censorship law had been repealed (1828) and was succeeded by Prince K. A. Lieven (1828–1833), who made an effort to maintain the principles of school articulation embodied in the Statute of 1804 but with no success. Lieven did, however, elicit a decree from Nicholas reviving the Main Pedagogical Institute of St. Petersburg (1828). He also protested against the removal of autonomy from the universities. But any hope that Nicholas had changed his mind regarding his educational policies was dissipated in 1832 by the suppression of the University of Vilna after the Polish rebellion and by the replacement of Lieven by Count Sergei S. Uvarov (1833–1849).

Uvarov, a cultured and learned man, had been a liberal in his youth. Even before his appointment as Minister of Education, in 1832, he reported to Nicholas that the only way to keep the subversive doctrines of western Europe from contaminating the Russian people was to set up a school system founded on "the truly Russian conservative principles of Orthodoxy, autocracy, and nationality, our last anchor of salvation and the best guarantees of Russia's strength and greatness." [48] This formula of orthodoxy-autocracy-nationality became the official basis for all educational work during the reign of Nicholas I. As he assumed the portfolio of education, Uvarov expressed his determination to apply his slogan in order to distinguish the Russian education of his period from that of Alexander's, which he subjected to devastating attack. The nature of his policy can also be determined from his statements that many intellectual dams were necessary "to hold up the flow of new ideas into Russia" [49] and that he would die a happy man if he "could succeed to retard the development of Russia for about fifty years." [50]

The Nicholas-Uvarov combination "did not promise much good for education." [51] Although the new minister opened the University of Kiev during the first year of his term of office, this was no step forward, since it was merely a substitute for the suppressed University of Vilna. In 1835 Uvarov, through the General Regulations of Imperial Russian Universities, further reduced whatever autonomy the higher institutions had retained. The new university code controlled the students through an independent inspector; made theology, church history, and church law compulsory studies for all students; and introduced the study of Russian history.

In spite of the pains taken by the government to maintain the aristocratic character of the universities, some students from the lower classes managed to get admitted. To prevent further trespassing by unwanted individuals, the government began charging tuition fees in 1839 and raised them in 1845 and again in 1848. It also set up other barriers.

The French Revolution of 1848 made the tsar's government even more alert to the need of keeping the universities in their proper place. Many repressive measures were taken. The number of students not receiving government stipends was limited to 300 in each institution, the curriculum was cleansed of several philosophical and legal courses, professors were forced to submit to the Ministry of Education advance copies of their lectures and collateral reading lists for their students, and teachers and all other educational functionaries were forbidden to travel outside Russia. All this proved too much for Uvarov, who was convinced that tsarist repression had reached new depths and wished to put in a good word for the universities. When he was restrained, he handed in his resignation. The condition of the universities remained at a low point, regardless of who headed the Ministry of Education, throughout the remaining years of the reign of Nicholas.

One cannot leave the era of Nicholas without taking cognizance of the growth of university scholarship and the phenomenal development of literature. Perhaps the outstanding Russian scholar, from the standpoint of world renown, was Nikolai I. Lobachevski (1793–1856), professor of mathematics and rector of the University of Kazan, who pioneered in non-Euclidean geometry. In 1846, during the professional persecutions inspired by Uvarov, Lobachevski was discharged from both of his positions.

That Nicholas failed to discourage excellence was evident from the fact that his reign coincided with the golden age of Russian literature. The most significant writers, each of whom won a world-wide reputation, were Alexander Pushkin, Michael Lermontov, Nikolai Gogol, Alexander Herzen, and the great literary critic Vissarion Belinsky.

The Split Among the Intellectuals.   The era was also characterized by a deep differentiation among Russian thinkers. Beginning in the 1840's, the intellectuals were divided into two camps. The Westernizers looked to western Europe for inspiration regarding science, constitutional freedoms, humanitarianism, and education of the lower classes. In this group were Herzen and Belinsky, the latter being radical enough to be considered by Lenin one of his intellectual ancestors. The Slavophils looked to the past of Russia. The leading Slavophils, Alexei Khomiakov and Ivan Aksakov, are hardly as well known as the chief Westernizers, but they were no novices in the art of intellectual exchange. In fact, they and their colleagues were "very well educated and highly cultured," and by no means unaffected by Western thinking.[52] The Slavophil approach to education was, first of all, via the home and society and then by the church and school. Aksakov felt that the only solution was "complete freedom of education: then schools will be formed which will be private, not state, which will belong to and reflect the needs of society; then each milieu will itself create the schools which it needs most."[53]

Both the Westernizers and the Slavophils desired a much broader base for education than had hitherto been vouchsafed the Russian people, but they differed radically as to the kind of education that was desirable. Although the views of the Slavophils in many respects coincided with the views of the government, they were not regarded as an unmixed blessing by the government, probably because of the periodic criticism of some official policies. A publication representing the Slavophils was banned in 1852 — an indication that the government was ready to clamp down on all forms of thought, Westernizer or Slavophil.

The Great Reforms and After

Like his immediate predecessors on the throne, Tsar Alexander II (1855–1881) started his reign with a reform movement and then, after a period of constructive change, reverted to reaction. Among the many reforms initiated, the emancipation of the 22,500,000 serfs, in 1861, stands out as the most significant. In education, the new tsar began to make liberal changes in the very year of his accession, when he abolished the restriction on the number of university students. Two years later, in early 1857, he permitted the reopening of private schools. The following year a law provided for the encouragement of secondary schools for girls.

The Great Reforms. The more penetrating reforms came after the appointment in 1862 of a liberal Minister of Education, A. V. Golovnin. Trying to restore order in the universities by methods other than the punitive ones used by his immediate predecessors, Golovnin drafted a new code for higher education. After sending K. D. Kavelin to examine at first hand the university situation in Germany, France, and Switzerland, and after exposing the proposed university code to domestic and foreign criticism, academic and journalistic, the government adopted this code in 1863. Under it the universities were finally allowed to exercise the autonomy they had received originally in the Statute of 1804. In each university the professors had the right to organize themselves into groups for administering the affairs of their institution.

The following year a Secondary Education Code and an Elementary Schools Code were promulgated. The former created a classical Gymnasium and a nonclassical Gymnasium, while the latter permitted the local communities to take the initiative in organizing and maintaining schools.

The inauguration of Alexander's rule was also marked by the publication of educational writings that attempted to point the way to pedagogical progress. An article by the great surgeon N. I. Pirogov, called "Questions of Life," appeared in the *Journal of the Admiralty* in 1856 and caught the eye of the Minister of Education, who put the author in charge of the Odessa School Region. Pirogov was thus able to put into practice many modern ideas for the improvement of education. Among his innovations were the opening of the first Sunday schools for Russian adults (1859), pupil self-government, and pressure for the abolition of corporal punishment (1863). The special periodicals for the dissemination of pedagogical ideas included *Zhurnal dlia Vospitaniia* (*Journal of Education*), *Uchitel* (*Teacher*), and *Pedagogicheskii Sbornik* (*Pedagogical Collection*).[54] In addition, literary journals began to pay attention to educational questions.

The Period of Reaction. The great reform era came to an end in 1866, when a university student made an unsuccessful attempt to assassinate Alexander II. The tsar replaced Golovnin with a minister of a totally different stripe, Count Dmitri A. Tolstoi, who once more combined the office of the Ministry of Education with that of the Chief Procurator of the Holy Synod. Tolstoi remained in office until 1880, almost to the end of Alexander's reign. He opposed all forms of academic freedom and freedom of thought and became "a sinister figure notorious for his savage persecution of Roman Catholics and his vicious opposition to the emancipation of the serfs."[55]

Tolstoi, assuming that the seeds of revolution could be traced to educational institutions, at once began a campaign to restore government control over the universities and the schools. As early as 1867 he curtailed the university faculties' freedom of action and imposed strict police supervision over students. This attempt at control, however, did not achieve the hoped-for results; "serious student disturbances took place in 1869, 1874, and 1878."[56] Tolstoi continued his plan to subject the universities to centralized imperial dictation. His effort, in 1872, to get the universities to give up the privileges so recently received was turned down, and his perseverance, especially through the Delianov Committee, led to continual conflict with the advocates of academic freedom and to the resignation of Rector S. M. Soloviev of the University of Moscow. At length Tolstoi had a charter that satisfied him and he presented it to the State Council in February, 1880. It was too stringent, however, and he was dismissed in April of that year, to be succeeded by A. A. Saburov, a liberal who worked in the spirit of Golovnin.

Saburov withdrew the proposed charter at once, but his successor, Count T. D. Delianov, enacted the provisions of Tolstoi's repressive code in 1884.[57]

Tolstoi's intentions toward secondary education were no different, but here too he encountered hostility. It was over the opposition of a majority of the State Council that Alexander II translated Tolstoi's proposals on secondary schools into law (1871). The new second-ary-school code made classical languages compulsory in all Gym-nasiums, thus creating a "Greco-Roman bondage."[58] It was not the languages themselves so much as Tolstoi's method of administra-tion that breathed autocracy — the Ministry selected all textbooks, dictated all aspects of content and methodology, and effectively gagged the teachers. Another law, in 1872, set up a new type of nonclassical, scientific Gymnasium, again over the objections of a majority of the State Council. This new secondary school was to furnish a rather narrow technical training for boys of the lower middle class, after which they might attend higher technical schools but not universities.

Tolstoi was also active in making changes in girls' education and the schools of the Holy Synod.[59] The attempt to centralize power over primary schools culminated in the New Code for Elementary Schools (1874), under which the control of the local schools was taken away from the zemstvos (district councils) and placed in the hands of inspectors of the Ministry of Education. What Tolstoi wanted was to lay down school policies and select teachers, leaving the local bodies to raise school funds. As at the other scholastic levels, he faced considerable opposition.

Higher education for women was promoted under Tolstoi, pri-marily because Russian girls had been studying in the universities of Switzerland and Germany and absorbing revolutionary doctrines propagated by Russian political émigrés. Accordingly, the Ministry permitted university facilities for women, who had been denied access to the regular universities under the code of 1863. Higher instruction for women was provided in Moscow in 1869 and 1871, and in St. Petersburg, Kiev, and Kazan later in the decade. Tolstoi drew the line at medical education in these schools, but Count Dmitri Miliutin, Minister of War, provided facilities for medical courses for women at the Military Medical Academy (1872).

Dmitri Tolstoi was a faithful servant of his master, so far as absolutist philosophy in educational administration was concerned. He has been widely and correctly judged as a reactionary, but it is necessary to keep in mind that his term of office also saw some beneficial developments in education. At least one scholar exempts him "from the charge of having arrested the progress of education or having abandoned the democratic principles in favour of class system in education." [60]

Cultural Development. Culture reached a high point in the age of Alexander II. In the sciences, Dmitri Mendeleyev, Elie Mechnikov, and Ivan P. Pavlov were conducting studies that were to make them world famous. The great men of Russian literature — Leo Tolstoi, Ivan Turgenev, and Fedor Dostoievsky — flourished during this period. Of equal impressiveness were the giants of music — Alexander Borodin, Modest Mussorgsky, Peter I. Tchaikovsky, and Nikolai Rimsky-Korsakov. Florinsky explains this phenomenon in a few words: "Science in Russia, like art (and in a smaller degree music), stemmed from a foreign tradition and was somewhat akin to a luxurious flower blossoming on the surface of a stagnant pool of ignorance and illiteracy." [61]

Revolutionary thought on social and educational matters were expressed in Alexander's reign by Nikolai G. Chernishevsky, Nikolai A. Dobroliubov, N. I. Pirogov, Dmitri Pisarev, and Konstantin D. Ushinski, all of whom occupy an honorable place in current Soviet pedagogical thought.[62] Ushinski (1824–1870), in particular, after ups and downs in Soviet estimation, has emerged as the "father of Russian pedagogy . . . the greatest scholar and pedagogical theoretician and practitioner" [63] and "one of the greatest pedagogues, not only of Russia, but also of the whole world." [64] His ideas, thwarted under tsarist Russia, reached their "full development in the Soviet pedagogy under the basic teachings of Marx, Engels, Lenin, and Stalin on the Communist education of children. The Soviet people value highly the historic progressive role of the theoretical and practical activity of Ushinski." [65] The importance of Ushinski is also acknowledged by a penetrating critic of Soviet education, George S. Counts, who describes him as "one of the truly great educators of Europe in the nineteenth century." [66] In other countries Ushinski has not attained similar recognition.

During the reign of Alexander the other Tolstoi, a most significant figure for Russian and world culture, produced his great works in literature, philosophy, and education. *War and Peace* (1869) is beyond any doubt one of the masterpieces of world literature, if not, indeed, the greatest novel of all time. In 1859 in Yasnaya Polyana, now a four-hour automobile journey from Moscow, Leo N. Tolstoi (1828–1910) opened a free elementary school for the children of the peasants in the vicinity. At the same time he began to issue a pedagogical journal in which he discussed his ideas for better education. As preparation for this venture, he visited schools and cultural institutions in Germany, France, Switzerland, and Italy. The Russian government, however, was in no mood to tolerate his school, and in 1862 a raid by the police served to discourage Tolstoi from further practical effort.[67]

It is worthy of recording, before leaving this period, that the manual training of Russia won international plaudits at the Philadelphia Centennial Exposition in 1876. American educators admired the exhibit of the work done at the Imperial Technical School of Moscow under the direction of Victor Della Vos. Two well-known leaders in technical training, President John D. Runkle of the Massachusetts Institute of Technology and Dean Calvin M. Woodward of the Engineering School of Washington University, wrote and lectured in praise of what had been accomplished in Russia in this field. Their enthusiasm was contagious and a number of cities introduced the Russian practices. Noteworthy is the fact that Russian technical instruction was derived from principles and practices of Scandinavian and Swiss origin.

Reaction and Revolution. The assassination of Alexander II in 1881, on the day he was to confirm some mild governmental changes, brought Alexander III (1881–1894) to the throne of the Romanovs. After some shadowboxing with the possibility of reform, he turned decidedly toward reaction and the policies of Nicholas I. The following year the new Minister of Education, Count T. D. Delianov (1882–1897), the right-hand man of Dmitri A. Tolstoi, began to take repressive steps against students after disturbances at various universities. With the support of the tsar, Delianov enacted a new University Code in 1884 over the opposition of the State Council. The new rules abolished the autonomy of the universities by centralizing all important functions, such as the appointing of professors and administrators, in the Ministry of Education, by revoking all student rights to act as a corporate body and imposing police and other forms of supervision over the students, and by sharply curtailing opportunities for the higher education of women. That these regulations did not achieve the government's aims was evident from the fact that in 1890 disorders took place in seven universities.

The power of Konstantin P. Pobedonostsev, Chief Procurator of the Holy Synod and tutor of Alexander III and Nicholas II, was often behind the reactionary measures in education, as in other affairs. Under his inspiration and instigation, Alexander apparently sponsored, and certainly did not oppose, the pogroms against the Jews in 1881–1882 and the anti-Jewish university rules of 1885–1887. The educational policy toward national and religious minorities became Russification, the prevalent policy under Nicholas I. The Russian language was mandatory, and the Ministry of Education took all except the Moslem schools under its direct administration. Other educational legislation concerned the promotion of the church parochial schools as a counterforce to the public schools (1884) and the non-admission of the children of the lower classes to the Gymnasiums (1887).

The cultural leaders who lived and worked during this era of autocracy included Leo Tolstoi, Anton Chekhov, Peter Tchaikovsky, and Nikolai Rimsky-Korsakov. One particularly free spirit was Vladimir S. Soloviev, son of the famous historian. A profound and original religious thinker possessing none of the anti-minority prejudices that characterized many Russian intellectuals, Soloviev has been called "the greatest philosopher Russia has produced," [68] and was to publish some of his writing abroad.

The most significant intellectual development of this period was, of course, the rise of the revolutionary movement. Marxian thought had already been made available in the Russian language through translation of the *Communist Manifesto* (1862) and *Das Kapital* (1872), and throughout the reign of Alexander III the revolutionaries, theoreticians and practical men, plotted and bided their time. The death of Alexander III concluded "a period of reaction and stagnation in education." [69] The attempt by the tsar and his mentor, Pobedonostsev, to make autocracy prevail in matters of the mind as in all other matters was successful for a time under his successor, but the first revolution was only a few years in the future.

The reign of Nicholas II (1894–1917) was marked by foreboding events — the Russo-Japanese War, the 1905 Revolution with Bloody Sunday, the extension of liberal and revolutionary thought, and World War I. Throughout these years, revolutionary steps were taken amid retrogressive movements. The regime could not prevent the activities of Georgi V. Plekhanov (1852–1918), leader of the Menshevik (minority) faction in the Social Democratic (Marxist) Party, or of Vladimir Ilyich Ulyanov — known as Lenin — (1870–1924), leader of the Bolshevik (majority) element in the Party. The Marxists had organized their party in 1898 in Minsk; they split in 1903 at the Second Congress, which took place in Brussels and London. The Bolshevik organ, *Pravda*, began publication in 1912. During this same period Paul Miliukov (1859–1943), the historical scholar who served as a spokesman for liberal tendencies in Russia, founded the Constitutional Democratic Party. In 1906 the first elective assembly, the Duma, began to deliberate and to offer advice to the government, but it had no legislative power and was often disregarded by the ministers and the tsar.

During the periods of freedom that existed on and off following the Revolution of 1905, which, according to Hans, "was only possible because of the great progress made in education during the preceding decade," [70] Anton Chekhov, Maxim Gorki, and Leonid Andreyev produced some extraordinary works in literature. In two other fields of culture, moreover, Russia continued to excel. Sergei Rachmaninoff and Igor Stravinsky were the chief contributors to the Russian reputation in musical composition, and many first-rank concert artists and opera singers added to her cultural luster. In the theater, Konstantin Stanislavsky was supreme, while the ballet of Sergei Diaghilef, Anna Pavlova, and Waslaw Nijinsky could not be duplicated anywhere.

The field of education was far less productive than was that of culture. In the first place, the entire period featured continual student disturbances. Even more significant for the future, general student strikes were characteristic from 1899 onward, affecting universities all over Russia. The universal strike of 1905 — the year of the Revolution — resulted at first in the closing of all universities, but later in the year the government authorized a University Statute restoring some of the privileges of the higher institutions of learning. In the same year an Academic Union of Professors was formed to protect the rights of university faculty members, who were at least as vulnerable to dismissal and persecution as were the students.

In an attempt to curb student unrest, the government made some concessions to the students, but these were too meager to stop the campaign. The universities remained to the very last hotbeds of revolutionary activity, despite the policy of expulsion, exile, and execution of students and faculty.

This is not to say that there was no positive side to Russian higher education. New higher institutions were opened during the era of Nicholas — the Psycho-Neurological Institute in St. Petersburg (1907), the Municipal University of Moscow (1908), the University of Saratov (1909), and several universities in various parts of Russia during World War I. Moreover, the student population increased threefold between 1895 and 1914.[71] Women students had their changes in fortune, with the new courses opened to them in 1907 and discontinued in 1908; in 1915 women were admitted to the universities on an equal basis with men students. The policy of repression in 1909 resulted in the drastic reduction of the number of Jewish students and the loss of institutional privileges under a new University Statute. Further persecution of students and faculty occurred in 1911, but in 1915, when it was too late to save the government, the universities were once more granted autonomy.

The secondary schools changed somewhat for the better. The classical emphasis in the Gymnasiums was curtailed in 1902, and Greek had practically disappeared by 1914. The number of students, boys and girls, in both the Gymnasiums and the Real Gymnasiums increased considerably, and a larger percentage of lower-class youth received opportunities for secondary education. From approximately 1895 to 1915 there was practically a threefold increase in secondary-school attendance.[72]

Primary education showed the greatest progress just prior to World War I. In 1908 the government approved a primary-education law that made school attendance free and compulsory between the ages of eight and eleven. This law was to go into full effect in 1922. Another law (1912) provided a system of higher elementary education, but few schools at this level were in operation by the time the war started. In 1915 the Duma considered a new bill for compulsory attendance, but the war situation and the coming revolution prevented any definitive action. "Several more years of progress at the same pace would have brought Russia to universal elementary education and to a democratic ladder system." [73]

It is instructive to consider the statistical figures. The only complete census in the Russian Empire revealed that the total population in 1897 was 125,600,000, of whom only 13 per cent lived in cities and towns. For the entire empire there was a literacy rate of 21 per cent, broken down as follows: 29 per cent men; 13 per cent women; 45 per cent urban; 17 per cent rural.[74]

The liberal Minister of Education, Count P. N. Ignatiev (1915–1916), claimed that in 1916 "91% of the children of the Empire attended the schools; the literacy of the total population was estimated at 56%." [75] His figures indicated that the estimated educational budget for 1916 was 6,244,553 rubles more than the 1915 budget, but that the estimate for 1917, "in spite of the war difficulties," was raised, "through Imperial sanction, by 30,000,000 rubles over the 1916 estimate." [76] To judge from these statistics, as well as from the detailed analysis of school and university attendance,[77] it would seem that more significant changes in educational policy would have been likely in the future. But the tsar did not live to see them. "The gulf between the educated classes and the masses was the basic and fatal weakness of Russia's social structure." [78] This gulf was the product of the history of the Russian educational system with its "two contradictory ideals: the ideal of a democratic ladder system and that of a class system of education, according to the origin of pupils." [79]

THE HISTORICAL SETTING
AFTER THE REVOLUTION

The Revolution of February, 1917, deposed the tsar and brought in the first provisional government. In July, 1917, after opposition by the Bolsheviks, this government was replaced by a coalition headed by Alexander F. Kerensky. The October, or Bolshevik, Revolution of October, 1917, led to the formation of a Soviet government, which, the following year, signed a treaty of peace with Germany at Brest-Litovsk.

During the very short life of the pre-Bolshevik government some educational developments did take place. One of the first acts of the provisional government was to secularize the church schools and to place all schools under the control of the Ministry of Public Instruction. The new regime was intent upon the eradication of illiteracy and it took immediate steps toward that end.

The Time of the Revolution

The Revolution of Lenin was accompanied by a Civil War (1918–1920) and by clashes with foreign armies. The Communists — as the Bolsheviks soon called themselves — did not, however, neglect, educational matters. In 1917 a People's Commissar of Education, the literary critic Anatol V. Lunacharsky, was named to replace the Minister of Education. The Narkompros (People's Commissariat of Education) was organized into seventeen departments, which dealt with universal compulsory education, autonomy of colleges and universities, home education and peoples' universities, aid to independent school organizations, experimental pedagogy and school medicine and hygiene, technical schools and polytechnical education, construction of new schools, and literature and publishing.[1] At about the same time, the local schools were put under the control of the regional and local councils (soviets), representing the citizen, which took over the educational functions of the zemstvos.[2] Another decree, on February 5, 1918, removed schools from the control of the church. The Constitution of the Russian Socialist Federated Soviet Republic, adopted on July 10, 1918, by the Fifth All-Russian Congress of Soviets, declared that, "for the purpose of guaranteeing to the workers real access to knowledge," the R.S.F.S.R. "set itself the task of furnishing full and general free education to the workers and the poorest peasantry."[3] It goes without saying that this objective was not immediately realized; well over a decade passed before the new republic had a well-organized, regular educational system.

Communist Education. The early years of the Soviet regime brought thoroughgoing changes in educational policy and practice. "When the Bolsheviks seized power in 1917 they repudiated all the major features of Tsarist education,"[4] and at once "began combing the world for suggestions."[5] The scope of the repudiation may be determined from Lunacharsky's first annual report:

> In place of schools of all varieties and kinds — which formerly were sharply divided into a lower school for the plain people, and the middle school for the privileged classes and the well-to-do people, and divided further into schools for boys and those for girls, into technical and classical secondary schools, general and special school institutions — the Commissariat has introduced the *Unified Workers' School*, covering the entire length of the course of instruction.
>
> The unity of this school should be understood in two ways: first, that the class divisions are abolished and the school adopts a continuous grade system. In principle, every child of the Russian Republic

enters a school of an identical type and has the same chances as every other to complete the higher education. Second, that up to the age of 16, all specialization is omitted. It is self-understood that this does not hinder the adoption of the principle of individual attention and of the greatest possible variety of forms inside each school. But specialization in the full meaning of the word is permitted only after the attaining of the age of 16, and upon the foundation of a general and polytechnical education acquired already. The school is declared an absolutely lay institution; diplomas, in their character of certificates granting special rights, are abolished. The classical languages are declared nonobligatory.[6]

The school was divided into two sections, a five-year program followed by a four-year program. In principle, this nine-year course was obligatory. Moreover,

> Our school will be in fact *accessible to all*. To attain this end, not only are all tuition fees abolished, but the children are provided with gratuitous hot food, and the poorest children with shoes and clothing. It goes without saying that all school manuals are offered to the children free of charge by the school.[7]

More than forty years later, the intentions of Lunacharsky have not yet been fully realized.

The recent resurgence of interest on the part of Soviet leaders in the value of polytechnical education comes to mind when one reads other sections of Lunacharsky's report. For instance, in discussing the basic aims of the school, Lunacharsky stated,

> The labor character of the school consists in the fact that labor, pedagogical as well as productive labor, will be made a basis of teaching. In the primary schools it will be mostly work within the walls of the school: in the kitchen, in the garden, in special workshops, etc. The labor must be of a productive character — in this way, in particular, that the children serve the needs of the community so far as their strength will permit them. . . .[8]

The secondary-school pupils aged thirteen and over should be able to perform in

> . . . an easy but *real* labor outside of the school; the participation in

factory or shop work, the helping in serious farm work, the co-operation in some business enterprise, the co-operation in some social or state undertaking.[9]

Another revolutionary change introduced by the new regime was a regulation, in 1918, concerning admissions to universities in the R.S.F.S.R. Signed by Lenin as Chairman of the Soviet of People's Commissars, this act comprised the following orders:

1. Every person, regardless of citizenship and sex, reaching the age of 16, can be admitted as a member of the student body of any of the higher institutions of learning without submitting a diploma or testimonial papers attesting graduation from a secondary or other school.

2. It is forbidden to demand from persons seeking entrance any certificates whatsoever, except their identification papers.

3. All school institutions of the Republic, in conformity with the decree on joint instruction, dated May 27, 1918, are thrown open to all, regardless of sex. All persons responsible for violating this decree shall be tried by the Revolutionary Tribunal.

4. Admissions of students (freshmen for the 1918–1919 course) already made on the basis of either school certificates or competitive examinations, are hereby declared void. New entrance conditions in accordance with the requirements of the general provision on the higher educational schools of the Republic, now in the course of preparation, shall be published not later than September, 1918.

5. Tuition fees in higher educational institutions of the Russian Socialist Federated Soviet Republic are henceforth abolished. Tuition fees already paid for the first half of the academic year 1918–1919 shall be refunded accordingly.[10]

The Eighth Congress of the Communist Party, March 18–23, 1919, formulated the aims, structure, and program of the Soviet educational system:

1. The introduction of free and compulsory general and technical education (instruction in the theory and practice of the principal branches of production) for all children of both sexes up to the age of 17.

2. The establishment of a system of pre-school instruction: nurseries, kindergartens, homes, etc., to improve the social development of women and assist in their emancipation.

3. Full realization of the principle of a uniform industrial labor school with instruction in the native language, with co-education for children of both sexes, free from religious influences; a school where teaching is closely connected with socially useful labor and which prepares members of a communist society.

4. The supply of all pupils with food, clothes, boots and school appliances at the cost of the state.

5. The preparation of a new staff of teachers who are imbued with the ideas of Communism.

6. Bringing the toiling masses to take an active part in educational work (the development of councils of public education, mobilization of educated people, etc.).

7. General state assistance to self-education and the intellectual development of workers and peasants (creation of a system of institutions for education outside of the schools, such as libraries, schools for adults, people's palaces and universities, courses of lectures, cinemas, studios, etc.).

8. Spreading on a large scale of professional education for persons from the age of 17, in connection with technical knowledge.

9. Making all universities accessible to all desiring to study, particularly to workmen; attracting all people able to lecture to become instructors in these universities; abolishing all artificial barriers standing in the way of young scientists reaching professorial chairs; financial support of students in order to offer the proletarians and the peasants the fullest opportunity to take advantage of the universities.

10. Opening and making accessible to the toiling masses all the art treasures which were created by the exploitation of their labor, and which were formerly at the exclusive disposal of the exploiters.

11. The development of the propaganda of communist ideas on a wide scale and for that purpose the utilization of state resources and apparatus.[11]

The resemblance to the Lunacharsky program of the previous year is obvious. The principles expressed in these statements are very revolutionary when compared to those prevailing in imperial Russia. In actual practice, however, the Communists had to make many adjustments and changes as they realized the gap between the professed theories of the Revolution and of the war communism (1917–1921) on the one hand and the facts of cold reality on the other.

It was this realization, as well as the consequent return to pre-revolutionary practices, that led one student of Russian and

Soviet education to observe that the 1917 Revolution "did not establish a complete break with the Russian past," that "the educational system since 1917 has borrowed now here, now there, from the pedagogical theory and practice of tsarist Russia," and that there was a "similarity between Tsarist and Soviet educational procedures." [12] Another student concludes that "the educational developments during the present [Soviet] regime were perhaps less revolutions in than continuations of policies widely implemented several decades before the revolution, vigorous as have been the efforts in recent decades." [13] Those familiar with Russian education also note that the early experiments carried on by the new government were reminiscent of the pedagogical thought of Leo Tolstoi.

Borrowing from Abroad. (We have indicated two general sources of Soviet education during the formative years of the regime — Tsarist practice and Marxism.) But the early development of the school system cannot be fully comprehended without an appreciation of the borrowing of foreign ideas and practices by Soviet educators. Even before the Revolution, Stanislav T. Shatsky, one of the pedagogues who were to become influential figures in Soviet education, drew upon practices and ideas which he had observed in Scandinavia, Switzerland, Germany, Belgium, and France (1910, 1913–1914), as well as upon the thought of John Dewey.[14] Very possibly Shatsky learned about Dewey from his co-worker, Alexander Zelenko, at the First Moscow Settlement, a transplantation of the American idea of Hull House in Chicago, where Zelenko had lived for some time.[15] Shatsky joined the Communist Party in 1926, an action that was "doubtless one of the most important successes of the Soviet education of that time." [16]

The early Soviet educators borrowed liberally from all kinds of non-Russian thinkers, "from Montessori to Kerschensteiner, from Dewey to Lay and to Decroly." [17] The government translated German, French, and English works on psychology and education, issuing thousands of copies of Russian versions of them.[18] In 1926, in fact, a lone visitor remarked that "Kilpatrick, Thorndike, Dewey, and other American educators are almost as well-known in the Soviet Union to-day as they are in the United States." [19] They were, however, largely misunderstood and misinterpreted. Much of the

Soviet interest in American education was concentrated on the project method, which was recommended by Nadezhda K. Krupskaya, the wife of Lenin, in 1924.[20]

At this point we might mention briefly the sources of the concept of polytechnical education, which was mentioned in Lunacharsky's first report and which has been given practical attention at various times in Soviet educational history, particularly since 1958. The idea came primarily from Karl Marx, but also from Friedrich Engels and later from Vladimir I. Lenin. The *Communist Manifesto* (1848) of Marx and Engels probably contains the first Marxian statement on polytechnical training. In "the most advanced countries," say the authors of this document, there will be a "combination of education with industrial production." [21] The instructions sent by Marx in 1866 to the delegates of the Congress of the First International at Geneva, which were accepted by a resolution in the same year, interpreted education as consisting of three elements: the mental, the physical, and the polytechnical,[22] the last of which

> ...imparts the general principles of all processes of production, and simultaneously initiates the child and young person into the practical use and handling of the elementary instruments of all trades. . . . The combination of paid productive labor, mental education, bodily exercise, and polytechnic training, will raise the working class far above the level of the higher and middle classes.[23]

The immediate source of Marx's thinking on polytechnical training was doubtless Robert Owen, who received his inspiration from the French social reformer Charles Fourier. In *Das Kapital* Marx stated his basic idea and his indebtedness as follows:

> From the factory system budded, as Robert Owen has shown us in detail, the germ of the education of the future, an education that will, in the case of every child over a given age, combine productive labour with instruction and gymnastics, not only as one of the methods of adding to the efficiency of production, but as the only method of producing fully developed human beings.[24]

The school program of the Eighth Congress of the Communist Party (1919), cited earlier, not merely accepted these views on polytechnical education but actually went beyond them.[25]

The Progressive Period: 1921–1931

The second postrevolutionary period of Soviet education, which extended from 1921 to 1931, has been described by Soviet educators as "experimental" and by George S. Counts as "romantic." [26] It was a time of change in all aspects of life and culture. Lenin introduced the New Economic Policy, the NEP (1921–1927), an economic and industrial compromise under which the speedy application of Marxist doctrine toward the creation of a socialist state was delayed. Time was now measured in accordance with the Gregorian calendar, which had replaced the traditional Julian calendar in 1918. The Union of Soviet Socialist Republics was established in December, 1922, and in 1924 the first U.S.S.R. constitution went into effect. In domestic politics, after the death of Lenin, in 1924, Stalin's star rose steadily, resulting in 1929 in the expulsion of Leon Trotsky from the U.S.S.R. The position of the Soviet Union in foreign affairs was greatly strengthened by full recognition by Great Britain and France and by various agreements with Germany.

Lenin was fully aware of the importance of education in the creation of a new society. Doubtless he was acquainted with the major movements in modern education, probably through Krupskaya, whose writings show much familiarity with pedagogical ideas and practices, from those of Rousseau and Pestalozzi down to such early twentieth-century leaders as Cecil Reddie, Hermann Lietz, and Edmond Demolins of the New School movement [27] and, interestingly, William James.[28] His deep concern for learning was evident from the advice he gave to the third Komsomol Congress in 1920: "Study, study, and keep on studying in order to become better Communists." [29]

The Komsomol, or All-Union Leninist Communist Union of Youth in its present full designation, came into existence in 1918 as the militant youth arm of the party. Led by members of the party, the Komsomol was called upon to provide indoctrination programs for its own membership as "the training school of the Communist party," [30] and also to perform a variety of other functions, including the supervision of the Pioneers, a Communist organization for children aged ten to fourteen (the age of admission was later reduced to nine). The Communist children's organization of the Young Pioneers in the Name of Lenin was set up in 1922 to replace the Boy Scouts, which had been dissolved. The Pioneers were in turn entrusted with the direction of the Union of Little Octobrists, an organization founded in 1925 for children below the age of nine and named in honor of the October Revolution. By July 1, 1926, the Pioneers numbered 1,832,587 and the Octobrists 273,909.[31] The later growth of the Pioneers was even more rapid, but the Octobrists languished behind as an organization until very recent years.

Workers' education was given much attention with the introduction of *rabfaks* (workers' faculties) in 1919 by M. N. Pokrovsky, the Deputy Commissar of Education. Through these, factory workers could take courses to enable them to gain admission to higher education. So far as the universities were concerned, the authorities discriminated in favor of admitting children of workers and peasants and keeping those of bourgeois parents out. This policy of the "proletarianization of the universities," according to von Rauch, resulted in "a quick decline of the general intellectual status to the level of adult education schools lacking a systematic curriculum and a depth of knowledge." [32] Before long the Soviet educational leaders discovered that the policy was too extreme and had to be modified. In general, however, the idea that academic standards must be subordinated, to an extent at least, to the immediate needs of the new society persisted for some time. This was true of the secondary schools as well.

The Struggle for Literacy. Immediately after the Revolution, the Communist regime devoted considerable attention to its most pressing cultural-educational problem — the "liquidation of illiteracy and ignorance." [33] Lenin supplied a wealth of slogans — "You cannot build a Communist State with an illiterate people" [34] and "You must remember that an illiterate, uncultured people cannot conquer." [35] Moreover, in his report to the Second All-Russian Congress on Political Enlightenment, October 17, 1921, which dealt with the theme "The New Economic Policy and the Problems of Political Enlightenment," Lenin made the following significant statement: "An illiterate person stands outside; he must first be taught the ABC. Without this, there can be no politics; without this, there are only rumors, gossip, tales, prejudices, but no politics." [36]

These and related expressions served as springboards for action.

On December 26, 1919, Lenin signed a decree issued by the Soviet of People's Commissars, "On the Liquidation of Illiteracy among the Population of the RSFSR," which required all illiterates from the age of eight to fifty to learn reading and writing in their native language or in Russian, as each desired.[37] This ambitious inauguration of the campaign for literacy in the Soviet Union was followed up with various types of action. The Narkompros set up an All-Russian Extraordinary Commission for the Liquidation of Illiteracy in July, 1920, with M. I. Kalinin as president, to coordinate the campaign.[38] The First All-Russian Congress for the Liquidation of Illiteracy, held in February, 1927, adopted a program of organization of courses and of publications, and the second congress, meeting the following year, resulted in the founding of the society Down with Illiteracy, again with M. I. Kalinin as president.[39] This new organization soon became very active, making use of a special publishing house and a journal, both named *Doloi Negramotnost!* (Down with Illiteracy!).[40] Within the exceptionally short time of about two years the society could boast of 1,600,000 members in 28,000 cells.[41] In all phases of Soviet life, particularly in the Red Army, the authorities pushed their campaign for literacy with great vigor.

The literacy drive, as can well be understood, was a fundamental function of the program for enlightenment or indoctrination of the vast Soviet population. The readers and other textbooks were saturated with Communist doctrine.

The Soviet leaders have constantly claimed that the literacy campaign achieved phenomenal success. By 1927 at least, the results were still less than astounding, to judge from the admission of Albert P. Pinkevitch, Rector of the Second University of Moscow, to the effect that "one of our most urgent problems in the sphere of adult education is the liquidation of illiteracy." [42] This situation probably was the outcome of the subordination of the literacy campaign to the program of political propaganda, with the Communist leaders getting very little satisfaction from either.[43] Visiting the U.S.S.R. in 1927, Counts, a member of the technical advisory staff of the first American trade-union delegation to the Soviet Union, heard "much about the liquidation of illiteracy," as well as "frequent references to the need for liquidating political illiteracy." [44] To Kalinin, however, there was no such thing as political illiteracy in the Soviet Union. In his address to the graduating students of the Sverdlov Communist University, May 30, 1926, he boasted: "With respect to political education, political activity of the masses, and political permeation, our Soviet Union very likely stands in front of all European and non-European countries." [45] That the problem of general illiteracy was still important by the time the First Five-Year Plan was under way can be seen from the fact that the liquidation of illiteracy was one of the plan's objectives. The drive was stepped up as in a military campaign and in 1929 Lunacharsky, the relatively easygoing educator who had won credit for saving art masterpieces in the midst of the Revolution, was replaced by Andrei S. Bubnov, who had won Stalin's favor as commander for the political administration of the Red Army. [46] By the mid-thirties, however, the goal had been generally attained.

Antireligious Indoctrination. Of great significance was the Soviet campaign to eradicate all forms of religious influence. As early as January 21, 1918, a decree was issued whereby the church was separated from the state and the school was separated from the church. [47] In 1921 the religious education of children and youth was banned, and forced labor was declared to be the penalty for such teaching. New textbooks openly reflected the hostile attitude of the regime toward religion. Furthermore, all religious literature was forbidden and monasteries and church schools of all types were closed. [48] A special organization, the Society of Militant Atheists, founded in 1925, undertook to coordinate all antireligious activities through propaganda, exhibits, and other methods. The major publicity medium of this society was a journal, *Bezbozhnik* (*Godless*), which was blatant in tone and rather inferior in content. [49] All these activities were carried out in the spirit of Karl Marx's oft-quoted statement that "religion is the opium of the people."

During the following years, the Soviet authorities forbade the teaching of religion except privately and allowed special religious schools only for persons over eighteen. [50] At the same time, the schools were required to indoctrinate children with antireligious views. In the syllabus appeared such statements as "The October Revolution, which dethroned the tsar of the earth, has made superfluous the tsar of heaven." [51]

The various religious groups resisted to some extent. A religious youth organization, called Baptomol or Christomol, attempted to compete with the Komsomol, but it only evoked more intensive action on the part of the antireligious elements.[52]

An American scholar, Professor Samuel N. Harper of the University of Chicago, who visited Russia in 1926, reported that the Soviet government enforced antireligious legislation most rigidly against the Russian Orthodox Church.[53] On the other hand, the Moslems "were allowed certain exemptions, particularly in the field of religious training of minors," and "Protestant churches have been less curtailed in both educational work and civic activities because their memberships have not been large and because, also, they have been persecuted under the old regime." [54]

In spite of the concessions and various temporary setbacks, the Communists proceeded with their war against religious influences. On April 8, 1929, a decree codified all previous orders into a general law containing sixty-eight articles. Under Article 18, "The teaching of any kind of religious belief whatsoever is forbidden in State, public or private schools." [55] The Narkompros promulgated various regulations in 1929 and 1930 on the implementation of antireligious teachings on all levels and in all subjects of instruction, including mathematics and foreign languages. This authority recommended all the literature of the Society of the Militant Godless, especially the periodical *The Godless in the School,* issued by the journal *Bezbozhnik.*[56]

From a campaign of this nature, which eliminated religious instruction to children and youth and resulted in the transformation of churches into Communist clubs and museums, one might have expected a rather large degree of success. The Communist leaders, however, had to admit that their goal was far from reached. In 1932, the president of the Society of Militant Atheists conceded in his report that close to half of the Soviet people still adhered to the beliefs of some religious denomination.[57] As late as the eve of World War II the regime realized the failure of its antireligious activities, which had aroused animosity toward itself and otherwise did not live up to the Communist objectives.[58] The schools continued, as effectively as they could, to indoctrinate opposition to religion, picking up the cue from the Society of the Militant Godless, whose influence grew weaker in the late 1930's. They did not concentrate on antireligion as such, however, but tried to prove that science contained the truth. This approach, coupled with the lack of religious teaching, served to keep the mass of Soviet Russia's youth away from religion. Where direct persecution led to moderate results, the positive method of the schools yielded richer dividends to the Communists.

A new and more favorable religious policy was adopted during World War II.[59] After the war, religion and religious education had their ups and downs, with antireligious attacks rising rapidly in 1954.[60] The post-Stalin thaw again yielded concessions to religious groups, but essentially the ban upon organized religious education to the young is still in force. On the basis of a study of 165 individuals who had fled the U.S.S.R. since World War II, Ivan D. London and Nikolai P. Poltoratzky concluded that "religious sentiment is not only widespread among the Soviet younger generation, but on the increase." [61]

The general aim of secularized education in the Soviet Union during the decade of the 1920's was clearly expressed by the educational authority Pinkevitch as "all around development of a healthy, strong, actively brave, independently thinking and acting man, acquainted with the many sides of contemporary culture, a creator and a warrior in the interests of the proletariat and consequently in the final analysis in the interests of the whole of humanity." [62] Counts, who was in the Soviet Union at about the time these words were written, stated that:

> According to official pronouncements, education in Soviet Russia embraces the threefold purpose of fostering the development of an efficient economic order, of promoting the organization of the political life of the Union, and of furthering the evolution of national cultures.[63]

In other words, the individual was to subserve the needs of the group and of the new Communist order. This was to be the new religion.

Pedology. "The axis of the Soviet educational system is the Unified Labor School," wrote Harper in the 1920's.[64] The term "unified" referred to an organization that made it possible for a child to go through all grades up to and including the ninth in a single institution. The term "labor" was in line with the concept that productive, socially helpful activity was the basis of all education. Through actual experience in work (in addition to studying it academically) the pupil was considered competent to live and thrive in a collectivist social order founded on labor activity. The basic procedure in this school was the complex method, defined by the great Soviet educator Paul P. Blonsky as "a central theme, in connection with which children receive the necessary information concerning nature, labor, and social life of mankind." [65] This means that the subjects taught in the elementary school were not compartmentalized but presented in an interrelated fashion.

The new school required a new psychological orientation toward the child. This was pedology, which meant to Blonsky "the science of the chronological development of the child under conditions of definite social-historical environment" and to Professor Bosov "the scientific synthesis of all that presents the actual results of different scientific disciplines studying the developing human, each from its own approach." [66] Pinkevitch defined pedology as a "science . . . concerned with the psychological and physical development of the child from birth to maturity," which "studies the biology and psychology of human growth" and furnishes findings enabling men to organize "methods for promoting the desired physical and mental development of the child." [67] Interest in this new field grew among educators, and no less than 2500 attended the First All-Union Congress of Pedology, December, 1927, through June, 1928. [68] The importance of this conference was evident from the fact that such prominent Communist leaders as Nikolai Bukharin, Lunacharsky, and Krupskaya took an active part. [69] Pedology continued to be popular until 1931, when a resolution of the Central Committee of the Communist Party started Blonsky and pedology on the road to oblivion, a journey finally completed in 1936.

By the close of the 1920's, the unified labor school had developed into the polytechnical school, following the "basic Marxian conception of polytechnical education." [70] The First All-Russian Congress on Polytechnical Education, which met in August, 1930, in Moscow, was addressed by Krupskaya and a member of the Central Committee of the Communist Party. This circumstance, however, did not prevent the Party from setting aside polytechnical education until 1952.

Blonsky was a victim of the 1936 purge; there are few references to him after that date.[71] It is believed that he died in 1941. He was probably the most creative educational thinker, in the international sense, in the Soviet Union — according to Counts, "perhaps the most erudite Soviet scholar in the whole field of education." [72] He was acquainted with the work of important American and other educators and, in turn, was known to them. As an educational psychologist, he drew considerably from the work of American behaviorists.[73] His tragedy, like that of Shatsky, was that he adopted the Communist *Weltanschauung* only to be repudiated by his new political faith. Even his labor school, which was declared by Schoenchen to be "a factory, not a school at all," and "a form of fanaticism," [74] did not save him.

Impressions of Foreign Visitors. The student of the history of Soviet education can also learn something from the contemporary reports of foreign educators and scholars. One of the first visitors to observe Soviet schools in the early 1920's, Anna Louise Strong, described the devotion to John Dewey's ideas. "Every new book by Dewey is seized and eagerly translated into Russian for consultation," after which the Russians "make their own additions." [75] Jawaharlal Nehru, who was in Russia in 1927, wrote that "to an Indian the most interesting and instructive aspect of her [Russia's] new policy is probably her attitude to education and especially her gallant fight against illiteracy"; his first impression was "of the enormous importance that is attached to the education of youth by the Bolshevik leaders and rank and file." [76] The latter statement is strongly reminiscent of the first conclusion reached by some of the American delegations visiting the U.S.S.R. in 1958.

Counts was impressed during the summer of 1927 by the Communist influence on education and by the various changes, especially in the organization of political and adult-education centers. Of particular interest are his conclusions that "there is perhaps no place in the world where new educational ideas receive a warmer welcome" and that "the educational authorities are prepared to give a hearing to any suggestions or theories which, of course, do not question those basic social aims which are the guiding stars of education in Russia." [77]

The judgments of his fellow visitor Carleton Washburne, then superintendent of schools in Winnetka, were very specific. Like

Counts, Washburne noted the American origin of many Soviet ideas and practices (Dewey's thought, the Dalton Plan, the project method) and complained that "all too swiftly they [the Russian educators] discarded the old and plunged into the new," but he was nonetheless convinced that "today Soviet Russia as a whole probably has the most modern and the most progressive school program and methods of any country in the world." [78] Despite this generalization, he observed the inadequate training of Soviet teachers, the insufficient schools and educational equipment, the meager amount of schooling available, the lack of a compulsory system of education, and the lowering of scholastic standards. Washburne called a spade a spade — "The schools deliberately and thoroughly indoctrinate children with communism and atheism." [79] In his conclusion to the chapter prepared for the labor delegation report Washburne emphasized that "a rapid growth and improvement" was "taking place both in material conditions and in pedagogical methods," and that "Russia is clearly on the road to an extremely interesting and efficient system of universal education," one, however, that "leads to a goal which most of the world will condemn — effective, loyal participation in a materialistic, communistic, workers' civilization." [80] In another essay on the same visit Washburne expressed an opinion that the Russian "system of experimental schools is admirable," but here too he balanced his generous praise with bitter criticism. Russia's "failure to recognize individual differences is stupid," he maintained, and "her thrusting of communism and materialism down the throats of her children seems to some of us criminal." [81]

John Dewey went to the Soviet Union in 1928 as a member of a delegation of twenty-five educators and wrote a series of articles for the *New Republic* in November and December, 1928, which were reprinted the following year, together with essays on other countries. In this report Dewey observed that, to the Communist leaders, "propaganda is education and education is propaganda," and that, moreover, "they are more than confounded; they are identified." [82] The distinguishing element of Soviet education with respect to other nations' systems and to foreign progressive schools ("with which they have much in common") was "precisely the conscious control of every educational procedure by reference to a single and comprehensive social purpose." [83] Dewey felt that "the Russian educational situation is enough to convert one to the idea that only in a society based upon the cooperative principle can the ideals of educational reformers be adequately carried into operation." [84] He found that Russian school children were "much more democratically organized than are our own" and that they received "through the system of school administration a training that fits them, much more systematically than is attempted in our professedly democratic country, for later active participation in the self-direction of both local communities and industries." [85]

Dewey seemed to lean toward a definite appreciation of the Soviet schools. Although admitting, in general, the limitations and difficulties of the system, he expressed amazement "at the progress already made," since it was "a going concern; a self-moving organism." [86] He confessed that, "while an American visitor may feel a certain patriotic pride in noting in how many respects an initial impulse came from some progressive school in our own country, he is at once humiliated and stimulated to new endeavor to see how much more organically that idea is incorporated in the Russian system than in our own." [87] It is possible that Dewey was here hinting at the remarkable reception of his educational thought in the Russia of that day.

Dewey's admiration for Soviet educational progress made him "deeply regret those artificial barriers and that barricade of false reports that now isolates American teachers from that educational system in which our professed progressive democratic ideas are most completely embodied, and from which accordingly we might, if we could, learn much more than from the system of any other country." [88] This rather lavish praise was tempered a little by one of his concluding remarks, which nonetheless expressed his faith in the future of Soviet education:

> There is, of course, an immense amount of indoctrination and propaganda in the schools. But if the existing tendency develops, it seems fairly safe to predict that in the end this indoctrination will be subordinate to the awakening of initiative and power of independent judgment, while cooperative mentality will be evolved. It seems impossible that an education intellectually free will not militate against a servile acceptance of dogma as dogma. One hears all the time about the dialectic movement by means of which a movement contradicts

itself in the end. I think the schools are a "dialectic" factor in the evolution of Russian communism.[89]

Dewey's prophecy is still awaiting fulfillment.

In view of the generous judgment of Soviet education by John Dewey, it is interesting to note how the Soviet educators reacted to him. In 1929 Pinkevitch praised him as one of "the bourgeois forerunners of the true labor school" and as coming "infinitely closer to Marx and the Russian communists" than contemporary German educators.[90] The Soviet pedagogical authorities urged that "every contemporary student of education should study his [Dewey's] writings" but should never forget that the American "is a representative of the bourgeoisie, albeit a talented one and one who has superior grasp of contemporary industry, and therefore in his ideology a stranger to us." [91] Yet only a few years afterward, for reasons not strange to one acquainted with the history of the period, Pinkevitch was able to write *Science and Education in the U.S.S.R.* (1935) without a single reference to Dewey.

Dewey's educational works were made available in Russian translations,[92] and his ideas were kept before the public. The 1931 edition of the *Bolshaia Sovetskaia Entsiklopediia* characterized Dewey as "an outstanding American philosopher, psychologist, sociologist, and pedagog" and discussed his thought at some length.[93] But 1931 was the year of the decision to throw the progressive educational practices out the window, and Dewey's reputation began to decline in the Soviet Union. The condemnation of Dewey by the Communists may be traced to Dewey's leadership in the investigation of Stalin's charges against Trotsky and to his exoneration of the latter.

The 1952 edition of the *Bolshaia Sovetskaia Entsiklopediia* contains a shorter article on Dewey and is far less complimentary. He is condemned as "a reactionary bourgeois philosopher and sociologist," as working "in the interests of the aggressive policy of the government of the U.S.A.," and as "spreading racial obscurantism, amorality, unscrupulousness. . . ." [94] Dewey is taken to task for using education for indoctrinating the idea of capitalism and a hatred of communism. The article concludes as follows:

The philosophy of Dewey is a philosophy of war and fascism.

Dewey is a proclaimer of contemporary American reaction, an ideologist of American imperialism, [and] a violent enemy of the U.S.S.R., the country of the people's democracy and of the revolutionary theory of Marxism-Leninism.[95]

Other examples of the denunciatory attitude on the part of Soviet philosophers and pedagogues toward Dewey have been cited by Levit. [96] Also, one cannot overlook what was recommended to members of the Comparative Education Society by the members of the Academy of Pedagogical Sciences as the best example of recent research on the history of educational theory. This work, *The Pedagogy of J. Dewey in the Service of Contemporary American Reaction,* by V. S. Shevkin, consists of five chapters, the first of which contains footnote references to Lenin, Marx and Engels, Stalin, Zhdanov, Kalinin, and Malenkov. Only one educator is quoted, Herbart, but not a single footnote is devoted to Dewey. The second chapter, "Pragmatism — Instrumentalism — the Philosophical Foundation of the Reactionary Pedagogy," is based upon Dewey and William James, but again with liberal citations from the writings of the Marxist-Leninist-Stalinist school. The third chapter deals with "The Pseudoscientific Meaning of Education in the Pedagogy of J. Dewey"; the fourth with "School, Pupil and Teacher as Represented by Pragmatic Pedagogy"; and the final chapter with "J. Dewey — the Henchman of Contemporary Imperialist Reaction." In these Dewey is cited, to be sure, but he is evaluated in the light of the Marxist-Leninist-Stalinist thinkers, who share the footnotes equally with the American educator.

The final paragraph of the fifth chapter is typical of the tone of the entire book:

> Dewey is the wicked enemy not only of the American people but also of all the freedom-loving peoples on our earth. The entire system of his views on the world, society, and the younger generation is, knowing no bounds, an apologia for American imperialism.[97]

By way of contrast, Shevkin mentions "the great leader of the Soviet people and of all progressive mankind, I. V. Stalin. . . ." [98] The fortune of Dewey had undergone quite a change in the Soviet Union since the time of his visit. One interpreter of Soviet life attributes the revised attitude to Dewey to the circumstance that:

Unhappily Soviet philosophers have weakened their own case by displaying a formidable ignorance of American philosophy, especially in their continued misunderstanding of the American school of Naturalism led by the late John Dewey.[99]

This is perhaps too simple an explanation.

The development of Soviet education in the 1920's was a process of constant change, which brought about "the disorganization of instruction." [100] It was doubtless the desire to bring order out of chaos that led the Communist Party leaders to abandon their experimentation, flexibility, and foreign pedagogical ideas in the next decade.

The Period of 1931 to 1941

The decade from 1931 to 1941 saw the completion of the First Five-Year Plan, the Second Five-Year Plan (1933–1937), and most of the Third Five-Year Plan (1938–1942). These plans converted the Soviet Union from an agricultural nation into one with a dual economy of industry and agriculture. The industrial development, however, did not change the nature of the regime. The average Soviet citizen gained nothing substantial either in material comfort or in personal freedom. In point of fact, Communist power was reasserted as never before. The assassination of Stalin's close associate Sergei Kirov, in 1934, became the point of departure for a series of treason trials, party purges, and executions of old Bolsheviks and other Communist leaders.

In the midst of this turmoil a new constitution (the "Stalin Constitution") was adopted, in 1936. This document proclaimed in Article 121 that "Citizens of the U.S.S.R. have the right to education" and that:

> This right is ensured by universal and compulsory education; by free education up to and including the seventh grade; by a system of state stipends for students of higher educational establishments who excel in their studies; by instruction in schools being conducted in the native language, and by the organization in the factories, state farms, machine and tractor stations, and collective farms of free vocational, technical and agronomic training for the working people.[101]

Nurseries and kindergartens were to be provided under Article 122 to enable women to enjoy "equal rights with men in all spheres . . . of activity." Under Article 124, which separates the church from the state and "the school from the church," "Freedom of religious worship and freedom of anti-religious propaganda is recognized for all citizens." It is noteworthy that the constitution did not include freedom of religious propaganda as one of the rights of the Soviet citizen.

An important milestone in the development of Communist indoctrination was the publication in 1938 of the *History of the Communist Party of the Soviet Union* (*Bolsheviks*): *Short Course,* a volume authorized by the Central Committee of the Communist Party and edited by one of its commissions. During the final years of Stalin's life the statement was frequently made that he was the author of this volume and it appears, in fact, as Volume XIII in his collected works. Stalin did order the writing of the book and annotated and corrected the manuscript, which was prepared by a committee of historians working under the supervision of A. A. Zhdanov. His actual authorship was confined to a section, "On Dialectical and Historical Materialism," in Chapter Four, a total of 32 out of 440 pages in the original Russian text.[102] The objectives of this history of the Communist Party were to establish the role of Stalin in the October Revolution and to provide historical justification for Stalin's personal dictatorship. Needless to say, this history formed the image of Stalin that was retained in the Soviet mind until his death and to a large extent until Khrushchev's downgrading speech in 1956.

On the cultural front, the Soviet Union could still boast of Maxim Gorki, Alexis Tolstoi, Boris Pasternak, and Mikhail Sholokhov, but very few others reached an audience outside the U.S.S.R. The Soviet composers Sergei Prokofiev, Dmitri Kabalevsky, Aram Khatchaturian, and Dmitri Shostakovich are an even more impressive array of talent. The excellence of Soviet ballet, of the Stanislavsky method of acting, and of the Sergei Eisenstein films was acknowledged all over the world.

Soviet foreign relations were very extensive during the period. The United States conferred *de jure* recognition on the U.S.S.R. in 1933; and from 1934 until 1939, when it was expelled for invading Finland, the Soviet Union was a member of the League of Nations. The economic and nonaggression pacts between Hitler and Stalin were doubtless significant factors in paving the way for the Nazi invasion of Poland. The sudden attack by Hitler upon his ally, on June 22, 1941, was a turning point in Soviet history.

The Decline of Progressive Education. In 1931 the growing dissatisfaction with various aspects of education and psychology finally came to a head. On September 5, 1931, the Central Committee of the Communist Party passed a resolution, "On the Primary and Secondary School," [103] ordering the schools to apply themselves more seriously to instruction. The charge was made that the schools had failed to teach the fundamentals of learning and to prepare students adequately for the technikums and higher educational institutions. According to Pinkevitch, "unfortunate results showed that the project method and the Dalton Plan do not provide sound and profound knowledge, and do not train the children to work systematically." [104] The Party accordingly determined to restore the Leninist line in education and to eliminate foreign techniques. This was the beginning of the decline of the influence of foreign educational ideas.

The second step in the modification of the Soviet school system was the enactment of a decree on August 25, 1932, by the Central Committee of the Communist Party, "On School Programs and Administration in Primary and Secondary Schools." [105] This decree criticized the teaching of various subjects and called for a rapid revision of all primary- and secondary-school courses of study. Special stress was laid upon the strengthening of school discipline and the restoration of the teacher as leader. This point was reiterated later in the year by Andrei Bubnov of the Narkompros when he told regional educational commissars and other functionaries that "our next task is to re-establish discipline in the schools," since "without planned discipline properly imparted to the students there will never be a real Soviet education." [106]

Still another stage in the process of eliminating progressive education was the decree by the Central Committee, February 12, 1933, "On Textbooks for the Elementary School." [107] The Party revoked the previous practices and demanded "real textbooks" rather than those that "do not impart systematic knowledge of the subjects of the curricula." [108] Two more decrees, both issued on May 16, 1934, and both signed by V. Molotov, Chairman of the

Council of People's Commissars of the U.S.S.R., and J. Stalin, Secretary of the Central Committee of the Communist Party of the Soviet Union, gave instructions "On the Teaching of Civic History in the Schools of U.S.S.R." and "On the Teaching of Geography in the Elementary and Secondary Schools of the U.S.S.R." [109] That the power of the Communist Party was predominant in the educational affairs of the country was hardly debatable. There could be little doubt that the new laws marked an emphasis "on the ever-increasing role of the teacher as a fighter for communist education of the new generation." [110]

These decrees were followed by one under the auspices of the Council of People's Commissars and the Central Committee of the Communist Party, September 3, 1935, "On the Organization of Educational Work and Inner Order in the Primary, Incomplete Secondary, and Secondary School." [111] In this directive the Party restored the system of grading that had prevailed during tsarist times: (1) — *ochen plokho* (very bad), (2) — *plokho* (bad), (3) — *posredstvenno* (satisfactory), (4) — *khorosho* (good), and (5) — *otlichno* (excellent). Precise instructions were given on evaluation for promotion and for entrance into higher schools. The grade of "5" in the major subjects and at least "4" in all the others entitled a secondary-school graduate to enter a higher educational institution without having to take an entrance examination. These practices, it should be noted, have now been greatly modified.

The death blow for progressive education finally arrived on July 4, 1936, when the Central Committee of the Communist Party issued its decree "On the Pedological Perversions in the System of the Narkompros." [112] Pedology was branded as pseudo-scientific and anti-Marxist; it was accordingly abolished and its practitioners were condemned. Intelligence and other psychological tests were discontinued, with the result that the function of psychology in the school was, for all practical purposes, eliminated. [113] The combination of reaction in politics and education, together with the resurgence of nationalism, brought about the disappearance and liquidation of leading educators, among them Pinkevitch, Lunacharsky, and Blonsky. As the stars of these pioneering pedagogues set, that of Anton S. Makarenko rose until he became recognized as "the outstanding Soviet pedagogue." [114]

Pinkevitch, during this period of change, expressed clearly the basic reasoning behind the drive for more systematic instruction:

> The Soviet Union has set itself the task of overtaking and outstripping the capitalist countries in the matter of technique and economics. It can fulfill this task only if it masters all the knowledge of science and technique to be found in the most advanced countries of Europe and America. It is in correlation with this task that the general and vocational schools of the U.S.S.R. carry out their work. Hence the need for discipline in the school.[115]

There were other educational developments of interest and significance during the decade 1931–1941. Paradoxically, after the liquidation of pedology "there began a period of more or less normal 'Western' pre-school policy, with stress upon play, music, etc. Toys, dolls, fairy-tales — all of which had previously been banished — reappeared, together with childish fun and laughter." [116] Conferences and special requalification courses for kindergarten teachers and workers with young children were held immediately to acquaint such personnel with the new Party line.[117]

In 1934 Stalin, reporting as Secretary General to the Seventeenth Congress of the Communist Party, enumerated recent cultural and educational advances but admitted "the intolerable fact that our pedagogical and medical 'faculties' are still neglected. This is a great defect bordering on the violation of the interests of the State. We must remove this defect without fail, and the sooner this is done the better." [118] At the Eighteenth Congress, the Party again expressed lack of satisfaction with the school system and clamored for more communism in education.

In October, 1937, Andrei S. Bubnov, the favorite of Stalin, was dismissed from his post as Commissar of the People's Education. Shortly afterward a new official was appointed, Vladimir Potemkin, historian, diplomat, and teacher. Potemkin, who founded the Academy of Pedagogical Sciences in 1943, served as head of the Narkompros until his death, February 26, 1946.[119] This move may have been a sign that the direction of education was regarded as properly belonging to a person whose qualifications included more than revolutionary and Party experience and loyalty.

The Rise of Juvenile Delinquency. The process of industrializing and collectivizing the Soviet Union caused considerable unrest in the 1930's. Large numbers of homeless children, plus those who could not be effectively controlled by their parents, contributed to social disorganization, which was not at all alleviated by the low standard of living and the collapse of moral codes. Even though progress was made with the homeless children, little could be done with children and youth who were delinquent owing to disrupted family life and broken homes. These factors were more potent than war or hunger in bringing about delinquency.[120]

The situation in the large cities was particularly bad. "In Moscow, from 1931 to 1934, juvenile delinquency increased 100%," with theft and similar offenses committed by two-thirds of the delinquents of Moscow and Leningrad.[121]

Even worse was the frequency of hooliganism, reported by the Soviet press throughout 1935. The young delinquents perpetrated acts of destruction and vandalism. "Sometimes the schools were besieged by neglected children; other times gangs beat the teachers and attacked women, or regularly fought against one another."[122] Some relief was achieved by the decree of April 7, 1935, "Concerning Measures for Combating Crime among Minors," making children over twelve punishable under the regular criminal code. The government considered punishment an educational procedure and refused to be lenient with delinquents.[123]

New Developments. Two important decrees affecting secondary and higher education were enacted on October 2, 1940. The first was the imposition of tuition fees of 300 to 500 rubles a year for higher education, with stipends to students who excelled in their studies, and of 150 to 200 rubles a year for instruction in grades eight to ten in the ten-year school. One very possible reason for this reversal of the policy of free tuition was the huge cost of educational development incurred by the Soviet government. The second law established the state labor reserve, under which young persons aged fourteen to seventeen (later nineteen) were given industrial training in special half-year and two-year schools at full state expense. Upon completion of this period of training, the youths were supposed to work by assignment four years in a particular job. Both decrees were instrumental in the creation of a new Soviet elite along intellectual, technical, political, managerial, and professional lines.[124]

The textbooks of the period constitute interesting source materials on what was taught. Shestakov's nationalistic text for grades three and four covers Russian history from ancient times and then sums up Soviet history. Nearly half of the book deals with the revolutionary movement from Lenin onwards. Lenin and Stalin were great heroes, but the country was constantly threatened by enemies without and within. "That contemptible enemy of the people, the fascist agent, Trotsky, and his contemptible friends Rykov and Bukharin, organized in the U.S.S.R. gangs of murderers, wreckers and spies," and "as long as the U.S.S.R. is surrounded by countries in which capitalism reigns, spies and wreckers will continuously strive to penetrate our country and cause us harm." [125]

Lenin and Stalin made their debut in the second of the three-volume history of Russia and the U.S.S.R. for grades eight, nine, and ten, the second edition of which appeared in 1940–1941 under the editorship of A. M. Pankratova. The third book begins with the year 1900 and is loaded with quotations and pictures of Stalin in various forms.[126] Lenin was not neglected, but Stalin's significance was not permitted to be overshadowed by that of the older revolutionary.

Bushtueva's English textbook for grade three of the incomplete and complete secondary schools contained reading selections dealing with the class struggle, unemployment, persecution of Negroes, and Soviet and foreign geography. In one passage the pupil was informed that in the U.S.A. "millions of people have no work and must starve." [127] The fourth-grade text for the complete secondary school, by the same author, had passages from Upton Sinclair, Jack London, Arnold Bennett, O. Henry, Charles Dickens, Shelley, Longfellow, and Mark Twain, but also from Stalin, Marx, and Engels. The exercises included sentences such as "The agitator spoke well, didn't he?" [128]

André Gide, who visited the U.S.S.R. in 1936, admired the unusual *élan* of the country toward education and culture but pointed out the monolithic nature of both, as well as the delimiting of criticism to trivialities. The Party line, he emphasized, was never questioned. The Soviet citizen was allowed, moreover, to remain in deep ignorance about foreign countries and was persuaded by his government that everything abroad was inferior to its Soviet counterpart. Gide also expressed his amazement that the Soviet students, who were required to learn a foreign language, spoke English and German "so badly." An upperclassman in a French *lycée*, he felt, had a better knowledge of languages.[129]

The Postwar Period in General Perspective

Chapter 4 will consider in detail postwar and current developments in Soviet education. The present section attempts only to reconstruct the general background of Soviet political and cultural history against which the postwar educational events have taken place.

The current period, from 1941 to date, may be subdivided into several sections. One dividing date would be the reimposition of Stalinist values in 1946, another might be the death of Stalin in 1953, and a third might be the formal repudiation of Stalin in 1956. This period saw the end of the Third Five-Year Plan in 1942, and the inauguration and completion of the Fourth (1946–1950) and Fifth (1951–1955) Five-Year Plans. The Sixth Five-Year Plan, which began in 1956, was terminated in 1958 in favor of a more ambitious program. The Seventh Plan was started in 1959 and is to last seven years.

World War II and Its Aftermath. On June 22, 1941, Hitler's armies invaded Soviet Russia and made rapid progress in their conquest of Soviet territory. After a period of resistance, the Red Army began an effective counteroffensive with the raising of the siege of Stalingrad in 1943. This proved to be the turning point of World War II on the Eastern Front. With help received from the Allied nations, as well as with the help of the military action on the Western Front, Russia managed to expel the Nazis from her soil, take over other, neighboring countries, and carry the war into Nazi Germany. During the prosecution of the war, the Soviet authorities disbanded the Comintern (1943), which, however, was revived in another guise in 1947 as the Cominform. They also made concessions to religious groups and authorized the re-establishment of the Orthodox Patriarchate in 1943.

As the war drew to a close, the U.S.S.R. took a leading part in international negotiations. It drew an "Iron Curtain" around certain countries — East Germany, Poland, Hungary, Rumania, Albania, Bulgaria, and Czechoslovakia — in which the local Communist Party had entrenched itself in power during 1945–1948 with the aid of the Soviet Army and political machinery. In eastern Europe only Yugoslavia, under the leadership of Marshal Tito, refused to follow Soviet leadership. In 1949 the Communist victory in China brought that vast Asian area into the Soviet orbit. The Korean War (1950–1953) confirmed the Communist domination of North Korea, and Soviet activity elsewhere in Asia has paved the way for the extension of Soviet influence in various parts of this continent.

The "Cold War" between the Soviet bloc and the West was intensified by the Berlin blockade, which began in 1948. The formation of the North Atlantic Treaty Organization further separated the Communist countries from the rest of the world. The tension has remained throughout the entire postwar period, with only occasional letups.

The Soviet rule behind the Iron Curtain was hardly an easy affair. There were insurrections in East Germany in June, 1953, workers' riots in Poland in June, 1956, and a revolution in Hungary in October–November, 1956. By and large, however, the Communist powers have maintained their sway over the many peoples inside the Iron Curtain.

Educational and Scientific Advances. On the inner front in the Soviet Union, numerous changes were made after World War II. Internationalism gave way to patriotism, the Russian past was glorified, and Stalin laid down the law in such fields as economics, history, and linguistics. The theories of Michurin and Lysenko, which stressed the primacy of environmental influences over human personality and character, were declared official doctrine in biology.[130]

Direction of the intellectual and cultural dictatorship was entrusted to Andrei A. Zhdanov (1896–1948), an old Bolshevik.[131] As far back as 1934–1938, Zhdanov had begun to exert influence on cultural activities in the U.S.S.R. It was due to his initiative that the Central Administration for Propaganda and Agitation was founded in 1938, that free tuition in secondary schools was abolished in 1940, and that the maturity examination was reintroduced in 1944.

Zhdanov's control of intellectual life in the U.S.S.R., "Zhdanov-shchina," began in 1946 and continued until his death, although the *Gleichschaltung* of Soviet culture continued at least until Stalin died. Zhdanov's address to the Central Committee of the Communist Party in September, 1946, demanded the elevation of Soviet cultural values and the elimination of foreign, especially Western, influences from Soviet life. The battle against cultural cosmopolitanism and objectivism was waged on all fronts — philosophy, economics, music, history, biology, psychology, and philology. Noted scholars and cultural leaders were forced to confess their previous "errors" and to repudiate publicly earlier works that did not conform to the Party line. Stalinism stifled scholarship, scientific research, and cultural creativity. The watchword "Slava Stalinu!" (Glory to Stalin) permeated the pages of *Pravda* and virtually all media of information.[132] The culture of the various nationalities in the Soviet Union was likewise affected by Stalinism. The dictator's slogan, "National in form, Socialist in content," was applied to the cultural development of the Ukrainians, Georgians, Uzbeks, Lithuanians, and other ethnic and linguistic groups. This meant that the minority could make use of its language only by learning about Marxism-Leninism-Stalinism.

The Twentieth Congress of the Communist Party, February 14–25, 1956, was an important milestone. Not only did this Congress adopt the proposals for the Sixth Five-Year Plan, as well as new educational and cultural directives, but after Nikita Khrushchev's now-famous speech condemning Stalin, the delegates passed resolutions against the "personality cult." The downgrading of Stalin, or de-Stalinization, caught Soviet citizens by surprise and it took them some time to recover from the shock. The following year, in his report to the Supreme Soviet of the U.S.S.R. on the fortieth anniversary of the Revolution, Khrushchev seemed to back down from his initial stand regarding Stalin, stating that "as a devoted Marxist-Leninist and a staunch revolutionary, Stalin will occupy a worthy place in history" and that "our party and the Soviet people will remember Stalin and pay tribute to him."[133] Portraits, statues, and busts of Stalin are still in evidence in many public places, including schools and universities, but the political content in school curricula has been decreased as a result of the downgrading.

The unexpected launching of an earth satellite on October 4,

1957, and of another the following month brought world-wide acknowledgment of the Soviet achievement in applied science and technology. Khrushchev congratulated and expressed his gratitude to the Soviet scientists, engineers, and industrial workers responsible for these exploits. His judgment concerning the Sputniks was shared by millions all over the globe: " . . . The fact that the Soviet Union was able to solve such intricate scientific and technical problems showed them [the enemies of the U.S.S.R.] the high level to which we have raised our science, engineering and industry." [134]

In preparation for the Twenty-First Congress, January, 1959, Khrushchev put together a set of theses outlining the objectives of the Seven-Year Plan (1959–1965). He stressed the expansion of the Soviet economy in raising industrial output 80 per cent and agricultural output 70 per cent, reducing the work week, increasing consumer goods and housing facilities, and providing for other improvements in the life of the Soviet citizen. "In the coming seven years, the U.S.S.R.'s economy, and above all its basic, heavy industry, will continue, as in the past, to advance at a pace many times faster than that of the economic development of the capitalist countries, including the United States of America." [135]

The Cultural Climate.   Culturally the most significant development since 1953 was the temporary relaxation of the policy of *Gleichschaltung*, somewhat parallel to Khrushchev's policy of industrial decentralization, and the inauguration of cultural and educational exchanges with other nations. The publication of a short novel, *The Thaw*, by Ilya Ehrenburg, gave a name to the brief period of relative freedom in the arts. Vladimir Dudintsev's *Not by Bread Alone* was a further illustration of the fact that it was now possible to write about Soviet life as it really was rather than as it was pictured in the official propaganda. However, any doubt as to the basic policy of the Communist regime regarding genuine freedom of literary creativity was eliminated by the violent reaction of the Union of Writers to Boris Pasternak after he had been awarded the Nobel Prize following the publication of his novel, *Doctor Zhivago*. Literature and other arts, it was clear, were to remain handmaidens of the Party's ideology.[136]

More promising, perhaps, was the change in official policy, in 1955, permitting Soviet scientists and historians to take part in international conferences. Later on psychologists, educators, and other scholars were given opportunities to visit foreign countries and to present papers at international congresses. Soviet cultural enterprises, such as the ballet, won the plaudits of foreigners. Soviet athletes, farmers, and industrial workers also were allowed to see life and labor in a foreign setting.

It is against such a background that the major educational changes of the postwar period described in the next and subsequent chapters have taken place. The increased expenditure for education, the movement to polytechnization, the creation of boarding schools, and the reframing of the organizational structure in 1958 may be cited as examples of the many major innovations the implementation of which still occupies the center of the stage in the Soviet Union. It is, indeed, a distinct positive characteristic of this period that these changes, unlike those of the previous era, are open to Western scrutiny.

4

THE CONTEMPORARY
SOVIET SCHOOL

We can now review in more detail the educational events from 1941 to the present. In the elementary and secondary schools enrollment was sharply cut in the second and third years of the war, in spite of the fact that, so far as possible, educational and welfare services were maintained in Moscow and Leningrad even while those cities were under Nazi siege. Outside the cities, where it was possible, children under fourteen were evacuated to the eastern regions, and the schools there became instrumental in furnishing food, shelter, and clothing for the evacuees and orphans. In 1942, as the military situation improved, the schools that had not been destroyed or devastated were reopened. During the same year the government began to restore school buildings, construct temporary schools, and manufacture school equipment.[1]

Many of the institutions of higher education also managed to stay open during the crisis, although here, too, the number of students sharply decreased, and most of those who attended universities and technical institutes were women.[2]

81

The War Years

The Soviet authorities devoted much attention to the military training of children and youth during the war years. In October, 1942, the Soviet of People's Commissars of the U.S.S.R. published two decrees "On Preliminary Preservice Military Training of Pupils from the First to the Tenth Class of the Middle School, Secondary School, and Technikum" and "On Military and Physical Training of Pupils in Primary Schools, and Those of the First Four Classes of Middle and Secondary Schools." The objective of these decrees was not only to provide military training for war purposes but also to suffuse all the subjects of the curriculum and all school activities with military values and virtues, love of the motherland, and hatred of the enemy.[3] This militarization program resulted from the disclosure that the Soviet schools had failed to inculcate in the pupil the "strong will, perseverance, stability, and other moral qualities necessary to the future warrior on the battlefield." [4]

The number of hours devoted to military training in the secondary school course rose from 596 in 1938, or 6.2 per cent of the entire course of study, to 1048 in 1942, or 11 per cent of the entire course. Military training was also given to pupils in grades eight through ten in two-week summer camps, where they were instructed in map reading, shooting, and battle formation.[5] In 1943 special military schools were opened for the children of military and naval officers and men who had been killed in the "Great Patriotic War of the Soviet Union." These secondary boarding schools prepared for the army or air force (Suvorov schools) or for the navy (Nakhimov schools).

New Developments. In October, 1943, the Academy of Pedagogical Sciences of the R.S.F.S.R., the famous research organization, was founded. Another significant occurrence the same year was the lowering of the age of compulsory school attendance from eight to seven, where it remains. In July, 1943, the Soviet of People's Commissars enacted a decree, "On the Introduction of Separate Instruction of Boys and Girls," to take effect in the ten-year schools of the larger cities. This unexpected move was a wartime measure due to the "necessity of differentiating the military-physical preparation of the youth of the two sexes." [6] There was no difference in curriculum, syllabus, and textbooks, but the separation of the sexes "made it possible to take into consideration the special characteristics of the physiological development of boys and girls, certain of their psychological characteristics, and differences in training and preparation of boys and girls for practical life." [7] Interestingly enough, these considerations had lost their importance by 1954, when the Soviet of Ministers of the U.S.S.R. passed a decree reviving coeducation.

Also in 1943, which seems to have been a most eventful year in Soviet education, the government founded a new type of evening school for the general education of the many young workers of fifteen or sixteen who had been forced by the war to discontinue their secondary-school studies and to work in industry and agriculture. A year later similar evening schools were opened for young peasants.

Revisions in Rules and Standards. On August 2, 1943, the Soviet of People's Commissars of the R.S.F.S.R., adopted "Rules for Pupils," [8] a document that was promulgated three days later by the Narkompros. Pupils of all schools were required to memorize and obey the twenty regulations, which concerned behavior in and out of school. Any pupil violating these rules could be punished and even expelled.

The question of standards came up during the war. On June 21, 1944, the Soviet of Ministers of the U.S.S.R. instituted special examinations at the close of grades four, seven, and ten, with the test at the end of the seventh grade covering the seven-year school. The matriculation examinations after grade ten were conducted by a commission of five persons, including the principal and someone from the regional department of education. Pupils with excellent results on the tests were given gold and silver medals entitling them to enter a higher educational institution without having to take the entrance examination, [9] a practice discontinued only recently.

The Postwar Period

After the end of the war education in the Soviet Union expanded rapidly. The educational budget rose immediately, the budget for

1946 exceeding that for 1940 by 17,671,000 rubles. The elementary-secondary attendance in 1946–1947 was 29,399,000, or 13.9 per cent more than in the previous year; the specialized secondary attendance was 1,030,000, or 22.9 per cent over the preceding year; and the higher educational attendance was 653,000, a rise of 22.6 per cent over 1945–1946.[10] By 1947 the R.S.F.S.R. had repaired and reopened more than 28,600 schools.[11]

Content Changes. The change in Soviet foreign policy after World War II necessitated corresponding changes in educational content and practice. On August 2, 1946, the Central Committee of the Communist Party adopted a decree, "On the Training and Retraining of Leading Party and Soviet Workers," which was intended to reorganize the schools in such a way as to heighten Soviet self-consciousness and to inculcate a bias against the West. The new system of Party schools consisted of three levels: the Party school, which offered a two-year course preparing members for lower Party and government positions; the higher Party school, which trained members for more important positions in the Party and the government; and the Academy of the Social Sciences, an institution of university rank, which prepared instructors in a variety of fields — international law and relations, political economy, history, psychology, literature, history of philosophy and art, and foreign languages — for higher educational institutions and trained investigators for research organizations.[12] It is not difficult to discern the direct relationship between the intensification of Party doctrine and discipline and the work of the Soviet schools and universities.

In view of this new system, it was hardly surprising to read, in 1950, that "the entire system of public education in the U.S.S.R. ensures the communist education of the youth, the education of a new, people's intelligentsia, the education of millions of active builders and defenders of communist society."[13] This education was reflected in the school materials of the period. In a secondary history textbook, the pupils were taught that "the theories of Marx and Engels were elaborated and raised to a still higher plane by the great leader of the world proletariat, V. I. Lenin, and his faithful disciple and associate, J. V. Stalin,"[14] and that "under the leadership of the Party of Lenin and Stalin, the Soviet people will carry out this historic task [of completing the building of socialism and of the gradual transition from socialism to communism] and usher in a new era in world history." [15] In a sixth-grade English text the pupil was taught, among other things, that Stalin, "the leader and teacher of the workers of the world," [16] was the one "who leads our country to Communism and shows the road to Communism to all the world." [17] Textbooks in other subjects were no less instructive in the glories of communism.

Sovietization of National Republics. During the postwar period there was a greater concentration on Sovietization of the culture of the national republics, probably because of the defection of citizens of the Ukraine and other non-Russian areas to the Germans during the war. The progress in culture and education in the Asiatic republics and other territories seemed to be satisfactory to both the Russians and the non-Russians. Stalin's policy respecting minority cultures was proving a success so far as the Communist leaders were concerned.[18]

From another point of view, the picture was far from rosy. According to a recent visitor, Associate Justice William O. Douglas of the United States Supreme Court, the Russians discriminate against the Soviet Central Asians in virtually every aspect of life, especially in housing and education. In spite of an egalitarian constitution, the Russians maintain separate schools for themselves and for the native Uzbeks or other Asians, thus bringing about the Russianization of Asian culture and the neglect of the traditional cultures of Asian peoples. "In short, the segregated public school system of Central Asia operates to favor the Russian and to disadvantage the native." [19]

Growth of the Schools. School enrollments showed a steady decline from 1950 through 1957, according to official Soviet statistics.[20] However, this did not affect adversely the construction of schools and the rising educational budget.[21] Soviet authorities attribute the decrease in the pupil population to the fact that "beginning with the 1949–50 school-year, schools enrolled children born during the war years, when the birth-rate, especially in occupied territories and the war zone, dropped considerably." [22]

Under the terms of the Fifth Five-Year Plan there was to be compulsory ten-year schooling for urban boys and girls by 1955, and for rural pupils five years later. It did not take the authorities long to realize that their aims were fanciful in the light of scholastic reality. With too many pupils failing to meet the rigorous standards, some downward adjustments had to be made in the curriculum and educational standards. To some extent, at least, the decision of the Nineteenth Congress of the Communist Party, in 1952, to reintroduce polytechnical training in the schools was related to the sobering educational experiences of the previous years.

After Stalin

The death of Stalin in 1953 may have been instrumental in introducing some changes in Soviet education, such as the revival of coeducation and U.S.S.R. membership in UNESCO during 1954. In the school year of 1954–1955, according to the official governmental report, "Soviet schools started to switch over to a new curriculum and new syllabi to cope with tasks connected with the introduction of universal secondary 10-year schooling and the implementation of polytechnical training and labour education of pupils." [23] The switch-over did not occur overnight; many textbooks continued along the lines of their predecessors, as did the syllabi. For example, the significance of Stalin was evident as late as 1956 in the prominent treatment he received in textbooks.[24] A number of syllabi retained their usual content; some still included required readings in the works of Stalin.

Although official reports, such as the one just cited, are valuable as sources of official information, it must not be forgotten that they seem to have been prepared for foreign consumption — in this case for the International Conference on Public Education convoked each summer in Geneva by the International Bureau of Education. To get a true picture of the period it is necessary to analyze such educational literature as *Uchitelskaia Gazeta, Sovetskaia Pedagogika,* the general and specialized pedagogical journals, and the newspapers *Pravda* and *Komsomolskaia Pravda.* Students of Soviet education — the Lazarévitches and London, for example — have investigated such writings to some extent, and their findings indicate that the Soviet educators engage in severe criticism of the practices and results of their schools.[25] Unfortunately, few writers and lecturers on Soviet education have utilized these important source materials.

The official report for 1955–1956 proclaimed that "the decisions of the XIXth Congress of the Communist Party calling for transition to universal secondary education under the Fifth Five-Year Plan have, on the whole, been successfully applied." [26] It also called attention to the abolition, as of September 1, 1956, of all tuition fees in the upper grades of secondary schools, by order of the Council of Ministers of the U.S.S.R. But almost in the same breath it announced the imposition of a tuition schedule for the new boarding schools to be established in accordance with the recommendations made by Khrushchev at the Twentieth Congress of the Communist Party. The report frankly acknowledged the "serious shortcomings in the work of the general education school, and particularly, the unsatisfactory state of polytechnic education . . . the lack of coordination between teaching and life, and the inadequate training of school graduates for practical work." [27] These criticisms applied equally well, according to this document, to higher educational establishments, including institutions for training of teachers. Similar sentiments, minus the forthright criticisms, were expressed in the official reports of Byelorussia and the Ukraine. [28]

Khrushchev's report to the Central Committee of the Twentieth Congress, February 14, 1956, contained boasts of the cultural and educational progress of the Soviet Union but also complaints about the slowness of educators in putting polytechnical training into practice, the need for boarding schools, and the inadequacy of the practical training of engineers and agronomists. [29] These ideas were formally and unanimously adopted in the resolutions and directives of the Congress on February 24, 1956. [30] The speed and direction of the educational reform urged by Khrushchev may be seen in the intensified effort in polytechnical training on all levels, the growing polytechnical stress in pedagogical institutes, and the opening of boarding schools in September, 1956. It is important to note here that Party leadership, not the ministries of education and culture or the educational profession, made these decisions.

The boarding schools, according to the report by Khrushchev, were primarily intended for the children of war widows and of working parents. From this it may be inferred that political indoctrination and possibly Communist leadership would become major emphases in the boarding school. Such aims would be easier to accomplish in a home-school environment from which the family influence had all but been removed. During visits of the Comparative Education Society to boarding schools, however, the political and leadership aspects of these schools were either ignored or denied by the principals and teachers.

Revisions in the Textbooks. Of particular significance at the Twentieth Congress was the address of Anna M. Pankratova, which reflected Khrushchev's just-expressed policy of stripping Stalin of his glory and prestige. Pankratova, who was also the editor of *Voprosy Istorii* (*Problems of History*), undoubtedly took her cue from Khrushchev's demand for a new Party history textbook "based on historical facts and giving a scientific generalization of the epoch-making struggle waged by the Party for communism and bringing the story up to the present day." [31] This is all the more surprising when one takes into consideration the fact that the *History of the Communist Party of the Soviet Union* (*Bolsheviks*): *Short Course,* which had served as the basis for Party propaganda since 1938, was written under the supervision and editorship of Stalin. There is some evidence that Pankratova had been primed for the impending changes prior to the Khrushchev report. At a conference of historians in Moscow in January, 1956, before the opening of the Twentieth Congress of the Communist Party, E. N. Burjalov, deputy editor of *Voprosy Istorii,* condemned those who had falsified Party history by the excessive glorification of some leaders and by other pernicious practices.[32]

Pankratova's address, accordingly, carried on the campaign against the "cult of personality" in history textbooks used in the seven-year schools, including the many edited by herself. She thus admitted publicly that her own textbooks had contained falsifications of history and that she was determined to rectify the errors in future editions.[33]

The new developments tended to disorganize the school program considerably. There were no examinations in history in grade ten at the conclusion of the school year 1955–1956. The textbook for the course in the history of the U.S.S.R. in grade ten was withdrawn, and history was taught without a text. In the school year 1956–1957 there was no instruction in history and literature in grade four, because the textbooks had been withdrawn and the revised editions were not yet available. Other subjects were also affected, and teachers given instructions on how to present topics in ways differing from the textbook treatments.[34]

Pankratova, in a pamphlet summarized in *Uchitelskaia Gazeta* on September 22, 1956, again confessed openly to historical heresies in her textbooks. She specified such sins as overstressing the significance of some princes and tsars, underemphasizing the part played by the masses in Russian history, accepting the colonialist-imperialist policies of the tsars, and overemphasizing the historical impact of Stalin. The policy of overcoming the cult of personality in the instruction of history in schools was, in effect, a revival of the discredited historiography of M. N. Pokrovsky.[35]

An example of what the new history was made of can be seen in a tenth-grade textbook published in 1957.[36] This volume begins with Lenin's journal, *Iskra,* in 1900 and ends with a quotation from Khrushchev at the Twentieth Congress in 1956. There is but one small photograph of Stalin and but passing references to the departed dictator, such as a less-than-two-line mention of his death. The customary chronological table, which appears at the end of all history textbooks, carries no mention of Stalin. This contrasts sharply with the large number of significant events in Soviet history that had been presented to the pupils in earlier editions of the history texts.

The distortion of history by omission was not a simple process even in the Soviet state. What had appeared at first to be merely a matter of deletion of Stalin material and the inclusion of some previously forbidden content became complicated by the Polish uprisings and later by the Hungarian revolt. It was clear to the Soviet authorities that the de-Stalinization program had been undertaken too fast. Consequently, another modification of the Party line was in order:

> The "un-rewriting" of history . . . now had to take into account not only the demotion of Stalin, but also Khrushchev's dictum that "We are all Stalinists when it comes to the struggle against imperialists." The ideological refreeze called for a more cautious approach to historical revisionism, so as to avoid the "Polish infection." [37]

These changes understandably made it difficult for history

teachers, research workers, and textbook writers to do their work with any degree of reasonable safety from a sudden reversal in Party line. Students too had their problems in this respect.

What appears to be the present Party line with respect to Stalin can be determined from Khrushchev's report to the jubilee session of the Supreme Soviet of the U.S.S.R. on November 6, 1957. In this document the leader of all the Soviets stated that "we Communists criticize the personality cult as being alien to the spirit of Marxism-Leninism, as something intolerable in a communist party, in a socialist society." Although Communists reject the "negative aspects of Stalin's activity," they must protect Stalin from slander. Moreover, "As a devoted Marxist-Leninist and a staunch revolutionary, Stalin will occupy a worthy place in history. Our Party and the Soviet people will remember Stalin and pay tribute to him. (Prolonged applause.)" [38]

Revision of Standards. Of additional interest to the student of Soviet education was the unexpected decree by Minister of Education of the R.S.F.S.R. E. I. Afanasenko, in September, 1956, that henceforth final examinations would be given only at the end of grades seven and ten and would be made easier.[39] Thus pupils ending all other classes would be free from the burden of special preparation. This would not substantially reduce the daily homework, however, about which there had been much controversy stemming from the feeling that excessive homework impaired pupil health. Promotion was to be based on the pupils' daily recitation grades and on reports by their teachers. This change will probably be adopted by the other republics, since the problem is Unionwide. There is also the possibility that the standards of primary-secondary education will decline, a hypothesis that becomes more credible when one reads the Soviet pedagogical periodicals.

The official report for 1958 indicated a 6.2 per cent rise in the 1957 state budget for education, science, and culture to 83.9 billion rubles (tourist exchange rate, 1 ruble = 10 cents) although only 38 billion rubles were spent specifically for primary and secondary education; an increase of 500,000 pupils in all types of general schools, making the total enrollment 30,624,900; the opening of 1700 new schools, making a total of 214,162 general schools of all kinds; an almost doubling of the boarding-school population to

104,500 children in 456 institutions; a 10.2 per cent increase in the number of kindergarten children to 2,088,200; and a vocational and other secondary specialized enrollment of "about 2,000,000." [40] The total registration, including correspondence students, in the higher educational institutions was given as "in excess of 2,000,000." The number of students in such institutions has been steadily increasing: 730,200 (1945–1946); 1,247,400 (1950–1951); 1,730,500 (1954–1955); 1,867,000 (1955–1956); [41] and 2,001,000 (1956–1957). [42] Except for these increases and for an intensified campaign in polytechnical training, "there were no changes in the Soviet system of public education in 1957/58." [43]

The New Reform

Such was the general educational situation during the early months of 1958, when the members of the Comparative Education Society were preparing for their visit to the U.S.S.R. But further reform had been under discussion for some time. There was growing dissatisfaction with the polytechnical program: formal instruction had to be reduced, pupils and parents did not respond with enthusiasm, and the Soviet economy had not benefited sufficiently.

The first public step in the process of reforming the Soviet school system was the address by Premier Khrushchev in April, 1958, to the Thirteenth Komsomol Congress. The projected changes had already been discussed in the Academy of Pedagogical Sciences, but Khrushchev brought them out in the open. His basic proposal was as follows:

> In the reform of the work of the secondary school, it might be advisable to consider using a form which has proved useful before, such as the schools in factories and plants. Pupils could study in the secondary schools up to a certain, definite class; and they would go to factory and plant schools to continue their education and to acquire work skills and a profession, which every person needs so that he will not only be prepared in subjects of general education, but also know life well, know production, and not confuse a rake with a shaft. [44]

In addition, "The work of universities, medical, pedagogic, and other higher educational establishments should also be more closely connected with life, with practical work." [45]

The latter point was reinforced in an article in *Pravda*, September 17, 1958, by Vyacheslav Yelyutin, Minister of Higher Education of the U.S.S.R. His statement constituted a blueprint for the reorganization of higher education and rested on Khrushchev's proposal that work experience should be a prerequisite and corequisite of higher education. The key to this reform lies in Yelyutin's words: "However substantial the achievements of the Soviet higher school may have been, in the world of contemporary demands they can no longer fully satisfy the growing demands of the national economy and of the culture of the country." [46]

On September 21, 1958, two days after the departure of the Comparative Education Society from the U.S.S.R., there appeared in *Pravda* an elaborate memorandum by Khrushchev. After specifying some of the achievements of the Soviet school system, he admitted that "there are big shortcomings in the work of our schools and higher educational establishments which can no longer be tolerated [and] the chief and basic defect in our secondary and higher educational establishments is the fact that they are divorced from life." Accordingly, he insisted that "the system of bringing up our growing generation in the schools must be reorganized drastically." To introduce a full ten-year school on a compulsory basis, as had been recently considered, was "inexpedient" under present circumstances. "In my view all pupils, without exception, should be drawn into work beneficial to society at industrial establishments, collective farms, etc., after they have finished seven or eight classes at school." Secondary education, declared Khrushchev, might consist of two stages: a compulsory school of seven or eight years concentrating "on instruction in the fundamentals of science, on polytechnical training and the teaching of work habits, and on education in communist ethics, the physical development of the children and on inculcating in them good aesthetic taste," and a course of two or three years in specialized vocational training in industry or agriculture. As far as the post-secondary schooling was concerned, "We must re-shape the system of higher education, draw it closer to production, and link it up with production directly. The higher educational establishments should enroll young people who already have some experience of life and have a record of practical work." With many young men and women engaged in production after the completion of basic education, if higher education was to develop, particularly along the lines of technical training, it had to "shift the emphasis more to evening and correspondence education." [47]

The reaction of Americans to Khrushchev's proposals for educational change was interesting. On September 22, 1958, the *New York Times* published a dispatch by its Moscow correspondent outlining the plan. Telephone and the postal communications began to hum. People wanted to have the "new" and "revolutionary" program interpreted. Specialists in Soviet education were asked many questions for some time afterwards. Evidently American interest in Soviet education was growing. Clearly, too, not many Americans had done enough reading in Soviet educational history, both recent and remote, to fully appreciate the context of the Khrushchev reform.

The Projected School Program.   Two months later, on November 14, 1958, Khrushchev issued, in *Pravda*, the theses of his report to the forthcoming Twenty-First Congress of the Communist Party on the targets of the new Seven-Year Plan. His fundamental theme, which appears in the form of slogans on posters and in other forms of publicity all over the Soviet Union, was that "in the coming seven years, the U.S.S.R.'s economy, and above all its basis, heavy industry, will continue, as in the past, to advance at a pace many times faster than that of the economic development of the capitalist countries, including the United States of America." [48] Once more he called attention to the program for "a radical improvement in the entire system of public education" and emphasized the government's plans:

> To effect a transition from seven-year to eight-year universal, compulsory education.
> To ensure the organization and necessary equipment of training centers at the eight-year schools, combining polytechnic labour instruction with the extensive drawing of school children into such interesting forms of socially useful work as they are capable of performing at their particular age.
> To organize the network of ten-year schools (their upper forms) into various types of urban and rural secondary labour schools, the pupils of which, by combining study with work at factories, on collective farms, and in special work shops, will receive both a complete

secondary general and polytechnical education and a special training for a mass trade, depending on the local needs of the personnel.

Considerably to extend the network of city and village schools which provide their pupils with a secondary school education while they continue their work.[49]

The impression that Khrushchev apparently wished to give was that, instead of backtracking from the goal of a ten-year school for all, the government was moving forward from a seven-year to an eight-year school.

Probably the major reason behind the reform was economy as a means to greater international power. In September, 1958, during a number of discussions with Soviet educators on the polytechnization of education from the primary grades through the university, the American visitors remarked that the projected educational reform would inevitably cause a weakening of the standards of scholarship. Soviet educators conceded that the concentration on labor, the deferment of entrance into the higher educational institutions, and the increased stress on correspondence and evening education would make it impossible for students to devote adequate time or possess sufficient energy to do justice to serious advanced study. They insisted, however, on the primacy of the immediate need for the Soviet Union to expand its economy by making the fullest possible use of its total manpower.

A later form of the new educational program, which has been described by a recent writer as the "Khrushchev School Reform" because of the premier's constant public advocacy of it,[50] was printed on November 16, 1958, in *Pravda* and in its final legislative form on December 25, 1958. This document consisted of the forty-eight theses of the Central Committee of the C.P.S.U. and the U.S.S.R. Council of Ministers. It drew its title and content from the September memorandum of Khrushchev, which had been "approved by the presidium of the central committee of the C.P.S.U. and [is] warmly supported by the Soviet public, which regards the reorganization of the school system as an urgent task."[51] The essential elements of this detailed document are the following:

12. *The first stage* of secondary education must be the *compulsory eight-year school,* set up in place of the seven-year school that exists at present. The compulsory eight-year school will be a considerable step

forward in developing education, as compared with the seven-year school. The young people who complete their studies at an eight-year school will have a greater general knowledge and, both psychologically and practically, will be better prepared for taking part in socially useful activities. Such a school will solve the problems of communist education and of labour and polytechnical instruction more successfully; it will provide the pupils with a wider range of knowledge, and will make it possible to eliminate the overloading of the pupils with studies that has existed in the seven-year school, and to organize in a more thorough way the physical training of children and the development of good artistic taste. The specific features of women's work would be taken into account in the work training given to girl pupils in the eight-year school.

In the process of instruction and upbringing the school is called upon to familiarize the pupils with the varied forms of work in our society and to help them discover their particular bent and make a conscious choice of their future occupation.

The eight-year school will be an incomplete labour polytechnical school providing a general education. Primary schools consisting of the first four forms should be preserved in small communities. When they have been through the fourth form at these schools the pupils will enter the fifth form at the nearest school.

On leaving the eight-year school, all young people must join in socially useful work at industrial establishments, collective farms, etc. This will create more equal conditions for all citizens as regards work and education, and it will be a good means of bringing up young people in the spirit of the heroic traditions of the working class and the collective-farm peasantry.

13. Young people will receive a complete secondary education during the *second stage* of instruction. A secondary education can be completed on the basis of combining studies with productive work in the following ways:

The first and main way is for young people, who upon finishing at the eight-year school go to work, first of all to receive initial vocational training and then, while working in production, to study at *schools for young workers and peasants*. These schools should give their pupils a complete secondary education and help to increase their vocational skill.

The second way is for young people who have completed their studies at the eight-year school, to be taught at a *secondary labour polytechnical school providing a general education together with production training* (of the type of factory or agricultural vocational schools) which, on the basis of nearby industrial establishments, collective farms, state farms, repair and service stations, etc., will combine instruction with productive work and give the pupils a complete secondary education and vocational training for work in a branch of the economy or culture.

The third way is to teach a section of the young people in *specialized secondary schools* which will function with the eight-year school as a basis, and at which the pupils will obtain a complete secondary education, a specialty and the status of specialists with medium qualifications.

The new system of education will enable every boy and girl to prepare for life better, to have a definite trade and to choose the way of obtaining a complete secondary education that suits them best.[52]

The other theses deal with the various aspects of polytechnical and vocational training, specialized (technical and agricultural) secondary schools, and higher education. The document repeats Khrushchev's statements on practical work as a prerequisite to entrance into higher educational establishments, on the expansion of evening and correspondence instruction, and on the necessary combination of higher learning with production and work for the national economy.

Training of Teachers.   Of special interest is the application of the principle of work to the training of teachers. "University students who are going to work in the schools should be given better methodological training and practical teaching work, for which the services of the best secondary school teachers should be enlisted." [53] Teacher training was emphasized in Thesis No. 41:

> The reorganization of the system of secondary education calls for a fundamental improvement in the training of teachers at *teachers' training institutes* and universities. These higher educational establishments must train teachers for the secondary schools who have a profound knowledge of their subject, possess adequate teaching experience, have a good knowledge of life, and can bring up the pupils in the spirit of boundless loyalty to the cause of communism. Teachers for primary schools should be trained at special departments in teachers' training institutes with a view of having all schools completely staffed with college trained teachers in the future.[54]

Ideological Indoctrination.   Another matter that received serious attention was ideological indoctrination, particularly in the higher educational institutions. According to Thesis No. 46:

> The educational importance of the higher educational institutions is great. The colleges must turn out people who have mastered their specialty well, who are active and passionate champions of Lenin's ideas and the policy of the Communist Party, who are bold and enthusiastic, and are profoundly convinced of the triumph of our cause.
>
> In fostering these qualities, a big part is played by studying the social sciences. Knowledge of the fundamentals of Marxism-Leninism is necessary for specialists in all fields. One must study Lenin and be able to apply his tremendous theoretical heritage in life, and to build up life along communist lines. Marxism-Leninism must be taught in a creative, militant way. Our youth must be brought up in the spirit of irreconcilability to bourgeois ideology and any manifestations of revisionism. Instruction in the social sciences must be conducted so that it is inseparably linked with the study of the natural sciences, and it must help to develop in the students a scientific method of cognition. The higher requirements with regard to teaching Marxist-Leninist theory in the colleges make it the duty of every teacher constantly and persistently to deepen his knowledge and closely link his work with practice, with current tasks.
>
> It is the job of all the professors and lecturers and of party, trade union, and Y.C.L. organizations to attend to the upbringing of the young people at higher educational institutions. It is their duty to inculcate in the students a Marxist-Leninist world outlook, a love for work, communist morality, and the habit of social activity.
>
> The colleges must imbue the students with a responsible attitude to their studies, with a creative approach to mastering the sciences, with independence in their work. They must eliminate the overloading of students with compulsory studies and must draw the senior students into scientific research work.[55]

This document, with its forty-eight theses, is nearly twice as long as Khrushchev's September memorandum. Because it covers the wide expanse of Soviet education, it may be regarded as a reliable expression of current educational aims. On December 24, 1958, it was approved and enacted into law by the Supreme Soviet of the U.S.S.R. with only minor changes. The reform will go into effect gradually, beginning with the school year 1959–1960, and will probably be accomplished within five years. Unless sudden change is introduced, the new law may be expected to form the framework of the Soviet school system from 1965 on.

Objectives of the School Program. Thus, the fundamental aims of the Soviet school have recently been clearly expressed. Premier Khrushchev's oft-repeated and unoriginally phrased demand for the education of "active and conscious builders of a Communist society" is being constantly echoed and re-echoed. But he evidently does not want to make a Communist Party member out of every person. The total number of full Party members, as of February, 1959, is 7,622,235, out of a total population of more than 208,826,000 (1959 census). In addition, there are 616,775 alternate members.[56] It is far easier to control a small membership than a large one. Khrushchev and his followers seem to be more interested in disseminating the principles of communism as widely as possible, so that Soviet citizens, youths, and children will be convinced that the Communist way of life is best for them.

From Khrushchev's recent speeches and writings it is evident that the current polytechnization of the curriculum is intended not only to "bring the schools closer to life," to use the official terminology, not only to make a permanent contribution toward the improvement of the national traditional Marxist-Leninist ideology of communism, but also to keep the masses of the population on a common social level. The rising repugnance to rigorous labor — indeed, to any form of manual labor — on the part of those who were making a career out of attendance at school and higher educational establishments was responsible for the stiffening of the Soviet attitude toward the person desirous of ensconcing himself in a white-collar job. The Soviet government does not want to see the development of a broadly educated elite remote from the population at large. The intellectual, the technologist, and the ordinary citizen must all have had similar work experience and must share a respect for hard work.

It is questionable whether the Soviet authorities have in mind turning back the clock — abolishing all differences in salaries and prestige according to achievement and position — although they have eliminated some of the substantial differences in the past year or so. Such differentiations doubtless led to a widening of the gap between the intellectual (not to say political) and the average man.

Some members of the Comparative Education Society have confirmed by observation what has long been reported to amount to social-class differences in income and level of service. Perhaps, by giving all a taste of toil, the Soviet leaders are trying to reduce the extremes of elitism.

Basic Features of the System

The long transition period assigned for the implementation of the reforms makes it uncertain what the final form of the Soviet system will be. The attempted changes will have to contend with entrenched educational traditions before they are successfully implemented, if, indeed, they can be implemented. For the time being, one can do no more than describe the system as the members of the Comparative Education Society found it in September, 1958.

Mme. L. Dubrovina, former Deputy Minister of Education of the R.S.F.S.R., has stated the aims of the Soviet school:

> to equip pupils with knowledge of the fundamentals of the science of nature, society and human thinking and to develop in them a scientific outlook;
>
> to acquaint the younger generation with the general outlines of modern industry, the fundamentals of modern technique, and to teach them to link the conclusions of science with the practice of socialist construction;
>
> to ensure development in pupils of firm moral convictions; to implant in them boundless loyalty to their native land, respect and love for other nations, humanism, diligence, honesty and truthfulness;
>
> to ensure co-ordination of the pupil's mental development with correct physical development; to bring up a generation of healthy, vigorous people;
>
> to provide for aesthetic education of pupils; to teach them to understand and appreciate art, develop aesthetic taste and cultivate creative ability.[57]

As of the summer of 1958, the school system of the U.S.S.R. serving this philosophy consisted of the following kinds of institutions: preschools — nursery schools and kindergartens; primary-secondary schools of four, seven, or ten years, depending on urban or rural location; evening and part-time schools for young workers and farmers; vocational schools and specialized schools of various types; semiprofessional schools (technikums); correspondence and evening schools for higher studies; universities, professional schools, adult schools; and out-of-school educational agencies. Special schools are provided for the physically and the mentally handicapped. Education is free, except on the preschool level, in the Pioneer summer camps, and in the new boarding schools.

All schools throughout the U.S.S.R. have substantially the same curriculum on their respective levels, although there are minor differences. The nationality schools in the non-Russian republics instruct in the native tongues, but all pupils are required to learn Russian as a medium of communication for the entire Soviet Union. A serious effort is made to have all the pupils obtain a uniform basic education by means of uniform teaching materials and reasonably similar methods of instruction, but, of course, the quality of the education cannot be made uniform by such measures.

Administrative Organization.   Decrees and laws concerning education originate as a rule in policies adopted by the Presidium and the Central Committee of the Communist Party. This is how the Marxist-Leninist ideology is made the basis for school policy and practice. The Supreme Soviet of the U.S.S.R. and the Council of Ministers of the U.S.S.R. then add their unanimous voices. All major changes in the school system are reviewed in this manner. Matters of lesser moment are dealt with by the ministers of education, doubtless also in accord with the tenets of the Communist Party.

There is no single ministry of education for the Soviet Union. Rather, each of the fifteen republics has a ministry of its own, which is responsible to the government of the republic. This arrangement gives the appearance of a decentralized system of schools, at least on the surface.[58]

Each ministry of education is in charge of the administration of the primary-secondary schools. Its work is accomplished by the central ministry office, the *oblast'* (provincial) departments and the *raion* or *gorod* (district or municipal) subdepartments. It is fully responsible for finances, courses of study, textbooks, appointment of teachers and other school functionaries, and supervision. On the various governmental levels, committees appointed by the corresponding soviets advise the educational administrative unit on school construction, finance, problem pupils, and related questions.

The Ministry of Education of the Russian Soviet Federated Socialist Republic, to take as an example the largest and most influential educational agency, is concerned with preschool education, the primary-secondary schools, adult educational institutions, and the like. Within its purview come budgets, buildings, all aspects of teaching, and supervision. It maintains the Gosudarstvennoe Uchebno-Pedagogicheskoe Izdatelstvo (Uchpedgiz), the State Pedagogical Publishing House, which publishes millions of textbooks on all subjects every year. With the changes in Party line and, consequently, in educational policy, it becomes necessary to issue revised editions at frequent intervals in many fields of study. Another probable reason why Uchpedgiz prints so many volumes is that many pupils buy and keep their textbooks, so that a new supply is necessary for each school year. The educational ministries of the other republics usually translate the R.S.F.S.R. textbooks into their native languages and make other slight adjustments, such as modification of the illustrations, to reflect the native culture.

The R.S.F.S.R. Ministry of Education also operates a State Publishing House of Children's Literature (Detgiz). Its Academy of Pedagogical Sciences issues pedagogical publications and a periodical, sets up research projects in educational theory and practice, and maintains a central pedagogical library in Moscow which is of great significance to research workers in education.

The ministries of the fourteen other republics are organized along the same administrative lines. As a matter of regular practice, they follow the lead of the largest ministry, as in the case of the textbooks. The Academy of Pedagogical Sciences of the R.S.F.S.R., because of the significance and magnitude of its research program, is frequently the source of professional inspiration and guidance for the ministries of the other republics.

Higher education has hitherto been generally under the control of the Ministry of Higher Education of the U.S.S.R. Before 1959, only one republic, Ukraine, had a subordinate Ministry of Higher Education of its own; now such a ministry has been established in all the other republics. The Ministry of Higher Education of the U.S.S.R. supervises the universities, professional schools, and research institutions. It determines the quota of enrollments, appoints professors and teachers, decides on methods and on instruction content, selects textbooks, and appoints graduates to positions.

Vocational and technical schools were until recently under the jurisdiction of the various specialized ministries concerned. A school preparing technicians in coal mining was administered by the Ministry of Coal Industry. Now, with the exception of medical technikums, such schools are supervised by the Ministry of Higher Education. Elementary vocational schools are controlled by the Chief Administration of Labor Reserves under the Council of Ministers of the U.S.S.R., which also directs vocational schools for various highly skilled occupations, as well as elementary factory schools preparing workers for mass occupations.

The Ministry of Culture of the U.S.S.R. is in charge of adult education, libraries, museums, houses of culture, theaters, radio, the cinema, television, literature, and the press. In addition, each of the fifteen republics has a ministry of culture, which, like the ministry of education, is divided into *oblast'* and *raion* levels.

Capital investment in the construction of educational institutions in 1957 showed an increase of 33 per cent over 1956. In that year, a total of 3285 schools was built for the use of 676,000 children.[59] In thinking about the Soviet educational budget, it is important to realize that it provides for not merely the education and training of children and adolescents and higher professional education but also children's homes, adult political education, the press, art, radio broadcasting, and scientific institutions.[60] A part of the school budget goes for the activities in the Pioneer palaces and houses, in which the young children enjoy supplementary education and training, recreation, and Party indoctrination. Since an exact breakdown of statistics is hard to come by, it is impossible to make comparative studies of educational budgets.

The total enrollment during 1957–1958 in all types of general schools — four-, seven-, and ten-year schools, schools for young workers and farmers, and adult correspondence schools — was 30,624,900 pupils in 214,162 institutions.[61] The higher educational establishments enrolled about 2,150,000.

Sequence of Preschool, Elementary, and Secondary Education.
Preschool education takes a child at the age of a few months and cares for him until the age of three in a nursery. From age three

to seven the child may attend a kindergarten. These preschools are useful for mothers who are employed and unable to supervise their very young children, who may remain at the school for as long as nine hours each day. The cost of attendance to the parent is about 25–35 per cent of the total expenditure. There are preschools in kolkhozes, factories, and various other establishments. Up to the present, however, preschool education has not been uniformly widespread in the U.S.S.R.

The child is developed physically, morally, mentally, and aesthetically in the kindergarten and is even given some labor training. He learns how to speak properly, sing, dance, and draw. In many instances he learns the rudiments of reading. The kindergarten, furthermore, teaches responsibility for cleanliness and order, care of plants and animals, and other skills that will be helpful to the child as he grows up.

Compulsory attendance begins at the age of seven. The first rung in the educational ladder is the first grade of the four-, eight-, or eleven-year school. Four-year schools are usually found in rural areas. The eight-year school is called the incomplete secondary school and the eleven-year school the complete secondary school. The successful completion of eleven-year education is a prerequisite to the entrance examination to the university.

The primary-secondary sequence is divided into three levels: (1) grades one through four, elementary, for children aged seven to eleven; (2) grades five through eight, intermediate, for those between eleven and fifteen; and (3) grades eight through eleven, secondary, for students fifteen through eighteen. Final examinations are given at the end of grade eight, in order to determine what kind of secondary education the pupil is eligible for. There are also final examinations at the end of grade eleven. Until the new reform is accomplished eight grades in the incomplete school and eleven grades in complete secondary school will not uniformly replace the old seven- and ten-year structure in all parts of the country.

Article 121 of the Soviet Constitution guarantees a seven-year period of compulsory schooling (that is, until the end of grade seven), now to be changed to eight years (end of grade eight). Youngsters may continue to study, if they possess the proper qualifications and pass an examination, in vocational schools for agriculture and industry, technikums for such professions as nursing and teaching, military and secret-police schools, and the complete secondary school, now to be transformed into a part-time school in grades nine to eleven.

Sequence of Higher Education. The regular course at a Soviet university is five years in length, with the engineering and medical courses lasting five and a half and six years respectively. Special institutes for the training of agricultural experts, primary teachers, and other professionals of similar status offer four-year courses. Higher education is also carried on in military academies, advanced secret-police schools, and higher Party schools. All institutions of higher education can be entered only by graduates of a ten-year school or of a technikum, after they have passed competitive examinations. A candidate for higher education may apply to only one institution during one year. If he fails to enter, he must wait until the following year before he can try again. Winners of gold and silver medals were not required until recently to submit to an entrance examination.

The courses of instruction in all types of higher education are completely prescribed. All students, regardless of their field of specialization, must study and successfully pass examinations in the full sequence of Communist subjects — history of the Communist Party, political economy, historical materialism, and dialectical materialism. A diploma is granted upon the presentation of a thesis or the passing of a state examination.

A student who is permitted to undertake postgraduate studies becomes an *aspirant* and after three years' work obtains the degree of *Kandidat,* provided that he is successful in the public defense of his dissertation before a faculty examination panel. At least four additional years of study and research, as well as a dissertation, are required before the doctoral degree is granted. As Nicholas DeWitt has observed, "For either degree the dissertation may be a published or unpublished work, a published textbook of outstanding quality, independently obtained findings of empirical or applied research, a contribution to the methodology of a given science, or theoretical treatment of a specific topic in relation to an existing body of knowledge." [62] Such flexible requirements inevitably result in an "uneven quality of advanced-degree requirements." [63]

It is significant that the Party exercises pressure, to some extent at least, on various phases of higher education, such as lectures, examinations, and research. A former Soviet professor has testified that a panel of faculty members conducting an examination "must be careful in handling particularly active Party members. Although professors can make a grade 'stick,' Party inquiry or some other embarrassing result may follow unfavorable grading." [64]

Such is the general outline of the Soviet educational system. With the spread of the Soviet zone of influence the features of this system have also been spreading. Since World War II the Soviet Union has been successful in imposing a rigid rule of Communist discipline on seven satellite nations — East Germany, Poland, Czechoslovakia, Hungary, Bulgaria, Rumania, and Albania. The teaching of the social sciences, philosophy, psychology, and other subjects in these countries has been deeply affected by Communist doctrine. As in the Soviet Union, students must pursue courses in Marxism-Leninism and related areas without regard to their field of interest. In this way the Soviet and satellite leaders hope that the students behind the Iron Curtain will form one solid phalanx of ideology. Another method of achieving uniformity and conformity is the teaching of Russian as a first foreign language. However, the Soviet authorities have not been able to maintain a strictly monolithic system. Thus, religious education in schools and some doctrinal deviation are permitted in Poland. Minority groups, such as the Jews, have more cultural and educational privileges in most of the other Iron Curtain countries than in the Soviet Union. On the other hand, after several years of dispensing with the required teaching of Russian, the East German government recently restored this language to its former place of prominence in the curriculum.

On balance, one might venture a judgment that at the time of the Comparative Education Society's visit the impact of Soviet educational practices upon the world was not growing as compared with the preceding decade and was, perhaps, about to diminish. Absorbed in the task of solving its own problems, which will be described in detail in succeeding chapters, the Soviet system has entered upon a period of uncertainty, which for the present should stay the hand of even the most ardent of its imitators.

PART

TWO

PART

TWO

5

SCHOOL ADMINISTRATION

The administrative theory under-
lying the management of a formal institution such as a school often
reflects the prevailing value system of its parent society. In the
Soviet Union this relationship between basic social values and
administrative structure is consistent and clear. Ostensibly a self-
governing democracy but in reality an autocratic society, the Soviet
Union carries the principle of one-man management into the administrative organization and supervision of its educational system.

Administrative Policy: Development and Implementation

Educational policy in the Soviet Union is determined by a relatively small group and is filtered down through succeedingly larger
administrative units until it is finally put into practice at the local
school level. Modifications of existing policy or innovations begin
in the Central Committee of the Communist Party and are transmitted to the Council of Ministers of the Supreme Soviet of the
U.S.S.R. for legal action. The Council of Ministers then issues instructions to the ministries of education in the fifteen republics of

the Soviet Union. Since some specialized branches of education are under the jurisdiction of other ministries, these instructions are presented to the appropriate ministry; for example, policies pertaining to the education of physicians are referred to the Ministry of Public Health. The Russian Soviet Federated Socialist Republic, the largest of the republics, usually works out the details for implementing the decree in cooperation with its Academy of Pedagogical Sciences and the Academy's related research institutes. When the details have been developed satisfactorily, each of the other ministries puts into effect, with a few local modifications, the educational policy of the Central Committee of the Communist Party.

In due time the ministries of education of the other republics receive the policy and plans for its implementation and transmit them, in turn, to regional, territorial, city, and district boards of education. They are then given to directors of local schools, who are responsible for working with their assistants and teachers to see that the policy is finally put into operation. Nicholas DeWitt has summarized this procedure as follows:

> In the Soviet Union, individual educational establishments or groups of facilities joined under certain branches of the educational administration have only limited autonomy in reaching day-to-day operational decisions. Such decisions are merely tools in the implementation of certain aspects of educational policy, and the over-all educational effort remains centrally co-ordinated and centrally supervised.[1]

The Central Committee of the Communist Party. The Central Committee of the Communist Party consists of a small ruling group elected by a congress of Party members. It has a special subcommittee devoted to school affairs, whose task it is to examine, formulate, re-examine, and reformulate educational policy. The decisions of this subcommittee are carried out by the permanent office on school affairs, which is linked to similar offices in the various republic Party organizations. Two recent examples of the great influence of the Central Committee on educational policy can be cited. The first of these was the shift, in 1952, from rigid emphasis on an academic program to reinstitution of the concept of polytechnical education, described at length in Chapter 10. The second example occurred in connection with the 1958 reforms described in the preceding chapter. On these two occasions outright directives by the Party forced changes upon the schools. But Soviet pedagogues are extremely reticent about the details of Party participation in educational decision-making. They contend that the role of the Central Committee is confined to "over-all supervision."

The Supreme Soviet. The Constitution of the Soviet Union contains sections devoted to the rights of Soviet citizens. Among the provisions for participation in government are the following:

> The Soviet Constitution provides that the people should be formally governed by Communist Party and non-Party members popularly elected by all Soviet citizens over 18 years of age from a single slate of candidates to serve a four-year term as Deputies in the Supreme Soviet of the USSR. This is a bicameral body with executive and administrative functions as well as judiciary and legislative ones. Because the Supreme Soviet itself meets only once a year to approve legislation, these responsibilities are delegated to and carried out by other organs whose members are elected by the deputies to the Supreme Soviet. After these meetings the deputies return to their homes and to their regular jobs in the various parts of the USSR, with news for the local population about what has been enacted and why.[2]

The Supreme Soviet consists of two bodies: the Soviet of the Union, which has one deputy for every 300,000 persons, and the Soviet of Nationalities, which has twenty-five deputies from each republic, eleven deputies from each autonomous republic, five deputies from each autonomous region, and one deputy from each national district.

The enactment of new educational laws, which have to be passed by both houses of the Supreme Soviet, is, as in the case of most laws, only a *pro forma* action.

Ministries of Education. A recent report on changes in educational administration in the Soviet Union draws some distinctions between the various ministries in the U.S.S.R. and its republics and identifies the relationships of one ministry to another.[3] There are three types of ministries: all-union, union-republic, and republic. The all-union ministries exercise direct control over the entire Soviet Union. Republic ministries are state organs that administer matters within the confines of the fifteen republics constituting the Soviet Union. The union-republic ministries are a combination in which some aspects of administration are concentrated in the union ministry while others are administered by ministries within each republic. The table below illustrates how the main ministries are related to each other at various governmental levels. In addition, the State Labor Reserves Administration and various specialty ministries control vocational schools. After the implementation of the 1958 reforms the latter will probably substantially increase in importance.

Soviet School Administration [4]

Level of Government	Type of Administration		
Union	Union Ministry of Higher Education	Union Ministry of Culture	—
Republic	Republic Ministry of Higher Education	Republic Ministry of Culture	Republic Ministry of Education
Province (*Oblast'*) or Municipality (*Gorod*)	—	Provincial or City Department of Culture	Provincial or City Department of Education
District (*Raion*)	—	District Department of Culture	District Department of Education

Of the three branches of administration, Higher Education was until 1959 most closely centralized, since only Ukraine had a ministry at the republic level (other republics are establishing such ministries at the present time). There are sixteen Ministries of Culture, one federal and fifteen republican. However, the organization of Higher Education and Culture stands in further contrast with the administration of primary and secondary schools.

There is no federal Ministry of Education but only fifteen Ministries of Education, one for each republic. These Ministries are also in charge of most, but not all, kindergartens and administer all professional institutions for the training of teachers in primary and secondary schools. On the other hand, they have no jurisdiction over technical and vocational schools, which are administered by various other ministries concerned. . . .

The so-called autonomous republics represent a special complication. They are not direct members of the federation but are themselves members of the constituent republics. There are seventeen such autonomous republics, thirteen of which are within the Russian republic. They administer their schools through their own separate Ministries of Education. But these are subordinated to the Ministry of Education of the constituent republic, as well as to their own government agency. Thus, the Ministry of Education of the Buriyat-Mongolian Republic is responsible to the Ministry of Education of the Russian Republic. If we add the autonomous republics, we come to a sum of thirty-two offices within the Soviet Union which are called Ministries of Education.[5]

The ministries of education of the constituent republics and their respective local bodies are responsible for developing budgets for public education, placing teachers, inspecting curricula, coordinating in-service education of teachers, approving textbooks and study aids, and administering the educational and organizational activities within the school.[6]

Regional, Territorial, City, and District Boards of Education. Each ministry of education administers primary and secondary education through local government units. As illustrated in the table on page 112, each ministry has departments at the provincial level, the *oblast'* or *gorod*, and these are in turn subdivided into departments at the local level, the *raion*. Within these:

. . . The local Soviets at all levels delegate one of their committees to deal with matters of education. Its members have some prerogatives in advising on building programs, bookkeeping, budget, living facilities for teachers, care of students who fail to make satisfactory progress, and the like. But the bulk of financing, the curricula, personnel management, and inspection — the four cornerstones of control — are completely in the hands of governmental hierarchy.[7]

In addition, the regional economic councils established in 1957 are to be invested with powers to regulate vocational education in their areas.

The city or district board of education has jurisdiction over the directors of the schools. Plans for the school quarter and school year must be submitted to it, and it is responsible for the quality of teaching and the level of student achievement.[8]

In Leningrad, for example, there are twenty-one district boards of education. They are under the jurisdiction of the city board of education, whose chairman is a member of the Leningrad City Soviet of Workers' Deputies. Thus a close relationship is maintained between the city board of education and other branches of the city government. The city board of education is also closely related to the Ministry of Education of the R.S.F.S.R.

The city board of education is responsible for the management of general schools, schools for young workers (labor schools), technikums of a semiprofessional nature, kindergartens, orphanages, children's sport schools, and children's parks.

Operating from the city board of education is a staff of inspectors, usually one inspector for every two districts. Their duties deal with the level of proficiency attained in schools throughout the district.

The district board of education maintains its own staff of inspectors, each inspector assigned to ten schools within his district. He visits each school twice during the year and checks on the proficiency of the director and his teachers. These inspections are thorough; the inspector may remain at the school for a period of from ten days to three weeks. His main concern is the proper implementation of educational decrees concerning program and instructional materials and methods. The inspector also makes himself available to teachers who need help. After his visit the inspector writes a report and leaves a copy and recommendations for certain improvements.

Improvement of methods is a major concern of the city and district boards of education. At the city level it is accomplished through the establishment of an *Institut Usovershenstvovaniia Uchitelei* (Institute for the Advanced Training of Teachers). At the district level, boards of education have departments of teaching methods, which conduct seminars devoted to better teaching.

The city board of education conducts monthly seminars for school directors, city and district inspectors, and chairmen of district boards of education.

Unlike the members of most boards of education in the United States, Soviet board members are appointed. Those on the city boards must have higher pedagogical education and a minimum of seven years of experience as an inspector of schools. District board members must have pedagogical training and five years of experience as an inspector of schools. Both the chairmen and members of the city board of education are appointed by the executive committee of the city soviet. The city board, in turn, appoints members to the district board of education. The district boards appoint their own inspectors (who are usually ex-teachers). They also appoint teachers, usually with the help of school directors.

The chairman of the city board of education appoints the director of schools and his assistant directors.

School Directors. The director of the school heads all of the educational training and administrative work in his school. His chief tasks are to organize teaching personnel, to work effectively with school organization, to study and analyze the work of the teachers and pupils, and to discover and rectify shortcomings in the educational program.

The assistant director schedules classes and teachers. To help the director handle training and educational problems, each school also has a pedagogical council, which consists of all the teachers of a school, the senior Young Pioneer leader, the librarian, the school physician, and the chairman of the parents' committee. The director of the school acts as chairman of the pedagogical council and has final approval or veto of plans developed by it.

The Central Institute for the Advanced Training of Administrators of Public Education, R.S.F.S.R.

Unlike their American counterparts, Soviet teachers are not trained to be administrators. Soviet educational leaders claim that teachers receive no advance preparation for educational administration but are picked on the basis of length of teaching experience and on teaching and organizational ability. They are first appointed to administrative posts and then sent to a central institute for advanced training of administrators of public education. There are many such institutes scattered throughout the Soviet Union and located in large cities and in each *oblast'*.

The Central Institute for the Advanced Training of Administrators of Public Education, R.S.F.S.R. (*Tsentralnyi Institut Usovershenstvovaniia Administratorov Narodnogo Obrazovaniia RSFSR*) is located in an old yellow building on the outskirts of Moscow. It is not an impressive building. Bare light bulbs illuminate its interior and it seems to be chopped up into a labyrinth of many little cubicles and rooms. It houses classrooms, living quarters, and offices for teaching and administrative personnel.

This institute trains ministers of education for the autonomous republics in the R.S.F.S.R.; directors for *oblast'*, *raion*, town, and city units; directors and inspectors of elementary, incomplete secondary, and complete secondary schools; directors of cabinets (departments); directors of institutes for the in-service education of teachers; and directors of institutions of defectology. Directors of institutes and departments are enrolled for a ten-day seminar. All other students are enrolled for a thirty-day course of approximately 200 class hours. The Institute has a student capacity of 300 and operates on a six-hour day. After a student leaves the Institute he attends monthly lectures conducted under the auspices of his city board of education for as long as he holds his administrative appointment.

Although the Institute has forty specialists on its staff, only three or four of them are permanent members. The remainder of the staff work on a part-time basis. Ministers of education, directors of institutes, inspectors of schools, superior teachers, and others are invited to deliver a series of lectures to the students during the course. The methodological specialist attached to the Institute works with teachers in the schools as well as lecturing at the Institute.

In addition to the classes, annual conferences are held at the Institute for directors of institutes. These conferences are planned to give the directors an opportunity to hear new ideas discussed on the administration of institutes of higher learning. The proceedings are published and distributed throughout the Soviet Union and to many foreign countries as well.

Program of the Institute. The enrollees in the Institute attend classes six hours a day, six days a week. They hear lectures in several areas, have an internship or a practicum, and engage in extracurricular work.

The areas comprising the basic training program are dialectical materialism, basic pedagogical problems of schools, content and work of the administrative post for which the student is being trained, work of union organizations and labor legislation, study of the rights of children under Soviet law, and study plans, programs, and basic questions of the method of instruction.

The tables below are taken directly from an *uchebny plan* (teaching plan) for the preparation of inspectors of schools and chairmen of *raion* and city boards of education.

Monthly Teaching Plan for Inspectors of Schools

Titles of Lectures	Number of Hours Devoted to Lectures*
General Cycle	
Ideological work in current times	8
Lenin's principles on Communist education of youth	2
Total	10
Basic Pedagogical Problems of Schools	
The connection of study with productive labor	4
Means of improving the effectiveness of the lesson	2
Educational work in the school	4
The work of Young Communist and Pioneer organizations in the school	4
Organization of the pedagogical process in small schools	2
Total	16
The Content and Work of the Inspectors of the District and City Boards of Education	
Lenin's statements on the mission of governmental control and how it relates to the basic work of the inspector	2
Planning and organization of work of the inspector, means of improving the effectiveness of inspection	2
Work of the inspector with the staff, participation in methodological work, progressive pedagogical experience	2

Monthly Teaching Plan for Inspectors of Schools [Continued]

Titles of Lectures	Number of Hours Devoted to Lectures*
Inspection of Schools	
Evaluation of teaching of general education and of the fulfillment of the national economic plan	2
Inspection of intra-school control and leadership of the pedagogical process	4
Inspection of instruction and the quality of knowledge and habits of the students	6
Inspection of polytechnical education and the work of the school according to the new plan of study	5
Inspection of the system of educational work of the school	6
Total	29
Work of Union Organizations and Labor Legislation Total	8
Protection of the Rights of Children Total	3
Study Plans, Programs, Basic Questions of the Methods of Instruction and Inspection of the Separate Subjects	
Russian language (Grades 1–4)	4
(Grades 5–7)	4
Literature (Grades 8–10)	4
Arithmetic (Grades 1–4)	4
Mathematics (Grades 5–10)	4
Physics	4
Chemistry	4
Biology	3
History	4
Geography	3
Handicrafts (Grades 1–4)	4
Practical work in shop (Grades 5–10)	6
Practical work experience (Grades 5–10)	2
Basis of production in Grade 9	4

Monthly Teaching Plan for Inspectors of Schools [Continued]

Titles of Lectures	Number of Hours Devoted to Lectures*
Knowledge of machines and electrotechnics	6
Mechanical drawing	3
Foreign language	2
Physical education	3
Total	68

Practicum in the School, Conferences for the Exchange of Experiences

Practicum in the schools of the city and *oblast'* of Moscow	16
Practicum in inspection of schools	24
Conferences for exchange of experiences	
On polytechnical education	6
On the inspection of schools and educational work	6
Episodanal lectures	
General information, travel experiences overseas, world affairs, and other cultural discussions	2
Total	54

Excursions beyond the Plan

Polytechnical museums, Museum of Lenin	—
Faculty lectures and practical work beyond the course of study	—
Inspection of national schools	2
Russian language in national schools	2
Inspection of schools for working and rural youth	2
Visit to boarding schools and to out-of-school establishments	6
Pedagogical works of N. K. Krupskaya (lecture and visit to an exhibit)	2
Total	14

* The total program comprises 25 study days per month and 202 class hours.

Monthly Teaching Plan for Chairmen of District and City Boards of Education

Titles of Lectures	*Number of Hours Devoted to Lectures°*
General Cycle	
Ideological work in current times	6
Lenin's principles of Communist education of youth	2
Total	8
Basic Pedagogical Problems of the Secondary School	
The connection of study with productive labor	4
Means of improving effectiveness of the lesson	2
Educational work in the school	4
The work of Young Communist and Pioneer organizations in the schools	4
Total	14
The Content and Organization of Work of the District Board of Education	
Lenin's statements on the mission of governmental control	2
Planning and organization of work of the district board of education	4
Implementation of the national economic plan and general education	2
Inspection of schools	10
Work of the district board of education with staff leaders	2
Methodological work in the district and the improvement of teacher qualifications	2
Leadership of preschool establishments	2
Work of professional organs and labor legislation	6
Protection of the rights of children	2
Finance of public education	2
Leadership in workers' schools and schools for rural youth	2
Total	36

Monthly Teaching Plan for Chairmen of District and City Boards of Education [Continued]

Titles of Lectures	Number of Hours Devoted to Lectures°
Basic Questions of Methods of Instruction and of Inspection of the Separate School Subjects	
Russian language (Grades 1–4)	4
(Grades 5–7)	4
Arithmetic (Grades 1–4)	4
Mathematics (Grades 5–10)	4
Physics	4
Chemistry	4
Biology	3
History	4
Geography	3
Handicrafts (Grades 1–4)	2
Practical work in shop (Grades 5–10)	6
Practical work experiences (Grades 5–10)	2
Basis of agriculture	4
Knowledge of machines and electrotechnics	6
Basis of production in Grade 9	2
Physical education	2
Drawing and mechanical drawing	2
Foreign language	2
Total	62
Practicums and Conferences	
Practicum in the schools of the *oblast'* and city of Moscow	32
Conferences for the exchange of experiences	
On polytechnical instruction in the district and city board	6
In the course of educational work in the school	6
Total	44
Episodanal Lectures	
Faculty lectures and practical work beyond the study plan	—
Leadership of out-of-school sections	2

Monthly Teaching Plan for Chairmen of District and City Boards of Education [Continued]

Titles of Lectures	Number of Hours Devoted to Lectures*
Leadership of kindergartens	2
Leadership in control of the work of non-Russian schools	2
Visits to boarding schools and out-of-school establishments	6
Total	12
Excursions beyond the Plan	
Polytechnical museums, Museum of Lenin	—
Faculty lectures and practical work beyond the course of study	14
Total	14

* The total program comprises 25 study days per month and 190 class hours. Both academic plans were translated at the Central Institute for the Advanced Training of Administrators of Public Education, R.S.F.S.R., Moscow, by William Benjamin and Herbert C. Rudman.

A. Malysheva, Assistant Director of the Central Institute, made it clear that those who are appointed to administrative posts receive basically the same preparation. Details may differ somewhat, but the pattern is always the same.

A variety of methods is used in preparing administrators at the Institute. For example, students take a basic block of lectures and seminars and, in addition, lead discussions — called episodanal lectures — in which they share experiences with their classmates. Trips around the community are planned and many hours are spent in observing seasoned administrators at work. Practice and theory are combined at every step of training.

A Day in the Life of a Student-Inspector. To understand better the kind of preparation undergone, let us follow for a day a typical student.

Mikhail Golodov has been selected by the Ministry of Education of the Dagestan Autonomous Republic to serve as Inspector of Schools. He is married, thirty-five years old, and an aspirant for the Candidate of Sciences degree. He lives in Machashkala, a city located on the shores of the Caspian Sea, and has taught school for seven years.

Mikhail has been awarded this singular honor because he has evidenced to the director and inspector of schools in his area an ability to work well with his fellow teachers. He has also shown great organizational ability in his work with classes and with teacher members of the Young Communist League. Now Mikhail has left his family to spend a month in Moscow, where he will receive advanced training to adapt him for the work he will take up when he returns home.

Mikhail arrives at the Central Institute in the late afternoon and reports immediately to the office of the director, somewhat awed by the businesslike atmosphere of the building. The director puts him at ease with a cordial greeting and exchanges pleasantries for a few minutes while recording Mikhail's name, his age, and the course of study he is to pursue. When he leaves the director's office, Mikhail notices the many colorful displays lining the hall on the way to his quarters. On the bulletin board are pictures of the life of Lenin — his arrival at Petrograd from Switzerland, his meeting with Stalin, his address to a crowd from an armored car, even his picture as a towheaded child. At the far end of the bulletin board are *uchebnye plany* (teaching plans) for the different courses of study available. By the time Mikhail reaches the far end of the display he finds himself at the door of his dormitory.

The dormitory contains twenty beds placed close together. After depositing his extra clothes in the wardrobe Mikhail proceeds to the dining room, where many of his new classmates have already gathered. The evening is spent in excited talk about the coming days.

Next morning Mikhail arises in time for an eight o'clock breakfast, after which he proceeds to his classroom for his first lecture. This first hour is devoted to dialectical materialism as currently interpreted by the Party theoreticians. N. K. Valadin, a staff member of the Party school, is this morning's lecturer. He greets his new charges as follows:

Comrades, you have been sent to this institute charged with a heavy responsibility. The State has entrusted you with the leadership of teaching-upbringing work, with developing the ideology of the State and Soviet society within students who are inexperienced in Communist ideology. You may be a successful leader of the education of children in the spirit of Communism only if you yourself are a Communist, a member of the Party or not. Your life, like that of the rest of our people, should reflect a dedicated commitment to the ideology of Lenin. The State has entrusted to you its people — its children, its future leaders of education, a new generation of Soviet people. This task is a complex and a noble one. You must present to boys and girls an example of wholehearted service to your native land and to your people.[9]

For the rest of the hour Valadin hammers home ideological point after point, as Mikhail's pen flies over his note paper recording the relationship of Communist doctrine to the inspection of educational programs.

During the second hour Mikhail hears a lecture on polytechnical education — the relationship of academic study to productive labor. The lecturer is a specialist in polytechnical education from one of the experimental schools in Moscow.

At eleven o'clock the student proceeds to his third class, where he is introduced to Lenin's concept of governmental control and its relationship to the basic work of the inspector.

From twelve to one he attends a lecture on the work of the Trade Union of Educational, Cultural and Research Workers of the U.S.S.R. Mme. Olga V. Nikolaevska, a worker in the Union offices, reviews the nature of the Trade Union and impending labor legislation, as follows:

> Comrades, as you know, the Educational and Scientific Workers' Trade Union is the largest union in our country. Its four million members include workers in the Ministries of Education, Higher Education, and all educational institutions. Our union stresses "production," not "profession"; professors, teachers, and all other school workers belong to our union. But, of course, these are things you already know about.
>
> Perhaps, however, you do not know of impending legislation which the union is presently sponsoring. We are working on laws to equalize pension benefits between the workers of heavy industry and our own workers. Presently our teachers get a pension after they have worked in our schools for twenty-five years. Women are eligible for this pension at age fifty-five and men at age sixty. We want this changed to coincide with conditions as they exist in heavy industry; we want our

woman to be eligible for pensions at age fifty and our men at age fifty-five. We think that in a few years this will happen.

Another area of legislation in which we are engaged is that dealing with privileges for rural teachers. We are advocating that all rural teachers be given apartments that are heated free of charge. We also want, and expect to get, new schools built near villages and especially near teachers' apartments.

Although we can legislate the material well-being of rural teachers we cannot, of course, regulate their social life. However, the union is finding a way of helping the teacher become a happy citizen leading a well-rounded life. We organize the Day of the Rural Teacher once or twice a month; a day in which rural teachers meet to exchange experiences, to sing and to dance and to come to know each other better. The rural teacher is isolated; she wants to know where she can meet a man. She wants the trade union to help, so we help her. You see, comrades, the union helps teachers in many ways.[10]

The lecturer goes on, mentioning new legislation for workers in research institutes and laboratories. Mikhail suddenly comes alert as she refers to a prospective change in the educational program:

Comrades, soon there will be announced new changes in the structure of our educational system and, of course, the curriculum will be changed. There need to be mass discussions by those who work in education. This is not a question for those who work for academies or institutes, but it is a question for the masses. The union is planning to organize conferences to discuss these changes and to present suggestions to the Council of Ministers. Of course we will also discuss this with the Academy of Pedagogical Sciences, but we expect a difference of opinion. The State will decide between us.[11]

A change that would develop an evident split between the Trade Union and the Academy of Pedagogical Sciences? Before Mikhail can ponder this question the lecture is ended and the class files out to eat dinner in the communal dining hall.

After dinner his group leaves for School No. 15, where they will have an opportunity to observe the director and his class leaders at work. Upon entering the building, the visitors are greeted by the director and his staff and led to the assembly hall on the fourth floor. The director introduces the assistant director for the educational program, the assistant director in charge of administrative details, and the class leaders of the school. A ten-minute description of the school, its faculty, its student body and student organizations follows. The group then observes a conference between the director and his staff as they plan the next quarter's work. The observation period lasts from two o'clock to six, when the group returns to the Institute for supper.

Following the evening meal the students go to one of the classrooms to hear an episodanal lecture by a student from the Tatar Autonomous Republic. He explains the work of the polytechnical education instructors, who coordinate the work of the ninth-grade students in the school and in the factory sponsoring them. In the ensuing weeks Mikhail will hear many such lectures and will probably deliver some himself.

Since this is Mikhail's first night in Moscow, he and two of his classmates leave the Institute and walk five blocks to the subway station where they board the train and in ten minutes are at the *Okhotnyi Riad* station. They go up the escalator and come out of the station built inside the Moscow Hotel. From here they can see Red Square and Lenin's and Stalin's tomb nestled against the red walls of the Kremlin. But a short distance from here is the Bolshoi Theatre. Like tourists anywhere in the world, Mikhail and his friends walk and talk the hour away. Eventually they retrace their steps to the subway station and to the Institute.

This day will be repeated many times during the next month. When Mikhail returns home he will continue his education by attending a monthly seminar conducted by his city board of education. Here he and the directors and assistant directors of schools will meet to discuss mutual problems and to broaden their horizons in the field of pedagogy.

The Work of the School Director

In form, the job of a Soviet school director is similar to that of his American counterpart, but in practice his main task is fulfilling the policies that have been established by the various governmental agencies and the Central Committee of the Communist Party.

Let us look at a typical school director.[12] Anatolii Zelenko, aged forty-seven, is director of School No. 23 in Leningrad. He holds the Candidate of Sciences degree from the Leningrad City Institute of Advanced Training for Teachers, received his training for the directorship at the Central Institute for Advanced Training of Administrators of Public Education, R.S.F.S.R., and has twenty-six years of experience, seventeen of them as director of School No. 23.

His school is a large one. He has fifty-two teachers, who are responsible for thirty classes, and 1140 pupils. School No. 23 still operates in two shifts. Twenty-three classes are scheduled for the first shift and seven classes attend the second shift. Grade one attends school from eight-thirty to eleven-thirty and grades six through ten attend school from eight-thirty to two. Grades two, three, and four attend school from two-thirty to five-thirty. Grade five attends school from two-thirty until seven-thirty.

Director Zelenko's day lasts from 8:00 A.M. to 7:30 P.M. To start the day he greets his teachers and students as they enter the lobby of the school. After the bell rings, he makes a quick tour of the building, visiting all rooms to be sure that all is well and that nothing is wanting in any classroom. He may stay for a time in one class to observe a teacher who is having difficulty with her pupils. Follow-

THE DIRECTOR IN THE SCHOOL HIERARCHY

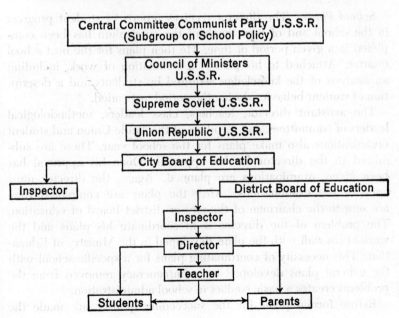

ing his morning classroom visit he meets with his administrative staff. Zelenko has two assistants, one in charge of the educational program and the other in charge of the various class leaders in the school. He and his staff plan their daily activities and may spend some time planning for activities in the succeeding thirty-day period.

Zelenko's duties have been clearly outlined for him.[13] His leadership responsibilities are centered in the following areas: development of school work plans, management of administrative details, development of a working relationship between the director and his assistant director for the educational program, staff meetings, selection and placement of personnel, responsibility for instruction, the pedagogical council, class leadership, out-of-school work, physical education of students, Pioneer and Young Communist organizations, work with parents of pupils, technical personnel, control and accounting of teaching-learning experiences, and maintenance of a good working relationship between the director and the district board of education. For nearly twelve hours a day the director has to cope with these problems.

School Plans. The director receives reports of student progress in the school and of how much of the curriculum has been completed in a given period of time. He then plans for the next school quarter. Attached to his plan is a summation of work, including an analysis of the knowledge acquired by students and a description of student behavior during the period just ended.

The assistant director, teachers, class leaders, methodological leaders of committees, and members of the Trade Union and student organizations also make plans for the school year. These are submitted to the director for his approval. Once his approval has been given, examinations are planned. Again, the director must approve the examinations. After the plans are completed they are sent to the chairman of the city or district board of education. The problem of the director is to coordinate his plans and the work of his staff with the plans developed in the Ministry of Education. This necessity of coordinating plans for a specific school with the general plans developed by a bureaucracy removed from the problems creates a basic conflict in school administration.

Before formal plans for the succeeding quarter are made the

director calls together his assistant directors for students and for administrative details, senior Pioneer leaders, the librarian, the school physician, the heads of methodological departments, representatives of the district committees, and representatives from the Party and Young Communist League organizations. At this meeting the director analyzes the educational program by subject areas, reviews the efficiency of individual teachers, and discusses other pertinent questions that will affect subsequent planning.

Management of Administrative Details. Soviet theory and practice dictate that there must be strict discipline exerted over all the workers and students in the school. As one textbook comments:

> When there is a tight work discipline in the school among educational faculties, the chief result appears to be success in the training and education of children. This has been confirmed by many years of practice in foremost Soviet schools. The establishment of such discipline and efficient internal routines in the schools is the major duty of the director.
>
> The standards which guide school life determine the regulations of internal routines. Every student and school worker's responsibility is to know and to strictly observe the rules. If such rules are not observed in the schools, if the director is unable to carry out his work, then all other measures for thoroughly establishing discipline cannot further desirable results in the school. To reiterate, careful administration of schools will do a great service for the means of education. It appears to be absolutely a necessary condition for the achievement of the best qualitative indices of instruction in education of children, for strengthening discipline, and for creating favorable conditions for work.[14]

The establishment of discipline and efficient administrative routines in the school is a major responsibility of the director. Every student and every school worker must know and strictly observe the rules governing staff and student behavior and work within the school. The director finds the basis for his local school rules in an educational directive entitled *Model Regulations for Workers in Elementary, Seven-Year and Ten-Year Schools in the RSFSR.*[15] He also determines the duties of students and administrative and technical workers on the staff.

The director is guided by Trade Union regulations in developing a satisfactory distribution of responsibilities between his assistant director and himself. Generally he determines all administrative policy, works with class leaders, student organizations, and parents' committees, supervises teachers and determines their placement, and works directly with the district school board. The assistant director, on the other hand, controls the implementation of the educational program, plans for examinations of students, is responsible for daily reports of progress of students, provides remedial instruction for slow learners, summarizes school progress for educational quarterly reports, and prepares materials for school accounts. He teaches some classes, develops schedules of lessons, schedules duty rosters for teachers and students, and organizes substitute lessons for absent teachers.

The director is responsible for statistics of school attendance:

> For the implementation of general compulsory education the director pays particular attention to calculating the children's population in the total school district. The director watches over and gives assistance to teachers, parents and older students. He makes a record of all of the children in the school district, including those who leave the district and those who return to it. In rural districts the director of school works closely with rural Soviets (councils). The director makes note of the trend in small districts of populations of children, carefully calculates all immediate terminations of elementary school programs, explains to collective farmers together with deputies of the rural Soviets about the obligation for future training of children and for finishing elementary school.
>
> If it appears to be a necessity, the director may organize in the school, or close by it, a boarding school for students, provide proper supervision for the students, help them in the preparation of lessons and organize their leisure time.[16]

Relations with the Staff. The director's responsibility for the selection of personnel is varied and extends beyond the mere placement of teaching staff. He strives for a balance in his faculty between young, enthusiastic, but inexperienced teachers, and older, more experienced teachers who provide a stable element on the staff. As one textbook comments,

> Some directors in the selection of teaching personnel invite only experienced teachers, those available with long teaching service. Ex-

perienced teachers in all schools and classes take pleasure in their work; teachers acquire this experience through pride in their work. However, it should be taken into consideration that young teachers show high quality in their work. The director should combine the skill and abilities of the experienced teacher with that of a young enthusiastic one.[17]

The director also selects leaders for the Pioneer detachments in the school. The Pioneer leaders are charged with developing a Communist philosophy among the students. The director places teachers and Pioneer leaders in positions with the specific help of the Young Communist League organization.

The director of schools must supervise instruction. Central to the Soviet concept of supervision is the belief that all educators must evidence continual professional growth. In order to keep teachers sensitive to their own levels of capability, the director relies heavily on classroom visitation, with conferences immediately following each visitation. During these conferences he refers to certain standardized guidelines in his discussions with the teacher.[18] He invariably keeps a written record of his visit, noting the teacher's strong and weak points. It is from this record that many of the suggestions for improving instruction come. There appears to be little evidence of a professional peer relationship in the conferences; the director, by virtue of his status, knows what is best, and the teacher, by virtue of his status, listens attentively and with respect.

The pedagogical council is the chief instrument for faculty consideration of major educational problems. The director of the school automatically becomes chairman of the pedagogical council. The council discusses the implementation of educational decrees emanating from the Ministry of Education. Since most teachers, and most directors, received their education before the 1952 decree of the Central Committee of the Communist Party introduced polytechnical education into the school program, it has been a problem of increasing proportion for teachers to adjust to the growing emphasis upon polytechnical education and to define its relation to the academic program. Although the director and teachers have nothing to do with the details of legislation, they do, nevertheless, discuss the possible ways that the Ministry of Education will choose to implement the new decisions. This kind of discussion helps them to anticipate some of the problems that they soon will face.

To help the director supervise teachers, an experienced teacher from each grade is appointed class leader by the director. The class leader organizes the teachers in his grade and attempts to coordinate the class activities with each of the various grades. If a teacher has need of some specialized help, as in the case of the teaching of reading, she may turn to her class leader for initial help.

The director holds weekly meetings with his class leaders, during which the work of various teachers in the school is reviewed, the conduct of students is evaluated, and standard school documents — such as the plans and anecdotal records of the class leaders — are reviewed. In addition to these weekly staff meetings, the director holds special monthly conferences to further the professional development of the class leaders. In essence, these conferences are in-service education for the teachers of teachers.

Attached to every school faculty is a group of nonteaching personnel. In many school districts within the Soviet Union, physicians are assigned on a half-time basis to two public schools. In addition to physicians and nurses, the school staff may have clerical, maintenance, and other technical personnel whose functions are basic to a good school program but who rarely come in contact with children in a teaching situation. The school director is responsible for the coordination of their work and for helping the nonteaching staff to relate themselves and their work to the activities of the school and its educational program.

The chart on page 127 shows the relationship of the director to the rest of the education hierarchy. This relationship is as pure a concept of line-staff connections as can be found anywhere.

Relations with the Students. One theme that permeates all Soviet education is that of control — control over the activities of the teachers, of the educational program, of the attitudes of parents and the values they convey to their children, of the actions of students. This control is complicated by the fact that many of the facets of control are intangibles and hence difficult to account for or to evaluate with any degree of validity.

Fortunately for the school director, this problem is recognized in official Soviet documents:

It is difficult to control the condition of educational work in the school. [For] here is not such a concrete criterion as can be found in students' work. As an example, [the idea of evaluating one's] knowledge of children. Regulations for students can be published yet it is difficult to know which regulations the students follow: it is impossible to make conclusions about good discipline in the class if the students in that class keep absolute silence, but do not study their lessons.[19]

In spite of this, the director is under pressure to control the conduct of students so that they behave properly not only in the presence of teachers but also when teachers are not there, and not only in the school but also in out-of-school activities.

Since one of the principal Soviet education demands is that all children enrolled in the schools partake of the same curriculum, devices that permit some individual interests to be served have been integrated into the educational system. The school circle, or club, is one such device.[20] Directions as to how these circles are to be organized and administered are clearly defined through Ministry of Education directives and syllabi. Since the staff for these school circles are specialists trained for just this purpose, the school administrator has added responsibility in coordinating their work with that of the classroom teachers.

The school director, with the help of his class leaders, organizes the physical education program. This program includes rigorous calisthenics and activities such as volleyball, soccer, and basketball. It is supplemented by periodic physical examinations by the school physician and by the development of a program of good health habits that is jointly supervised by teachers and the school physician.

The director works closely with leaders of the Young Communist League (Komsomol) and the Pioneer organizations within his school. The Twelfth Plenum of the Young Communist League, on April 30, 1944, was a bench mark in the establishment of a close relationship between school administration and these student Party affiliates. One of its directives states that "work in the school Young Communist and Pioneer organizations shall appear as an integral part of all educational work in the school conducted by the director and teachers." As a firm basis upon which to define the operational relationship between these organizations and the director, the Plenum decreed that "The director of the school has the right to stop the implementation of erroneous decisions of the school

Young Communist organization and to give the district committee of the Young Communist League reasons for canceling its decisions." It is clear, however, that the director has the responsibility of using mature judgment any time he does exercise his veto power.

In order to maintain close daily ties with the various student organizations, the director devotes a considerable portion of his time to attending regular meetings. He meets with the organization leaders periodically to discuss school activities and to plan new activities with them.

Parents' Committees

Soviet educational theory maintains that if the school is to work effectively with children it must establish close ties with the children's families. The degree to which parents' committees actively participate is open to question, but Soviet administrators and Soviet educational literature describe the role of parents' committees as helping school authorities enforce compulsory attendance, conduct extracurricular activities, improve school facilities, and the like:

> Active participation of Soviet citizens in the discussion of questions of educational problems and the nation-wide aid to the schools, kindergartens and extra-school institutions is an important feature of Soviet public education. . . .
> Parents' lectures in schools, parents' committees on administrative details of the school councils for the promotion of polytechnical training, and other public organizations, have been set up in the USSR.
> Problems of public education are discussed at trade-union and collective-farm meetings and in commissions of public education under local Soviets; they are given extensive publicity in the pedagogical press and in radio broadcasts.[21]

The difference between Soviet educational theory and American educational theory is that the Soviet home must help instruct its children in those values that the school deems important. The director gets his cue in maintaining good school-family relations from directives such as the following:

> In our time, when there still is a conflict with the vestiges of capi-

talism that still exist in people's minds, the significance of close contact of family and school is particularly important. The director ought
to . . . propagandize among parents . . . Communist attitudes.[22]

Every school, by decree of the Ministry of Education of the
R.S.F.S.R., must have an elected parents' committee, with at least
five permanent subcommittees — for insuring the education of all
children, for teaching and upbringing, for pedagogical propaganda,
for cultural mass work, and for sanitation. Other subcommittees
may be formed as needed. This decree dates from 1947.

Members of the Comparative Education Society nowhere found
evidence that the subcommittee for the general education of all
children is still in existence; possibly its work is no longer considered
necessary, at least in the cities.

The subcommittee on teaching and upbringing is responsible for
helping the school attain the maximum amount of success with
the children in their work. This subcommittee works with the
principal and the class leader. If a child receives more than two
marks of "2" in a week, the teacher or the director may give the
parents' group his name. This subcommittee may then call the child
to the school — either with or without his parent — to take him
to task and warn him to study better. Parents are also warned that
their child is not doing as well as he should. If this does not produce
the desired result, the parents' subcommitte may inform the trade
union or Party committee at the place of work of the parents. The
Party or trade union then may call a meeting, where the parent of
the pupil is publicly shamed for his failure as a parent and where
advice is volunteered by his comrades as to how to make his child
succeed in school. Such drastic procedures are probably not re-
sorted to very often.

The subcommittee on pedagogical propaganda organizes lectures
and meetings. It is responsible for the organization of the
quarterly plenary meetings, and it provides the lecturers for these
evenings. It further organizes a lending library in this school and
publishes a bulletin. The committee may ask teachers to explain
teaching methods and helps answer the questions other parents may
have on school procedures. In the period before the recent school
reforms, such committees were busy with the discussion of the proposals published almost daily in the press.

The subcommittee on cultural mass work helps organize children's circles, evening parties of pupils of the higher grades, and concerts for the school. It also organizes one money-raising event a year; the money raised goes toward providing hot lunches and uniforms and textbooks for children who cannot buy them. Since the parents' organizations are not allowed to levy dues on their members, this yearly event is the only source of income they have. This committee also provides escorts for the children on the school excursions and trips to the movies, museums, and the theater.

The subcommittee on sanitation checks on the school lunchroom, helps with the doctor's examinations of the children, checks on sanitary conditions in the school, and organizes the lengthened-day program. It also sees that there is a parent working full-time in the school each day — on hall duty, lunch duty, and other tasks of this nature.

To assure the proper socialistic attitude among parents the director arranges and conducts Sunday lectures on politics and on the agricultural themes of the school's educational program, stimulates parental participation in district Party organizations, and holds general meetings devoted to child-rearing topics, such as problems of discipline. The director often calls parents for consultations in the school and occasionally visits parents in their homes.

An interview with the chairman of the presidium of the parents' committee of School No. 1 in Moscow elicited the following information:

At the beginning of the school year the director calls the parents of all school children together, classroom by classroom. Usually a committee of three is elected from each classroom to form a parents' committee. These parents elect a presidium of eight to ten members, with a representative of each grade level. The presidium elects a president. In this particular school, the following subcommittees exist: for teaching and upbringing, for cultural mass work, for pedagogical propaganda, and for sanitation. The presidium plans the work for one-half year in advance. The director works with both the parents' committee presidium and the pedagogical council of the school. Class committees of parents work with the director and the pedagogical council also. There is no over-all city organization of parents' groups. There is a parents' meeting once every quarter in the school year. The presidium meets every two weeks. Class parents' committees may attend classes to see what goes on. When asked about the relationship between the school and the parents, the chairman of the parents' committee presidium maintained that no conflict ever developed between the two organizations:

> Parents are satisfied with the work of the school and have no complaints. As the parents and the schools have the same aims in the education of the children, no conflicts are possible. Besides, the teachers are the experts and the parents must take their word for it in any problem of school work.

During their meetings the parents first have a plenary session, where they hear a lecture, then meet in the individual classrooms, where the class teacher in the primary grades or the class leader in the secondary grades presents a progress report. Each pupil is mentioned by name and his progress or nonachievement is discussed. After this, the teacher may give a short talk on some topical subject, often a theme that has been suggested by the parents themselves.

Judging by an interview with yet another parents' committee in Moscow, the activities of the committees are about the same in every city school. In this committee, the teaching and upbringing subcommittee had organized a special homework session for children who did not do well in school or for children whose parents could not spare the time to supervise their homework. There, each day, a parent is on duty in a special room and sees to it that the pupils do not leave until they have done their homework conscientiously. Further, in this school the parents' committee does not need to organize a lengthened-day session, as there are no unsupervised children at home. Apart from these minor differences, the work of the parents' committees was the same as that in the first school.

Conclusion

No attempt has been made here to draw detailed comparisons between the administrative structure of schools in the Soviet Union and that of schools in the United States, for comparison without a prior examination of the societal forms and value systems that determine the basis of these administrative structures would be fruitless. It should be clear that the principle of one-man management is central to the administrative behavior of those who work in the Soviet administrative hierarchy. The question that needs to be considered at this point is "How effective is this management for the attainment of the aims set forth by the Central Committee of the Communist Party?"

Surely no one can speak with authority about so complex a question after a four-week visit in so vast a nation as the Soviet Union. But certain specific impressions can be reported. It would appear that there is little lag between educational theory and educational practice in the Soviet Union. The Soviet school is sensitive to the needs of its parent society — as the government interprets these needs — and can move rapidly to meet them.

Again, there is a close relationship between life in the Soviet Union and the educational program in the Soviet school. In 1952, when the Central Committee issued its statements about introducing polytechnical education into the school program, two conditions existed in Soviet life: the schools had no vocational preparation in the complete secondary schools, and the Soviet Union was suffering a serious shortage of skilled workers. In 1958, all schools had extensive programs of polytechnical education, and institutions of higher learning were busily familiarizing teachers with polytechnical education. By 1958 the shortage in the skilled labor supply had eased somewhat.

Unquestionably, for the attainment of Soviet aims the school administrative structure is effective. So long as the goals are clear and directives for attaining these goals are forthcoming, the various elements of the administrative hierarchy function smoothly and well. From the Soviet's point of view this is all one can ask for. However, through an American's eyes this is not enough, for the system has a serious flaw, evident even during a brief visit to the Soviet Union: lack of initiative on the part of agencies or individuals within agencies to improvise if a plan does not work in a given situation. The many detailed directives that are issued to an increasing number of individuals at the lower end of the administrative structure make it almost impossible to deviate from a given plan without taking great responsibility for the consequences of that deviation. Few are willing to do this, and what often started out as a purposeful plan ends up as mechanical manipulation with little understanding on the part of those called upon to implement it.

Nevertheless, the Soviets have developed a system for administering their educational system that is completely consistent with their own values. In a society where the emphasis is on what the individual can do for the state and not what the state can do for the individual, the principle of autocratic management is an acceptable administrative theory.

6

PRESCHOOL EDUCATION

Immediately after the October Revolution a Directorate of Preschool Education was established within the new People's Commissariat of Education. Nadezhda Krupskaya, Lenin's wife, was the moving spirit in the education of the young child in the beginning years of the Soviet government. During this period enthusiasm ran so high that the Commissariat of Education of the Russian Republic even made plans for universal preschool education. These ambitious plans have not yet been fulfilled.

In spite of the postrevolutionary enthusiasm no progress was made in the field of preschool education from 1917 until the introduction of the first Five-Year Plan, in 1928. In the years following this step, pressure to include as many children as possible in preschool institutions grew stronger as the rapid industrialization of the country progressed and as factories and plants clamored for more and more labor. Women had to be freed from family cares to work in the new enterprises, and this meant that young children had to be cared for.

General Characteristics

At the present time there is renewed emphasis in the Soviet Union on the importance of preschool education, and plans are being made for the expansion of preschool institutions as new economic plans make the employment of an increasing number of women imperative. The Soviet government does not emphasize the importance of preschool education for economic reasons only, however; it is also the belief of the authorities that a child is the more easily influenced the earlier he is enrolled in an educational institution. The twofold aim of Soviet preschool education was expressed well by Deputy Minister Markushevich of the Ministry of Education of the R.S.F.S.R.:

> We believe in the importance of pre-school education: children who have attended kindergarten work better in school, they adjust better to life in a collective and to school discipline. Further, pre-school institutions are necessary to families where both parents work. Finally, many families do not yet know how to bring up their children correctly; especially, many peasants are not educated enough for this.[1]

Extent of Preschool Education. Although there has been considerable development of preschool education in the Soviet Union since 1917, existing facilities fall far short of accommodating all children whose parents need or want to place them in nurseries or kindergartens. The period of greatest advance was between 1929 and 1940 and coincided with the period of most rapid industrialization. From 1940 to the present there have been only slight gains. Enrollment in crèches (*iasly*), which take children from the age of a few months to 3 years, cannot be precisely determined. In general, however, it seems safe to say that facilities even in the big cities are nowhere near adequate for the existing needs. For kindergartens (*detskie sady*), which include children from three to seven years of age, a Soviet publication quotes the following figures: in 1955 there were 31,596 kindergartens in the Soviet Union with an enrollment of 1,730,900 children, as against 2155 kindergartens with an enrollment of 107,500 children in 1927.[2] The Twentieth Congress of the Communist Party approved a plan to enlarge attendance in preschool institutions for the next planning period up to 45 per cent. It should be emphasized, in amplification of these figures, that by far the greater part, about two-thirds, of these preschool institutions are located in urban areas.

Members of the Comparative Education Society were told in every preschool institution visited that the number of available vacancies each year was not sufficient to accommodate all applicants. Figures quoted to questioners differed considerably, but it seems safe to conclude that only 10 to 20 per cent of eligible children go to kindergartens. While the inspector for preschool institutions in the department of education in Leningrad said that in her district 40 per cent of all eligible children go to kindergartens, the director of Kindergarten No. 1 in Kiev maintained that 90 per cent of the children attended in her city. Mme. T. A. Markova, Director of the Pre-school Section of the Sector on Education of Children in the Family, Institute of the Theory and History of Pedagogy, Academy of Pedagogical Sciences, R.S.F.S.R., gave another figure: "As the Ministry undoubtedly told you, only 20 per cent of the eligible children go to preschool institutions in the Soviet Union."

We must keep in mind the fact that these figures do not always apply to the same institutions — Mme. Markova was talking of preschool institutions in general, the other two informants were confining themselves to kindergartens; she was speaking of a national average, they of attendance in their cities (large and progressive ones). These examples show only how far information differed on this point. Whatever the true figure, there is general agreement that many more preschool institutions are needed. The chairman of the Leningrad department of education reported that in his city fifty-six new kindergartens were to be built in the near future.

Variations in Form. Although the government educational plan provides for the expansion of preschool institutions, Soviet law also permits plants and collective farms to establish nurseries or kindergartens from their own funds.[3] Indeed, creation of preschool institutions through local initiative is widely encouraged. In 1956, for instance, a district of the Leningrad *oblast'* declared a period of "socialist competition" between collective farms of the area, to see which one could best organize the preschool education of children. The collective farms were helped in this project by the workers of the surrounding industries. The movement was recommended to other regions of the country.

Nurseries and kindergartens cater to a maximum of 20 per cent of the age group. Now supervised by the Ministry of Education in each republic, until 1959 they were managed by the Ministry of Health. Though neither the nursery nor the kindergarten is part of the formal system of education, they do serve an important role in industrial plants and in the cities. Many working mothers deliver their children in the morning and pick them up after work; if both parents work at night, children may sleep at the nursery. Children are usually kept at home if relatives are available, but nurseries accept babies only a few weeks old and care for the children until they are three years of age. Fees vary according to the parents' ability to pay.

The future aeronaut in his first space ship is tended with 160 other toddlers.

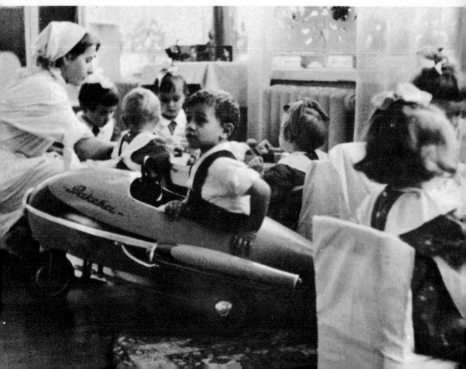

Nursery School

Children receive individual attention. Meticulously clean surroundings have a home atmosphere, with plants, pillows, and toys strewn about.

Nurseries provide toys and drawing pads. Children are dressed according to age groups, and clothes are the color of the playroom walls.

Boys are not above playing with dolls in this nursery in the Red Banner Factory in Leningrad.

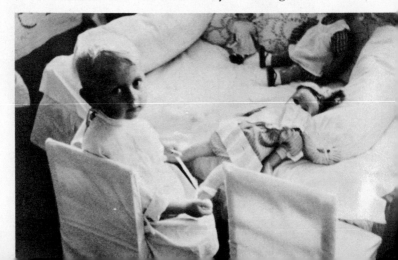

Kindergarten

Above: These boys, playing in a Leningrad kindergarten sponsored by a factory, are under conditions resembling formal schooling. Below: Girls are given periods to play with dolls but playroom activities are supplemented by instruction in reading readiness.

Above: Each kindergarten usually has a music room, in which the children receive training in singing, dancing, group formation, and music appreciation. At right: The picture of Lenin is displayed conspicuously. Respect for Communist leaders is inculcated early in life.

Outdoor exercises include play in an airplane model appropriately named *Druzhba* (comradeship) since it is used to teach teamwork. Large boats and playhouses are frequently built on the play lot.

PRIMARY EDUCATION

Children enter primary school after passing the seventh birthday, and uniforms, brief cases, and books become the part and parcel of everyday life. For four years all Soviet children receive training in fundamentals and preparation for a senior cycle of education. It is at this point that childhood gives way to youth. The child-centered emphasis of the preschool institutions disappears. Now the emphasis is on drill, industry, and basic learning.

Classrooms generally are old-fashioned and severe, with long rows of double desks. Correct posture and discipline are strictly enforced.

On the opening day of school children receive flowers from their parents, in congratulation, and these flowers are in turn presented to the teachers.

School attendance is represented as a joyful privilege. On the opening day girls don white aprons, which are also worn on other festive occasions. This first-grade class in Kiev is having a lesson in drawing.

Posters on billboards and in shop windows urge children to do well. This slogan reads *Uchus na PIAT*, "Learn for Five" ("5" is the Russian equivalent for a grade of A).

The Party's demand for closer union of school with life begins to yield fruit. Girls learn to sew and iron in a Home Economics class. As training in school service, the boy shown here delivers pastry to a school cafeteria in Tashkent.

Contrasts between new and poor school buildings remain great. Above: This school in Moscow represents the best in school construction. Primary-grade children have their classes on the top floor. Below: An outdoor fountain is the only running-water facility for this ten-year school in Tashkent.

The number of preschool institutions established by plants and factories seems to be quite considerable. N. Kova, Assistant Chairman of the department of education of Leningrad, reported: "We have 257 kindergartens in our city, but only 148 were established by the Ministry of Education." Many plants establish nurseries, which include, among other things, provisions for the convenience of the nursing mother; such women may be excused from work at stated periods to nurse their babies in the nursery rooms adjacent to the plant.

Preschool institutions differ not only in sponsoring agencies but also in type of service offered. They may be permanent or seasonal, depending on the needs of the locality. For instance, in many cases the preschools established by collective farms are organized only for the harvest period, so as to free the mothers to help with the farm work at that time. Other institutions are organized for the school year, still others for the whole year. Another form of preschool organization is the summer play group (*letniaia ploshchadka*), which is something on the order of the supervised playground in the United States.

Factories or farms that establish preschool organizations are responsible for financing them — for the upkeep, repair, and equipment of the school buildings; but the ministries supervise the work done with the children, make the educational plans, and enforce compliance with their regulations through a staff of inspectors attached to the various local departments. The ministries of education check on the work of the kindergartens under their jurisdiction through the preschool departments of their district systems of inspection. Inspectors, who are attached to the local education departments and visit the kindergartens regularly, not only criticize but also suggest changes and help make improvements.

Nurseries are concerned mainly with the physical care of the child, with health and bodily development. The personnel includes a doctor, and some of the staff have a certain amount of medical training. Hardly any educational work is done in these institutions. For this reason, they have hitherto been administered by the ministry of health in each republic and have had nothing to do with the ministry of education.

Since nurseries and kindergartens were under the jurisdiction of different ministries there was rarely any contact between the two institutions. The complaint was often found in Soviet literature on preschool education that there was no continuity of the work between the two levels. Nurseries tended to retain children past the proper age, and kindergarten authorities complained that they were insufficiently informed about the problems of each child when they did transfer. Although nurseries kept elaborate records about each child, these records did not accompany the pupil to kindergarten. The ministries of health kept all records, and kindergartens, as they came under a different jurisdiction, had no access to them. Thus, there tended to be a sharp break in the rhythm and methods of teaching in the two institutions. For this reason a decree published in *Pravda*, May 28, 1959, merged nurseries and kindergartens into one institution under the direction and supervision of the republic ministries of education.

It is in the kindergarten that the formal education of the child — his training in how to live in a socialist society — commences. In the later years children are also given a certain amount of academic education and knowledge. The teachers are supposed to have some pedagogical training; and the curriculum is prescribed by the Ministry.

Admission to preschool institutions is determined mostly on the basis of need. In cases where both parents work and there is no relative to care for the child, the family is given priority in admission to nurseries or kindergartens; however, institutions established by plants or collective farms naturally admit children of their members or employees. As stated by the director of Leningrad Kindergarten No. 31, which was established by a leather factory,

> Our kindergarten is meant in the first place for the children of our workers. Of course, we would not refuse to admit children from other families, if we had room for them, but there has never yet been a vacancy for children of parents who do not work at the factory.

Preschool institutions are not free of charge, as are the schools of the Soviet Union. Parents are charged a fee, which is related to the cost of upkeep and varies with the amount they earn. Maximum and minimum amounts are fixed, but these charges seem to vary from city to city, or even from one institution to another. In Kindergarten No. 31 in Leningrad the minimum fee was reported to be 25 rubles a month, the maximum 100 rubles. The nursery run by the Red Banner factory in Leningrad charges a minimum fee of 30 rubles a month, with the maximum 100. Kindergarten No. 1 in Kiev has a maximum fee of 100 rubles a month and a minimum expressed as 30 per cent of the cost of the food for the child. Kindergarten No. 314 in Moscow charges a maximum of 125 and a minimum of 60 rubles a month. Informants agree, however, that some families do not pay anything at all, if truly in need. In such cases, the trade-union committee at the parents' place of work may pay all or part of the cost of tuition.

The Soviet Nursery

Let us look at the nursery of the Red Banner factory in Leningrad — a textile plant manufacturing underwear. This nursery takes care of 160 children ranging in age from two months to three years. In 1958, the budget for the physical up-keep and equipment of the nursery was close to a million rubles, part of which was paid by the parents.

Visitors to the nursery are given white disinfected robes to wear over their street clothes. The staff all wear similar uniforms and the premises are kept scrupulously clean. Children are received in a "medical room," where they are examined and accepted. They are then assigned to one of the groups, divided according to age. The youngest group is two months to one year old, the middle group is one and a half to two, the oldest is one and a half or two to three. Each group is kept separate from the others.

This nursery has altogether eight groups, each with its own "apartment" — a playroom, bedroom, and washroom with a toilet and washbasin — where the children play, eat, and sleep. Each apartment is decorated in its own color scheme; one was painted white and blue, another white and pink, yet another white and red. Children are dressed in the colors in which their rooms are painted. The clothes are provided by the plant. The building has its own infirmary, where children can be treated for minor illnesses and kept isolated from the rest of the nursery. When there is a serious illness, the child is taken to the hospital.

The nursery is in the charge of a director, who is assisted by a clerk for administrative matters. A pediatrician is always in attendance, as are two professional nurses. The kitchen is staffed by three cooks and three dishwashers and is supervised by a doctor in charge of dietetic matters. Each group of children is cared for by two teachers and two assistants. There are usually fifteen to twenty children in the younger groups and twenty to twenty-five in the older groups. As the nursery runs on a twenty-four-hour basis — although not all children stay the whole day — doctors and nurses alternate in six- and seven-hour shifts, respectively. The director, the teachers, and the assistants work eight-hour shifts.

The staff is fully trained. The director, although originally a specialist in economics, took a special training course in nursery education at a pedagogical institute. The teachers have completed the ten-year school and a short-term course in nursery education. The nursery also employs a music teacher, who has completed the course at the Conservatory.

The nursery is well equipped with a variety of toys. There are tricycles, trucks, playhouses, blocks, picture books, dolls and doll carriages, and so forth. The furniture is scaled to the children's size. Contrary to previous reports,[4] the toys are of a small size so that each child can play with his own individually.

There is no set program for the nursery. Children are allowed to play as they like, and teachers and assistants merely supervise. The atmosphere is relaxed, warm, and cheerful. The children all looked healthy and happy. The oldest group was interested in visitors and proved quite ready to sing and dance for strangers.

An extremely careful and detailed record is kept of each child. A city district clinic makes a medical examination of the child, which is turned over to the nursery when he is admitted. The record includes birth certificate, health certificate, growth charts from birth, and reports of illnesses and their treatment. A nurse visits the family before the child is admitted to the nursery and gives the mother advice on child care. The data on the family are then added to the child's record, as is also a record of the mother's hours of work, the parents' salaries, the number of children in the family, and any other relevant information. During the child's stay in the nursery the record is kept up to date, and special eye and ear examinations, vaccinations and immunizations, skin test, X-ray treatments, and chest examinations are entered as they occur. The growth and weight record also is kept. Finally, the record contains information on the behavior and progress of the child in the nursery.

When he is absent for any reason, a nurse visits the home and records the reason. When the child goes on to kindergarten a summary record is sent with him, but the original, detailed file stays in the nursery. This nursery is certainly one of the best equipped and best staffed in the Soviet Union. It probably represents a model for other nurseries to imitate as far as their conditions permit. Several good nurseries have now been reported to be in existence in different regions.

The Ministry of Health publishes a pamphlet for mothers whose children attend nurseries. Every mother with a child in a nursery is required to take the course on child care contained in this publication. It consists of a series of twelve lectures given in evening classes at the nursery. If the mother prefers, she can take the course by correspondence, but she must pass an oral examination on each lecture as she finishes it. The mother's record is kept with that of the child and when the second child is admitted to the nursery the mother is urged to take a refresher course.

The government controls the work of the nursery through inspectors. Inspection is also carried out by doctors, who may come without advance notice. This insures that the provisions laid down by the authorities are followed in practice.

The Kindergarten Program

With admission to kindergarten, the education of the Soviet child begins in earnest. Kindergartens are more widespread than nurseries, and their program is closely related to that of the schools. Several of the agencies of the R.S.F.S.R. Ministry of Education take part in determining the nature of kindergarten activities.

Art and Music Instruction. The Institute of Art Education — one of the constituent institutes of the Academy of Pedagogical Sciences of the R.S.F.S.R. — through its Sector for Preschool Education develops the program for kindergartens and suggests changes and new departures. As stated previously, the decisions of the Academy have validity not only for the Russian Republic but for the Union as a whole.

Art is a major part of the kindergarten program. Vice-Director Sakulina of the Institute of Art Education stressed the importance of aesthetic education for preschool children as follows:

All aesthetic education begins at the preschool level. It is important not only for its own sake but also because it contributes so much to moral education. It is through aesthetic education that we develop such qualities as collectivism, perseverance, purposefulness and the joy of life, all qualities which children must acquire.

The all-round development of children is assured by giving them artistic skills as well as knowledge commensurate with their age. Children are taught drawing, singing, dancing, and marching to music. Games with a musical accompaniment are also played.

Drawing lessons are formal and the resulting pictures concentrate heavily on ornamental patterns, painstakingly drawn and meticulously colored. Children draw with pencils rather than crayons and use very small pieces of paper. Nowhere did the visitors see easels, such as are used in United States kindergartens for the children to paint on, and nowhere were they shown large drawings or paintings. Free drawing and painting is sometimes allowed, and charming pictures may result. Visitors to Kindergarten No. 31 in Leningrad, for instance, were shown drawings that the children had made while spending the summer period at a farm. A teacher present at a meeting at the Institute of Art Education showed her collection of "free" drawings of her preschool pupils. Although all the drawings were very concrete, some of them were remarkably fresh and imaginative. Children are also taught to work in clay and plasticine. Kindergarten No. 1 in Kiev had an exhibit of plasticine animals that the children had made after a visit to the zoo. These were so good that one had difficulty believing that the children had made them unaided. The director seemed surprised at the visitors' incredulity. "This is nothing unusual; all our children can do work like this at that age," she repeated over and over again.

Music instruction in the Soviet kindergarten consists of marching, a form of group dancing, musical games, and group singing. Visitors to Kindergarten No. 1 in Kiev heard a music lesson in which about twenty-five children sat in orderly rows on small chairs in front of the piano and sang a few songs. The older children sat in back, the younger ones in front. The song they were learning was about the sun and its work. Another song was called "Vova's Drum" and told of a little boy who was the proud possessor of a drum and illustrated what noises the drum made for him. In a music period in Kindergarten No. 31 in Leningrad children entered marching in single file to the sound of the piano; then a game was played in which one child, in the middle of a circle, pretended to be sleeping, while all the others circled around him singing. When he woke up, he tried to get out of the circle. The music teacher in this class was asked whether she ever did free rhythms with the children. Her answer was in the affirmative, but when pressed she seemed to have no very clear idea of what was meant by the term. In no kindergarten did visitors see individual instruments for children, such as are used in the United States.

Provisions for Mental and Physical Health. The Institute of Psychology, another of the institutes of the Academy of Pedagogical Sciences, carries on research on the activities of preschool children. A. Smirnov, Director of the Institute and Vice-President of the Academy, stated,

> We observe children at play and judge the extent to which the child performs correctly a role which he has chosen for himself. If, for example, a child, in playing doctor, chooses a stick to play with and goes through all the motions of administering vaccinations, or of taking temperatures, then we can conclude that the child has formed a "correct" concept of the work of a doctor. Much can be told of the child's inclinations by watching him at play. Teachers are also urged to observe the kind of things children will do at different age levels. Psychologists work closely with educators in such projects. They also help in finding means to develop reading readiness in preschool children.

As there are still very many children who cannot enter kindergarten for one reason or another, the Academy of Pedagogical Sciences is concerned with teaching the family how to educate the preschool child at home. The Sector on Education of Children in the Family, part of the Institute of Theory and History of Pedagogy, publishes books and pamphlets on such subjects as what to teach the preschool child at home, how to bring up the child in the family to love and respect work, and games for the child of preschool age. These publications may be written by specialists of the Academy or by mothers who want to share some experience with other parents. Parents of preschool children who do not go to kindergarten are often invited to attend lectures arranged by the Sector in plants or in kindergartens. This is done in an effort to provide some of the advantages that children enjoy in kindergarten for the child who has to stay at home and to prepare him for school in somewhat the same manner.

Concern for mental health is closely connected with the interest in medical care. The health of the children is watched over very carefully and great emphasis is put on a strict regimen and plenty of fresh air. Dormitories in the kindergartens are airy and sunny and the children sleep with the windows wide open even in the winter. Special attention is paid to children with physical defects or weaknesses. If the doctor of the kindergarten certifies a child as not yet ready for school at the age of seven, the kindergarten may keep him for an additional year. Children who are physically handicapped are referred to special schools.

"Academic" Instruction.   In the opinion of the director of Leningrad Kindergarten No. 31, the most important task of the kindergarten is to prepare the children for the work in the first grade. For that purpose, reading readiness is developed, not by formal teaching, but by games that acquaint the children with letters and with certain combinations of letters. Counting and simple arithmetic are also taught by games. For example, the teacher may distribute little flasks — one to one child, two to another, three to another, and so forth. Then she will go to the other side of the room and call out, "All children with two (or one, or three) flasks run to me!" Children learn to add and subtract by helping the teacher take attendance.[5] They learn to speak grammatically and well by telling a story the teacher has read to them or describing a picture the teacher has discussed with them. Kindergarten teachers read stories chosen from the best classical and modern authors. In listening to and repeating these stories, the children not only develop an appreciation of the great writers but also improve their language and learn to understand basic moral values.

Teachers in the Preschool Department of the Gorki Pedagogical Institute in Kiev drew the attention of visitors to the fact that the program for kindergartens had recently been revised in the Ukraine in the direction of more intellectual training. In 1952 the Ministry of Education of the Ukraine republic had tried out a new program for preschool children. Youngsters were taught a series of accomplishments throughout the kindergarten years by the method of didactic play. Results were verified and inspected throughout the republic; the program was found to be a success and has since been formally adopted for all kindergartens. According to this program, children are now expected to be able to do the following things by the end of their kindergarten years:

Speak their native language well and pronounce it correctly.
Be able to tell a story grammatically and fluently.
Speak in sentences.
Name various objects in their environment.
Know the names of several books.
Be able to count to ten and to do simple oral adding and subtracting.

These skills are developed in "learning periods" (*zaniatiia*) of fifteen to twenty minutes' duration each, which are scheduled in kindergartens every day.

Description of the Soviet Kindergarten

Several kindergartens visited will now be described. Kindergarten No. 1 in Kiev is a government-run institution with a budget of one million rubles and an enrollment of 200 children. It is housed in a three-story building standing in its own grounds. Kindergartens in the Soviet Union are divided into three age groups: the youngest consists of children from three to four and a half, the middle one of children from four and a half to five and a half, and the oldest one of children from five and a half to seven. There is, of course, some overlap in each group. Each age group here has its own apartment, consisting of a playroom, a dormitory, a washroom, and a dining room, and is kept apart from the others, as was done in the nurseries.

The ground floor has a large music room, with a piano and several small chairs, which is used by all of the groups alternately. The top floor has a large room for physical culture, equipped with bars and ladders for Swedish gymnastics, which is also used by all groups in rotation. On this floor is a small library for the use of teachers and parents. Finally, there is a large playroom with a fountain and sand piles, which is used in the winter by all groups in succession, so that the children can play in the sand even when they cannot go outdoors. The individual playrooms for each group are equipped with a variety of toys, ranging from animals big enough for the children to ride on to dolls, trucks, picture books, and colored pencils. Blocks are of the small variety. The oldest group has a counting chart and an erector set.

The play area outside is also divided into sections, each with a large piece of equipment (a playhouse for one group, a steamboat for another, an airplane for a third), swings, climbing equipment, sand boxes, and toboggan slides. The oldest group has a garden plot where each child can raise something on his own allotment of land.

Kindergarten No. 31 in Leningrad is run by a leather factory. It has a budget of 600,000 rubles and an enrollment of 125 children. Although the house which this kindergarten has stands on its own ground and is fenced off from the street, it has only a small yard around it. Even the little space available, however, is subdivided into play areas for the different groups. The equipment here is very sparse; there are sandpiles and a toboggan slide, but nothing else. Inside the building the groups are divided as usual, each with its own dormitory and playroom, but the children have their meals on the tables in the playroom. Washrooms are not part of each apartment. Here, as in the Kiev kindergarten, the children's lockers are marked by pictures, so that each child can identify his place by his picture. All playrooms have Persian rugs on the floor. Toys are plentiful and varied. Each playroom has a doll corner with every size, variety, and color of dolls, doll furniture, and dishes. Other toys include blocks, building sets, trucks and cars, picture books, and games. Each room has a profusion of green plants and a cage with one or two birds. The music room in this kindergarten is on the top floor and does double duty as the physical-culture room. It is equipped with a piano, some gymnastic equipment, some tricycles and hobby horses, and a few large balls. A large painting of Lenin surrounded by red flags dominates the room.

Kindergarten No. 314 in Moscow is run by a biscuit factory and has a budget of 700,000 rubles. The arrangement of the age groups is the same as in the other two kindergartens and the equipment, though not elaborate, is adequate. In addition, this kindergarten has a dramatics room equipped with a puppet stage. The playground outside has a summer house, three sandpiles, a toboggan slide, two platforms with steps for climbing, and two large boats.

To give a better idea of the work of a Soviet kindergarten, extracts from the yearly plan of this institution follow:

THE PLAN OF WORK FOR KINDERGARTEN NO. 314
FOR THE SCHOOL YEAR 1958–1959

General Directives

The kindergarten is made to accommodate 175 children, of which 90 stay there day and night. All children will be divided into seven groups. The staff of co-workers is complete. New teachers came to the kindergarten — four without experience or any sort of training in education. Five teachers had a little experience and are in need of methodical help. Six teachers have great experience and know preschool work.

The principal problems of work of the kindergarten:

Striving for a high attendance of the children of the kindergarten.

Increasing the quality of work by a division of physical exercises.

    a. To carry on the gymnastics of the older groups in the fresh air.

    b. To do the gymnastics right after the children get up.

Increasing the work in all age groups by training in cultural-hygienic habits.

    a. To teach the children to wash carefully in the morning and in the evening before bedtime, and, in addition, to teach the necessity of washing the hands after any soiling.

    b. To teach the children to wipe their hands carefully.

    c. To remove the towel from the hanger before wiping.

Improving the manners at the table.

    a. Tablecloth should be clean and well ironed.

    b. Breadbaskets should stand on the table for the bread.

    c. Teachers, as well as children, should make use of the napkins during the meal and after.

    d. To bring up the children with an understanding that they are to start eating when, and only when, all their comrades are at the table.

    e. To use during mealtime a polite manner of speaking; "Please," "No, thank you."

Continuing concentrated effort in the matter of bringing up the children in the older groups with a love for work. Play as a help in developing comradeship in the middle group.

Continuing the improvement of the quality of work in expressive speech. To carry out practical applications with the teachers.

Increasing the literacy of the two older groups.

Strengthening the work with the family in developing in the children moral qualities.

THE PLAN OF WORK FOR KINDERGARTEN No. 314
FOR THE SCHOOL YEAR 1958–1959 [*Continued*]

Pedagogical Consultations

Fundamental Measures	Time of Fulfillment	Executor
1. Contents and manner of the work with the parents concerning joint education of moral qualities in the children in all the older groups. Ways of hardening the character.	September 8	Head of kindergarten Tokar and head teacher Rosenbaum
2. Report on summer work in moral education of older and younger groups. a. Bringing up with a love for work with nature. b. Games as a means for creating comradeship.	October	Head teacher
3. Pedagogic consultation concerning the holiday of the great October Social Revolution.	October 28	Music director and Mrs. Generaloff
4. The system of distributing on application the program material.	December	Mrs. Boodka
5. Development of motion in children.	November	Music director and Mrs. Generaloff
6. Discussion of the scenario for the holiday of "New Year Fir" [equivalent of the Christmas tree].	December	Music director, Mrs. Generaloff, head teacher and teachers
7. Games and activities of the younger children in the open air.	January	Mrs. Sergienkova
8. Planning with parents.	February	Mrs. Saidook

THE PLAN OF WORK FOR KINDERGARTEN No. 314
FOR THE SCHOOL YEAR 1958–1959 [*Continued*]

9. How I teach the children poetry.	November	Mrs. Sokolova
10. Preparation of the children in the older groups for the Lenin days.	April	Music director, Mrs. Generaloff, and teachers
11. Preparation of the children for the holiday of first of May.	April	Music director, Mrs. Generaloff, head teacher and teachers
12. Summing up the work of the teachers for the autumn-winter-spring period.	May	Head of kindergarten and head teacher

General Meetings with the Parents

Fundamental Measures	Time of Fulfillment	Executor
1. Report concerning the work during the summer. Problems for the autumn-winter-spring period.	September 13	Head of kindergarten
2. Choosing the parental committee.	September 13	Parents
3. Physical condition of children.	December	Dr. Novikov
4. Parental committee's report concerning their work.	December	Parental committee
5. Preparation for departure to the country place.	April	Head of kindergarten
6. Departure to country place.	early June	Head of kindergarten

THE PLAN OF WORK FOR KINDERGARTEN No. 314
FOR THE SCHOOL YEAR 1958–1959 [*Continued*]

Group Parental Meetings

Fundamental Measures	Time of Fulfillment	Executor
1. Physical development of a three-year-old child. Schedule for the day.	October	Doctor, the first and second younger groups of parents,
2. Training in self-reliance and cultural behavior.	October	Third younger group of parents, head teacher Rosenbaum and teacher Saidook
3. Introduction to literacy and arithmetic.	October	First and second older groups, teachers
4. Training of cultural behavior in the kindergarten with parental participation.	October	First and second middle groups, teachers
5. Report on the progress of children leaving for school.	March	Older group, teachers
6. Concerning children's recreation and leisure time.	March	Middle group and teacher
7. Concerning training in cultural-hygienic habits.	March	Younger group and teacher

The Raising of Ideological-Political Level and Pedagogical Qualifications

Fundamental Measures	Executor
1. Seminars on literacy, arithmetic, constructive games, and on the other parts of the program.	Head teacher Rosenbaum and teachers
2. Reading of articles from newspapers concerning the rearing of children.	Head of kindergarten, head teacher
3. Work on methodological literature.	Head of kindergarten, head teacher

THE PLAN OF WORK FOR KINDERGARTEN NO. 314
FOR THE SCHOOL YEAR 1958–1959 [*Continued*]

Administrative-Housekeeping Work

Fundamental Measures	Time of Fulfillment	Executor
1. Preparation of plants on plot for winter.	September–October	Head of kindergarten, Zavkhoz (vice-director in charge of housekeeping)
2. Increase of study materials and toys.	September	Head of kindergarten
3. Acquisition of more chairs, tables.	August–September	Head of kindergarten, Zavkhoz
4. Repair of domestic tools.	August–September	Zavkhoz
5. Acquisition of mattresses.	August	Zavkhoz
6. Repair beds for country place.	October	Zavkhoz
7. Preparation of new marks for closets, clothes, and towels.	September	Head of kindergarten
8. Preparation for departure for the country place.	February–May	Zavkhoz
9. Planting of flowers in town and at the country place.	May	Zavkhoz
10. Repair of place in town and of the furniture.	July–August	Head of kindergarten, Zavkhoz

In each of the three kindergartens described above the children were divided into groups of twenty-five, with a teacher and a nursemaid in charge of each group. This seems to be standard practice. The teacher and the nursemaid work six-hour shifts. All three kindergartens were organized on a twelve-hour basis, although not all kindergartens in the Soviet Union are twelve-hour institutions. Some children do not stay the full twelve hours, depending on the work of the parents, but some children stay all night, if the parents work on night shifts. The kindergarten in Kiev and the one in Leningrad are twelve-month establishments. The latter takes its pupils to the country for a period in the summer.

Kindergartens are always administered by a director, who is assisted by a vice-director in charge of the housekeeping. Apart from the teaching staff, there is a kitchen staff, consisting of one or more cooks and some kitchen helpers, and one or more laundresses. A doctor comes in for three hours each day and a dentist visits the kindergarten twice a week. Kindergarten teachers have some pedagogical training, either at a pedagogical institute or at a technikum.[6] Pedagogical institutes offer four-year courses for kindergarten teachers. The nursemaids, who help the teachers, have no pedagogical training. Their task is to help with the physical work, cleaning, meals, dressing and undressing of the children. The salaries of teachers and nursemaids differ accordingly; teachers are paid 450–500 rubles a month, nursemaids only 300 rubles a month.

In none of the kindergartens described was there transportation service for the children. Either the children were brought by their parents, or, if they were old enough and lived near by, they came by themselves.

A typical day in a Soviet kindergarten is organized along the following lines:

7:30– 8:00	arrival of the children
8:00– 8:30	chores, watering of the plants, physical exercises
8:30– 9:00	doctor's inspection
9:00– 9:30	breakfast
9:30–11:00	play and learning periods
11:00–12:30	play outside or walk
12:30– 1:30	dinner
1:30– 4:00	rest
4:00– 4:30	snack
4:30– 7:00	walk, play
7:00– 7:30	supper
7:30	parents pick up the children, boarders go to bed

This time schedule may vary according to the parents' hours of work but in essence it holds for all kindergartens.

The children get four meals a day. Breakfast will consist of fish or eggs, bread and butter, coffee, and sometimes cereal. Dinner consists of soup, meat and potatoes, bread and butter, and fruit. The snack after the children's nap generally includes sweet tea and cakes. At suppertime there is an omelet or salad, bread and butter, coffee, and sometimes a compote. The "coffee" served the children is mainly milk.

Each kindergarten has a parents' committee to help with the repair of toys and the upkeep of the building. Teachers are required to keep in close touch with the families of their charges. Even before the child is admitted to the kindergarten the teacher is expected to visit his home and to acquaint herself with the conditions in his family. Teachers report to the parents on the progress of their children orally at the quarterly meetings of the parents.

Aims and Methods of Kindergartens

The Ministry of Education of the R.S.F.S.R. states the aims of preschool education in the Soviet Union as follows:

> Kindergartens help to realize the task of achieving the all-round development of children of pre-school age, bring them up to be healthy and sturdy, full of the love of life, and educate them in the spirit of Communist morality. Kindergartens broaden the children's horizon, give them knowledge and skills commensurate with their age, develop their thinking and their speech and prepare them for school.[7]

Activities in the Soviet kindergarten aim at achieving all these goals. Kindergarten must contribute to the shaping of good communists:

> Our most important task is to bring the children up in the spirit of collectivism, to bring them up to love work and to develop in them a good sense of discipline, so that their adjustment in school will be easy and quick.[8]

This was the way Mme. J. Petrovskaya, director of Kindergarten No. 1 in Kiev, defined her task. She went on to explain that collectivism was developed in children by day-to-day living and playing in the group. Also, duties are assigned to the children which they must fulfill either in the group or for the group. Thus, the oldest group will be asked to shovel snow from the playground of the youngest group, so that they can go out to play, or one or two children will be assigned the task of "monitors" to set the table for dinner, to clean up the playground when the group has finished playing, and so forth. Both kinds of tasks develop the feeling of collectivism and the feeling of the individual's responsibility to the collective. Visitors to Kindergarten No. 1 saw a four-year-old girl sweeping the sand back into the sandbox and cleaning up the playground while the rest of the group got ready to leave.

Love of work is developed in various ways. First and foremost, the children are taught respect for the work of their elders. The youngest group may be taken on an "excursion" to the kitchen of the kindergarten, where they observe the work of the cook. The teacher will draw the children's attention to the importance of such work for the whole institution. Or the middle group may be taken for a walk to a public park, where gardeners are caring for the trees and flowers. The oldest group may go to a construction site and watch the various forms of labor going on there and discuss them with the teacher.

Another way of teaching children to respect work is to make them perform certain tasks in the kindergarten. The work of monitors has already been mentioned. In addition, in the words of Mme. Petrovskaya, "We teach children to care for the plants in their rooms, to keep their rooms neat, and to be careful not to add to the work of the nursemaids." Children must learn to wash their hands carefully, so as not to spill any water on the floor, which the nursemaid would have to wipe up. They learn to do this in a series of prescribed steps — "First turn up your sleeves, then take the soap, then take a little water . . ." This carefully observed order also teaches them certain work habits.

The importance of games and play is stressed again and again in Soviet literature on preschool education. The teacher will organize a "content" game; for instance, the children will all be urged to build a steamship with blocks, or to play at being on a chicken farm. Anything that is a part of the children's own experience and that will help to arouse their interest and enthusiasm will serve. When the subject of the game is agreed upon the teacher helps the children decide upon a distribution of the various roles that will have to be played. Thus, in the steamship, one child will be the captain, another the engineer, others the crew, and so on, all the way down to the cook. In the course of the game the teacher will try to develop in the children not only respect for each of these occupations but also team spirit and the collective idea. At Kindergarten No. 1 in Kiev, the director gave an account of an elaborate game played by the oldest group in the winter-time, when they became Arctic "explorers" and went to the South Pole on the school grounds just like the explorers written about in the papers. This game reportedly lasted several days and held the children's interest very well.

Another method of developing "collectivism" is to suggest to the children that they enact a fairy tale or a story that the teacher reads to them. The children must be taught that not everybody can play the most important part in the story, that other parts are also important, and that the main point is the production as a whole, not the individual success.

Developing patriotism is a major part of Communist education. Children are made aware of the lives and deeds of the great Soviet heroes, and learn to sing patriotic songs and recite poems. As mentioned before, pictures of the leaders decorate every room in the kindergartens. Sometimes children will be taken on excursions to the patriotic museums — the Lenin Museum in Moscow, for example — to develop their love of country and communism.

Discipline in the kindergarten is fairly strict but not oppressive. On the first day of school in Kiev, pupils of Kindergarten No. 1 who were three years old and in kindergarten for the first day were taught to go for a walk two-by-two, in line, and slowly, without running. Two four-year-olds were sent back outside by the director, because they had come into the building running and making noise. They returned walking decorously and slowly, but still laughing. A good deal of independence is expected of the children. The director of Kindergarten No. 1 maintained that in her school every three-year-old could dress himself quite alone (even tying his shoes) by the end of his first term. Older kindergarten children are taught how to sew on buttons, how to care for their clothes, and how to wash themselves and do their own hair.

In general, the atmosphere in a Soviet kindergarten is warm, friendly, and calm. Discipline is perhaps stricter than the American observer is used to — in the learning periods, for example, children are made to sit still and finish a set task before starting on another one — but it is not as rigid as in the upper schools. The children seem happy and unafraid, even in the presence of strangers. Equipment and physical appearance must surely vary a great deal throughout the Soviet Union, but the better kindergartens are certainly well equipped and adequately staffed.

Kindergartens supposedly use only the native language of the child; however, Kindergarten No. 1 in Kiev was a Russian-language kindergarten that had a number of Jewish, Polish, and Ukrainian children, all of whom spoke Russian. Mention should also be made of a kindergarten-orphanage inspected in Tashkent, where the children, aged three to seven, were being taught a foreign language on an experimental basis. Teachers would not say whether this had proved to be a success but said that there were several such kindergartens in existence in their republic.

When asked what changes she would like to see introduced into the kindergarten program in the future, Mme. Sakulina of the Academy of Pedagogical Sciences replied,

> We would like to see kindergarten groups reduced in size, so that teachers can spend more time with individual children. The "activity" of each individual should be encouraged more. Also, toys should be more plentiful and varied. Finally, it would be a good thing if the teaching of reading were introduced at the kindergarten level.

This statement represents as well as anything one can find in recent publications the direction that the development of Soviet kindergartens is likely to take.[9]

7

PRIMARY EDUCATION

In 1903 Lenin wrote, "Only the free and compulsory education of all children can free the nation, even if only partially, from its present ignorance."[1] The party he was to lead, then called the Russian Social Democratic Workers' Party, endorsed his stand in the same year. In the program adopted at the Second Party Congress, the Social Democrats called for free and compulsory education of all children of both sexes and for the use of state funds to supply needy children with food, clothing, and school materials.[2]

In 1918 the first education act of the new Russian republic set up a system of decentralized schools with locally determined curricula, which were to admit all children without pay.[3] The basis of school instruction was to be "polytechnic education," centered around labor. In the program of the Communist Party, promulgated in 1919, the Bolsheviks reiterated these same tenets and affirmed their steady adherence to the principles of the newly established "unified labor school."[4] During the first years of Soviet rule, however, not only was the establishment of universal education made impossible by the confusion, destruction, and poverty resulting

163

from the years of war, revolution, and civil war, but, since education was regarded as a means to an end, the changing concept of "state interest" also militated against realization of the ideal proclaimed by the party program.

With the advent of the New Economic Policy, a new school policy became necessary. The partial re-emergence of the middle class made some discrimination in educational matters imperative. In the new system established in 1923,[5] children of proletarian origin were given preference in admission to schools. Other changes were made to insure proletarian domination of the educational facilities; for example, children of nonproletarian origin could be charged tuition fees.

Although plans had been made as early as 1918, not until 1930 was a law passed calling for universal compulsory elementary education. This coincided with a series of decrees reforming the entire school system and setting up a new educational organization. By a decree issued on September 5, 1931, the Central Committee of the Communist Party abolished the unified labor school and established a system of primary, incomplete secondary, and complete secondary schools. The period of primary education was lengthened from three years, the term of primary education under the Tsarist regime, to four years, although the program was not expanded.

With the reorganization of the system went reorganization of the curriculum. A rigid, centrally determined curriculum was established for the whole Soviet Union and "stabilized" textbooks were introduced. Teaching methods were reorganized and the lecture was proclaimed the basis of instruction. Discipline, which had suffered from constant interference by political groups, was reinforced and the authority of the teacher affirmed.

It was not until the early forties that universal compulsory primary education could be said to have been achieved, and even today the Soviet press exhorts the population to see that all children actually do go to school at the compulsory age.[6]

It should be repeated here that although enrollment in primary schools, urban as well as rural, increased steadily between the years 1928 and 1941, the declining birth rate during the war years has led to a considerable drop in enrollment in the elementary schools in recent years. The number of children enrolled in the primary schools of the Soviet Union fell from 21,370,000 in 1940–1941 to 13,600,000 in 1955–1956.[7] This decline probably had a favorable effect on the quality of primary education.

General Features

Compulsory education starts at the age of seven.[8] All children who have passed their seventh birthday by September 1 (the first day of school) must go to first grade unless they are certified as physically unfit by the doctor in charge of their medical examination.

Primary school is an integral part of the complete secondary school and whenever possible is situated in the same building as the secondary school. In rural districts the primary schools are sometimes the only institutions available in the villages. In sparsely populated regions a primary school may be so small that classes have to be combined. As explained by Director Savetkin of the Institute of National Schools of the Academy of Pedagogical Sciences,

> If one teacher has to take two grades, we will combine grades 1 and 3, 2 and 4. The first and fourth grades are both considered to be hard classes to teach; one is the first school experience for the children, the other is the preparation for the secondary school. Thus we let the teacher combine an easy class with a difficult one.

In very small schools, one teacher may have to take over all four grades at once.

Clearly, the problems of rural and urban schools are quite different. It must be recognized also that the quality of the urban primary school, which is a part of a secondary school, is far superior to that of the rural elementary school, which in many instances exists by itself. Members of the Comparative Education Society did not see any rural primary schools. The reader should keep in mind that the following description applies only to urban primary schools.

Primary-school children start in the first grade with one teacher, who teaches everything except singing and physical culture. This teacher moves up with the class through the fourth grade; in this way, it is believed, teacher and pupils get to know each other thoroughly and work together more easily and efficiently.

The great majority of primary-school teachers are women. The roster of one Moscow pedagogical technikum visited revealed only seven boys out of a total enrollment of 540 students. Visitors to the technikum were told by its director that this proportion of male students is typical for Moscow, although in the institutions training elementary-school teachers for the national schools in the national republics the proportion of men students may go up to 40 or 50 per cent. Male teachers of primary grades were, in fact, more frequently encountered in the Uzbek schools. One such teacher, at School No. 22 in Tashkent, reported that he had been teaching elementary school for thirty years.

Primary classes in the secondary schools are placed mostly at the top of the building, usually on the fourth or fifth floor. Various reasons are given for this arrangement. Director I. P. Franko of School No. 29 in Leningrad claimed that the smallest children are more isolated in this way and can concentrate better than if they have to mix with older children. The director of School No. 717 in Moscow had a different explanation: "If we put the older boys at the top of the building, the whole school would shake."

Classrooms are generally quite bare and cheerless. They measure about fifty square meters and contain three or four rows of double wooden desks fixed in metal runners. Each desk is equipped with one inkwell, which is shared by the two pupils — usually one boy and one girl — who occupy the desk. Each desk also has a flap that lifts up to accommodate books and pencil boxes. In some classrooms desks were equipped with hooks for the boys' uniform caps. In the classrooms where there were no such facilities the boys were in continuous trouble with their caps, which were constantly falling off desks. At the Institute for Physical Education visitors were told, "We are trying to develop a new, single desk, adapted to the child's body; before the overcrowding in the schools is abolished, however, we cannot install these seats in the schools."

In the new House of the School Child in Moscow, which the Comparative Education Society had a chance to study only from pictures, the new seats seem to have been already installed.

The rows of desks in the classrooms are faced by the teacher's desk. On the wall behind the teacher's desk there is a rather small blackboard. It is lined horizontally and diagonally in the first two classes; in the last two classes it is lined only horizontally. The rooms are lighted by tall windows, and the window sills, if any, serve as space for the green plants that are the only decoration in the classrooms. The walls, usually painted in light colors, are bare, except for the ubiquitous pictures of Lenin and other leaders, such as Voroshilov, Stalin, and Khrushchev. The classrooms are not equipped to store materials or visual aids. Everything that is needed has to be procured from a general storeroom. Some classrooms, however, do have number charts and an abacus beside the blackboard.

Children's work is not displayed in the classrooms, but the corridors are often decorated with drawings and paintings that the children have made. Thus School No. 29 in Leningrad, for example, displayed illustrations by the children of Pushkin's fairy tales.

There are usually between thirty and forty children in an elementary-school class. They are required to wear uniforms. The girls wear brown dresses with black pinafores on ordinary school days and white pinafores on special days. The first day of school, for example, is a day for white pinafores. The boys wear military uniforms, gray or blue, belted at the waist, and with visored caps. The visitor sees many boys without the uniform. Mme. O. L. Maksimchuk, Director of School No. 57 in Kiev, explained that "The old uniforms for boys are unsatisfactory and new ones have been designed, of which there is not yet a good supply." Since the uniforms are also extremely expensive — one, in Moscow's principal department store, carried a price tag of 640 rubles — the old-fashioned style of the uniform may not be the only reason why boys do not wear it.

Children in elementary school usually come to school at eight-thirty. The first class has only three lessons and goes home at eleven-thirty; older classes have four periods. Periods last forty-five minutes each and have ten- or fifteen-minute intermissions. Children whose parents both work and who would be unsupervised if they went home after school can stay in many schools for the so-called "lengthened day programs." They get hot lunch in school and a teacher takes charge of them, makes them rest, takes them for walks, supervises their homework, and plays games with them until it is time for them to go home. If children go to a school that is on two shifts, they may not start school until two-thirty.

Curriculum of Primary Schools

Curriculum in the primary school is, with minor local differences, the same throughout the Soviet Union. As a general rule, the pupils in grades one through three are taught Russian language (thirteen lessons a week), arithmetic (six lessons a week), physical culture (two lessons a week), and singing and drawing (one lesson a week, respectively). In addition, throughout the first four grades, one lesson a week is now devoted to "labor," this being, in fact, the beginning of polytechnical education.

The fourth grade is regarded as the preparatory stage for the fifth and for the secondary school. It is, therefore, treated somewhat differently from the other three grades. Three new subjects are introduced to prepare the children for secondary school, where there is complete departmentalization. These subjects are history, geography, and natural science. Two hours each are devoted to the new subjects every week, and the number of lessons in the Russian language is reduced to nine.

Exceptions to this curriculum are found in national schools, which teach in the native language. Here Russian is introduced, usually in the first or second year. Pupils in the national schools are thus burdened with more subjects than are children in the Russian schools. Another exception to the general curriculum is found in the experimental language schools, discussed in Chapter 9.

A closer look at the subjects taught in primary school will show the extensive scope of the program.

Russian Language. The most important subject in the primary school is Russian language. This includes not only reading and writing but also instruction in grammar, speech, calligraphy, and spelling. Reading and writing start in the first grade, but some children come to school knowing their letters and able to spell out their names. Some kindergartens have a readiness program in their highest age group and many other children are taught their letters at home. Thus, in the first grade on the first day of school (School No. 57) in Kiev more than half the class were able to write their names on drawings they had made. This is probably not true of schools in rural districts.

Reading and writing are taught by acquainting the children first with parts of letters, then with individual letters, with syllables, and finally with whole words. Director Shapovalenko of the Institute of Methods at the Academy of Pedagogical Sciences explained the Soviet method as follows: "We use the analytical-synthetic method of teaching reading. Pictures are also very important in the teaching of reading; the children are shown the pictures and by and by they learn the word underneath."

The first-year reading book shows parts of letters, letters, syllables, and words, all written carefully in the lined space underneath the pictures on each page. Pictures are plentiful and colored, but they seem rather small and there are too many on each page for American taste. The pictures vary according to the locale of the school; for instance, in an Uzbek school, children and adults shown in the pictures are dressed in the Uzbek style.

Writing is taught in the same manner as reading. Children use pens from the beginning. These are usually quill pens, although a recent reform permits the use of fountain pens. They are taught to write carefully with the aid of horizontally and diagonally lined exercise books, which impose strict and observable limits upon each letter. Penmanship is taught in the first three grades, and in the third grade the children are expected to be able to write well without the aid of the diagonal lines. In a third-grade penmanship lesson in School No. 143 in Tashkent visitors observed pupils being called to the blackboard to demonstrate how to write certain letters. If the pupil made a mistake, the whole class was called on by the teacher to make the correction; otherwise the children sat and watched the answering pupil until the teacher asked them all to copy in their exercise books the letter that had been demonstrated on the blackboard.

Correct speech and pronunciation are also emphasized in the Russian-language lessons of the primary classes. Starting in the first grade, children must reply to the teacher's questions with whole sentences, and they must speak correctly and express themselves well. In a Russian-language class in the first grade in School No. 29 in Leningrad, children had not only to answer the teacher's questions in complete sentences but also to explain the reason for their answer. For example:

"What do we see on this picture?"

"We see summer."

"That is not a full answer."

"We see summer on this picture."

"Why do you say that you see summer on this picture?"

"We think we see summer on this picture because there is no snow."

So went one exchange. When one little girl, in answer to a question, stated that "The radio tells us stories," the teacher corrected the answer to "The announcer on the radio tells us stories."

Another way of learning to express oneself is the "composition," which is written by the whole class. The teacher will choose a subject and ask for suggestions from the class on what to write about it on the blackboard. The suggestions are corrected and elaborated and then the teacher writes the finished sentences.

Grammar instruction is started as early as first grade. In the first-grade Russian-language class observed in School No. 29 in Leningrad, the children were taught the concept of a sentence. The teacher asked them to think of sentences with two words, then with three words, and the homework was to think of two sentences of two and three words respectively.

Expressive speech is also stressed as early as the first grade. Pupils of the first grade in School No. 57 in Kiev were busy the first day of school learning a poem of four lines entitled "September First." It told of the great joy and honor to a child of becoming a school pupil and of the love of the Soviet children for their beautiful schools. The poem was recited by the teacher with great expressiveness and the children repeated it after her with a similar emphasis. Homework for the class consisted of learning the poem well by repeating it to the family at home. The same procedure was followed in the first grade of School No. 29 in Leningrad with a different poem, entitled "Things." It told of the importance of being careful of all things in school, as they were all made by human labor and should be respected. Here the children had already learned the poem and individual pupils were called on to recite; each one recited the poem with identical emphasis and inflection.

Spelling is taught by dictation and by learning lists of difficult words. There is a constant repetition of these exercises. The teacher may hang lists of words next to the blackboard so that the children will see them constantly and get used to them.

Instruction in Russian language, however, does not consist solely in learning how to read and write and spell. It also includes "explanatory readings" by the teacher. These are meant to acquaint the children with the great works of Russian literature suitable for their age group and to give them first concepts of geography and history and general facts about their environment.

Thus, in the first two grades children get to know the fairy tales of Tolstoi and Pushkin, they learn about Lenin's boyhood, they recognize and identify local trees and flowers, and they may go on excursions to the local post office, the station, and the farm. In the third they learn to identify the local field crops, they learn about the lives of local heroes and the meaning of local historical sites, they learn about the weather and what causes it, and they go on excursions to study the countryside, the elevations, and the watercourses. They also continue with readings in Russian literature for children.

Arithmetic. Arithmetic is the next most important subject in the primary curriculum. Children who enter first grade from kindergarten know how to count to ten. In the primary grades children learn how to add and subtract, multiply and divide, numbers of many digits; they work with weights and measures and, as an innovation, with elementary concepts of geometry. By the end of the fourth grade the concept of one unknown may be introduced, although formal algebra does not start until secondary school. Observers of a first-grade arithmetic class saw children take squares, rectangles, and circles out of a box and carefully trace their contours in their notebooks. Director Shapovalenko explained such exercises in the program of elementary-school arithmetic in this way:

> In line with the program of polytechnic education it was found expedient to introduce some concepts of geometry into the primary classes. Also, we find that we want to give primary school pupils more direct experience in their arithmetic lessons; this means that in learning measuring concepts, for instance, they should go out and actually measure a space in the school yard.

Visual aids are limited in the teaching of arithmetic. Children are taught number concepts with the aid of an abacus. Sometimes the teacher will have little red flags to help the children count. One teacher, in School No. 22 in Tashkent, taught the concept of "3" with the aid of pictures of three dolls, three rabbits, and the like.

In the fourth grade the pupils' knowledge of arithmetic is systematized. At the beginning of the school year observers saw fourth-grade children in School No. 35 in Moscow working in numbers going into millions. Also, problems such as the following were introduced:

> A train makes 90 km. an hour. How many km. does it make in 3 hours?
>
> There are 12 shelves and 72 kgm. of apples. How many kgm. can go on 5 shelves?
>
> Pioneers plant 96 trees in 4 days. How many days would it take them to plant 72 trees?

These problems were worked out at the blackboard by one child, who explained each step of what he was doing as he wrote. When he had finished, the rest of the class wrote the problem and solution in their notebooks. During this class, children were asked to pose problems in simple computation to the pupil at the board. Such problems had to be worked out in the child's head. In another class, in Boarding School No. 13 in Moscow, children were working on division of numbers of five digits. The teacher called on children, one at a time, for the answer. When the answer had been found, the whole class repeated in unison what the correct procedure was and arrived at the solution.

By the end of the fourth grade the children are supposed to work well with whole numbers and with measures and weights. They are expected to master all four arithmetical operations. However, there have been many recent complaints that children do not really know what measurements and weights mean and that they are not too well grounded in arithmetic when they enter secondary school. The remedy is seen in more practical work with measures and weights and in more training in oral arithmetic operations. Teachers are exhorted to have the class repeat in chorus ways of arriving at solutions of problems and to give the children more training in quick mental counting and figuring. Teachers are also urged to make sure that the children know in practical terms what they are talking about when working with weights and measures.[9]

Music. To the two observers who spent much time visiting classes in music it was evident that considerable emphasis is placed on music education in the Soviet schools. It has a very definite place in the courses of study. The formal instruction is generally carried on by teachers who specialize in music, although in grades one through four it may be done by the regular teachers.

One part of the program is elementary sight reading. The children are given instruction in note reading from the first grade on, by rote methods and by drill. A second part, taught simultaneously with the first, is choral work. The Soviet school directors stated that each school has at least one chorus. The choral singing, which was quite impressive, featured songs with a patriotic or nationalistic theme, sung with tremendous vigor, enthusiasm, and assurance. There are special songs for special occasions and holidays, and folk songs. The Pioneer organization has its own special song, which the Pioneers learn when they reach the age of admission. One hardly ever hears any voice strain or off-key singing. There are no popular "hits" of the Western type in the Soviet Union and certainly they have no place in the school curriculum.

The equipment for teaching music is apparently meager. Not a single piano was observed, nor were there any rhythm instruments. Instrumental music, nevertheless, seems to be a significant part of the music program. Each school, the visitors were told, has an orchestra and a band. The school supplies the instruments to pupils who wish to try out for membership in these ensembles. The music is of the concert variety and aimed toward "self-improvement." The observers saw no marching bands. Music appreciation is integrated with other music instruction on each grade level. The teachers make use of record players and tape recorders to get pupils to understand and love good music.

The music teaching of the school can be fully understood only in connection with the work of the amateur music circles, which correspond loosely to the music clubs in American high schools. Soviet students, however, are much more serious about what they do in these clubs. The music teaching in the circles appears to parallel the music program in the schools, but in a less formal and more practical manner. Persons who direct the music circles receive a salary from the school and work closely with the music teachers. Sometimes, the music teachers of the schools also direct the music circles.

In all schools there are attempts to discover music talent, mainly by observation of musical performance. A child with exceptional talent is sent to a special music school. Pupils may study music during the summer vacation at the Pioneer palaces. Another possibility is to obtain opportunities for practice under the sponsorship of a factory or a trade union.[10]

Other Subjects. Drawing lessons take place once a week. The children are taught how to draw step by step, in a very systematic way:

> We believe that only children who have mastered the techniques of drawing can be permitted to do any free drawing. Also, children must learn to reproduce what they see around them with reasonable accuracy. This teaches them the correct approach to material reality. This does not mean that the drawings must be photographic reproductions of reality, but it does mean that the significant features of reality must be reproduced.

This is the way Mme. Shatskaia, Director of the Institute of Art Education in the Academy of Pedagogical Sciences, explained her theory of the teaching of drawing. She showed her visitors a book for the drawing teacher in elementary school, which prescribed what the children should draw in the first lesson, how much should be added at the second lesson, and so forth. The end result of this particular series of lessons was a beautifully drawn and colored tree, with symmetrical branches and leaves; all drawings were exactly alike.

The lessons also include drawing from nature. During the period before the New Year's holiday, for instance, children in primary school are asked to draw a branch of a fir tree. They also draw some rigid patterns, which are then painstakingly colored. In the fourth grade children learn how to draw geometric and round figures. For further variation of the program, children may be asked to draw illustrations for some story that they read in class. This serves the double purpose of teaching them how to draw and making the story come alive for them. Drawings on the subject of songs that have been studied in school are often assigned and sometimes given as homework. All drawings are made on comparatively small pieces of paper, mostly with colored pencils.

Physical culture takes place outside or inside the school building. Outdoors there are running games, races, obstacle races, and competitive sports. Indoors, all gymnasiums observed had equipment for Swedish gymnastics. Children also do military marching, accompanied sometimes by singing. There is much emphasis on training in formation.

In the fourth grade, as already mentioned, special subjects are introduced for the first time. Material touched upon in the explanatory readings with the teacher in the Russian-language lessons in the first three grades is now taught formally. In natural science in this grade children are taught the elementary facts about inorganic nature. They carry out experiments with water, steam, air, ice, and snow. They also learn about the properties of the soil and about various mineral resources.

In geography, fourth-grade pupils are given elementary facts about the geography of the Soviet Union. They are taught about various climatic zones, about the populations in these zones and the ways they make their living. Also, excursions may be undertaken to study, for instance, the local river and to learn about its significance to the community. Excursions may be made to local plants or farms where pupils can really see production. During their history lessons, pupils of the fourth grade learn about the history of their country, from the ancient Slavs to the Twentieth Congress. The textbook for this course [11] is divided into eight chapters; when they have studied each chapter, the children are expected to be able to answer a series of questions. For example:

How did the people of ancient Kiev live?
Make a diagram of the battle against the Germans and Swedes.
Find Novgorod on the map.
Tell about the life and toil of peasants of the 16th century.
Who needed the First World War?
Why is that war called a "World" War?
What is the difference between the toil of the workers under tsarism and today?

What is the significance to other peoples of the victory of the Soviet
Union in the Great Patriotic War?

Give some examples of the peace-loving policy of the Soviet Government.

Throughout the first four grades the children have one lesson a week in "labor." In the first grade this may consist of nothing more than learning how to use scissors and how to cut out and paste. Children may, under the direction of the teachers, make a notebook of decorations for the New Year's tree. In the next grade they may learn how to use a ruler and a triangle. They are also taught how to make an object without having the model in front of them constantly. In the third grade they are taught how to use a needle for sewing. Throughout these grades, the children also work with papier-mâché, clay, and plasticine. In the fourth grade they may be introduced to simple machines; a well-equipped school may even have a sewing machine. They make models of simple machines in clay or papier-mâché. Visitors to the school saw no evidence of machine-model construction, although this may have been because the visits took place at the beginning of the school year.[12] "Labor" also includes working on the school plot and doing "socially useful" work. This may consist in helping to make something the school needs, helping to repair some piece of equipment, or participating in some communal activities, such as gathering scrap metal for the sponsoring plant.

Quasi-School Subjects.   A word may be said here about the quasi-school activities in the primary school, for which the teacher of the primary grades is required to have a planned program. For example, during the explanatory readings of the first grades the teacher should include readings on the greatness of the Soviet Army with the object of inculcating patriotism, love and respect for the army, and love of peace. "The Soviet Army stands on guard to protect the peaceful toil of the Soviet People," runs the tenor of one of these readings.[13] The teacher also encourages the children to discuss their readings in class. During these discussions, she should inculcate the feeling of Soviet patriotism. For instance, during the discussion of a book on the boyhood of Lenin the pupils' attention is drawn to Lenin's fine qualities and the great things he did for the Soviet motherland. The same procedure is followed in discussion of the various national holidays.

The teacher is urged to encourage the children to put out a wall newspaper as soon as they are old enough. In this newspaper space is reserved for school business; books and movies can be reviewed, and the bad behavior of children in the class can be held up to ridicule. All this is part of the teacher's work in the primary school. Such "upbringing" work is later concentrated in the Pioneer organization, although the teacher still plays an important part.

Finally, teachers may organize expeditions to local points of interest — museums, plants, farms, or the railroad station.

Methods and Procedures

Curricula are rigid in the Soviet Union and the teacher's work must be carefully planned. As the director of School No. 57 in Kiev put it, "There is a school plan for every year and for every term and for every month; the teacher must plan his work for every week."

Lesson Procedure. Each lesson must be organized. The usual procedure is to have the children report on their homework at the beginning of the lesson. The teachers call on individual children to answer questions and on the rest of the class if a pupil is unable to answer. The amount of homework that can be given is prescribed by the ministries of education. N. Kova, Assistant Chairman of the Kiev board of education, reported that in the first grade homework is optional and no specific amount is required; in the next three grades, homework should amount to about an hour and a half daily. The children who are called on individually to account for homework come up to the blackboard to recite or rise to answer the question of the teacher.

After the children have answered questions on their homework the teacher introduces the new material for the lesson. If there is time the children answer questions on the new material, and finally the homework for the next lesson is assigned. A definite amount of material must be covered in each lesson if the teacher is to keep up with plan requirements. This often leaves little time for thorough explanation of subject matter that the children find difficult. Visitors to a fourth-grade arithmetic class in School No. 35 in Moscow saw an extremely kind teacher try to explain a problem to a little boy who was having difficulty. However, she could not stop long enough to make him understand fully. "Never mind, you will understand when you think about it at home," she consoled him before going on with the lesson.

Lessons center around the teacher, and very often children do not participate at all. They sit quietly and listen, speaking only when asked a question. When the teacher asks whether anyone has a question about the new material, pupils may bring up their difficulties, but never does a child volunteer a remark. Children write notes in their notebooks only on the express command of the teacher.

Children bring their own equipment to school. A bulletin board on display at the beginning of the school year lists everything a child will need in school — a pen and pencil box, an eraser, notebooks, a briefcase. This equipment they carry back home at the end of the school day. When they forget part of their equipment, they are apparently literally incapacitated for participating in the lesson. Visitors saw a little boy in the second grade do nothing at all throughout one lesson because he had forgotten his pencil and pen box.

Children in the primary grades, especially in the first two years, are still very young to sit still and to concentrate for forty-five minutes at a stretch. From time to time during a lesson the teacher will have them do a series of exercises to relax them and release some of their surplus energy. The children may be asked to get up and step out into the aisles between the rows of desks; then they are put through several exercises with their arms, swinging them up, sideways, and down. Some exercises are designed to relax the hand and consist of flexing the fingers of the hands, while the children remain seated. True relaxation takes place during the intermissions between lessons, when the children are allowed to go out into the corridors and when they can move about freely. These intermissions can be quite noisy.

Each child has a daybook (*dnevnik*) in which he lists his homework as it is assigned. When he is called on by the teacher to recite, he brings his daybook to the front of the class and puts it on the teacher's desk. When he has finished reciting, the teacher puts a mark in his book, informing him at the same time what grade he is receiving. Marks range from "5," excellent, to "1," failing. At the end of the week, parents are expected to sign their names at the bottom of the page in the daybook to show that they are following their child's progress. If a pupil receives more than one "2" a week, the parents' committee or the teacher may ask the parents to pay more attention to their child's homework and to the marks which he brings home.

All children in one classroom are treated exactly alike and are expected to perform more or less uniformly within the range of the five marks meted out for effort. Soviet teachers were repeatedly asked what was done about the slow learner in a primary-school classroom. The answer was always the same:

> All children can do what we ask of them. If they do not do it, they are lazy or they do not get enough supervision at home. It may also be that the teacher is not doing all she can. A child may be a little slower than his comrades, but with the right kind of help he will do as well as the others.

On the whole, observers got the impression that the average teacher did not apply the marking system too rigorously. Often the teacher did not give a mark to a child who had not done very well on his recitation. In other cases, marks would run consistently good, even if the performances were not quite up to the marks given.

Discipline. Discipline in the Soviet schools is extremely strict and enforced from the first day of school in the first grade, although the first day of school is a kind of holiday for the pupils. Mme. Maksimchuk, Director of School No. 57 in Kiev, emphasized this: "Pupils who come to school for the first time today are welcomed especially. We try to make them feel proud that they may call themselves 'school pupils' now."

Girls come to school in their festive white pinafores and many children bring bouquets of flowers to school, thus brightening up the classrooms.

However, there was nothing festive in the way a first-grade

drawing lesson was conducted that day. The children were taught exactly how to sit at the desks. Their feet should be on the footrest, and their shoulders should be straight and kept away from the back rest. The teacher showed the children how to check whether they were sitting correctly by passing their closed fist between body and desk. When they read or write, they were told, the correct posture is insured by putting the tips of the fingers to the temple, with the elbow resting on the desk. The head should not be inclined more than this gesture permits. After the children all understood this, they were constantly reminded of it by the teacher, as they would forget the prescribed gestures while doing something else. When the drawing lesson started in earnest, the children were told to wait for the teacher's command before taking out their pencils and paper. All did this at the same time. Then they were told exactly where to put their pencil, eraser and paper.

When the children are not busy, they are expected to sit at their desks with arms folded on the top. If they want to speak to the teacher, they raise their right arm from the elbow; no more movement is permitted. When the teacher calls on them, they rise and must wait for the teacher's permission to sit down again. They also rise when the teacher or any other adult comes into the classroom. Discipline was so perfect in the first grade on the first day of school that the children did not even look around at the foreign visitors sitting at the back of the classroom.

This discipline is enforced everywhere in the same way. The atmosphere in the classroom naturally depends a great deal on the personality of the teacher, but the demands made on the children do not vary much. In a first-grade room in School No. 29 in Leningrad, a little boy was reduced to tears because he was made to stand up in front of the class to tell what he had done wrong. The child was not conscious of any fault but did his best to guess where he had erred:

> "I held up my hand in the wrong way," he mumbled, hanging his head.
> "No, that is what you did yesterday," said the teacher. "I want to know what you did wrong today."

Only when the boy was crying did the teacher tell him what he had done — he had spoken without waiting for permission.

Children from the first grade on are taught to obey the "Rules for Pupils." [14] The teacher in primary school keeps a record on each child, which is sent on to the fifth grade with him. The form includes data on the child's behavior, marks, attendance record, illnesses, and family background. The following is a summary of a typical record, taken from the files of a Kiev school:

> *First Grade:* Pupil learned to read and write and count. At first he was not so good, because he was not very interested and he missed several lessons because he was ill. He is not a very good pupil, his average is satisfactory, but not excellent.
>
> *Second Grade:* He attended school systematically and was more obedient. He was able to work without help. However, sometimes he did not do his homework and his handwriting remains poor. He could study better, but he is lazy. His parents should pay more attention to his school work.
>
> *Third Grade:* He attended school systematically and listens to his teacher with interest. He does homework but often he does not do it very well. He was ill part of the year with a bad throat [there follows an account of symptoms]. The parents should pay more attention to his education.
>
> *Fourth Grade:* He has good marks. He took part in social life. He was ill with appendicitis and often had headaches. The teacher visited his home several times and talked about the correct upbringing of children with the parents.

These records were characterized by the teacher as "pedagogical, not psychological."

The pupils themselves are called on to help the teacher enforce certain rules. From the first week the teacher appoints some children to the "sanitary committee," whose members are responsible for the cleanliness of their comrades and the classroom. "Row leaders" are appointed, each one in charge of one row of desks. Thus, when, for instance, the teacher wants to collect finished papers, they are passed from the back to the front, each child receiving them from the pupil behind him without turning around; when they reach the front desk, the row leaders pass them to the teacher's desk. When the children get used to school procedures they elect these "officials," but in the first period they are appointed by the teacher. With such strictly disciplined behavior demanded of the children from the first moment of their school life, it is not surprising that

Soviet educators find that many children are not ready for the school experience when they enter first grade. Professor Smirnov, head of the Institute of Psychology of the Academy of Pedagogical Sciences, reported on this problem:

> We consider the readiness of the child for school activities. Many children find it difficult to concentrate on the teacher's words and to obey her commands. We are doing special work on how to help a child pay attention and answer questions. We have special methods which the teacher uses to help the child get used to the school work.

However, no special methods were observed in any primary classes. The children in every instance were treated exactly alike and the same performance was demanded of all. This applied even to a boy, in the first grade of School No. 57 in Kiev, who was the son of the Czech consul and, according to the teacher, did not know Russian very well.

The Institute of Psychology, however, has a Laboratory of Child Study that does research on basic problems of the young child with a view to relaxing some of the school regimen. Mme. Mentchinskaia, an official of the Institute, explained the work of this laboratory:

> We are studying the problems of perception in young children. Concrete and abstract thinking in school children is being studied; attention is also being paid to the psychology of writing and grammar. Further, we study various ways of remembering. For instance, in an experiment, two groups of children were given words to remember, one group in play, the other in study. It was found that the group who was given the words in play remembered them better.

A problem currently occupying Soviet researchers is how to make children participate more actively in the learning process. Academician Shapovalenko explained that the most important method of enriching the school experience is participation by the children in amateur circles and that these will continue to be encouraged.

> We plan to increase the number of excursions for children in the primary grades and to bring learning closer to their own personal experience. More visual aids will be produced for the primary grades and children will be taught to apply what they learn in actual practice.

Thus even during school hours time devoted to experiments and demonstrations will be greatly increased.

Experiments and Reforms

Even though such activity is confined to the central level, the Soviet school system is vigorously experimenting.

There is, first of all, an awakened interest in testing, although Professor Smirnov explained that the Soviet psychologists do not believe in using tests to determine aptitudes and peculiarities of the child. But for special purposes tests, not standardized but made up anew for each occasion, may according to the Soviet view, be a help to children with specific difficulties.

There is also great interest in experimentation in teaching foreign languages. The Institute of Methods is considering introducing a foreign language in the fourth grade instead of the fifth, as is the practice at present. A word should also be said about the special language schools, which introduce a foreign language at the primary-school level and which aim to teach several subjects in the foreign language at the secondary level. It was obvious that instruction in these schools aimed at abandoning the chalk-and-talk method. Second-grade language classes were taught by means of games and some visual aids. The children in one second-grade English class played a game of guessing: one child was sent out of the room, while the others decided on an object for him to guess. When he came back to the classroom, he had to guess, in English, what the object was. In another game the pupil pretended to be the teacher and conducted an English class. Children also acted out assigned roles (they were pretending to be various animals) and the rest of the class tried to guess who they were. Another method used was to teach the children poems in the foreign language:

> Up and down on skis we go
> To and fro, to and fro;
> Crystal air, the sun and snow
> Away we go, away we go.

The primary school seems to be only lightly touched by the

recent reforms. The emphasis on polytechnical education has brought an increased stress on arithmetic in the primary grades, but that is the only definite change.

There is a recurring demand for changing the compulsory school age from seven to eight years. Again and again we read complaints from primary-school teachers about the difficulties of working with seven-year-olds. On the other hand, there have been voices demanding the admission of six-year-olds to the primary school. The demand for changing the admission age died down in 1958 after the reformers decided not to change the age limit. However, preparatory classes for six-year-olds and the seven-year-olds who are not admitted to primary school because of their birth date are still being urged. Many such classes are said to be in existence.[15] Some pedagogues suggest that the teacher could get to know his future pupils in the preparatory classes and could separate the quick learners from the slow. Then he could work with the children in two separate groups when they enter school and improve his instruction. This is certainly an innovation, so far resisted by Soviet teachers who insist that all pupils can do the same work at the same time in the same class.

There was some discussion during the period when the reforms were being debated whether the elementary-school period should be lengthened to five years or shortened to three in the new eight-year school. This also died down as soon as the reform was decided. The period of four years is now accepted as final in discussions of the primary school.

One proposal that persists is the suggestion to abolish geography, history, and natural science as separate subjects in the fourth grade and to let the children get the necessary knowledge from the explanatory readings. This suggestion, however, is violently disputed. A more readily acceptable proposal, judging from the way in which it is discussed, is to combine geography and natural science into one subject, to be known as "nature study."[16] There are also repeated proposals that specialized subjects in the fourth grade be taught by different teachers to get the children used to more than one teacher before they go on to secondary school. The suggestion most frequently heard is that teachers of "parallel" fourth grades, if any, should divide the special subjects between them, so that each one will be taught by a different fourth-grade teacher.

Many demands are also heard for the introduction of a more balanced curriculum in the primary grades, with less emphasis on Russian language and arithmetic and slightly more on such subjects as singing, drawing, and labor. There must also be, some feel, smaller classes.

An innovation that has actually been put into practice on an experimental basis in Boarding School No. 13 in Moscow is the introduction of a new subject, called "Cultural Behavior" (*Kultura Povedeniia*), which is to acquaint children with basic norms of Communist morality. One lesson a week in the upper three grades of primary school is to be devoted to this in the proposed new curriculum. It cannot be a separate subject in the first grade, as the pupils are too young. This is an interesting indication of the new emphasis on "upbringing."

Yet another departure, aimed at solving the problem of unsupervised children, has been undertaken in Moscow recently. This is the House of the School Child (*Dom Shkolnika*), a cross between a boarding and a nonresidential school. Its purpose is to take care of school children in grades one through five while they are not in school and while the parents are at work. Children are either brought in the morning by their parents or collected from school at the end of the day, according to the shift they attend at school. At the House of the School Child children are given hot meals and supervised in their homework, and circles are organized for them after school hours. The House in Moscow has 420 children, 210 in each shift, and employs fourteen educators, all with at least a middle pedagogical education and most of them reportedly with a higher pedagogical education. Parents pay 10 per cent of their salaries for the upkeep of their children; however, if the parents are truly needy, they do not pay anything. The new institution is praised in the press as a valuable aid to "Communist education" as well as a great help to working mothers.[17]

SECONDARY EDUCATION:
A GENERAL DESCRIPTION

Secondary school (*srednaya shkola*) in the Soviet Union can be of several types. The secondary stage of the general school starts with the fifth class and consists of the incomplete secondary school, grades five through seven or eight, and the complete secondary school, grades five through ten or eleven. The recent addition of one year has grown out of experimental schools that have kept their pupils for an eleven-year secondary course, to allow for new subjects of a polytechnical nature. Children who do not finish the complete secondary school may complete their education, while working, in the schools for rural and working youth or in lesser vocational schools and courses. Graduates of the incomplete secondary school may go on to a specialized secondary education in the technikums. This chapter will concern itself only with the secondary schooling offered in the general schools, as they functioned in September, 1958.

After the Nineteenth Congress of the Communist Party, the Soviets maintained that the seven-year school was universal and compulsory throughout the nation. The Congress proclaimed the goal of making the ten-year school universal and compulsory throughout the nation. The Twentieth Party Congress, tacitly acknowledging the difficulties involved, amended the goal to the establishment of ten years of *schooling* (in or out of school) for every Soviet citizen. Even so, Khrushchev, in his September, 1958, memorandum on educational reforms, was forced to admit that "in spite of the fact that the seven-year school is compulsory, a considerable part of our people not only do not get a finished secondary education, but do not even finish seven grades."

General Characteristics

Although the goal of compulsory and universal secondary education — complete or incomplete — is still far from being reached, there is no doubt that great strides have been made in recent years. "The expansion of Soviet school enrollment from its abysmal decline in 1922 to its present very large size . . . has been most impressive in spite of the fact that it has consistently trailed behind official promises." [1]

Extent of Secondary Education. Statements by Soviet officials on the extent of secondary schooling must be carefully weighed for accuracy. Deputy Minister Markushevich, for instance, in an interview with members of the Comparative Education Society, said,

> The ten-year school is compulsory and universal in all the big cities; the seven-year school is compulsory and universal throughout the rest of the country. In the big cities 75 to 80 per cent of all children finish ten grades; in rural areas 50 to 60 per cent of all children finish ten grades.

But a few weeks later, Mr. Khrushchev wrote in his memorandum that only about 80 per cent of all children who enter first grade finish the seventh grade, and this includes all repeaters. An official of the Pedagogical Institute in Tashkent in the republic of Uzbekistan was asked what the most pressing educational problem of the republic was. He replied, "Our greatest problem is to make seven-year education universal in our republic." Mr. Petrokeevich, Chairman of the Leningrad department of education, claimed universal ten-year education for his city, but made a distinction between ten years of education and the ten-year school graduates:

In our city general ten-year education is realized. This means that all children get ten years of education; those who cannot finish the ten grades of the ten-year school go to technikums after the seventh grade, or they finish their education in evening schools.

An interesting statement was made on this subject by a school official in Tashkent, who was asked what determined whether children stayed on through the tenth grade. "It all depends on the social position of the parents," he replied. Unfortunately, he could not be questioned further on what precisely he meant by this statement.

Statistics published in a recent book on Soviet education cite an enrollment of 13,600,000 pupils in elementary schools in the school year 1955–1956; grades five through seven with an enrollment of 9,300,000, and the last three grades of the ten-year school with an enrollment of 5,200,000. Clearly, the drop in school enrollment caused by the war years is still making itself felt in the higher grades.[2]

On the problem of drop-outs from the secondary schools, Deputy Minister Markushevich stated:

> The figure is very low for the lower grades of the secondary school. I would say that about 5 per cent of the pupils drop out of the three lower grades of the secondary school. The causes for this are generally illness or mental retardedness. In the upper three grades the drop-out amounts to about 8 per cent; these children may go to technical schools or go to work and they may continue their education in evening courses.

School directors were reluctant to give figures on the problem. The director of School No. 1 in Moscow admitted to a 5 per cent annual drop-out for the ten-year school but did not break this figure down into the lower and upper grades and did not give any reasons for it. The director of School No. 92 in Kiev maintained that in the school year 1957–1958 only one pupil had dropped out of the secondary school in his institution. The director of School No. 20 in Tashkent reported that of the sixteen classes in the secondary school, eleven were in grades five and six and only five classes accounted for grades seven through ten; these figures argue a fairly high rate of drop-out from this school.

Length and Content of Programs. Although the chairman of the city department of education in Leningrad did not admit to the existence of a single seven-year school in his city (he said that Leningrad had 470 ten-year schools), the assistant chairman of the Kiev department of education reported that his city had 144 ten-year schools and 12 seven-year schools. Total enrollment in Leningrad was quoted as 382,000 pupils, in Kiev as 126,000 pupils.

Until fairly recently the upper section of the ten-year school served as a preparatory course for entrance into universities and other higher educational institutes. Only in the last years, with the increase in the number of ten-year schools, has the need arisen for converting it into a general educational institution with broader aims. According to Deputy Minister Markushevich, "Only some 20 per cent of the graduates of the ten-year school can be admitted to universities today. The others must go to work from school." Hence the increasing emphasis on the importance of polytechnical education, which keeps the pupils in school for an additional year and trains them for a special job. Conversation with at least one of the pupils in the eleventh year of such a school elicited the opinion that this was an excellent idea: "I spend half my time in school and half in the nearby factory, which makes television parts. I enjoy the factory work very much and I will have a good 'trade' when I graduate from school." These were the words of a young boy in Leningrad while his mother, a history teacher of many years' standing, nodded approvingly. But one must doubt whether such sentiments are very representative.

Graduates from the seven-year schools need not consider their education finished. They can go on to technical schools or continue their education while they are working. There are sixty-one schools for working youth in Kiev, and Leningrad has 70,000 pupils enrolled in such schools and evening courses. As reported by Deputy Minister Gerashenko of the Ministry of Higher Education of the U.S.S.R., 4.5 per cent of the graduates of the seven-year schools continue their schooling at semiprofessional schools.

Although the administration of secondary schools is decentralized in theory, the curriculum of the secondary schools is the same, by and large, throughout the Soviet Union. It was estimated that 80 to 85 per cent of the curriculum was identical in all republics. Minor differences due to local demands do exist. As one high education official explained regretfully, "National schools teach in the native languages and stress the local geography and history; thus, as far as that goes, there cannot be complete uniformity." Such uniformity, he emphasized, is desirable, since it enables any pupil who graduates from a ten-year school to apply for admission to a higher educational institution anywhere in the Soviet Union.

Since 1956, secondary education in the Soviet Union has been free throughout the ten grades. The children are required to buy their textbooks, but these are very cheap. Children are also supposed to wear uniforms, but, as has been stated before, many do not wear them.

For the last few years all secondary schools have been coeducational. Visitors were often struck by the preponderance of one sex or the other in the higher grades of some schools in the larger cities. They were informed that this was the result of the recent return to coeducation. A school that had been a boys' school will have more boys than girls in the upper grades, and vice versa.

School supplies and equipment are centrally manufactured and distributed by a special network of stores, situated in republic, regional, and district centers. These stores sell writing equipment, laboratory equipment, school furniture, and shop equipment — in short, everything a school needs. Exercise books, pens, pencils, and so forth must all conform to a standard laid down by the Central Committee of the Communist Party and the Council of Ministers. The Central Committee of the Trade Union of Educational, Cultural and Research Workers and the Academy of Pedagogical Sciences organize an exhibition of teaching equipment every summer, during the holidays. This exhibition includes not only the equipment produced by the various plants and factories according to the plan, but also the instruments and visual aids constructed by individual teachers and even by some pupils. Since 1954, collective farms, plants, and factories have been empowered by the Council of Ministers to give to the schools equipment and machinery that they cannot use in production and that will be useful in polytechnical education. Komsomol organizations, parents' committees, and the general public are also expected to help the schools with equipment.

Description of a Typical School

A good, though not necessarily representative, ten-year school in a city — and it should be understood that these are better schools than their rural counterparts — is housed in a four-to-six-story brick building. It may be surrounded by a little garden, where two or three white plaster statues of Pioneers are displayed — boys or girls at work or performing some athletic feat. In the downstairs entrance hall there is generally a cloakroom and a patriotic stand with flags and a bust of Lenin. The hall may have a bulletin board, which is used to display the work of the parents' committee and to post announcements of general interest. Just before the opening of school, for example, a list of the things a child would need to take to school is posted. The walls of the hall and passages are decorated with pictures of last year's graduates and of gold and silver medal winners, with the "honorary documents" that the school, the Pioneer brigade, or some special class has won, with slogans — generally quotations from Lenin, Stalin, or Gorki — exhorting children to learn and emphasizing the importance of knowledge, and with reproductions of famous paintings of scenes from Soviet history. The picture of Lenin addressing the Third Komsomol Congress and emphasizing the importance of learning appears frequently. Stalin speaking to a meeting or surrounded by school children is another favorite. There are scenes from the Russian past and photographs of great leaders (Marx, Engels, Lenin, Voroshilov, and Stalin) and of great scientists (Darwin, Michurin, and Lomonosov).

Classrooms, on the average, measure 22 feet by 28 feet. Secondary-school classrooms differ from those in the primary grades only in the fact that here the blackboard is not lined. The walls are bare except for the picture of Lenin or some other leader and floors are wooden and invariably painted dark brown. The only decorations are the green plants, which are in every classroom, although there is little room for them. The schools are scrupulously clean, but even the new buildings look old and dilapidated. Fire escapes seem to be nonexistent, but every school has fire-fighting apparatus on every floor.

Every school has a gymnasium, usually 30 feet by 50 feet. The walls are lined with equipment for Swedish gymnastics, and the floor may be marked off for games. Some schools have an outside play area, where physical-culture lessons sometimes take place.

The auditorium is often on the top floor. It may be large or small and is filled with benches, folding seats, or chairs. At the front of the room there is always a raised dais, sometimes with a piano on it. The back of the dais is invariably draped with red cloth or red banners, in the middle of which appears a picture or a bust of Lenin. Slogans such as the following are prominently displayed:

Discipline beautifies the collective and each separate member of the collective. (A. S. Makarenko)

Study, children, prepare to be the masters of your enormous, inexhaustibly rich country; it needs 100,000 clever heads, 100,000 clever hands. (M. Gorki)

Long live Communism — the Future of the Whole of Humanity!

These are typical examples, the first two from School No. 29 in Leningrad, the last from School No. 717 in Moscow.

Laboratories, workshops, and special rooms are variously equipped. Some are extremely impressive, others astonishingly poorly supplied. Thus, in the ten-year school in Yasnaya Polyana, Tolstoi's country home, the children themselves built a planetarium for use in their study of astronomy. It shows the heavens as they appear throughout the night, complete with the movements of the Sputnik, and ends the night by showing sunrise over the skyline of Moscow to the accompaniment of deafening music. On the other hand, the biology room in this same school has no equipment at all.

Physics and chemistry equipment in the various schools also varies considerably. School No. 57 in Kiev had a modern chemistry laboratory with double worktables equipped with sinks, electrical outlets, and gas jets. On the walls were chemical charts as well as pictures of famous Russian scientists. There were two large exhaust fans and a high demonstration table. On the other hand, the chemical laboratory at School No. 29 in Leningrad had only two sinks and four faucets, there were no outlets for Bunsen burners, and the supply cupboard contained only a periodic chart. The physics room of School No. 57 in Kiev was well equipped, whereas the physics room in School No. 717 in Moscow merely had charts of jet engines and television sets. The biology room in School No. 35 in Moscow had only a few charts, while the biology room in School No. 6 in Kiev had eleven cases of stuffed animals, four cases of skeletons, and models of the eye, ear, throat, heart, and so forth.

Every school has a "Pioneer room," which serves as a meeting place for the brigade council and, if it is large enough, as a recreation place for the children. Here are kept the banners of the Pioneer brigade and mementos of Pioneer heroes. The room always has a large center table, used for council meetings. If there is space, there will be smaller tables for games and displays. The Pioneer room of School No. 57 in Kiev had a corner devoted to Gulia Karaliova, after whom the brigade was named. Gulia Karaliova was a young Komsomol heroine who lost her life in the siege of Stalingrad. She had been a pupil of this school, and a glass case, between the banners of the brigade, displayed her uniform coat and cap. The director, after telling her story, said, "We also preserve, in a sacred way, her mess kit and her Komsomol card."

Along the side of this room was a display of work done by the children. They had been making a study of the life of Lenin and they had made models of the room he lived in when he was a boy, of the Winter Palace when it was stormed during the October Revolution, and of the room in which Lenin lived in his last years. On the wall of the Pioneer room was a large map, with red thread connecting Kiev with the cities in which the children had school correspondents. "Write to us. We will get some more red thread and there will be threads running from Kiev to the United States," said the director. In the Pioneer room of School No. 29 in Leningrad there was a corner for Octobrists, a little table with signs displayed above it: "We are happy little children, we are called Octobrists," or "Only those who love labor can be called Octobrists!" In addition, on little tables through the room there were games children could play in their leisure time — chess, checkers, table football, and the like.

Some schools have a "methodology room," where materials and equipment are kept. One teacher explained its use this way:

Each teacher is expected to write something on a particular problem she has successfully solved and file it away in the methodology room.

Then, when other teachers need advice on this problem they can profit by the experience of teachers.

These are usually small rooms, with racks of maps and cupboards of other materials.

There is a teachers' room in every school, usually with a couch and a few chairs, sometimes with a sink with running water and a towel. The room is rarely very big or comfortable. The walls are often decorated with displays of children's work.

Many schools have cafeterias where children can get hot lunches. These are usually situated in the basement and may be quite small. Indeed, it is sometimes difficult to imagine that many children can be served with such restricted facilities.

Most schools have libraries, which stock books by Russian and foreign authors and occasionally some periodicals. The library of School No. 717 in Moscow, although quite small, claimed to have 5000 books and had several periodicals on display. The books included sets of the Russian classics — Pushkin, Tolstoi, Gogol, Gorki, Chekhov, Turgenev, Lermontov, and many more; sets of foreign classics in the Russian language — Heine, Goethe, Schiller, Dickens, Victor Hugo; and books in English — Mark Twain, Howard Fast, and Jack London, to name three. English editions are all published in Moscow. The library of School No. 150 in Tashkent claims to have 1683 books in Uzbek and 96 books in Russian, and the school plans to acquire some books in other foreign languages.

Every school, even in the cities, is supposed to have a small plot for agricultural work. These plots, it would seem, are often not close to the school, as none were shown to visitors. Every school visited, however, said that such a plot existed and showed samples of the plants the children had grown on the allotment.

Every school has a "sponsor," a plant, collective farm, or other organization, which helps it with equipment and other needs. As stated by Mr. Kisov, head of the Visual Aids Department of the Institute of Methods in the Academy of Pedagogical Sciences, "If a school needs more equipment or material and its own funds for this are insufficient, the sponsoring organization may help either with money or with their own work. Many sponsors donate equipment to the schools."

Mme. Zoya Timofeeva, Director of School No. 35 in Moscow, reported that the machine shop in her school had been donated by the sponsoring plant, which also furnished the instructors. These were workers of the plant who had no pedagogical training but were learning how to teach while working at the school. It was a reciprocal relationship: "The plant that sponsors us furnishes the raw material for the metal working shop, and the school, in return, makes certain simple things that the plant needs." The school in its turn sponsored a kindergarten, and the pupils made toys for the smaller children in their woodworking shop.

There is generally no need for transportation services for the schools in the cities. Children go to the school nearest their home, usually not too far away. One director told us, "There is an in-creasing tendency to build schools for the new apartment houses in the middle of a complex of houses, so that the children will not have far to walk and will not have to cross the street on their way to school."

In the country, however, children sometimes live too far from school to walk, especially in winter. The school in Yasnaya Polyana, for example, admits children from three or four different villages. Children who live too far away from school to walk are furnished transportation by collective farms. This was reported by the direc-tor of the school in Yasnaya Polyana as well as by the Minister of Education of Uzbekistan.

Enrollment in a ten-year school of a big city will be 1000 to 1500 children. This number includes the primary grades, since they are an integral part of the complete secondary school. Most grades have two or three "parallel" classes and some schools, where enrollment is particularly large, run on more than one shift. According to Direc-tor O. L. Maksimchuk of School No. 57 in Kiev, "After the war, all schools in Kiev ran on two or three shifts. Now we have eliminated the two shifts from almost all schools in Kiev itself and we aim to do the same for all the schools of the Ukrainian republic."

If the school is on one shift, it will start at 8:30 A.M. and end at 2:15 P.M.; the afternoon, from 4 P.M. on, will be devoted to ama-teur circles. If the school is run in two shifts, the second shift will run from 2:30 P.M. to 7:30 P.M. Class size is regulated; in School No. 717 in Moscow, the visitors were told, "We try to keep classes within the approved norms; these are thirty to thirty-five pupils for the first three grades of secondary school, twenty-five to thirty in the three top grades." Observation confirmed that classes were held to more or less that size in the secondary school. The enrollment in this particular school, which had 30 classes and 56 teachers, was 1000 pupils. Other schools visited had an enrollment of 1200 pupils, 31 classes, and 45 teachers (No. 29 in Leningrad); 950 pupils, 23 classes, and 59 teachers (No. 57 in Kiev); 1073 pupils, 34 classes, and 52 teachers (No. 150 in Tashkent).

Curriculum

The curriculum for secondary schools is almost uniform throughout the Soviet Union, although theoretically in the hands of separate ministries in each republic. In the school year 1956–1957, the curriculum in the secondary school in the Russian republic was as follows: in grades five to seven children were taught Russian language and literature, mathematics, history, geography, biology, foreign language, physical culture, drawing, and singing. Physics started in grade six and chemistry in grade seven. At the end of the sixth grade drawing and singing were dropped, although they could, of course, be carried on a voluntary basis. Drawing was replaced in the seventh grade by technical drawing. Finally, in grade ten, geography and biology were dropped and Constitution of the U.S.S.R., astronomy, and psychology were added. Physical culture and "labor" were given throughout the ten grades, and there was some time set aside for excursions. Recent changes have tended to intensify the emphasis on science and practical work at the expense of courses in the humanities.

Variations. There is some variation in the work of the national and the Russian schools in the national republics. An example is the curriculum for the secondary schools in the Kazakh republic, where the language of instruction is Kazakh.[3] The curriculum differs in only one respect. From the first grade, two languages are taught, Russian language and literature and Kazakh language and literature. While in the lower grades more time is devoted to the native than to the Russian language, in the sixth grade both languages get equal time and from the seventh grade on, Russian language and literature begin to draw ahead. The other subjects are distributed in the same way as in the schools of the Russian republic, with very minor time differences. The only other notable difference in the curriculum of the two republics is that in the Kazakh schools no time is given to psychology or to excursions.

An example of another variation is the plan of the Russian schools in the republic of Azerbaijan,[4] where the native language is taught for two hours a week from the third grade on and psychology is again omitted from the tenth-grade curriculum. However, these schools do include excursions.

The plan for the Ukrainian and Russian schools in the Ukrainian republic for the school year 1955-1956 reveals that there are other variations by republics. Here the curriculum is the same for the two kinds of schools, with the single difference that in the Ukrainian schools more time is devoted to the Ukrainian language than to the Russian language up to sixth grade.

An additional important difference between Russian and national schools seems to be that children in the secondary grades of a national school must learn two foreign languages instead of one — Russian and whatever foreign language is introduced in fifth grade. This tends to overburden the children even more than in the ordinary schools. There has been much discussion recently on how to abolish this additional demand on the pupils of the national schools.

General Perspective. On the whole, the basic curriculum is very similar in all kinds of schools. While a more detailed account of it will be given in the next chapter, here we limit ourselves to a general perspective.

In the second cycle of the secondary schools (grades five through seven), history is taught according to the following plan: grade five, ancient history through the conquests of Alexander; grade six, ancient and medieval history from the rise of Rome until the feudal period of the tenth century; grade seven, medieval and early modern history through the seventeenth century.[5]

The biology course in grades five and six consists of botany, while the one for grade seven is devoted to zoology.[6] Physics is taught in grade six and deals mainly with mechanics. In grade seven, the course content is made up of heat and electricity.[7] Chemistry is introduced in grade seven.[8]

An important addition to the curriculum in grade five is a foreign language, usually German, English, or French. The course comprises vocabulary, grammar, phonetics, reading, and spelling.[9] It is interesting to remember that the non-Russian pupil begins his native tongue in grade one, Russian in grade one or two, and a non-Soviet language in grade five.

The curriculum of the second cycle also includes practical shopwork,[10] drawing (grades five and six),[11] singing,[12] and physical training.[13] In the school these subjects are not given much time. The Pioneer houses, palaces, and camps, however, carry on where the school leaves off. In most cases, the facilities and instruction of these institutions are far superior to those of the school. In addition, young pupils can often get more and better training in the very well-equipped science laboratories and practical workshops in these establishments, administered and supervised by the Komsomol.

In the uppermost cycle of the ten-year school, grades eight through ten, the major fields of study are Russian literature, history, mathematics, and physics. Russian literature in grade eight starts with a short over-all view of the medieval period and then concentrates on the eighteenth and nineteenth centuries. Although lesser figures such as Radishchev and Griboedov are given some attention, the emphasis is on Pushkin, Lermontov, and Gogol. The grade-nine literature course concentrates on Turgenev's *Fathers and Children* and Tolstoi's *War and Peace* but also covers some of the writings of Goncharov, Ostrovski, Chernishevsky, Nekrasov, and Chekhov. Two hours are given to the world significance of Russian literature and ten to Western literature, five to Shakespeare's *Hamlet* and five to Goethe's *Faust*. Grade ten is concerned with Soviet literature, especially Gorki, Mayakovski, Sholokhov, and Fadeyev. This course also includes six hours on the literature of the peoples of the U.S.S.R. after the October Revolution as well as four hours on the basic features of Soviet literature in its world significance, that is, its ideological aspects. It concludes with twenty-two hours of review and generalizations on the literature of the nineteenth century.[14]

Mathematics in grade eight consists of further work in algebra and geometry; in grade nine of algebra, geometry, and elementary trigonometry; and in grade ten of advanced algebra and trigonometry.[15] The 1958–1959 syllabus for mathematics did not include any provision for introductory calculus.

Biology in grade eight deals with the anatomy and physiology of man. In grade nine the subject is called "Foundations of Darwinism." The final four courses treat *The Descent of Man* and include some attention to "racial differences of mankind and a critique of racism" and "the antireligious significance of the conclusive animal descent of man." [16]

The physics course in grade eight is mainly concerned with the mechanics of motion and energy. In grade nine this topic is continued, but the majority of the time is given to molecular physics and heat. Physics in grade ten consists of electrictity, electromagnetic shaking and waves, optics, and eight hours of atomic construction. In addition, the students in grade ten have a thirty-four hour course in astronomy.[17] Interestingly, the number of hours of instruction in physics is 69 (grade six), 102 (grade seven), 102 (grade eight), 136 (grade nine), and 148 (grade ten). Chemistry rises from 66 hours in grades seven and eight to 99 in grade nine and 116 in the final grade (including fifty-four hours in organic chemistry).[18]

A short course in psychology is taught in grade ten. The thirty-three hours are apportioned among perception and reception, attention, memory, imagination, thinking and speech, sensation, volitional action, and the psychological character of personality. One of the subtopics is "the teaching of I. P. Pavlov on the higher nervous activity — the natural foundation of psychology." [19] As the members of the Comparative Education Society were repeatedly told, Pavlov's work is the starting point of all psychology teaching and experimentation in the Soviet Union.

The history program in grades eight and nine consists of two parts, history of the U.S.S.R. and modern history. In grade eight, sixty-six hours are dedicated to each field. Soviet history begins with the primitive period, proceeds through the medieval era, and concludes with the close of the seventeenth century. Modern history starts with the "English bourgeois revolution" in 1642 and includes the war for independence in North America and the formation of the U.S.A., the "French bourgeois revolution," the Napoleonic era, the Congress of Vienna, the 1848 revolution and its international influence, "the Civil War in North America," China from the seventeenth through the nineteenth century, and other topics through 1870. Significantly, adequate attention is paid to Communist ideology, "the rise of scientific Communism: K. Marx and F. Engels (until 1848)," in six hours. "The activity of K. Marx and F. Engels in the revolution" in Germany is also singled out for treatment. At the end of the year pupils spend three hours on the First Internationale from its rise in 1864 until 1870, in which the significance of the early congresses and Marx's *Capital* are discussed.[20]

In grade nine, seventy-four hours are devoted to Russian history and only fifty-eight to modern history. Russian history extends from Peter I, the Great, at the turn of the eighteenth century, until the close of the nineteenth century. The section of the syllabus on "bourgeois reforms in the 1860's" considers Lenin's views on these events, as do other sections. Modern history starts with the Franco-Prussian War and concludes with the end of World War I. The five hours on history of the U.S.A. during this period cover economic development, the political regime, the labor movement, and "the aggressive foreign policy." Under the last-named topic the students learn about "the intensification of the expansionist policy of the U.S.A. in the period of imperialism," "the enslavement of the countries of Latin America," and "the U.S.A. imperialistic policy in China." Chinese history is presented in three hours, as "the international labor movement and the Second Internationale" and "imperialism as the high point in the recent stage of capitalism." It is hardly extraordinary that World War I history includes an emphasis on the October Revolution.[21] What is surprising, however, is that the two history courses in grade nine are not parallel, although there is some overlap that permits correlation of content.

History in the final grade consists of only one course of 115 hours on twentieth-century Russia and the Soviet Union. The prerevolutionary period is taught in twenty-seven hours and the syllabus makes no mention of Stalin.[22] One hour a week in grade ten is devoted to the Constitution of the U.S.S.R., a course that stresses the governmental processes and functions, the role of the Communist Party in the nation, and the superiority of the Soviet way of life over that of any other country.

Geography is taught in grades eight and nine only. In grade eight, the course offers eighty-two hours of instruction on the economic geography of foreign countries in Europe, Asia, North and South America, Africa, Australia, and Oceania. The coverage is obviously comprehensive, but the syllabus allots only one hour each to Hungary, Rumania, Bulgaria, Albania, Yugoslavia, Spain, Finland, Sweden, Norway, the Mongolian People's Republic, Korea, Viet-Nam, Pakistan, Burma, Southeast Asia, Afghanistan, Iran, Turkey, and Oceania. The geography of seven countries in the Middle East is taught in two hours and all of Latin America in three hours. The country that receives the most time is China (seven hours), followed by the U.S.A. (six hours) and Great Britain (five hours). The economic geography course in grade nine deals exclusively with the U.S.S.R., in ninety-nine hours.[23]

Foreign languages are continued in grades eight to ten. The emphasis is the same as in earlier grades. The syllabus does not provide for the inclusion of the foreign civilization, that is, literature, customs, culture, and so forth.[24] Nor does the textbook on the methods of teaching the German language treat this phase of language teaching.[25] At most, this content may appear in the form of "readings" paragraphs and illustrations. Some foreign-language textbooks contain distorted material on such foreign countries as England and the United States, literature by Lenin and Stalin in translation, and information on the U.S.S.R., but very little on the genuine culture whose language is studied.[26]

Other subjects taught in grades eight–ten are singing,[27] practical training in machine and other skills,[28] and physical training.[29] Military training, which is not mentioned in public, is given from grade seven through grade ten during one of the two hours of physical training each week. Only for boys, the military-training class teaches close-order drill, various weapons, and military regulations and courtesy. In grade ten, students learn to use live ammunition in target practice with rifles and submachine guns. Military content also appears in such subjects as geography, mathematics, physics, chemistry, and literature. Finally, military training gets much emphasis in the extracurricular summer training camps for boys about to enter grade ten.[30]

Soviet educators maintained that the decision as to which foreign language each school would teach was up to the parents. It is doubtful, however, that this is really correct, as government planning and supply of teachers and textbooks must also play a considerable part. The major foreign language used to be German, but English is now gaining the upper hand. The director of a ten-year school in Kiev reported that the new trend was to teach only one foreign language in each school and for all children to learn this language.

Methods of Instruction

All instruction centers around the class lecture. A lesson begins with recitation of the homework. Pupils are called on in the same way as they are in the primary grades and are given marks for their response to questions on the work done since the previous lesson. Sometimes written homework is also inspected. When the homework is disposed of, the teacher introduces the new material for the lesson, usually by straight lecture, with the children taking notes only when told to do so. If there is time the teacher discusses the new material with the children; however, in several classes observed the whole time was spent in going over the material from the last lesson and nothing new was offered at all. At the end of the class, the new homework is assigned and the children write it down in their daybooks. The amount of homework is prescribed by the Ministry of Education. N. Kova, assistant chairman of the department of education in Kiev, reported that "Homework for the first three grades of the secondary school should be about two to two and one-half hours daily; in the upper three grades, it should amount to about two and one-half to three hours daily."

Most Soviet textbooks are published by a publishing house in Moscow, the Uchpedgiz. Though the textbooks may be in the Russian or a native language, their content does not vary. To Western eyes, they are for the most part quite dull. Illustrations are few and of bad quality, and the text is wordy. The ministries of education of the various constituent republics have their own publishing houses to publish additional textbooks for national schools. These also must correspond to specifications determined in Moscow. In recent years efforts have been made to make textbooks easier to read and better illustrated. Also, new textbooks have been written for the newly introduced polytechnical subjects.

Examinations and Standards. At the end of the seventh and

tenth grades examinations are held for all pupils; those at the end of tenth grade are for the "certificate of maturity," which entitles the pupil to take entrance examinations for a higher educational institution. Examinations are prepared by the state education authorities and are quite independent of the individual school. This is how the director of School No. 171 in Leningrad described the examinations at the end of the tenth grade:

> There are seven examinations, lasting from May 28 to June 20. The difficult subjects require more days of preparation than easy ones. The first examination is usually a written composition in the subject of Russian literature on one of three subjects. For this, the pupils have six hours. All other examinations are oral. They have to be taken in algebra, trigonometry, geometry, physics, chemistry, and a foreign language. The pupil draws a ticket with three questions on it. He is given a certain amount of time to organize his thoughts, and then he gives his answers to a committee of examiners. This takes him about fifteen minutes for each question.

There is no doubt that pupils in the secondary schools are made to work extremely hard and that this burden increases with the higher grades. There have recently been many discussions by Soviet educators and doctors on how to lighten the tasks of the pupils. As Deputy Minister Markushevich put it, "Our pupils are too tense and many teachers and parents complain about this." Research is being done to determine how to reduce this tension. Visitors at the Institute for Physical Education were told that a study was being organized to determine the time when pupils are most tired during the day. Attempts to reduce the burden imposed on the pupils often fail owing to pressure from the teachers. Thus, officials at the Institute for Physical Education complained, "We have determined the correct amount of homework for each grade, but many teachers do not follow our recommendations and give more homework than is good for the children." However, they said that last year the teachers had agreed among themselves not to give homework on Saturdays.

The causes of failure on the part of many pupils are also widely discussed. The editor of the *Teachers' Gazette*, Mme. N. Parfenova, said, "We proceed on the assumption that every student can achieve well if he only tries. But the fact remains that many fail at the end of the year and have to repeat that year and we are trying to find out the cause for this." Soviet theory is forced to accept the fact that the only causes for failure that are officially admitted are laziness, illness, insufficient work on the part of the teachers, and insufficient supervision on the part of the parents. Thus, methods of avoiding failures include more supervision of the child and, in extreme cases, extra work with the child by the teacher or parent or sometimes by a member of the parents' committee. The director of School No. 717 in Moscow reported that in the school year 1957–1958 40 out of 1200 pupils failed in his school. The director of School No. 112 in Kiev reported that in the last year 16 out of 620 pupils had to repeat a grade; these pupils were mostly in grades four and six. A pupil has to repeat a grade if he receives unsatisfactory grades in three or more subjects. If he gets bad marks in only two subjects, he can take the examinations over again. For instance: "Pupils can take the same grade twice. In exceptional cases, when there has been illness, or some other good and valid reason, a pupil can take the same year three times. Otherwise, he has shown that he is not capable and must be referred to a special school."

One must add to the above a report by an official of the Institute of the Theory and History of Pedagogy that every effort is made to prevent failures. At Schools No. 717 in Moscow and School No. 6 in Kiev, both directors stated that their teachers often stayed after school with slow pupils to help them over their difficulties. At the Institute for Art Education, the deputy director reported that the same efforts are made to teach untalented children singing. She cited a case of a girl who just could not sing; the teacher worked with her for several years until she finally was brought to sing correctly. However, no concessions as to subject matter are made to slow children. All children have to master the same material and there are no electives in the secondary school.

"There are sweet and bitter medicines; for many children mathematics is a bitter medicine, but that does not mean that we can let them off learning it," replied Deputy Minister Markushevich, himself a mathematics professor, in answer to a question asking what happened to the children who had great difficulties with mathematics. There now seems to be some prospect that polytechnical subjects might become elective in the future. Director Shapovalenko of the Institute of Methods mentioned this possibility in an interview. This means not that pupils will be able to decide whether they want to take polytechnical courses in general, but that they may be given a choice as to the type of work they want. Director Timofeeva of School No. 35 in Moscow reported that in her experimental polytechnical school girls were given some choice as to whether they want to continue with sewing and embroidery lessons beyond the stage when these are compulsory.

Discipline. Discipline in the secondary grades is enforced in much the same way as in the primary grades. Work on the enforcement of the "Rules for Pupils" is intensified, and more is expected from the secondary-school child than from the younger pupil.[31] Children wear the same uniforms as in the lower grades and conform to the same behavioral standards. However, it would seem that the rules are not enforced quite as strictly in the highest grades. The director of School No. 143 in Tashkent explained that she did not make the pupils in the highest grade wear uniforms if they did not want to, and visitors noticed that the overwhelming majority of boys did not wear them. Discipline in the tenth grade in this school was noticeably more lax than in the lower grades, although the teacher conducting the class was very strict. Many of the pupils simply had not done their homework and this was not treated as an extraordinary occurrence by the teacher; she simply assigned the same homework all over again. Moreover, the pupils moved about and talked in class with much more freedom than had hitherto been observed in the lower grades. It is, of course, impossible to generalize from such isolated observations.

Methods of enforcing discipline were discussed with the director of School No. 6 in Kiev. She reported that, if there are any disciplinary problems, the teacher may call a class meeting where the pupil's behavior is discussed publicly. Another method of helping a child is to give him some "social work," which will make him aware of himself as a member of the collective. Finally, if the child persists in bad behavior, he may be transferred to another school or even expelled. Asked whether such cases frequently occurred, the school director replied; "We hardly ever expel any child. In fact, it happens so seldom that I can't even remember when it happened last."

Records. As in primary-school years, records are kept throughout the secondary grades listing the achievements and social behavior of the pupils. These records include:

Name
Date and place of birth
Place of work of the parents, names of parents and siblings
Who is living at home with the pupil
Nationality
Year of entering school
Birth certificate and home address
All marks received
Marks received for behavior
Record of lateness to school
Record of practical work carried on during the school years and after
    school
Membership in circles
Socially useful work done
Health
Physical-culture activities
Participation in sport competitions
Medals of honor received for the work
Bad behavior, measures taken and punishments given
Characteristics of the pupil during the various grades

The following are summaries of two sample records from the fifth grade, taken from the files of a Kiev school:

She has had excellent marks during the year. She is generally capable, likes to study, and learns well; also, it is very important to her to do well. She goes into the material deeply during lessons. She is a pupil who is polite, well brought up, and clean. She reads a lot of books. She always helps her friends and takes an active part in social life. In class, she wants to clear up everything, she wants to know without any doubts and hesitations. She works in an embroidery circle and her work has been exhibited. During the summer she had agricultural practice and did excellent work.

*   *   *

He has done better throughout the year. He received a "3" in history and botany and a "4" in other subjects. He is not talkative in the presence of grownups and teachers, but among pupils he is very lively and friendly. He is stubborn. He breaks rules and when the

SECONDARY EDUCATION

Secondary schools are the main testing ground of the quality of Soviet education. Here the majority of students receive terminal training for Soviet production (though schools associated with factories often supplement this training). At the same time, this level of education supplies a substantial proportion of youth with a springboard to academic and professional careers. While the secondary schools are currently undergoing substantial reorganization, the general atmosphere of the schools presented in the photographs below may be confidently predicted to remain unchanged.

Potted plants are found in halls and classrooms.

Students stand for recitation and when the teacher or visitors enter the room.

Each school has its library.

Attention to lectures is rapt in this history class in Tashkent. Girls sit together, presumably in deference to a surviving Moslem custom.

Extremely neat notebooks for
each subject are closely checked
by the teachers.

Flaxen hair and round Slavic faces predominate in
this Leningrad class. Students pay attention to the
teacher even when they are photographed.

As an "Honored Teacher," this Leningrad instructor wears a medal indicating his status. The title is bestowed upon outstanding teachers by election of the teaching body.

Old and young teachers in Tashkent

The editor of the *Uch telskaya Gazeta* (*Teache Gazette*) answers questio through an interpreter.

The new polytechnization reform urges the development of industrial skills. This poster tells students to acquire the habit of manual work.

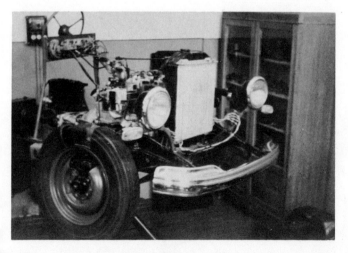

Polytechnization brought driver education and a car model into the secondary school.

This is a typical school chemistry laboratory. The number of bottles on display
never fails to impress visitors.

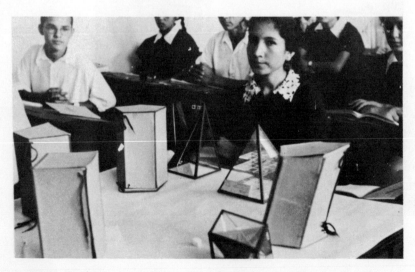

Trigonometry is studied with the aid of models, many
constructed by the students themselves.

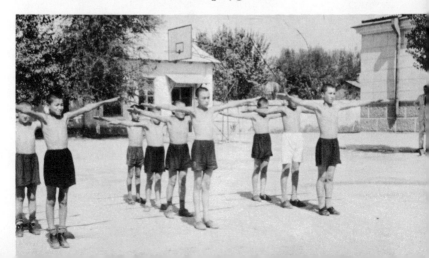

During good weather, physical education classes in
Tashkent exercise on the playground.

Factory Schools for Working Youth

This chemistry teacher in the School for Working Youth at the Lukacho Auto Works in Moscow is dressed in "revolutionary" Soviet costume.

A young worker studies geography in the Lukacho Auto Works School.

class leader tries to talk to him, to find out the reason for this, it is very hard to talk to him. If he is in a group with good pupils, he will be good, if he is in a group with bad pupils, he will be bad. He can work by himself if he wants to. His handwriting is poor. He likes to read and re-tell stories. He comes to school daily. The parents do not come to school often; it will be necessary for them to come more often and speak with the class leader. They should be made to be more interested in the boy's achievement. During the summer he worked on a collective farm.

Boarding Schools

In February, 1956, the Party Congress, acting on a suggestion by Khrushchev, established the boarding school. This school was to be radically different from the boarding facilities that already existed in some regions to provide accommodations for children who lived too far away from their school to go back and forth every day. The original plan was for boarding schools to provide an education and upbringing for children from the earliest years to their graduation from school. They were to be situated in healthy country districts and they were to give preference in admissions to children of war invalids, to children of needy families, and to children who were orphans or semi-orphans.

Function of the Boarding Schools. By 1958, boarding schools had been in existence for two years. They were much praised by Soviet educators as providing a new and better method of bringing up children and as a means of freeing the parents for work in production. Soviet educators interviewed by the Comparative Education Society almost unanimously denied any special educational function of boarding schools. It was emphasized again and again that these were not schools for the privileged, as had been speculated in the Western press. Deputy Minister Markushevich made a point of this:

> Boarding schools exist in all regions and districts but they are in a minority as compared with the regular schools. Their sole purpose is to provide for children whose home life is unsatisfactory and whose families are in need. Far from being schools for the privileged, they are schools for the underprivileged. Families who are well off do not need boarding schools.

It was stated further that there would be only as many boarding schools as were required to take care of all needy children; for the time being no plans were to be made to convert the rest of the schools into boarding schools, even if that were materially possible.

This, in general, was the view expressed by most of the educators interviewed on this subject. A notable exception was the Deputy Minister of Education of Uzbekistan in Tashkent, who stated:

> Boarding schools are not meant only for orphans and semi-orphans or children of needy families. There are orphanages and children's homes for such children. Boarding schools are intended mainly for the children of parents who think that the schools can do a better job of bringing up children than they can. Many parents think this and want to send their children and there are always more applications than can be handled.

This view of the purpose of boarding schools led observers to suspect that they sometimes got the children who could not successfully be integrated into the general schools. This view was confirmed in an interview with V. Gmurman, the official in charge of boarding schools in the Institute of the Theory and History of Pedagogy, of the Academy of Pedagogical Sciences in Moscow. When questioned on this issue, Gmurman stated:

> It must be admitted that the academic level of boarding schools, generally speaking, is lower than that of the ordinary schools. This is attributable to the fact that boarding schools often get pupils who have been rejected by the ordinary schools, pupils who have proved to be hard to handle. Much work must be done with such children, before they can be expected to catch up with their contemporaries in the ordinary schools.

Application for admission is made by the parents or guardians of the child to the district department of education. A commission named by the city department of education decides on the applications. All informants stated that there were always more applications than there were vacancies. The director of Boarding School No. 12 in Moscow said that in the year 1958–1959 he had 140 applications for 30 vacancies.

Characteristics. The boarding schools that were inspected by members of the Comparative Education Society were all situated in big cities and were very far from being the healthful country institutions described in Khrushchev's speech. It was explained that they had had to be established in a great hurry and that there had been no time to build schools expressly for them. Boarding schools for the time being had to be situated in buildings converted from the ordinary day schools. However, more boarding schools are planned for the future and these are meant to be in special buildings.

The staff of boarding schools consists of teachers and "educators" (*vospitateli*). As a general rule, the teachers do the academic work while the educators concentrate on the physical and moral upbringing of the children. It is clear that these functions often overlap. The literature on boarding schools is full of discussions on the delimitation of the function of the two types of staff members. Teachers in boarding schools are paid according to the number of hours they work, while educators are paid a fixed salary. When pressed on this issue, informants admitted that such educators were paid much less than teachers and that they did not have the education and training of the teachers. Although staff members at the Maxim Gorki Pedagogical Institute in Kiev maintained that their institute offered a special course for educators in boarding schools, it proved impossible to get information on this course, to obtain the textbook reportedly used in it, or to talk with a professor who teaches it. The vice-director of the Lenin Pedagogical Institute of Moscow stated that his institute had as yet no special courses for educators in boarding schools, although a course was planned, and that teachers for the boarding schools were trained in the same way as other teachers.

The curriculum of a boarding school is essentially the same as that of an ordinary school. A few differences can be noted, most of which are due to the fact that the children spend their whole day in the school. Because homework is supervised, educators maintain that less time is spent on homework in general. Some boarding schools continue to teach singing all through the ten grades of secondary school; some introduce the teaching of a foreign language in the third grade of the primary school.

When asked about the relation of the boarding schools to the families of their pupils, informants unanimously maintained that the boarding schools did nothing to estrange the children from their parents. The general attitude was stated by Gmurman in the following way:

> Boarding schools exist not to destroy but to help the Soviet family. The schools help the families bring up their children in the spirit of Communist morality. Many Soviet families are not yet on a high cultural level. If the child sees drunkenness and fighting at home, if he sees his mother come home from work too tired to pay him much attention, the family is weakened. If the child is in a boarding school, where he only sees his parents when they are rested and at liberty to pay him attention, the family is strengthened.

All informants emphasized that parents could see their children in the boarding schools at any time they wished. They may have them at home during the summer vacation if they wish — though it is desirable to keep the school "collective" together in a camp, said one educator — and they may have them at home for the week end.

Although boarding schools supposedly exist only for needy families, parents who send their children to these schools must pay a fee in most cases. The amount depends on the parent's salary. According to the director of Boarding School No. 1 in Tashkent, the minimum is 30 rubles a month, the maximum 250 rubles. However, if the family is truly in need, it does not pay at all. In this school in Tashkent, 40 per cent of the children pay nothing, and in School No. 13 in Moscow 37 out of 180 children are also exempt from payment. The others in this school pay from 30 to 300 rubles a month. On the basis of this information, it seems probable that a great proportion of the children in boarding schools do not come from extremely poor families.

According to the director of Boarding School No. 12 in Moscow, there are as yet no boarding schools with children of preschool age. This is not yet economically possible, he stated, although it would be highly desirable from the educational point of view to get the children as early as possible.

Boarding schools are coeducational, and the director of Boarding School No. 13 in Moscow said that friendships and social contacts were encouraged. "We like to think that our pupils may even marry each other later on," he mused.

The director of Boarding School No. 12 in Moscow said that one of the most important problems of the boarding school was how to replace the family atmosphere. In his school an older child is attached to a younger one, to simulate to an extent the influences of a sibling. The school had a bulletin board where photographs of the older children with their "brothers" and "sisters" were displayed. Other schools, said the director, were experimenting with mixed Pioneer detachments to achieve the same effect. Older children would be in one Pioneer detachment with younger ones, and this would accustom the children to getting along with pupils of different ages.

Pioneer and Komsomol groups are organized on the same plan as they are in the ordinary schools. There is also a student government, organized into committees with representatives from each class, which takes care of the social and "cultural" life of the school, as well as systematizing the care of the school building and grounds. Pupils are expected to take care of a large part of the cleaning and upkeep necessary in the school.

Pioneer and Komsomol organizations as well as the student government committees play a large part in the moral upbringing of the pupils. The director of Boarding School No. 12 in Moscow reported that the children themselves took care of infringements of the rules of Communist morality. The guilty pupil is summoned to stand in the middle of the room and is judged by his fellow pupils. This method is very effective, sometimes too effective, said the director. "Children tend to be much stricter than adults, and the punishments are sometimes so severe that the adults must interfere." As in all Soviet schools, corporal punishment is strictly prohibited.

Boarding schools are expected to grow in number in the future. According to the director of Boarding School No. 12 in Moscow, there were nineteen boarding schools in Moscow in 1957–1958, with twenty-six new ones planned for 1958–1959. Four new boarding schools were planned for the city of Leningrad for 1958–1959, according to the chairman of its department of education. Gmurman stated that the over-all plan was to have one million pupils in boarding schools by the year 1960. The figure currently most often referred to is two million.

In general, Soviet educators seemed enthusiastic about the new boarding schools, although they maintained that it was too early to evaluate them realistically. There are those who point out the great expense involved and urge better use of these funds in improving existing day schools.[32] On the other hand, Minister of Higher Education V. Yelyutin, during his recent visit to the United States, expressed his belief in the desirability of boarding-school education for *all* Soviet children.

9

SECONDARY EDUCATION:
SUBJECT AREAS AND METHODS

Soviet educational authorities do not look upon the educational process as a matter of content versus method, but rather as a compound of both. This point was made time and again in the pedagogical institutes, the schools themselves, the Moscow Institute for the Improvement of Teachers, the ministries of education, the Trade Union of Educational, Cultural, and Research Workers, and the Academy of Pedagogical Sciences, particularly in its Institute of Methods of Teaching. A general outline of what is being taught in the Soviet secondary grades was given in Chapter 8. The following pages will discuss in greater detail the content and methods of instruction.

Science and Mathematics

Although the members of the Comparative Education Society were not able to visit technikums and vocational schools in which science and mathematics receive applied emphasis, several did observe science and mathematics in the general schools.[1]

Mathematics. In mathematics, which is required of all pupils, the unknown quantity is introduced as early as the fourth grade. The formal study of algebra, however, does not begin until grade five. This teaching of the unknown, which was regarded by one observer as "an excellent approach in moving toward algebra," is not without difficulty. Another American educator, who watched a class in fifth-grade arithmetic at School No. 1 in Moscow, reported that "at various points in the lesson different pupils showed confusion over the function of x in the equation." The teacher approached the unknown by writing a simple arithmetical equation in which she substituted a numerical value for the unknown. This particular lesson began with a step-by-step description by various pupils of how they solved the homework problems. The teacher then asked the pupils to open their textbooks, and some of them traced all the steps necessary to solve a particular problem. Although a pupil would go to the blackboard now and then to perform an arithmetical operation, the teacher did most of the work, writing down each step as described by the individual child.

Difficulties in teaching the unknown were also discernible in School No. 153 in Leningrad. In one fifth-grade arithmetic class, pupils did well on problems that involved simple addition and subtraction. In problems of combining quantities in addition and subtraction, many were unable to find the solutions by themselves. The young teacher, who was in his first position, gave directions on how to solve the problems but did not explain the basic principle or try to get the pupils to see why they were performing the operations. Very few members of the class seemed to understand the meaning of $x + 32 = 64$. Most of the pupils who worked on this kind of problem at the board did not find the solution. Thereupon, the teacher directed them to write down $x = 64 - 32$ and to subtract. When the observer walked around the class to examine the pupils' notebooks, he noted great variations in ability to do the problems. Some students had the work done before it was completed on the board; others were following the board work. At no point did the teacher explain any operation. He did not write any marks in the grade book of the pupils who did not give correct answers.

Another observer noticed similar difficulties in a different class in the same school. One pupil at the blackboard could not begin on a problem involving an equation with an x. After some discussion on the part of the class, the teacher dictated the answer and the child wrote it down, but he still did not understand. Nor did he comprehend the teacher's explanation on the board.

An eighth-grade mathematics class in School No. 6 in Kiev was engaged in factoring quadratic equations. The teacher, who impressed the visitor as "excellent," provided various exercises to show the relationship between algebraic and arithmetical computations. The pupils who were sent to the blackboard did well.

In the following period, the same teacher had a ninth-grade mathematics class. First he conducted a discussion on the differences among parameters, functions, and constants, and then the algebraic and graphic solution of simultaneous equations. In both classes, "the students assiduously copied what was put on the board into their notebooks."

Another visitor noticed "no student participation in a sense of three, four, or five students solving a given problem or being asked to work on something else that the class has not been able to work out." Most of the pupils in the arithmetic classes visited were very good, but there were many basic errors in fundamentals, especially in long problems involving division, multiplication, and addition. In one class, eight out of fourteen pupils who went to the blackboard received a grade of "3," one was marked "2," and the rest received "4" and "5"; and half of the class sat with a bored expression while the teacher helped a pupil solve an equation with an unknown quantity.

One observer was quite impressed with both the quality and the quantity of the visual aids used in teaching mathematics. He was less impressed by the ability of pupils to answer their teacher's questions in an arithmetic class. This teacher had the pupils who made errors stand until someone gave the correct answer. The teaching of geometry, according to the observer, stressed measurements, volumes, shapes, and various figures, rather than formal proof.

The mathematics specialists in the Institute of Methods of Teaching of the Academy of Pedagogical Sciences and in the Moscow Institute for the Improvement of Teachers indicated their dissatisfaction with the program of teaching mathematics. The experts in methodology admitted that there were many problems in getting all the boys and girls to learn mathematics. The big question, as one visitor phrased it, was "whether you gain anything by having all students study mathematics all the way through in order to get a few who can succeed in it."

Biology.   For the first lesson of the fall semester in grade seven at School No. 6 in Kiev, the teacher wrote several questions on the board, such as "What is the significance of zoology for our economy?" The pupils copied these questions into their notebooks. Then, with the aid of a picture of a Siberian tiger, the teacher explained the relationship between climate and the habitat of animals. A new word, *environment,* was defined at this point. The teacher pointed to a picture of a whale and described its anatomy, means of locomotion, size, and other features. She then continued to a mounted bird. All through her presentation, which lasted twenty minutes, the teacher emphasized that animals were very important for the Soviet economy. The rest of the lesson was devoted to a question-and-answer period on the hunting and trapping of animals, the differences between tame and wild animals, and the economic significance of animals. Although there was formality during this part of the period, the lesson in general was far less formal than any others witnessed by the observer.

Two educators attended an eighth-grade class in Darwinism in School No. 20 in Tashkent. They heard a full-period lecture on Darwin, the theory of evolution, and the problem of natural selection. On the blackboard were pictures of Darwin and Pavlov. The students listened attentively but took no notes.

A visitor to the biology laboratory used by grade five in School No. 57 in Kiev noted various visual aids, flower models, specimens in jars, a stuffed rabbit, diagrams, skulls, and so forth. She also counted thirty-nine microscopes, one for each member of the class. Other educators likewise commented on the excellent quality of the biology teaching aids.

Chemistry.   Chemistry is taught with emphasis on the basic laws and the mathematical approach. The student in the laboratory is not trying to make a new chemical discovery but rather seeks to fix the law in his mind. Although the materials used in the chemistry laboratories were very poor, the teaching seemed quite good. The content of the chemistry course is far more rigorous than its American counterpart. "I was fooled on one of our visits. . . . I thought we were going into the tenth-grade class in chemistry and it seemed perfectly logical according to what they were doing, but then we found it was the eighth-grade class," wrote one observer.

In a chemistry class in grade seven in School No. 6 in Kiev the teacher began the first lesson by talking about the nature of chemistry and explaining the names and uses of standard chemical equipment — a burner, flasks, test tube, and ring stand. Then she discussed and demonstrated the differences between physical and chemical properties. Some of the demonstrations were done by the students themselves; others were done with the help of the teacher, who gave directions in either case. To demonstrate physical change, the teacher asked a girl to bend a glass tube. Chemical change was shown when the teacher burned some potassium chlorate and inserted a smoldering splint to show that oxygen was produced. The teacher called on almost every child during the lesson. The homework assignment was the reading of the first two pages of the textbook. The chemistry room had many bottles of chemicals, but the desks had no outlets for burners, indicating that there was not much individual laboratory work.

The same teacher taught the grade-ten chemistry class. The lesson, which dealt with the chemistry of metals, began with a review of the periodic chart of the elements. The teacher sent a pupil to the chart and asked him to describe the nature and meaning of the various columns. Since he did not give full answers, the teacher had to draw him out by questioning. She pointed to the positions of the metals on the periodic chart and talked about the changes in electron structure of the various groups in the chart. In addition, she wrote several equations showing electron balance on the board and discussed them with the pupils. There was also some discussion of atomic and electron numbers. After a question-and-answer period, the teacher assigned four pages of reading as homework. In this particular class there was not much class response without some coaching and coaxing on the part of the teacher.

In a seventh-grade chemistry class in School No. 151 in Moscow one American educator noticed that the teacher had the class wound up like a top. First there were the "arise" and "sit" recitations. Then the teacher performed a demonstration, and the pupils repeated the experiments at their desks.

Physics. Emphasis on the basic laws and the mathematical approach is also characteristic of the teaching of physics. The equipment in this field is completely adequate and "will hold its own, compared with what we find in the better schools in the United States." The visual aids, however, did not strike the visitors as being adequate. About one-third of the filmstrips examined dealt with automobile mechanics but were labeled "physics."

The course in physics begins in grade six with an elementary introduction to the subject. In grades six and seven the pupil learns elementary mechanics, heat, and electricity. The basic principles of light and sound, which were once taught in these grades, are now being reconsidered as content for later grades. In grade eight the course is devoted to a systematic study of mechanics and sound. Grade nine offers instruction in mechanics and heat; and grade ten is concerned with light and atomic structure. In every grade, some work is done in electricity. Ohm's law is taught in grades six and seven, problems involving the equation $I = E/R$ are taught in grade eight, and the cosine law is used in problems in grade ten. The weekly time given to physics is two hours in grade six, three hours in grades seven and eight, three and a half hours in grade nine, and four and a half hours in grade ten.

Laboratory experiments are compulsory. In grades six and seven the pupils repeat the teacher's demonstrations, but in the higher grades the pupils are supposed to work on individual projects, at least five a year. The ninth-graders test Boyle's law in their experiments, and the senior students study Joule's law and measure the current, resistance, time, and amount of heat to find the constant in the formula. Apart from their own experiments, the senior pupils also get a chance to watch demonstrations by the teacher.

The physics course requires at least two excursions a year. Each excursion lasts three hours and the teachers are notified where they will take the pupils. The trips may be to an electric station, an industrial plant, or a factory, so that the pupils may see the practical applications of what they have learned in the classroom.

The Institute of Methods of Teaching recommends that the teacher first demonstrate a simple machine, then show the motor part of the machine, and then demonstrate the whole machine again. In general, theory precedes practical application.

The formal teaching of physics is supplemented by voluntary

out-of-school circles. The construction of a telegraph set, for instance, would be carried out in a circle rather than in the classroom. Pupils who do not do well in class are not permitted to join these clubs.

At School No. 57 in Kiev the grade-ten physics class contained twenty-five girls, who "seemed rather free and talked at times among themselves — not noisily." There was adequate equipment for demonstration purposes. All desks had gas outlets. The pupils seemed free to ask questions and some made voluntary contributions.

A physics teacher in grade ten in School No. 6 in Kiev presented a lesson on the fields of force surrounding an electric charge on the first day of school. With the aid of the cosine law and vector analysis she demonstrated the resultant force of two like and two unlike charges on a given point. Most of the class, which was made up of thirteen girls and eight boys, seemed to do well, but their work was almost straight formula substitution. The method consisted of teacher explanation, student recitation, and student work on the blackboard. That the teacher was inactive was probably due to her sprained arm and to the fact that this was her first year of teaching. There was no audio-visual material in the room, but the laboratory equipment stored in the cabinets was adequate. The lack of audio-visual aids may have been due to the circumstance that the teacher had not yet had an opportunity to prepare such material.

At School No. 171 in Leningrad one visitor noted a variety of equipment in the grade-eight physics class: an opaque projector, a six-foot screen, cradle gas jets at each table, four large diagrams on transfer of energy (steam boiler) and three on practical application (steam locomotive), beaker stands, a very simple sink, and a small water heater on the wall over the sink. The thirty-five students sat at fourteen tables, many tables crowded with three occupants. The teacher's lecture was interspersed with questions to the students. The students wrote down the content of the lecture and the teacher reviewed by means of questions and answers.

In a grade-ten physics class in School No. 151 in Moscow the teacher asked, "What forces operate and in what direction, concerning the behavior of molecules?" The student replied, "Molecules are a combination of two different charged particles, and they are dipoled." From time to time the teacher called upon students in their seats to help those reciting at the blackboard. The teacher then began a rapid-fire explanation: "Now let us begin the next topic. Today we have the theoretical theme and I think the most difficult one. It regards potentials and the difference of potentials." The observer commented that he never saw any teaching in the Soviet Union that was not rapid. Part of the reason, he felt, was attributable to the fact that "in the Soviet Union teachers have little time to prepare their lessons, and, obviously, practice stimulus-response teaching. . . . No one thinks or reasons; he merely responds like a parrot."

A grade-six physics class in School No. 1 in Moscow had forty-one students, twenty-two of them girls. The lesson was on the measurement of area and volume. Each pupil, who was given a rectangular piece of wood and a short meter stick, was instructed in procedures of measuring the length, width, and height of the wood and told how to calculate the area of the long surface and the volume. The lesson was organized as a laboratory exercise, with the pupils supposed to perform the experiment four times and to record the data in their notebooks. The teacher used blackboard demonstrations and a question-and-answer technique before the experiment began. Students were asked to measure various items in the room and calculate, at the board and in their seats, the areas and volume. The observer noted that, even though each pupil was to work on the experiment by himself, there were "several instances of the collective in operation." He also looked at four or five of the notebooks and found that all had "the same data for each of the four measurements" of the experiment.

In a grade-ten physics class in the same school the pupils were studying fields of force surrounding static electrical charges. Their objective was to solve several problems on the strength and direction of the force by means of two isolated charges — two positive, two negative, or one of each. The teacher called three students to the blackboard to do the homework exercises. The rest of the period was spent in solving the problems and correcting the work of the students. Not one of the three students was able to solve the assigned problem. The teacher lectured and asked questions while developing the correct solution.

It is evident that teaching physics is not an easy matter in the

Soviet schools. Even advanced students have some difficulty in learning and teachers have to expend much energy in explaining a point. A clue to this situation may be found in a statement made by a methodological specialist in the Academy of Pedagogical Sciences. The Soviet educator admitted that one of the basic problems in teaching physics is to obtain a sufficient number of well-qualified teachers, especially for the rural schools. He made it quite clear that there were enough teachers of physics, but that they varied greatly in quality.

Humanities and Social Studies

Members of the Comparative Education Society had no opportunity to study methods of teaching in Russian language and literature. What follows is the account of their observations of the teaching of other subjects in the humanities.

Geography. The teaching of geography has not been unaffected by the recent changes in Soviet educational policy. Thus, according to Anatol V. Darinsky, head of the Department of Geography in the Herzen Pedagogical Institute at Leningrad, all the geography textbooks were undergoing thorough revision during 1958, in line with the renewed emphasis on the polytechnical element. Henceforth all geography textbooks, particularly those in economic geography in the upper grades, would stress even more than in the past the industrial development of the various countries and such problems as labor relations.

Map making was the subject of one lesson in grade-five geography at Boarding School No. 13 in Moscow. To begin with, the teacher discussed the significance of a scale in measuring distances on a map. Then she took up the metric system and showed how to measure by means of meter sticks and meter tapes, distance pacing, and large wood dividers. The class was interested, or appeared so. Although the teacher talked most of the time, she did ask questions and gave about half of the class an opportunity to answer. The class went out into the school yard. Each row of students formed a group to measure off three different lengths in the school yard in the four ways they had just learned: meter stick, tape, dividers, pacing. During the time of measurement "there was the usual romping around and lack of teamwork, and only a few of the more conscientious ones kept at the task. Others paced off the lengths with exaggerated steps, much to the amusement of the others." Since the teacher worked with one group at a time, it was not possible for her to watch all the groups. The class finally returned to the classroom to compare results.

At the experimental School No. 1 in Moscow an eighth-grade geography class was studying the economic geography of foreign countries in the English language and from an English translation of the standard Russian text. The teacher of this class was a man in his thirties, quite competent in English, rather severe in manner. Except for a large wall map of Europe the room was barren. After giving some details about Polish industry the teacher sent a pupil to the front of the room and asked him several factual questions on the rank of certain industries and metals, temperatures in specific places, the location of the Vistula, and so forth. At the end of this pupil's recitation the teacher said he was "sorry," he could only give him a grade of "3," since he "did not locate the Vistula quickly."

The teacher continued to ask about the Polish chemical industry and agriculture. He was trying to get the pupils to give quick answers. One pupil standing in front of the room was asked, "Where are the principal copper ore deposits?" Since the reply was slow in coming, the teacher said, "Read the map — it is like a book. You cannot find the swamps, you get the same mark as Ivan, a '3.'" He went on to lecture on Polish agriculture. The directions by the teacher were sharp. As a rule he spoke English. Only once did he break into Russian. A quiz on the imports and exports of Poland then followed. One pupil, who could answer only some of the questions, was told by the teacher, "Sorry, it is no more than a '3.' You usually answer much better."

This part of the lesson was evidently a review of what had been learned previously. The teacher now began to lecture on Czechoslovakia. After giving the class some facts on the geographical features of the country he ordered the pupils to put down their copybooks and assigned reading in the textbook as homework. He ended the lesson by asking questions on what he had just told the class about Czechoslovakia.

The same observer visited an eighth-grade geography class in School No. 171 in Leningrad. The teacher announced that the lesson was on the people's democracies and that the pupils were not to take notes. One boy who was asked to locate the people's democracies on the political map of the world had some difficulty in finding the countries. Others, therefore, volunteered to show the proper locations not only of the European people's democracies but also of the Mongolian People's Republic. The teacher then lectured on Czechoslovakia, especially on the political, economic, and cultural reforms that have taken place since that country became a people's democracy. She also referred from time to time to Poland and Bulgaria by way of illustration and comparison. The role of the U.S.S.R. in the development of these countries was stressed. An occasional question by the teacher interrupted the lecture. One question, "What are heavy industries?" failed to elicit a correct response from the pupil who was asked, but others volunteered the answer. During the entire lecture the students were "very tense and very stiff . . . scarcely moving a muscle and taking no notes." The teacher then announced that "in the next lesson we will study the natural conditions of Poland." She dictated a systematic outline for the study of any country and concluded the lesson by assigning particular pages in the textbook for homework.

Another section of grade-eight geography in this school was visited by the same observer. The teacher, the methods, the maps, and the lesson were the same, but the class met in the physics room. "The instructor knew the lesson by heart, the students took no notes during the lecture, the teacher asked the students to recall what was the content of the lecture." In this class the observer noticed "somewhat more free response on the part of the students" than in other classes and schools he had visited. "Often after a question had been asked, there was a kind of murmur of response until the teacher called on someone," as a rule adding the word *pozhaluista* (please). "Sometimes the teacher forgot to tell the students to sit down, so the students sat down when they felt the question had been answered. Sometimes there was a murmur in the class while one was reciting, especially if the class felt that the response was not correct."

The teacher took special pains to spare the pupils any embarrassment when they did not have the correct answers. No grades were written down in their books following their recitations, as happened in most of the classes which had been visited by the

Americans. The observer did not feel that the teacher was putting on a pedagogical performance. "The personality of the teacher was such that this was most likely the normal class routine."

It was evident that this teacher was trying hard to get the pupils interested in the subject matter of the lesson. Nonetheless, "some students did not pay very close attention. Some were looking at other maps in a packet at the back of the room. The teacher did not observe or did not interrupt." The observer felt that this situation might have been the result of "the interruption of the normal class routine by the visitors."

Whenever the teacher dictated, she repeated phrases for the benefit of pupils who were not able to keep up with her. Although the day was rather cloudy, she did not turn on the lights.

From the reports on the teaching of geography it is clear that formal procedures of instruction are not universal. Apparently, some teachers allow more leeway to their pupils in the classroom than do others. This may not be news to the professional pedagogue, but it is necessary to make the point, inasmuch as the impression seems to have gained ground that the teaching in Soviet classrooms is identical, regardless of instructor or place.

History. Academician Alexander M. Arseniev, Director of the Institute of the Theory and History of Pedagogy of the Academy of Pedagogical Sciences, gave the American educators some interesting replies to questions concerning the function of critical analysis in history classes. According to him, bourgeois history textbooks were used until about fifteen years after the October Revolution. The secondary and university students had numerous opportunities to criticize the anti-Marxian viewpoints expressed in those books and they were in a good position to compare bourgeois and Communist values. The pupil was free to take any position, however wrong, on historical matters. The teacher, on the other hand, was confined to the limits of the truth. He must teach the truth; he has "no right to be wrong." Should the teacher give the monarchist or aristocratic — hence, untrue — interpretation of history, his superiors would tell him that he was deceiving the young people in his charge.

The teacher is supposed to take into account individual differences among his pupils. He is told to stimulate discussion and not to undertake any "strict measures" against pupils who present different viewpoints on historical events. Although the teacher is encouraged to employ various procedures in stimulating pupil discussion, he is not permitted under any circumstances to use a false position to get pupils to participate in discussions. In practice this theoretical position results, as in other subjects, in a rigid content.

In the grade-seven history class in School No. 151 in Moscow the pupils had desk atlases to help them follow medieval Russian history. A girl was called to recite in front of the class. She was nervous and had to be helped by the teacher and other pupils. She received a grade of "3" after the weaknesses of her recitation were pointed out. Another girl was asked to write on the board while still another pupil was reciting, but she did not know the answer, apparently because she had not done her homework. The teacher kept her standing for some time and the girl broke into tears. As she sat down, the teacher walked over and talked to her. The observer remarked, "I don't know if she was comforting her or what, but it was rather cruel treatment of a child, I thought, particularly when there were visitors present."

All through the lesson, which dealt with the social structure of the Slavonic tribes of the ninth through the eleventh centuries, there was much stress on the means of production, the nature of property, the master-slave relationship, and similar matters. This procedure illustrates again the strong use of history and social studies for indoctrination of the concept of Marxism and the Marxist interpretation of social development from earliest times.

Formal methods marked the instruction of grade-six history in Boarding School No. 10 in Moscow. The teacher lectured and raised questions on thirteenth-century Europe. The pupils recited orally, apparently from memory, in front of the room.

In the grade-six class at School No. 171 in Leningrad, the fourteen boys and seventeen girls were learning about the structure of Roman society. The teacher asked questions on the homework. Various pupils would volunteer answers when the pupil being quizzed was having trouble. Much use was made of the small historical desk maps that are included in the history textbooks. In part, this explains the lack of wall maps in many history classes, somewhat surprising "since in the map stores there was an enormous quantity of very good maps." As the pupils recited, the teacher glanced through some of the homework books and wrote down grades. After every recitation she entered the mark in the grade book, following the usual Soviet practice, but she also gave reasons each time she gave a low mark.

The pupils in the Ukrainian capital seemed to be more at ease than those in schools of the Russian republic. On the opening day of School No. 6 in Kiev grade-six pupils received an introduction to ancient history in the form of a lecture. The material dealt primarily with the geography of ancient Italy and neighboring countries and was presented through use of the blackboard and map. The pupils pointed out various places on the map. The teacher then read some sources from a textbook and ended the lesson by explaining the homework assignment. In general, the teaching of history in Kiev did not make much of an impression on an American specialist in social studies instruction. He felt that "classroom performance by teacher or pupils was not up to our best practices."

History teaching in Tashkent, Uzbekistan, was not basically different from that in any other part of the U.S.S.R., except that the Uzbek language was the medium of instruction. In School No. 20 in Tashkent the teacher in grade eight asked questions and the pupils recited in front of the map. The answers by the pupils tended to be rather long. In School No. 143 in Tashkent the tenth-grade history class was studying the Revolution of 1905. The teacher lectured for the greater part of the period on the Bolsheviks, Mensheviks, Lenin, and others, and the pupils copied from the board the factual data written down by the teacher. After the lecture, the teacher asked questions on the content. This was a "catechism routine . . . rather than questions on the meaning."

To a specialist in audio-visual instruction, the history films used to improve the qualifications of teachers in actual service seemed to have many faults — poor sound track, "quite ametrical photos," no real sets, no real acting, lip synchronization sequences of poor quality, evidence of editing splices. The film on the history of the Petro-Pavlovski Fortress in Leningrad had no actual scenes. The content was shallow and did not seem suitable for grade nine, for which it was intended.

One of the American visitors analyzed, grade by grade, the content of the geography and history courses. In grade five the pupils study the physical geography of the U.S.S.R. and the history of Greece and Rome. In grade six geography deals with physical characteristics of other countries, while history is concerned with the ancient and medieval world. Grade-seven geography covers the U.S.S.R. in a more advanced way, whereas the history class is still in the Middle Ages. In the eighth grade the pupils learn about the economic geography of the world with some stress on the people's democracies and the capitalist countries. The history course deals in the first semester with the ancient Russian period and in the second semester with European history from the seventeenth century. In grade nine the economic geography of the U.S.S.R. is again studied, while history extends from the development of capitalism up to World War I. The final grade substitutes the Constitution of the U.S.S.R. for geography. The development of the Soviet Union since the Revolution comprises the history course.

It would appear, then, that as a general rule the course in geography is not correlated with the course in history. Certainly, the teachers in these fields make cross references (as do the textbooks) to the other disciplines. The fact that the contents of the two courses are not parallel may be due, in some measure at least, to the fact that geography is considered related to the physical sciences rather than solely to social sciences. In any event, it seems that the elements of history and geography might be brought closer together by reducing the differences in content at each grade level.

Foreign Languages

The teaching of foreign languages, like the teaching of mathematics and science, is generally assumed to be of a superior order. The present writer was one of the few Americans who seriously questioned this assumption. After his first visit to the Soviet schools, in December, 1957, he described his disappointment at the results of Soviet foreign-language instruction as observed in several schools, the First Moscow Foreign Language Institute, and the Lenin Pedagogical Institute.[2]

Other members of the Comparative Education Society also expected to see exceptional work in foreign-language teaching. Instead, some students who presumably had had language in school and in the foreign-language institute did not speak with any fluency. Others had great difficulty producing anything but the simplest phrases and did not understand complicated vocabulary or complicated sentence structure. "With the exception of those who specialized in a particular language, general language teaching is not very much better than it is in the United States."

But English teachers, in particular, were greatly interested in talking with the American educators, since only a few of them ever had any opportunity to practice English outside of their classrooms. Two English teachers with whom one member of the Comparative Education Society talked for some time during a couple of hours at a restaurant in Leningrad told him of their thrill at being able to talk with people who spoke the language as natives. One of them said that it was only the fourth time in his life that he had had a chance to talk with somebody who spoke English, although he had been teaching English for eight years. English is taught with the English accent and those who speak it well speak very well. On the other hand, a number of the English teachers met were limited in their vocabulary and their choice of words, although they were easily understood. The school director who could converse in a foreign tongue was a rarity.

There are also language teachers who lack not only fluency but a knowledge of grammar. At the Moscow Institute for the Improvement of Teachers the writer met one German teacher whose conversational ability was quite good; however, she made more grammatical errors than one would expect from a teacher of the language.

At the Institute of Methods of Teaching, Director Shapovalenko expressed the dissatisfaction of Soviet educators with the state of foreign-language teaching:

> We are not satisfied with the teaching of foreign languages because pupils who complete the course have trouble expressing their thoughts and reading rather simple matter in special fields. We do have an increasing number of schools that are achieving satisfactory results in foreign languages. One line we are taking is to begin in the fourth rather than the fifth year in a few schools. And as we are going to extend school, it is clear we will add one or two years of foreign lan-

guages. Direct contact with other people will naturally lead to improvement. Our country is profoundly interested in the expansion of contacts with other countries and that explains our interest in foreign languages.

This statement reveals clearly that language learning has hitherto been below the expected level.

Shapovalenko was talking of an eleven- or twelve-year school when he mentioned that the language program would be extended by one or two years. He also said that during the Moscow Youth Festival of the previous year the Soviet young people had showed sufficient linguistic knowledge to get along with the foreign youth delegations.

The major emphasis in language instruction, according to Shapovalenko, was oral facility, although formal grammar was not to be neglected. One visitor commented, however, that he had heard the same statement from other Soviet educators but had not observed "a single instance of conversational method being used in language classes."

Out of the 625 regular schools in Moscow, a total of 400 offer the English language, while in the R.S.F.S.R. at least 50 per cent do so. Prior to World War II, 60 per cent of the pupils in the ten-year school studied German and 40 per cent English. At present, the tendency is for greater emphasis on English. All students of engineering, biology, and physics in the higher educational institutions study English.

According to the experts in the Institute of Methods, records have been widely used in language training and tapes are now being introduced. Apparently this is the extent of the utilization of audio-visual aids in foreign-language instruction. At the Institute for the Improvement of Teachers, however, it was said that "we use tapes and films, and our children write to children in the United States in order to practice" the English language.

Russian as a Foreign Language. The teaching of Russian in the non-Russian republics presents numerous difficulties. In effect, Russian is a foreign language to Georgians, Tadzhiks, and so on. The Academy of Pedagogical Sciences recognizes this problem and its Institute of National Schools deals with the techniques of teaching Russian to the non-Russian nationalities.

In Tashkent, the capital of Uzbekistan in Central Asia, the American educators had an opportunity to observe this problem at first hand. In School No. 143, as elsewhere in the non-Russian areas, study of the Russian language is begun in the first grades. The teacher of Russian literature in grade ten was a Russian woman who was particularly severe and formal. The theme of the lesson was Gorki's life and writings. The pupils, when presenting their homework reports, "would not look at the class and the rest of the class seemed rather bored. The entire work was conducted in Russian. The director of the school was in the class for about half of the period. As soon as she walked out there was considerable relaxation in the class."

An account of the same class was given by another American observer. The homework on the postrevolutionary writings of Gorki had not been done by three or four of the twenty students, and none of them had an explanation or excuse. "The teacher was very strict and hard," and she called on one pupil after another in an effort to evaluate the homework. They had to reply in good grammatical Russian and made many mistakes in declensions and conjugation endings. The answers also had to be expressed in the correct formulas, being repeated again and again until they were completely satisfactory. One part of the lesson required the students to summarize the ideological content of Gorki's writings. Through her questioning, the teacher elicited biographical details about Gorki — his close friendship with Lenin, his chairmanship of the Writers' Union, his winning of the Order of Lenin, and the change in name of the city of Nizhni-Novgorod to Gorki. Reference was also made to Gorki's earlier literary works.

Each pupil asked to recite had to answer questions on Russian-Uzbek and Uzbek-Russian vocabulary. The teacher asked such words as "greatness" and "worsening," and many pupils had difficulty with these, even after they had been repeated in class many times. The pupils tended to make frequent mistakes in using prefixes of Russian verbs; thus, one said *prodavat'* ("sell") for *podavliat'* ("suppress"). The teacher told the girl who made the mistake not to be nervous, but, when the girl became even more nervous, the teacher brought her to the verge of tears and then gave her a poor grade because she was nervous. "You could have done much better if you hadn't been nervous," she remarked.

The homework in preparation for the next lesson was to write an essay on Gorki, to prepare a chronological table of Gorki's life and works, and to sum up the ideological content of each of his writings. This was the same assignment as for the current lesson, but since it had not been properly done by the class, it had to be repeated.

The observer "was amazed at how poorly the pupils spoke Russian." She was equally astonished at the ignorance of many pupils in this grade-ten class about Russian literature and Soviet history. One boy "was completely ignorant" of the history of the Soviet Union before 1945. He did not know what Fascism meant and could not explain why Gorki had attacked it. Moreover, "many children in the class did not know about historical events in the Soviet Union between 1917 and 1930. Even the date of Lenin's death caused some hesitation, although in the end the children remembered it."

French. It is interesting to review language lessons in experimental language schools. School No. 6 in Kiev is a "French" school. French, the only foreign language, is taught by seventeen teachers. The pupils observed began French in grade one, started a textbook in grade four, and were now in grade five, using a grade-six textbook. The class was divided into very small sections. The entire class was conducted in French, and the teacher spoke with an excellent accent. After a preliminary statement on the significance of the first day of school, the teacher asked the children some questions, such as what they had done during the summer and what books they had read. She made use of picture cards in order to develop vocabulary. Giving the French name for an object on the card, she would repeat it two or three times and then ask various pupils to give the meaning of the word. The teacher wrote some words on the blackboard and the pupils copied them into their textbooks. In the left-hand column went the Russian and Ukrainian translations, and in the right-hand column some information about the word — antonym, meaning of the prefix, and the like. A pronunciation chart was used to review some of the difficult sounds in French.

The next part of the lesson was taken up by reading in the textbook. The children read a passage in the first lesson, with the teacher paying particular attention to the pronunciation, then made up sentences on what they had read and wrote them on the blackboard. Next the teacher narrated a brief story about a boy in a picture that she showed to the class. She asked comprehensive questions, paying special attention to pronunciation and vocabulary in the pupils' answers. Two children were then instructed to ask questions of each other about the picture. Whenever a mistake was made in pronunciation the teacher had the child repeat the word correctly.

For all the formality, the American observer was impressed with this particular teacher, her ability to move the class along at a rapid rate. There was a good deal of variety in the work being done, and the children seemed interested.

Another observer attended an eighth-grade French class in the same school. Since the system of a one-language school beginning with an early grade and utilizing very small sections had been in existence for only three or four years, these children had not started to study French until grade five. At first there were twenty-six pupils in the classroom but later the class was divided into two groups. According to the teacher, it was too difficult to teach a foreign language to a large number of pupils. The instructor spoke French throughout the lesson. The pupils gave the day of the week and the date of the month in French, and these were written on the board by the teacher. She also wrote in French, "We have prepared all our lessons" and "We have rested in a Pioneer Camp," which the children read aloud. The next part of the lesson took up the conjugation in the compound past tense of *parler* with the aid of a large chart showing the verb forms. This was followed by having individual pupils read a few lines of a French story. The bell rang before all the pupils had had a chance to read. Moreover, they had few opportunities to ask or answer questions based on the story. As they read, the teacher walked around the classroom and gave assistance to pupils having difficulty with pronunciation. There was no assignment at the conclusion of the period.

In grade five in School No. 29 in Leningrad the forty-three pupils were studying French for the fifth day. The classroom had one picture on the wall, the only audio-visual learning device "aside from the built-in hearing aid, the 'squawk box' from the director's office." Some pupils were at the board writing *pr, ec, m,* and *n.* The others were at their desks copying words from their textbooks into their notebooks. They copied one word many times. "The handwriting is excellent. And in a nation where the typewriter is about as nonexistent as a cash register, first-class handwriting is indeed an advantage." The children were drilled on the alphabet; several pupils in succession went to the board and drew a letter or two.

The entire textbook contained nineteen verbs and about 450 words. It had few illustrations. The highest level of difficulty in this text, which was published in 1958, were the following sentences:

> Les vacances commencent. Maman apporte deux grandes valises. Elle dit à Marie: "Marie, apporte tes robes. Prends-tu tes livres?"

German. About ten Americans, each a fluent speaker and reader of the German language, visited School No. 117 in Kiev. Opened in 1955, this became a "German" school in 1957.

The first class visited was grade five, with twenty-six pupils beginning their second year of German. The instruction was carried on in the Ukrainian language but occasionally the teacher would use a German classroom expression. There was much mechanical drill, with identical sentences being used over and over again. Some minutes were spent in drilling the pupils on how to stress the initial syllable in *Schultasche.*

The teacher then read a German paragraph and translated it into Ukrainian. She called upon several pupils, one at a time, to stand next to her desk and read and translate the same passage. The children stood stiffly at attention during the recitation.

Pupils were encouraged to ask questions of other pupils on the text, with the teacher correcting any mistakes they made in German. At various times the children copied from the textbook and from the board while the teacher walked around the room and checked the copybooks.

In the next portion of the lesson the teacher read another paragraph in German. Her pronunciation was reasonably good, but she was not fluent in conversation, although she had received the title "Honored Teacher" for excellence. After the reading she called for volunteers to retell the passage in Ukrainian. Since no one could do this she asked the children to translate the individual sentences into Ukrainian. The homework assignment was to read and translate one paragraph in the textbook. At no time in the period was any reference made to German life or culture, not even to that of East Germany.

The Americans also visited a grade-four class with eleven pupils studying third-year German. The contrast with the first lesson was very marked. The teacher, a younger woman, spoke German with ease and grace, if with a mild Slavic intonation. She gave the directions in German and the pupils had much oral practice. From time to time, there were translations from German into Ukrainian. As a basis for oral drill the teacher used pictures of summer and winter scenes. Her usual procedure was to ask, "Was ist das?" and for the pupils to reply, "Das ist ein Baum." This practice occupied the major portion of the period.

A vocabulary game followed. One pupil, the leader, asked, "Was ist das?" holding up a card with a picture of a fruit. Upon getting a correct answer, he gave the child the card. The pupils did well on the whole. The teacher made a serious effort to get them to speak and understand spoken German. Sometimes she gave her explanations in that language. Yet even she was hampered by mechanical methods.

In conversation with the teachers of German, observers noted wide variation in ability to speak and comprehend. Teachers did not seem to be particularly well grounded in German literature, history, or culture. Some said that they read the Communist writers of East Germany; most did little or no reading in the German classics or contemporary non-Communist writers. No newspaper other than *Neues Deutschland,* the Communist organ of East Germany, was read.

English. There were various reactions to the English teaching. One observer reported that some ninth-grade students of English "talked reasonably well, but others had difficulty expressing themselves" when he tried to converse with them. "I felt that all such students had considerable difficulty in understanding English when we spoke to them. I suspect that the situation in Russia may be somewhat like that of our students studying foreign language." Two other educators remarked, "We were under the impression that many of the young people could speak

English; but frequently in Moscow we asked questions that many young people could not understand. Our impression is that they are now beginning to emphasize the teaching of English but that so far they have not achieved good results."

The writer visited a grade-seven English class in Boarding School No. 10 in Moscow. The teacher called some of the twelve pupils of this section to her desk to read and translate passages into Russian and English. Directions were given in both languages. The teacher wrote the new words on the blackboard and added the phonetic signs and the Russian meanings. There was a drill on the principal parts of "go," "see," "throw," and "can." Finally, the pupils were given conversational practice through the question-and-answer technique. In all, this was a routine and uninspired lesson.

In an eighth-grade English class in the School for Labor Youth, School No. 143 in Moscow, an American educator observed a group of six boys and four girls who read aloud in English and then translated into Russian. On the board was the proclamation in English, "We Stand for Peace." After a review of the past indefinite of "to be" and "to know," the teacher read two paragraphs of new material. No pupil showed a spark of knowledge or understanding. The teacher, who seemed to have a small, rotelike knowledge of English, asked a student to stand and to explain to him word by word what the reading passage meant.

In School No. 153 in Leningrad, the only foreign language studied is English. According to the director, however, the pupils did not speak English satisfactorily, inasmuch as too much stress was laid on the teaching of formal grammar. But he also stated that the teachers were trying out other methods, particularly translation and conversation. The grade-six English class started its work with reading drill, the children repeating after the teacher. Then came reading by individual pupils, followed by translation into Russian. The teacher gave directions in English and Russian. After the reading there was drill in conversational vocabulary. The pupils asked and answered in English, "What is the English for (Russian word)?" The questions were identical and mechanically formulated. There was drill in the conjugation of "to have," as well as drill in vocabulary. The pupils worked on textbook exercises in their seats while one of them copied from the textbook on the blackboard. The teacher was very formal, but her pronunciation and fluency in English were reasonably good.

The showplace of English specialization is School No. 1 in Moscow, also known as an experimental school and as the "English" school. Here English is begun in the second grade. The experimental nature of the school dates from 1949. Pupils in the lower grades have five hours of English per week, while those in the senior grades get seven hours weekly. English becomes the medium of instruction in geography in grade eight and in literature in grade nine. All the other courses are taught in Russian. English is also practiced in several circles or clubs.

The thirty-five pupils in grade-five English were divided into three sections. The period began with a recitation of Thomas Hood's poem "The Song of the Shirt." Pupils asked questions about the title of the poem, its theme, the life of the author, and so forth. Then came the checking of the homework, which involved the writing of five sentences, such as "I want to play football," "I want to fly to the moon," "I want to shoot," "I want to read an English book." At this point the teacher announced, "Please shut the notebooks. Ivan will collect them."

The next part of the lesson was the reading of the story "The Spider That Went Around the World." Some of the children read parts as in a play. The teacher, in the meantime, used her hands — and feet — to prompt the pupils to pronounce the English words correctly. Both teacher and children spoke with a British accent. There were some corrections in pronunciation and diction. Conversational games, more or less formal in nature, a spelling game, and a homework assignment on the story brought the lesson to an end.

One of the visitors to this class said that "the teacher was animated, enthusiastic, with a sense of humor and a wide smile. She used praise judiciously.... The class was conducted entirely in English. Teacher and students speak very clearly, almost an exaggerated enunciation. Everyone in the class participated in the recitations."

Grade-seven English in the same school had two sections, each with fifteen pupils. First the homework notebooks were collected by the teacher. He called out the name of each pupil, who stood up and listened to the correction of his errors and to an explanation of the reason for the teacher's grade. The grades ranged from "1" to "5," with the lower marks being given mainly for errors in tense. The teacher's comments were punctuated by such expressions of praise as "Very clever" and "Excellent" for those pupils who did not make any mistakes.

The next activity in the lesson was listening to a recording of a small portion of Mark Twain's *The Prince and the Pauper*. The pupils followed the decidedly British accent of the recording in their readers. When a pupil was called to the front of the room she recited almost verbatim what she had just heard, while the other children jotted down in their notebooks the errors she made. Another girl who was called upon to recite verbatim seemed embarrassed, and she faltered in trying to repeat the text. Both recitations were followed by children's questions and by drills in the formation and pronunciation of the past tense. Finally, the teacher asked a pupil to state the rule distinguishing the pronunciation of such past-tense forms as "lived," "worked," and "wanted." Since the child was having difficulty expressing it in English, the teacher allowed her to use Russian, explaining that the rule had too many technical grammar terms.

An analysis by a specialist in geography of an eighth-grade class in economic geography, taught in the English language in School No. 1 in Moscow, has been reported on earlier in this chapter. It is interesting to record the comments by other observers on the quality of the English in this class. One American, a specialist in social studies, noted that the students spoke English very well and the teacher, though he was a Russian, spoke it almost perfectly. "This was the best English instruction which I saw anywhere in the Soviet Union." However, this wasn't a very good lesson. "The instructor was quite poor according to our standards."

School No. 29 in Kiev is another "English" school. In grade-two English, a game was played in which the children identified various objects in the classroom. The general procedure could be described as a "Schnitzelbank" method, after a German song:

TEACHER (pointing): Is it a blackboard?
PUPIL: No, it is not a blackboard.
TEACHER: Is it a book?

PUPIL: Yes, it is a book.
TEACHER: Is it a lamp?
PUPIL: Yes, it is a lamp.

This game aimed to develop the children's oral speech and vocabulary, but it was played "in a rote-like fashion." The other games and conversational activities were of a similar nature.

In an eighth-grade English class in the same school, one American found that "only a couple of students could hold a simple conversation in English." In another grade-eight English class "the teaching was very rigid, formalized, and repetitious. When the pupils were asked questions, they had to repeat the answers in the exact form that was given either in the book or in the phrasing of the teacher." This observer felt that the homework assignment, the writing of a theme on "My Summer Holidays," did not offer the pupils an opportunity for any creative or original thinking. Rather, it was evident that the teacher expected a routine kind of theme. Another visitor to the same class noted the mechanical drill, the teacher's and the pupils' errors in pronunciation, and the introduction of propaganda about "new Soviet construction." This particular educator commented on the discrepancy between practice and theory: "The school is known as an English school and we were told before we went to it that classes were taught in English. When we got there we found that only one class was taught in English. This happened to a number of visitors in a number of schools."

Evaluation of Language Training. The weaknesses of the teaching of English in the Soviet Union appear in the teaching of other languages. The Soviet prediction that all studies will be conducted in the foreign languages in the foreign schools in three years must surely be overoptimistic. Considerable labor by really superior teachers is necessary, together with gifted pupils, before such an end can be achieved. The Soviet authorities have made up their minds that schools teaching all languages must be created. Since a decision from above must be carried out at all cost, wishful thinking seems often to be taking the place of actual implementation.

Over-all evaluations of Soviet foreign-language instruction were not favorable. There is a certain rigidity about the method. Emphasis on correct pronunciation is so great that to some extent one feels the children are inhibited in trying to say things when they are not sure of the pronunciation. There is little of the informal give-and-take of the American classroom, although this, of course, varied with different teachers. While classroom procedures are rather similar in foreign-language teaching — and in most other subjects — methodological approaches, teachers' personalities, and results achieved in teaching vary. In other words, on the surface it might be possible to feel that the teachers are alike; yet on the basis of visits to many classes in schools in widely spaced localities it is necessary to emphasize the significant differences in teaching methods. The objective may be the same for all the schools in the Soviet Union, but the teachers differ in ability, attitude, and performance.

The accent in foreign languages was very good so far as some of the teachers were concerned and these teachers seemed to be competent in their job. In other cases they were limited by their own lack of knowledge of and experience in the foreign country. There were conversational classes held at times of the day when the visitors were not in school, but one observer noted:

> Certainly . . . , for example, in the French school in Kiev, after having attended what I thought was an excellent French class, when I wandered around in the corridors and tried to strike up a conversation in French with the children, I got very little response. Other people had the same difficulty in German and in English. Some of this, of course, might have been embarrassment.

Generally speaking, there seems to be very little projection of speaking ability beyond the content learned in textbooks.

The summarizing judgment is that the over-all effort is enormous, the time spent is considerable, and the whole approach is commendable, but as far as technique is concerned the Russians still have a long way to go. Nevertheless, Soviet leaders are determined to continue along the course they have charted. Even if the language program has been something short of a success, the aim of conversation will henceforth be made paramount. The Soviet educators are optimistic about raising the level of their teacher training and, as a consequence, about the status of language instruction in their secondary schools.

10

SECONDARY EDUCATION:

POLYTECHNIZATION

One of the most interesting and meaningful phenomena in the present Soviet educational scene is the reintroduction of polytechnical education. Professor Litvinov of the Maxim Gorki Pedagogical Institute in Kiev, who wrote his thesis on this subject, made the following statement:

> If you ask what is the most outstanding feature of education that has developed in the last forty years in the U.S.S.R., it has been the search for the true relation of general and polytechnical education.

The evolution and present status of polytechnical education in the U.S.S.R. are due to the crucial importance attached to it by the Directives of the Nineteenth Party Congress, which were drafted by M. Saburov in 1952.[1] It was then that the Party ordered the reintroduction of polytechnical instruction in the schools. But the slight progress made in this direction during the next four years led to Premier Khrushchev's impatience at the Twentieth Party Congress:

> Although the Directives of the Nineteenth Party Congress for the Fifth Five-Year Plan called for measures to introduce polytechnical

240

instruction in the schools, this matter is moving ahead very slowly. Many educationalists and numerous workers of the Academy of Pedagogical Sciences are still busy with general talk about the value of polytechnical instruction instead of doing something to put it into practice. They must be quicker about going over from words to deeds.[2]

Khrushchev's speech outlined a series of proposals for education that included part-time work in factories, construction of school workshops and experimental gardens, and introduction of polytechnical subjects.

Meaning of Polytechnical Education

What is polytechnical education? Does it have the same meaning in the U.S.S.R. as it does in Europe or the United States? In France, *école polytechnique* is a term reserved for a school of engineering. The English, on the other hand, have restricted the term "polytechnical school" to those educational institutions that provide vocational and instructional facilities for young working youth. The usage in the United States differs from both of these; here it commonly means a post-secondary educational institution offering a variety of curricula in technology, science, and agriculture. In the Soviet Union, however, the term "polytechnical" is intimately bound up with the Marxian-Leninist interpretation of communism.

The leaders of the Soviet state introduced polytechnical education shortly after the Revolution of 1917. Litvinov recommended that Book I of *Capital* be read to discover the Marxian basis for polytechnical education. Marx reveals there his belief in the greater effectiveness of formal education if taught conjointly with manual labor:

> The success of the clauses of the English Factory Act proved for the first time the possibility of combining education and gymnastics with manual labor, and, consequently, of combining manual labor with education and gymnastics. The factory inspectors soon found out . . . that the factory children, although receiving only one-half as much instruction as the children of the regular day school, yet learnt quite as much and often more. . . . The system on which they work, half manual labor and half school, renders each employment a rest and a relief to the other; consequently, both are far more congenial to the

child than would be the case were he kept constantly at one. It is quite clear that a boy who has been at school all morning cannot (in hot weather particularly) cope with one who comes fresh and bright from his work.[3]

Another reference to polytechnical education was made by Karl Marx in his instruction to the delegates to the First International. Marx pointed out three main elements as basic to an education, namely, the mental, the physical, and the technical. The latter he described as polytechnical education or getting acquainted with the scientific basis of production and developing a command of the tools of production.

Lenin advocated polytechnical education and supported the position that a close relation must exist between the mental, or theoretical, and the practical. One of the important addresses given by Lenin at the Komsomol Congress in 1920 stressed this principle. The Soviet leader asserted that there must be a close relation between schools and industrial plants, and that instruction should be intimately bound up with concrete production work. This meant, to Lenin, that each pupil must study industry generally and come to an understanding of the processes of all industrial activity.

Throughout the U.S.S.R. today there is a revival of interest in the writings of Nadezhda Krupskaya. In her essays and speeches on education she emphasized that the distinctive feature of Soviet schools should be their intimate and close relationship with labor.[4] As early as 1917 she stressed, in *People's Education and Democracy*, the need for a close relationship between mental and physical education. Consequently, with the policy decision to return to polytechnical education Krupskaya once again is being quoted and praised in education circles.

The American visitors were told many times that the aims of polytechnical training are to acquaint children with the most important branches of modern industrial and agricultural production, to impart skills in handling a great variety of materials and tools, and to develop related labor skills and endurance. The Soviet government hopes to achieve all this by combining theoretical with practical subjects, and these two with socially useful labor.

From the descriptions of postrevolutionary education in the

U.S.S.R., it is apparent that the emphasis upon polytechnical education was carried to an extreme during the 1920's. All theoretical learning was condemned unless intimately related to practical work experiences. As a result, training for engineers, physicists and chemists tended to develop low-grade technicians. Then, in 1931–1934, there was a revolt against polytechnical education; it was reduced to a separate, extremely specialized vocational training for those not pursuing a general education in a ten-year school.

Professor Aleksei Markushevich, Deputy Minister of Education of the R.S.F.S.R., sketched this period in the following words:

> The leaders of our state proclaimed polytechnical education right after the Revolution. It was developed through the twenties and thirties. During this time not enough attention was given to the theoretical development of teachers and pupils. Many experimental projects were undertaken then that interfered with the development of polytechnical education. So, in the late thirties and forties, the emphasis was upon the theoretical. Polytechnical education was de-emphasized.

Professor I. A. Kairov, President of the Academy of Pedagogical Sciences, described the reaction to the excesses of the 1920's:

> In the 1930's the Soviet schools were assigned the task of preparing youth for entrance into technical schools and institutions of higher learning by giving them a good grounding in the basic sciences. This was dictated by the necessity of preparing, in the shortest possible time, hundreds of thousands of young specialists for the nation's economy and culture. For the past 25 to 30 years, the schools have been working on the fulfillment of this task, and for the most part they have been successful.[5]

In the face of this success, one might wonder why the reintroduction of polytechnical instruction was necessary. Perhaps it was because, as might be expected from the nature of all bureaucratic systems, the professional educators were slow in putting their words into practice.

Reasons for the Revival of Polytechnical Education

The Dogmas of Karl Marx and Lenin. The highly theoretical and academic education that developed after the 1930's contradicted the early utterances of Marx, Lenin, and Krupskaya, but today posters and wall newspapers in classroom after classroom remind students not to restrict themselves to school learning but to link their education and knowledge with the labor of workers and peasants. In slightly different words, Academician A. M. Arseniev, of the Academy of Pedagogical Sciences and former Minister of Education of the R.S.F.S.R., reaffirmed the ideological soundness of the return to polytechnical training:

> We are seeking an understanding of the development of heavy industry and agriculture. This classic position was approved by our Sacred Father Karl Marx when he set forth three guiding principles for education. Education must be concerned with the mental, physical, and polytechnical development of the child.

In conferences the visitors heard again and again this direct quotation from Lenin: "To wed universal productive labor to universal education, it is evidently necessary to obligate everyone to participate in productive labor."

The Materialistic Mind.　At the Institute of Theory and History of Pedagogy, the Soviet school is viewed as an instrument for molding the naturalistic and materialistic mind of the child and for inculcating an empirical approach to truth. All knowledge should be derived from a study of matter. The foremost aim of life is to discover how matter operates, to establish relationships, and to formulate laws that will contribute to man's control over his environment. Academician Arseniev described the dialectical and materialistic nature of Soviet education:

> Our theory of knowledge is marked by two characteristic features, namely, theory of reflection and dialectics. Under our theory of reflection, ideas or knowledge reflect the objective world. Mind does not give birth to ideas, it merely reflects the world. In the foundation of the nervous system of man is a reflective state of conditioning. . . . We believe in dialectic reflection. Dialectic reflection has two characteristics: a constant state of flux or change and activity. A book that describes this is Lenin's *Materialism and Empirical Criticism*.
> Truth is everything that is correctly reflected. This is Absolute and Truth can be secured. . . . We believe the human mind can reflect properly the phenomena of nature and society.

Consequently, the reintroduction of polytechnical education is an attempt to reinforce the scientific, naturalistic, and pragmatic approach to all learning and to all questions and problems in life. As a means to this end, the number of hours devoted to practical and laboratory work, as well as the time given to field studies and factory or farm work, is being increased.

Universal and Compulsory Education. The ideal of a universal and compulsory ten-year school for all Soviet youth was proclaimed by the Central Committee of the Communist Party in 1951. With the primary purpose of preparing for the matriculation certificate, however, the junior and senior divisions of the ten-year school had taken on most of the characteristics of the prerevolutionary Gymnasium. Now with post-primary schooling compulsory for all Soviet youth, there was obviously a need for comprehensive reconstruction. Khrushchev, in the Party Central Committee report of February 24, 1956, made known the Party's dissatisfaction with the aim and content of present Soviet secondary-education practices. The report included a warning that "no small number of those leaving will at once start to work" and schools must introduce subjects that will prepare them for work.

The need for reform in the ten-year school was buttressed by statistics given to the American observers by the Ministry of Education of the R.S.F.S.R. In 1950, some 290,000 youths were supposedly enrolled in the last year of the ten-year schools. In 1951, about 350,000 students were admitted to institutions of higher learning. It is obvious that all who were admitted could not have been graduated from the regular ten-year school. The situation was radically changed by 1957–1958. Secondary-school graduates numbered 1,600,000 whereas higher institutions admitted only 440,000. Over the years a smaller and smaller percentage of ten-year school graduates were being admitted to institutes and universities. As the secondary-school enrollment continued to expand, so did the number of graduates who entered factories or worked on farms. The kind of instruction given to these students in the senior school encouraged them to think of themselves as destined for "white-collar" jobs rather than for assembly lines and collective farms. Soviet educators, therefore, were confronted with problems not too different from those that faced our own educators at the turn of the twentieth century, when the secondary school was made universal and compulsory in the United States.

In many conferences the visitors heard generalizations of which the following are typical:

> Our country has reached a level of industrial and cultural development at which the existing educational system can no longer be satisfactory to either parents, school children, or the state.
>
> In the present form Soviet secondary and higher schools lag behind the requirements of life. Their principal fault is a certain gap between the theoretical instruction given to school children and productive labor.

One of the Soviet answers to this problem is a return to polytechnical education and a kind of life-adjustment curriculum.

A Doctrinaire and Threadbare Idealism. Over the years, a constant repetition of clichés and slogans relative to the glory of work, the wonders of communism, and the benefits derived from being freed from the exploitation of an employer class is bound to result in a certain amount of indifference and callousness. Their effectiveness in motivating behavior to higher and higher standards is dubious. Khrushchev admitted this on the final day of the Comparative Education Society's visit to the U.S.S.R., when he said:

> A number of ten-year school graduates unwillingly go to work at factories, mills, collective farms, state farms and some of them even consider this to be below their dignity. . . . This lordly-scornful, wrong attitude toward physical labor is to be found also in some families. If a boy or girl does not study well, the parents and the people around them frighten the child by saying that if he does not study well, fails to get a gold or silver medal, he will not be able to get into the university and will have to work at a factory as a common laborer. . . . Such views are insulting to the working people of the socialist society.[6]

Later in this same memorandum Khrushchev revealed the hope of the Party that the introduction of polytechnical education might help youth recapture the spirit of the proletarian revolution. The goal is not only to have polytechnical education recover or establish a respect for labor but also to have laboring youth inject into the life of the factories an enthusiasm for the ideals of communism.

In addition, the Party hopes that this, in turn, will increase the quality and quantity of agricultural and industrial production.

Deputy Minister of Education Markushevich summarized it in this way: "By having students secure work experience in plants we hope to raise the qualifications of workers in factories. Requiring students to work a year or two will set a high tone in these factories."

Khrushchev was much more vocal on the point and demanded students who would know their work to perfection. Through such perfection in training these students "will be able to work more efficiently and show the workers how best and most productively to do the job."

The Integration of School with Life. While many American people are advocating a return to the abstract and the academic in curriculum content, the Party is demanding a practical type of curriculum. One is told everywhere, "The most important problem facing the ten-year school is how to strengthen the connections between school and life."

Khrushchev has devoted many words to this subject, but the memorandum of September 21 was the longest and most detailed:

> The chief and root defect of our secondary and higher schools is the fact that they are divorced from life. For this shortcoming the workers of public education and of higher schools have been criticized time and again.
>
> Our ten-year schools, however, at present are not accomplishing this task of training youth for life and are only training for entering college. . . . The greater part of them, upon finishing secondary school and receiving a matriculation certificate, turn out to be unprepared for life and do not know where to go. . . . Hence, a considerable section of the youth and parents are dissatisfied with such a state of affairs. And this process, far from relaxing, is intensifying with time. I think that this situation should invoke in us grave anxiety.
>
> Nor can we forget the specific features of the women's labor. In our country, where labor is the same in amount and quality men and women receive the same remuneration. Still, due to specific everyday conditions the woman has many other obligations which are, moreover, quite inevitable. This is to know how to nurse a child, keep house and do some amount of cooking. . . . Therefore, while at school the girls

must be taught cooking, dressmaking, needlework, and other female occupations. This must all be provided for in school curricula.[7]

The last sentence implies that this requirement could not be adequately met by an amateur circle for the few who might have an interest in one of these activities. Under the extracurricular program of the Young Communist League, opportunities were provided in the afternoon for such interest groups. These were elective, however, and chosen by only a small minority of the students.

Since the Party edict of 1956, the schools have begun to revise their curriculum to include in polytechnical education those subjects dealing with fundamentals of technology and agriculture, work experiences in school shops and in school gardens, on-the-job experiences in factories and on farms, home economics, and driver education.

The Proletarian Class. A possible danger in overemphasizing the academic program and separating the theoretical from the practical in the school is the development of two classes, the intelligentsia and the workers. Soviet educators directly and indirectly in conferences evidenced fear of the growing social distance within and between the new classes in the U.S.S.R. The word *class,* however, is not used in the Soviet Union to identify this stratification. Marx defined classes in terms of those who used private property for private gain, as opposed to those who owned no property and were exploited by the private operator. Since no one is permitted to use private property for profit-making purposes in the Soviet Union, the assumption is that there are no classes. Actually, there are great differences in private income and there exists a very definite social stratification on the consumer end of the economic system. Khrushchev referred briefly to this fact in his September memorandum to the Presidium of the Communist Party:

> . . . And, lastly, we must not ignore the fact that we still have a small number of workers' and collective farmers' children at the higher establishments. At Moscow colleges, for instance, children of workers and collective farmers comprise but 30 to 40 per cent of the student body. The rest are children of the office employees, of the intelligentsia. Such a situation is clearly abnormal, let alone the fact that the workers and collective farmers themselves are very rarely full-time students.[8]

The implication is that if this upper economic, social, and intellectual stratum is permitted to continue and is not thoroughly grounded in labor experience and in a proletarian orientation in thought, the destruction of communism is only a matter of time.

Professor Litvinov summarized this for the Comparative Education Society very well:

> The person who is inclined to be intellectual must understand the process of work and the worker as a person. This mutual understanding and respect are basic to socialism. The intellectual and the worker are both proletarians. For this reason the word "professional" is often used as synonymous with "vocational."

Polytechnical education, therefore, is an attempt to provide a grounding for the proletarian mind. At the Institute of Theory and History of Pedagogy of the Academy of Pedagogical Sciences, the visitors were told that there is nothing to be feared from such stratification so long as the upper social and economic stratum of the Soviet society, hand in hand with the lower stratum, works for the common end of bettering the collective state. It is when the upper stratum loses touch with and has few, if any, labor experiences in common with the lower stratum that class consciousness results and the capitalistic mind develops.

Several members of the Department of Pedagogy of the Lenin State Pedagogical Institute explained why this problem was so pressing:

> There has been developing a negative attitude toward physical labor and an intelligentsia has developed that has not had the experience of working with its hands. So now the aim is not only to give theoretical knowledge but also to develop the necessary love for labor and identification with labor. The real aim should be to educate people who will work with their hands as well as their minds.

I. Grivkov, President of the Trade Union of Educational, Cultural and Research Workers, analyzed this situation from the standpoint of teacher education as follows:

> If the teacher has never worked, it is very dangerous in a socialist society. All ten-year graduates should have some work experiences for two or three years and then selection for higher education should take place. If a teacher is not acquainted intimately with the life and

labor of the people, he has little in common with his pupils and he will not be able to relate his teaching to their lives.

That Khrushchev had a real concern for developing the proletarian mind is clear from the many references he made to it in the September memorandum. For example:

> We can no longer tolerate such a fallacious situation when in our society people are brought up with no respect for physical labor. . . . In a socialist society, labor must be esteemed for its usefulness, must be stimulated not only by remuneration but also, and this is important, by high respect of our Soviet public. It must be constantly inculcated in the youth that the chief thing for society is that by which society lives, namely, productive labor, because it creates material values. Work is a vital necessity for every Soviet man.
>
> I think all pupils, without exception, should be drawn into socially-gainful labor at industrial establishments, collective farms, etc., after they finish seven or eight classes. Whether in city, village, or factory settlements, all school graduates should be placed in production and no one should skip that. In the first place it will be democratic, since there will be more equal conditions for all citizens. Neither the standing of parents nor their solicitations will release anyone whatever from productive labor.[9]

The Americans were told that for the school year 1958–1959 80 per cent of all first-year registrants in institutes and universities were required to have had at least two years of work experience. Actually, there was some evidence that this rule was not rigidly adhered to in spite of general statements to the contrary.

Collective Attitudes, Habits, and Skills.   Professor Ivan Ogorodnikov, Chairman of the Department of Pedagogy at the Lenin State Pedagogical Institute, cited another reason for the introduction of polytechnical education:

> There is a need for much emphasis upon the collective in the school. In the class itself, however, there is little or no collective work. This is especially true of the humanities. . . . The collective is emphasized in the amateur circles. Some twenty-five years ago we used it widely in the classrooms. Students formed small groups and worked together. Then the experts in education reached the conclusion that such a method did not give the results expected of children. The laboratory brigade methods were used. We experimented with them but con-

cluded they did not work well in the classroom. In the humanities we used to give a whole group the same tools to work with in a laboratory. It did not work. We can, however, use this method in workshops, in industrial practice, and in agriculture. . . . Learning demands some individual work. Only when each member can find his place and contribution in group work can there be a collective.

Professor Markushevich emphasized this same point and in doing so anticipated another reason for the introduction of polytechnical education into the schools:

Labor is basic to moral development. Education in a collective and labor in a collective are both necessary conditions for the moral upbringing of children. Polytechnical training fosters the collective habits and skills.

The Soviet society has always emphasized the sense of brotherhood and common cause inherent in common manual labor. It is now making another attempt to involve its schools in this emphasis.

Moral Conditioning. A nation is able to universalize secondary education only as it becomes technologically able to release a large number of young hands from productive effort. With this release, the period of adolescence is lengthened and problems of juvenile delinquency invariably arise. In the transition to an economy of abundance, parents in greater numbers tend to indulge their children, as is evidenced in the Soviet Union in the appearance of the "jet set" and the *stilyagi*. This poses a dilemma to the Soviets, who look upon labor as a necessary condition for the development of morality. From what the visitors read and heard in the U.S.S.R., there can be little doubt that this situation is a strong reason for a renewal of interest in polytechnical education. Academician A. M. Arseniev expressed his belief as follows:

Labor has a tremendous moral and educational importance for children and adolescents. We want the younger generation of our country to combine harmoniously rich intellectual development and moral integrity with physical perfection.

At the Institute of Theory and History of Pedagogy, the same sentiments were stated:

"From each according to his ability, to each according to his need." The attainment of this great ideal does not mean that under communism labor will not be respected, that laziness and idleness will prevail. On the contrary, communism regards labor as the first vital necessity of man.

Finally, Professor Ogorodnikov emphasized the collective features of polytechnical education and the ways in which the collective is essential to character development:

> The collective does exert a disciplinary effect upon students, especially in terms of misbehaving in class, in lagging behind in class, and in preparing homework. The collective is a means of discussing problems or a form of self-criticism that is needed for moral growth.

There is no doubt that work is acknowledged to be an indispensable form of therapy in the period of growing abundance that the Soviets now face.

Economic Necessity. There is some evidence that immediate economic needs had a share in dictating the directive of the Party on polytechnization. The Soviet Union has reached a low point in its labor force because of the very small birth rate of the war years. This occurs just at a time when secondary education is being made universal and compulsory and in the face of a new Seven-Year Plan of agricultural and industrial production, the most comprehensive blueprint ever drawn by the Soviet Union in its economic competition with the Western world. The goal is to overtake the United States not only in volume of production but also in output of products per capita.

For years the authorities have encouraged graduates of the ten-year school to work in industry before going to higher institutes of learning. An employee in Radio Moscow made clear how this pressure was resisted:

> Because of the war years, I did not complete the ten-year school until 1950. The graduates of my class were encouraged to enter the factories. I chose to enter the Institute of Foreign Languages and I took the examination given by the English Department. Most of my classmates also preferred the higher institutes to work experience.

In many of the ten-year schools and higher institutions for the school year 1957–1958 an attempt was made to discourage this practice. Each establishment of higher learning was supposed to have selected from the applicants for admission only 20 per cent who had not had at least two years of work experience. There was some question as to how rigidly this regulation had been enforced. In School No. 171 in Leningrad, for example, the director reported that about 50 per cent of the graduates of that school in 1957–1958 had entered higher institutions. This was much less than the percentage in the previous year, but it was typical of the figures given in the various schools that were visited.

There is no question of the future intention of the Soviet leaders to do something to force students into manual work. Proposals for educational change were published in full in all of the newspapers during the months of August and September of 1958. Public as well as professional discussions concerning them were held throughout the U.S.S.R. The new law, the outcome of these debates, makes certain that for the next decade millions of young workers will, while they study, be placed on jobs both for production and for educational purposes.

The present output of engineers and theoreticians is evidently sufficient. It appears that the greatest deterrent to the achievement of the new Seven-Year Plan is the lack of skilled workers and technicians. Premier Khrushchev called for a sharp upgrading in the preparation of skilled workers and technicians in his September memorandum to the Presidium of the Central Committee of the Party. At the Academy of Pedagogical Sciences the American observers were given an excellent description of how this junction of general and specific vocational education was to be achieved:

We consider polytechnical education closely related to general education and not narrow vocational education. It does not mean a narrow specialization. The graduate of a ten-year school should know all of the common branches of industry and agriculture. At the same time, it does not exclude special development in one area. For example, in some of our 50 experimental schools the pupils work in school shops. Then they go out and actually work in factories, not on one job, but in a variety of work experiences. Or they may be put into a variety of plants or into various industries. In this way they will learn the common purposes and features of industry as well as the unique features. While working at one of the plants, they may develop rather narrow specializations. For example, they may work at metal fabrication or they may specialize at lathe turning in a metal machine factory.

Much of the new productive work will take place on the eastern frontier, that vast area stretching between the Urals and the Pacific, where the U.S.S.R. has the least of its population. This will necessitate movement of labor into the iron beds of Kazakhstan, the coal fields of Siberia, the steel mills of Novosibirsk, and the virgin lands around Alma Ata. The proposed plan for on-the-job work experience for all youth may be one means of getting vast numbers of adolescents to go where the work demands are the greatest.

Another economic reason for polytechnical education is that under present technological conditions rapid changes create all kinds of labor dislocations. Academician Arseniev pointed out that polytechnical education is an attempt to meet such disruptions:

> Conditions of technical progress and forms of labor change quite often. For example, a man operates one machine for years and then automation replaces him. One worker is needed instead of ten. What will be the fate of these workers? . . . Workers must be able to change their specialties. This is one of the chief reasons for polytechnical education, namely, training to give background for change.

Childhood, Adolescent, and Adult Needs. Anyone who teaches soon discovers that children and adolescents learn certain concepts and skills best at certain age levels. The Soviets have found that much of their curriculum content was not determined by this principle. It was taught too early and often without any meaning to the student. Polytechnical education will attempt to correct some of these difficulties. Professor Shapovalenko, Director of the Institute of the Methods of Teaching of the Academy of Pedagogical Sciences, cited this need: "There is a need for studying the peculiarities of children and correlating them with the peculiarities of the subjects to be taught."

Mikhail Melnikov, Secretary of the Presidium of the Academy of Pedagogical Sciences, indicated that the Department of Child Psychology in the Institute of Psychology was studying the problems that children of all ages encounter, as well as the characteristics of each age level, as a basis for curriculum change. Furthermore, new content had been added to existing courses to make them more lifelike and of more practical worth to the student. Director Shapovalenko gave an illustration of this type of change:

> One of the new changes that took place during the past year is the introduction of some elementary geometry into the primary school. We now have a special interest in polytechnical education and this requires some knowledge of geometry and measurements. So we give them knowledge of measuring lengths, volumes, and solids. Then some practical tasks are frequently given. Mental arithmetic and oral counting are being stressed because they are important in life.

He reported, moreover, that significant changes had been made in the content of many of the subjects.

The visitors were told many times that since physics and chemistry played a very important part in polytechnical training the new curriculum devoted more time to these subjects. The new courses in physics, chemistry, and biology provide a more extensive acquaintance with the use of the laws of these sciences in modern production. This led to a reduction in the number of hours devoted to the humanities. Moreover, it placed greater emphasis on the age peculiarities of the pupils than did the former curriculum.

Obviously, such changes demand a lengthening of the total number of years of schooling if the previous scope of the curriculum is to be retained. Professor Shapovalenko put it in these words:

> The length of the school period will have to be increased to eleven or twelve years to enable students to get a good general education, polytechnical education, and a mastery of some vocation or profession so that they can go directly into industry, agriculture, construction, and such work activities or go on into a high school.

The trend, however, seems to be toward establishing a basic eight-year school divided into two stages, namely, the primary and secondary divisions. Both stages will be obligatory for all children and will provide a general educational and polytechnical grounding for further years of specialization and practice.

Guidance Function. Most Americans have an idea that there is little freedom on the part of the adolescent in the Soviet Union to select his future vocation. Perhaps this was truer in the past than it is today. There was ample evidence that Soviet educators were concerned with identifying individual abilities, developing them, and utilizing the best guidance techniques in the process. From the American point of view, it is unfortunate that the Soviet educators are reluctant to use any objective tests and measurements to assist them. However, the various issues of *Pedagogy and the People's Education in Foreign Countries,* the Soviet digest of educational literature throughout the world, reveal that major attention is being given to articles on educational and vocational guidance.[10]

There is also pressure from the Party to affect a better system of guidance and selection of students for higher institutions of learning.

Soviet pedagogues freely express their doubts and problems in this area. As Mr. Grivkov put it,

> How to select for the various schools and what specialization shall we have? These are real problems. The aim of the U.S.S.R. is to achieve equal rights. Hence, special schools create a real problem. How can the state, dedicated to equality, direct children to such schools or to labor?

Of the many attempts to answer these questions only a few are cited here. They all, however, were closely related to polytechnical education. Deputy Minister Markushevich offered this answer:

> When students graduate, as a result of polytechnical training they will have some idea and understanding of the work they will enter. Students at seventeen are still young. Polytechnical training will help them mature. They will be older when they graduate, since the course will be extended, and this maturity will make for better learning. In some fields this training is not needed and bright boys will be admitted to the university without work experience in factories.

Academician Arseniev analyzed the problem in a similar way:

> Taking into consideration the multiplicity of individuals, we must

have general polytechnical education rather than early specialization. A young man can appreciate his special ability at only about fifteen or sixteen years of age. So until the adolescent is seventeen, we develop all sides to locate his special abilities.

The Minister of Higher Education, V. Yelyutin, approached it from the point of view of university administration. The suggestion made is that all entering students must work for at least one year while they attend classes. As Yelyutin stated,

> The first year or years of combined instruction and work will make it possible to discover the most able and the most diligent people who have really become fond of their future profession, and who have a strong desire for the continuance of education in a chosen specialty.
>
> Those people who find themselves by chance in a given field and who do not manifest diligence and ability in the work and in the study will leave in this first stage of education. The most deserving young people will continue their studies.

Experiments in Polytechnical Education

Combined work-study programs are not new to Soviet education. There are engineers, scientists, and agronomists working at almost every plant or farm who have done their studying while holding down a full-time job. There have been all kinds of factory and agricultural arrangements of an experimental nature. Moreover, the schools for the past several years have been experimenting in relating polytechnical education to general education. Many of the republics have introduced polytechnical vocational training of various types and at levels that conform to regional conditions. The task now is to consolidate, to coordinate, and to refine these many experiences.

Moscow. The Ministry of Education of the R.S.F.S.R., in cooperation with the Academy of Pedagogical Sciences, designed an experimental syllabus in polytechnical education and introduced it in 500 of its schools in 1956–1957. Thirty of these experimental institutions were made into eleven- and twelve-year schools. In the academic year 1957–1958 the syllabus was introduced in 25 per cent of all schools in the R.S.F.S.R. During 1957–1958, fifty of the schools were freed to experiment with students of the

upper three grades, who spent three days a week in class studying general subjects and worked in industries the other three days.
Upon graduation, these students were given certificates attesting their level of skill in a particular trade.

Members of the Comparative Education Society visited Schools
No. 1, 35, and 717 in Moscow to observe their programs in polytechnical education. Seven of the thirty rooms in each school
were given over to polytechnical instruction. In the first four
grades training was largely devoted to manual work and activity
of a very elementary kind. Organized classes in polytechnical
workshops began in the fifth grade. The first course required of
all boys and girls was carpentry and woodworking, together with
some gardening. This is what one observer reported:

> The fifth-grade class for polytechnical courses was divided into two
> groups, each with eighteen pupils. Elementary classes in metalwork
> and locksmithing followed in the junior divisions. Starting in the
> eighth grade the course included machine repair and power lathes
> together with some agriculture. In the ninth grade, students were sent
> to factories one day each week for four hours. During vacation, work
> experiences were provided in plants. Every tenth-grader took a four-
> hour course in automobile and electrotechnics. The school had its own
> car for driving practice. Parts of the car were strewn all over tables
> and the floor. One room contained all of the mechanical parts of the
> car and the other room contained all of the electrical parts.

Here is an excerpt from a more detailed report on the automobile and electrotechnics course given in School No. 717:

> The automobile course apparently was considered a highly important
> operation because it contained all kinds of parts and gadgets. On
> one of the walls were road signs that were all electrically hooked up
> so that one could push a button and flash individual signs. Moreover,
> there was an electrically controlled engine and an actual truck, com-
> plete with plastic hood so that one might view the engine as it operated.
> We were informed that this was a required subject and that one might
> obtain his driver's license after taking the course. This is quite an
> accomplishment because a license can be obtained only if one is able
> to disassemble a motor, reassemble it, and install it in a vehicle.

In every one of the schools visited ordinary classrooms were
turned into workshops. Equipment was jammed into classrooms

or basement areas that were never intended for such activities. In some of the workshops the equipment appeared to be adequate and good, while other workshops were poorly supplied or had either low-quality or old equipment. The equipment at the school in Yasnaya Polyana is typical:

> A quick visit to the workshop revealed the lack of refinement in equipment found in Soviet schools. They still use wooden planes and frame saws in their woodshop work, and, in addition, I noticed carpenters on the job using the same type of tools. Part of the shop projects in this school, however, consisted in having students make their own tools.

In School No. 35 the visitors observed a workshop in woodworking:

> The class was making wooden shelves to hold flower pots. The boards from which they were made were of extremely poor quality and would have presented a challenge to a skilled carpenter to plane them into a decent condition. Several old cans, without lids, and with a thick scum, contained the paint that was used on the completed product. The workmanship standards in this particular class were exceedingly poor.

Another report was submitted on a fifth-grade class in woodworking in School No. 1:

> The class was taught by an old man who spoke German. For thirty years he had been a shipbuilder and a sea captain. He had been teaching polytechnical courses for the past two years but he had had no special training for it.
>
> The boy and girl pupils wore little aprons. They were standing before their benches, each with a small piece of wood. The teacher was issuing planes from a cupboard when I entered. There was an atmosphere of great enthusiasm and informality. Some of the children were searching in another cupboard for additional pieces of wood. The teacher paused to scold the pupils for pushing and for getting the extra pieces of wood. There was much noise, disorder, and shouting.
>
> Of the sixteen children present out of a class of twenty, six were girls. The teacher, shouting instructions, could not be heard due to the confusion. He said to me, "They do not understand anything. They are working only for the second time this year." This was a two-

hour period once a week with a ten-minute recess at the end of a forty-five-minute period.

No attempt was made to explain to the children what they were to do or what tools were needed. While the teacher demonstrated to one of the pupils how a plane was put together, several of the children got into an argument. There were only seventeen benches for the twenty students. The teacher complained that he had been waiting a year to get the other three.

A school for laboring youth at the Likhachev Auto Works in Moscow was also visited. Schools like this one are operated on three shifts so that those who work in the morning can attend later in the day or those who work the afternoon shift can attend in the morning or in the evening. These schools, organized when secondary education was declared compulsory in 1956, are under the direction of the Ministry of Education of the R.S.F.S.R. and have the regular course of study of the junior and senior divisions of the complete secondary school. Graduates have the right to enter universities and institutes. In fact, under the policy of preferring students with two years of work experience, these graduates have an advantage over the nonworking students. Since these schools will no doubt be greatly increased in number in years to come, a short description of the Likhachev School follows:

> The school had more than 1000 students, with a graduating class in 1957–1958 of 160. The senior class for 1958–1959 numbered 220. Classes started with the fifth grade for those adults who were deprived of an opportunity for an education during and after World War II and for those adolescents who preferred to combine study with work. All students in this school were sixteen or over; some were forty years old. Youths of sixteen and seventeen were part-time workers; all others were full-time workers. The part-time students worked five hours for six days and attended classes five hours for four days. Full-time workers had to work seven hours a day for six days a week. The teaching methods consisted of study and recitation in the classroom with no assigned homework. Music, physical education, and polytechnical workshops were not required of these students. Teachers were supposed to relate whatever they were teaching to the life and labor experiences of the students. The director estimated that half of the graduates entered institutes and that about one-third of the student body were girls.

Leningrad. The well-organized program in School No. 171 in

Leningrad started its formal courses in polytechnical education in the fifth grade. It differed in many respects from that found in other Soviet cities. For example:

While boys work in workshops, girls take home economics. An experimental course of three years in sewing, apartment management, and cooking has been designed for the girls. After a course in theory and practice in machine for eighth-graders, ninth-grade boys are assigned to factories for one day each week. The main purpose is to acquaint the pupils with the processes of production, organization, and management of a particular plant. In the tenth grade there are two courses in polytechnical education. One is in electrical machinery, to give a practical knowledge of everyday electrical appliances, and the other is in automotive machinery, to give an understanding of the construction of engines. During vacation periods, students in the eighth grade are sent to collective or state farms for three weeks of work. The ninth-graders are sent to factories. These pupils are supposed to work at definite jobs under the direction of an experienced worker to get knowledge of and special skills in a job. An examination is given at the end of each vacation work experience and those who do well receive a certificate of specialization. Tenth-graders do not participate in such work experience because they must prepare for and take examinations for the maturity certificate and also examinations for entrance into institutions of higher learning.

Another observer tells of a visit to a fifth-grade class in metalwork on the day of its first meeting of the school year:

The teacher exhibited the basic tools and materials that the class would use during the school year. There were twenty-two boys in the class. Most of the students had notebooks in which they recorded the lecture word by word. All but a few of the boys wore black aprons. The teacher identified a number of files. Then he drew a picture of each and explained their functions. After this, by questioning, he reviewed the content of the lecture and demonstration.

Still another observer visited a class studying electricity:

An engineer from a nearby factory was lecturing the pupils on the subject of electricity. The pupils were standing at their benches taking notes. There were some wires and plugs on the benches. To one side of the room there were several large machines. One was a circular saw about eight inches in diameter without any protective guards whatsoever.

This shop was typical of what I observed elsewhere in the Soviet Union. The machinery was often used and worn, brought from the cooperating factories in order that children might have a first-hand experience in learning how to use it. I was told by one of the instructors that many machines were made by the pupils in the senior school.

Kiev.   Professor Litvinov reported that in the Ukrainian republic six schools had been engaged in an experimental program since 1954 and that in the fall of 1958–1959 an experimental eight-year work-study program was introduced in twenty-eight schools. This latter program covered technology of materials, electrotechnics, agriculture, machines and tools, and farm implements. Starting with the fifth grade, girls were given domestic science as a regular subject.

In the regular ten-year schools, a special polytechnical course covered three years, and certificates were issued after the completion of specialized work experiences and a successful examination. In 1958–1959, over 18,000 children were involved. Some 1500 certificates were issued in building construction, while others were issued in electricity, textile, and metal engineering.

The professors at Maxim Gorki Pedagogical Institute described what they thought was the most suitable form for polytechnical education to take in the first four grades:

> Polytechnical education in the first four grades should be organized in the most simple way in terms of the abilities of children on each grade level: papier-mâché, paper-cutting, planting and caring for flowers and vegetables, and such activities. Games should be organized in which use of simple tools and means of production are taught. Elementary reading materials should deal with the value of labor and the various means of industrial and agricultural production.

In the last two years of the ten-year school, Kiev experimented with and developed a program of polytechnical training quite different from that of Moscow or Leningrad. On-the-job training and experience were provided, not with the view of making a particular job a life vocation, but to help adolescents to understand work processes better, to appreciate the role of labor in life, and to identify their abilities and interests. Youths were sent directly to jobs or to production centers sponsored jointly by several schools and cooperating industries. Factories sent representatives to the centers to assist in organizing the workshop, providing equipment, and developing courses. They also provided experts for demonstrations and lectures and, during the summer vacations, accepted students for work assignments. If the students were sent to factories instead of centers, special training sections were created under the direction of supervisors. In effect the basic operations of the factory were concentrated in one central place for the purpose of instructing youth.[11]

The Americans visited School No. 112 in Kiev and were given this picture of its experimental plan in operation:

> Once a week for two hours a representative from the factory comes to the school to teach theory behind industrial practice. Four hours are given to industrial practices once a week in a factory. When students complete the last year successfully, they are granted two certificates. One is a certificate of maturity, which certifies that the student has reached a satisfactory level of general mental and physical development. The second certificate certifies that the graduate has had satisfactory practice in a specialized vocation together with a level of theoretical understanding. Two separate leaving or maturity examinations are given to qualify for these certificates.

School No. 117 presented a somewhat similar polytechnical program:

> None of the polytechnical classes was in action on the third of September, only the third day of the new semester, but one of the teachers was checking materials in the metalwork and carpentry shops. He said that the fifth-grade class was divided into two groups. Half of the children were given theoretical instruction in the use of metals and in the skills to be learned. The other half of the class were engaged in woodworking in another shop for three hours a week. Last year, the children of the fifth grade made a large number of little spades, about one foot in length, with wooden handles; for kindergartens in their own and other school districts of the city. When the school was in repair last year, one of the classes made 200 right-angle braces as its contribution to the reconstruction.
> The director told the visitors that the students were taken in groups around the factory under the leadership of a teacher. After some

weeks of observation, each pupil was assigned to a worker in one of the departments of the plant.

In order to make these arrangements, the director and the educational representative of the school district go to see the plant management to discuss the organization of the work of the pupils. The chief engineer of the plant is called into the conference. Experienced workers are selected and given the responsibility of working with the students. They are called together and instructed in their educational responsibilities. For assuming these responsibilities, workers are given extra pay. At first, workers use pupils as helpers but later students are given regular work assignments.

Tashkent. The practice in Tashkent in a few experimental schools appeared to consist of two hours of theory each week and three hours, after regular classes, of labor in various workshops. School No. 143 had labor practice for the boys and embroidering and sewing for the girls. All students were given experience in agriculture. All visitors agreed that the program of polytechnical education in Tashkent had not progressed very far.

Other Experiments. In conferences members of the Comparative Education Society heard many times about the experiments in Stavropol territory where the children in the upper grades were organized into teams. They participated in agricultural work and learned about farm machinery maintenance and operation. During the winter and early spring, students studied in a traditional school situation and during the other months they pursued practical courses on the state and collective farms. Members of the Society also heard about the work-study farms that had been created in a number of stock-breeding regions. Collective farms provided the schools with animals and sheds. The pupils assumed the tasks of caring for and feeding the animals in addition to their theory classes. In various regions of the U.S.S.R. schools had been created with their own work-study shops where students filled orders from neighboring factories for metal articles and tools. They built furniture for local sale and sewed clothing for children at local nurseries and children's homes.

Polytechnical Teacher Education

Unfortunately, there was not enough time to explore teaching-training programs for new developments in polytechnical education.

Professor Nikolai Alexandroff, Director of the Lenin State Pedagogical Institute, made several references to the problem of teacher preparation in this area:

> One of our problems is whether to have teachers highly specialized or teachers who are prepared to teach several subjects with a broad general background. We prefer the latter but as yet we have not had much progress in this direction.
>
> There has been a lack of relationship between the theoretical and the practical. The professors here are working on this problem of proper and adequate theoretical preparation for higher schools and at the same time for practical life.
>
> Considerable change has taken place at this institute. The faculties of physics, chemistry, mathematics, geography, and biology not only train in the discipline itself but also study electrical engineering, radio, machine operations, carpentry, plumbing, and such occupations. Teachers of mathematics must take mechanical drawing. The faculty of natural sciences gives training in agriculture, cattle breeding, and plant care in addition to the usual courses in industrial practice.
>
> Students of the first and fourth year must have one month of training in industries where they perform as workers or the biology majors go to state or collective farms. The main idea is to have students who will know not just books but who will have had many rich life experiences.

At the Herzen Pedagogical Institute in Leningrad the subject of polytechnical teacher training was discussed only briefly. The Institute emphasized polytechnical education in all of its courses where it was applicable. There were workshops and an agrobiological station, field trips to factories and farms, and six weeks of practical work in plants during the summer vacation. Physics teachers, for example, were taking courses in electrical engineering and metals.

In School No. 171 in Leningrad there were three special teachers of polytechnical education. One volunteered the following information about his training:

> I was a graduate of a technikum that prepared teachers for the specialized polytechnical courses. This technikum admitted students at the end of the seventh year of the ten-year school and required four years for graduation. Three weeks of student teaching and several courses in pedagogy comprised my professional training.

Proposed Reforms in Polytechnical Education

Over the past three years there have been many discussions and experiments relative to the nature and content of polytechnical education. The Party has demanded that something much more concrete and comprehensive be achieved. Mme. Pidtitchenko, Director of the Maxim Gorki Pedagogical Institute in Kiev, gave this summary of the thinking at the Institute on this subject:

> Pedagogical institutes, ten-year schools, and parents are all discussing polytechnical education. Our institute is working at the problem of how to prepare the teachers to direct the polytechnical education of the pupils.
>
> Some of the specialists propose to create a school with an eight-year course of polytechnical education and then all to be sent to work to get on-the-job experience for one's future life work. There are others who insist that on-the-job experience is not enough beyond the eight years. Youths should continue with either correspondence courses or study at night school. Still others are advocating extension of the ten-year school with a large polytechnical content in all courses.

Detailed outlines of the various kinds of school organizations and possible work experiences were published in all the leading newspapers of the Soviet Union in the period of September through December, 1958. A variety of proposals was suggested and legislated for the reconstruction and reorganization of the senior division of the traditional ten-year school.

New Kinds of Schools. The Soviet educators had discovered, just as we in the United States have discovered, that a number of youths either have no desire or little aptitude for continuing formal secondary schooling. It was suggested that such students might be given, after completing the eight-year school, trade training for three years in schools of three types.

The first would be schools for young workers or farmers, attended while students worked in factories or on farms. They would be made possible either by the use of two shifts, by a shorter working day, or by two or three days off work each week. Vocational part-time education, in this case, would supplement general education.

A more extreme proposal suggested that all students be forced into two or three more years of labor at the end of eight years of schooling. It was estimated that this would make available some two or three million adolescents for productive work.

A second type of school would be a general polytechnical establishment somewhat like the existing general schools with workshops. This school would be attached to an individual plant or to a state or collective farm. All youths who completed the basic school could work in factories or on farms part-time or could attend this school for three years, take workshop practice, and receive a general as well as a technical education. Where a school was not available, correspondence courses might be substituted. Many of the graduates of this kind of school would enter higher establishments of learning.

A third kind of secondary institution would be the technikum. Technikums are specialized schools in their own right, often attached to large enterprises. However, they would now provide a general and a technical education together with a specific technical skill. From these schools would be graduated skilled workers and technicians who could also go on to higher technical institutes.

A fourth type of secondary school would be for the intellectually gifted children, patterned somewhat after the existing schools for children talented in music, art, dancing, and sports. Many members of the Academy of Pedagogical Sciences appeared to favor schools for those gifted in mathematics, physics, chemistry, and biology. Provisions for these schools were eventually dropped from the Education Law of December 24, 1958.

A fifth possibility might be an increase in the number of boarding schools, which would be much like the present ten-year schools but extended for a year or two because of a greater emphasis upon general and specialized polytechnical training.

All these possibilities are now being considered. Contrary to the views expressed in American circles, Soviet educators argue that their intention is not to deprive great masses of Soviet youth of post-eight-year schooling. Rather, the new multiple-track system is an attempt to remove the hurdles created by the present single and highly academic ten-year school and, therefore, to make it possible for the great majority of Soviet youth to complete successfully some kind of secondary education. The fact is, however, that the majority of the fifteen- to eighteen-year-old youths will be deprived of any reasonable nonvocational education — and not through their own choice but because the educational system will be set up in such a way as to channel them into schools that have a primarily vocational orientation. A clear-cut picture of what will happen to Soviet eighth-grade graduates is now beginning to emerge. About 60 to 75 per cent of them will be inducted into direct employment and asked to study in schools for working and rural youth or "alternating-shift schools." About 15 to 30 per cent will be permitted to go into the ninth grade of the three-year senior schools, which will be called general polytechnical labor schools. The remaining 10 per cent will be allowed to enter technikums.

Problems of Polytechnical Education.   Many problems have already been created by the return to polytechnical education and still more will come into being with the changes introduced in the 1959–1960 school year. The problem of the large financial outlay for the program was mentioned in several conferences. School No. 143 in Tashkent, for example, had not moved very far toward introducing a polytechnical curriculum, as its director admitted: "The big problem we face is that of broadening the polytechnical education and providing work experiences on the job. We have done some things in agricultural training but little in the industrial." Those who visited the schools in Tashkent needed no imagination to tell that lack of finances was one of the obstacles in the way of inaugurating the programs being tried in Moscow, Leningrad, and Kiev.

The financial problem was not confined to Tashkent. The chairman of the city board of education of Leningrad indicated a concern over this matter:

> We are introducing new programs of home economics. Sewing workshops and laboratories for apartment management and cooking are being developed for girls. Some are of the opinion that these subjects should be introduced for boys as well. The city board of education must supply the material and the equipment for this new program. We are also having to buy much new equipment and material because of the introduction of polytechnical education in other grades and classes. The cost for such classes is much greater than that for general education.

The per-pupil cost of polytechnical education is increased by the need for smaller class sections. The average class size in the cities is about thirty pupils. Dividing these classes for specialized poly-technical courses doubles teacher costs. In addition, on-the-job pro-grams require administration and supervision which are much more costly to the local school system. Inevitably, the per-pupil costs of education in the Soviet Union will rise steeply.

The proposal to excuse those who are gifted from the work-experience programs was not well received by many in the Soviet public, to judge from the number of letters in *Uchitelskaia Gazeta* opposed to it. The opinions were that the establishment of special schools for the gifted would place a particular group of chil-dren in a privileged position and would cause many overzealous fathers and mothers to fight to get their children admitted to such schools.

Another difficulty is the dependence of the school upon the fac-tory or farm that is near the school. This tends to tie the school program too narrowly to the limited resources of the community, which, in turn, may lead to a narrowing down of the educational opportunities of the pupils. The creation of a central industrial workshop or a model agricultural farm may obviate this difficulty. If individual talents are to be respected and cultivated, however, it is evident that the program will not only be very costly but may also require boarding pupils.

Khrushchev has shown that he is aware of the many obstacles that are likely to be encountered. In his memorandum of Septem-ber 21, he indicated his concern over the present polytechnical labor practices:

> Production practice should be pursued more deeply, not as it is done now. Today, students doing work practice spend much time loitering around the factory. One works while ten or fifteen of his comrades only look on, themselves afraid to come near the ma-chine.[12]

There are many reasons why enterprises do not like practicing students. Beyond the usual reasons given, such as that they are nuisances, there is the consideration that many Soviet factories oper-ate on a quota basis. If production exceeds the quota, all employees and the manager share in a bonus. Workers often operate on a piece-work rate and the weekly wage is based upon production units. Khrushchev in this same memorandum dealt with the dislike of many factory managers for student employees:

> The managers of enterprises, too, little trust the practicing students, because they have no qualifications. If they be given the task of operating a machine, there would be a waste in productive capacities and productive possibilities. The enterprises do not like such practicing students.[13]

Obviously, the changing of content and methods will require a new kind of teacher. This will call for a complete overhaul of pedagogical institutes and the re-education of the teachers now on the job. The seriousness with which this problem is being attacked is illustrated by a letter that the Comparative Education Society received from Mr. Grivkov, President of the Trade Union of Educational, Cultural and Research Workers:

> It is necessary to prepare new curriculums and textbooks, to revise methods of teaching of many subjects, and so forth. Besides changes in content of education and its methods, a wide network of courses must be established to enable teachers to raise their skill. To fulfill these great tasks it will be necessary for all educational authorities, trade union and other public organizations, and everybody in schools, higher educational establishments and scientific institutions to carry out a very large amount of work.

Finally, the centralized nature of Soviet education will have to undergo a change. The proposals for polytechnical education will require each republic and, in turn, each region and city to work out its polytechnical program in accordance with the specific possibilities and limitations of the economic, cultural, and geographical resources of the area. This will call for an administrative flexibility and a professional creativity on the local level that, in the past, have not been encouraged in the U.S.S.R.[14]

11

HIGHER EDUCATION

The aims of Soviet higher education are formulated in the charter for higher educational establishments, as follows:

In accordance with Article 121 of the Constitution of the USSR, higher educational establishments put into practice the right to education of all citizens of the Soviet Union and have as their aim the preparation of cadres capable of mastering the latest science and techniques, armed with knowledge of scientific socialism, ready to defend their Motherland and utterly devoted to the cause of building a communist society. [1]

Higher education consists, for the most part, of five years of training beyond the ten-year school. It has none of the characteristics of the American liberal arts education. Rather, it is highly specialized and turns out qualified professionals.

General Characteristics

Graduates of the general schools and the best graduates of the technikums may continue their education at the various institutions of higher learning — universities, technical institutes, medical institutes, conservatories of music, institutes of fine arts, pedagogical institutes, and many other establishments offering high-level training for specific professions.

Administration.   Over-all control of institutions of higher learning is vested in the U.S.S.R. Ministry of Higher Education. This is a union-republic ministry, having a central ministry in Moscow for the whole union and subordinate ministries in each of the fifteen constituent republics. Until 1959, however, only the Ukrainian republic had established a ministry of higher education on the republic level, perhaps because in the other republics there were not enough universities or institutes independent of the control of other ministries to warrant separate administration. Other republics are reported to be establishing such ministries at present.

The current trend toward combining administration of institutions of higher education with that of the technikums is forcing administrative change. A further shift toward the republic level of administration may be foreseen from the decision of the Council of Ministers, published on June 27, 1959,[2] to rename the Ministry of Higher Education the "Ministry of Higher and Special Secondary Education" and to combine the administration of higher institutions and special secondary schools. The Union Ministry of Higher and Special Secondary Education is to *assist* the republics in research, supply of educational aids, finance, and construction. Actual decisions on policy and program are to be in the hands of the republic councils of ministers and republic ministries of higher and special secondary education. At the time of writing, these plans have not been fully carried out. The discussion that follows describes, therefore, the situation in force at the time of the visit of the Comparative Education Society.

The Ministry of Higher Education of the U.S.S.R. has thus far been responsible for curricula and academic standards for all institutions of higher learning in the Soviet Union; it also controls textbooks. Boris Gerashenko, Deputy Minister of Higher Education of the U.S.S.R., explained that:

> The Ministry of Higher Education, through its Scientific Council, made up of fifteen permanent members, makes all the decisions on curricula. For example, recently, the Council, aided by prominent

mathematicians, decided to increase the number of lectures on mathematics at the expense of those on technical subjects, in certain fields. However, specialized institutes can make their own curricula.

Final decisions in the Ministry are made after an examination of the suggestions and recommendations of the academic councils of the universities and institutes.

There are some exceptions, notably engineering schools and such large schools as the University of Moscow, which are permitted to structure their own curricula.

The Ministry of Higher Education controls directly many academic institutions and exercises supervisory and regulatory powers over those it does not directly control. Many institutions of higher learning are connected with the ministry responsible for the industry or profession that they serve. Thus, medical institutes are under the jurisdiction of the Ministry of Health, institutes of fine arts or conservatories of music use the facilities of the Ministry of Culture, institutes of agriculture are under the Ministry of Agriculture, and so forth. This, explained Mr. Gerashenko, is a convenient arrangement for the students:

> Imagine how inconvenient for the students of a medical institute, if they could not go straight from the lecture room to the hospital to do their practical work. They would have to go to the telephone from the lecture and ask the hospital; "Please tell me where the heart and lungs are!" Or the students of a drama school would have to beg the Ministry of Culture for a stage to practice on and this would lead to a great deal of red tape.

Apart from the institutions controlled by the Ministry of Higher Education, and those controlled by the ministry most concerned with the work they train for, there is a network of higher Party schools. According to Gerashenko,

> The Ministry of Higher Education does not administer these higher schools. We merely supply them with their curricula, but their work is independent of our ministry. They train journalists, magazine writers, specialists in political economy, and so on.

Extent of Higher Education. In 1958 there were 2,061,000 students enrolled in institutions of higher learning in the Soviet Union. Of these, 758,000 were registered in technical institutes or faculties, 770,000 were in pedagogical institutes, 184,000 were studying political economy and 178,000 medicine. Gerashenko made the following statement:

> As of nine o'clock this morning [August 25, 1958] there are 727 higher educational institutions other than universities in the U.S.S.R.; 198 of these are under the jurisdiction of the Ministry of Higher Education. Of the 727, 200 are technical institutes, 200 are pedagogical institutes, 100 are agricultural institutes, 70 are medical institutes, and 30 are institutes of railroad communications. The rest are conservatories, institutes of physical culture, drama schools, and so forth.

There are thirty-nine universities in the Soviet Union, at least one in each republic, and Mr. Gerashenko reported that in 1958 five new universities had been chartered.

Higher education in the Soviet Union is open to any student who has finished the ten-year school, who is under thirty-five years of age, and who satisfies the entrance requirements of the institute or university he chooses. Until recently entrance requirements consisted only of a series of competitive examinations. Recently another requirement has been added. The number of vacancies each year is determined by the needs of the economic plan, and a steadily increasing percentage has been reserved in recent years for applicants who have had two years of work experience after graduation from the ten-year school.

The reasons for this requirement and the practical limitations of its operation have been stated in previous chapters. In addition to manpower needs and the fear of growing social divisions, another reason given by Professor Markushevich and emphasized by many Soviet educators is the following:

> We believe that at seventeen a ten-year school graduate is not mature enough to choose his future profession wisely. If he goes to work for two years before he goes on with his education, he will know a little more about life and he will pick his future specialty with more wisdom.

Considering the highly specialized training given by Soviet institutions of higher education, this argument seems sound and valid.

Higher education is free, and needy students receive state stipends. The amount of the stipend varies according to the type of institution and to the number of years the student has attended the institution. As the student advances from one year to the next, his stipend increases. Mr. Gerashenko reported that stipends varied between 250 and 750 rubles a month. However, these figures were not completely in agreement with others quoted by various authorities and officials. The rector of the University of Central Asia, in Tashkent, said that the lowest stipend his students received was 220 rubles a month; on the other hand, the Gorki Pedagogical Institute in Kiev reported that the starting stipend for students there was 300 rubles a month, and at the University of Leningrad the starting stipend was quoted as 290 rubles a month. Students must do well in their academic work to retain their stipends. If a student does failing work or if he does not conform to social behavioral standards, he may lose his stipend. An honorary stipend for excellent achievement can be awarded to an outstanding student, over and above his regular provision.

In addition, students are provided with free or very cheap housing if they cannot live at home. Students of the Kiev Institute must pay only fifteen rubles a month for accommodation in the student hostel. At the University of Moscow student apartments, consisting of two rooms and a bath, are free; each student has his own small bedroom, which is furnished with a bed, chair, desk, and bookshelves, and each floor has a kitchen where students can make tea and snacks. Those students who live far away receive free transportation.

Higher educational institutions have full-time day divisions, and evening and correspondence divisions. The latter are maintained for the benefit of students who want to complete their education while working. Evening courses are generally given by the same faculty as the full-time courses and have the same curricula and standards. The only difference is that evening students take one year longer to complete their studies. Correspondence courses are usually given by a special faculty and the curriculum differs from that of the full-time and evening programs. Correspondence students come to the institution twice a year for special lectures and examinations. The course of study is adjusted to their needs. Hence, the official in charge of the curriculum of correspondence courses for the natural sciences at the University of Moscow felt that his offerings were an answer to the new Soviet educational postulates:

One advantage of correspondence students over full-time students is that they need less laboratory work, as they have so much practical experience gained in the course of their work.

Admission to evening and correspondence courses is by competitive examination, as in the full-time division. The only difference in admission requirements is that applicants are not confined to the age limit of thirty-five years. Students get special leaves of absence from their jobs (without loss of pay) to come to the institutions for entrance examinations and the twice-yearly lecture and examination sessions. Soviet educators maintain that there is no difference in academic standards between these several divisions.

Universities

Staff. Universities are headed by a rector appointed by the Ministry of Higher Education. He is assisted by a prorector. The executive organ of the university is the academic council, headed by the rector and consisting of the heads of the various faculties and prominent department heads. The academic council of the University of Moscow comprises sixty members. It determines academic plans within the framework of the regulations laid down by the Ministry and coordinates those plans for the whole university. It also elects professors and docents, subject to confirmation by the Ministry, and appoints the minor staff members — the instructors and assistants.

Universities are divided into faculties according to the various fields of specialization. Each faculty is headed by a dean and has its own academic council, which makes decisions for that faculty. Faculties, in turn, are divided into "chairs" (*kafedry*), or departments, headed by prominent professors or scientists. The University of Moscow, for example, has thirteen faculties, six in the natural sciences, seven in the humanities, and two hundred chairs.[3]

The teaching staff of a university consists of professors, docents, instructors, and assistants. The last two are appointed by the university academic council from persons who show a special aptitude for teaching. Professors and docents are elected for a period of five years. When a position falls vacant after five years, the university publicly announces a "competition" for it. The announcement is given wide publicity in the newspapers and all who are qualified may apply. It is not quite clear of what the "competition" consists. It seems safe to assume, however, that it takes into account scientific achievement in the candidates' special fields. The prorector of the University of Moscow put it this way:

> It is true that every professor, without exception, must compete with others for his position every five years. However, with some professors competition is not possible. For instance, we have Professor Nesmeyanov [the president of the U.S.S.R. Academy of Sciences] on our faculty. It would be hard to find anyone who can compete with him. Thus, great professors are always re-elected unanimously.

All professors are expected to do some independent research. The vice-rector of the Shevchenko University in Kiev stressed that "the principle of work at the universities is the correlation between teaching and scientific work." Many professors have contracts with industrial enterprises to help them solve specific problems. For this kind of work a professor is paid over and above his regular salary. In Kiev, according to the vice-rector, during the year 1957–1958 the university was given 4.5 million rubles to finance research by industrial enterprises.

It is difficult to determine the exact teaching load of a professor. Although he is supposed to work six hours a day, six days a week, it is hard to find out how this time is allotted between actual teaching and other duties. The information from Mr. Gerashenko was that

> We no longer tell a professor how many hours he should teach. Some are better at lecturing, some excel in research; it all depends on the wrinkles of the brain. We believe that each man should decide for himself how much time to devote to teaching and how much to other work.

Since work at the university must be planned and organized and the requisite number of lectures delivered, this statement must be received with some skepticism.

Salaries of the university teaching staff vary according to rank. At the University of Leningrad visitors were told that an assistant starts at 1500 rubles a month, a docent at 3200 rubles a month, and a professor at 4500 rubles a month. A chairman of a department receives an additional 500 rubles a month. Additional outside income may range up to one and one-half times the base salary.

Admissions and Curricula.   A person eligible for admission to a higher educational institution may apply to any faculty of the university of his choice. All applicants must pass an entrance examination in Russian language and literature. In addition, each applicant must take an examination for the particular faculty in which he wishes to study.

As there are always more applicants than vacancies, the examinations are very competitive. The prorector of the University of Moscow reported, for instance, that in the year 1957–1958 the University had 8000 applications for 2800 vacancies. Gold and silver medal holders from the ten-year schools used to enter the universities without examinations; now they must pass the examinations, but they are admitted ahead of the other competitors. All others are graded and are admitted according to their performance. All applicants must pass all examinations. If a candidate fails to reach a passing grade on one examination, he is ruled out of the competition. A candidate who fails the entrance examinations one year is permitted to try again as often as he likes.

At the University of Moscow, 16,000 out of a total of 24,000 students are enrolled in the regular full-time division, about 6000 in evening and correspondence courses, and about 2000 in graduate programs. At the Shevchenko University in Kiev 11,000 persons were enrolled in all divisions, while the University of Leningrad reported 9000 day students, 3000 evening school students, and 3000 correspondence students. The University of Central Asia had 4000 full-time and 1000 correspondence students.

The Soviet university generally has six schools (*fakultety*): physical and mathematical sciences, biology, chemistry, geography, philology, and history. Other schools that are found in some Soviet universities are economics, jurisprudence, and geology. Most specialized higher educational institutes, where the greatest number of young people study, are divided into five classes: engineering-industrial, agricultural, socioeconomic, education and the arts, and health and physical education. In all, about sixty training programs are administered by the universities and institutes in the U.S.S.R.

A student in a higher educational institute takes from 4500 to

5500 hours of instruction in twenty-five to thirty-five subjects during his period of study. Curricula in all faculties are rigid and highly specialized. Students are trained for a specific profession and no general educational courses are offered with the exception of the courses in history of the Communist Party, Marxism-Leninism, dialectical and historical materialism, and political economy, which are compulsory for all students. Every student must also take military training, two years of physical training, and two years of a foreign language. Students must take general courses in their field of specialization for the first two or three years. Specialization within that field is permitted in the third or fourth year of study, according to the faculty. The academic year is divided into two semesters. The few electives appear only in the years of specialization. Science students are not allowed any elective courses. For the first two years, a science student takes biology, chemistry, physics, mathematics, and other scientific subjects, but most of his higher education is devoted to the science or sciences constituting his specialty.

G. I. Nekrasov, the official in charge of curricula for the natural science faculties of the University of Moscow, gave the American visitors a sample curriculum for the chemistry faculty. In the first semester of the first year a chemistry student must take a course in Marxism-Leninism, a foreign language, inorganic chemistry, some laboratory work, and physical culture. In the second semester of the first year physics is added. In the second year he carries Marxism-Leninism, a foreign language, analytical chemistry, organic chemistry, physics, higher mathematics, and physical culture. In the third year the courses are political economy, a foreign language, higher mathematics, physics, and various branches of chemistry (radio chemistry, chemical technology, physical chemistry, molecular structure); in the fourth year, dialectical materialism, inorganic and analytical chemistry, physical chemistry, chemical technology, colloidal chemistry, and chemistry of crystals. It is in this year that the student chooses one of four specialties: inorganic and analytical chemistry, physical chemistry, organic chemistry, or radio chemistry. He now starts on his specialization, gets a special place of work in his department, and is assigned his own scientific adviser. At this stage also he starts work on his diploma project. In the first semester of the fifth year the student finishes all his lecture courses and current work. He also takes a course in the history of chemistry. The second semester is devoted to the diploma project. In June of the last year the student must defend his diploma work and pass one state examination.

At the end of each semester all students take examinations. In addition, during the semester there are various checks and controls. If all "control assignments" and examinations are satisfactorily fulfilled, promotion to the next year is compulsory. Visitors were informed by Soviet educators again and again, "We don't believe in the 'eternal student'; all students must move up from year to year or give up their studies." At the end of each year the student also must complete a small independent work, called a course paper. This paper must deal with a different course each year.

To sum up the sample curriculum for the Chemistry Faculty of the University of Moscow: of a total of 4600 study hours, 500 are spent on the social disciplines, 270 on a foreign language, and 136 hours on physical culture. The rest of the time (3694 hours) is devoted to the special faculty field.

The work load changes with the year of study. In the first year in the Chemistry Faculty the student must attend lectures for thirty-six hours a week (this includes laboratory work and seminars) and work at home for three to four hours daily. In the second year this load is reduced to thirty-two hours and in the third year to thirty hours a week with one day left free for the student to do independent work. The latter applies to the fourth year as well, and the best students are no longer compelled to attend lectures. However, all students have to complete all control assignments, papers, and other requirements and must pass all examinations.

Examinations are usually oral. The student draws a ticket with three questions on it. He has a little time to prepare and organize his thoughts and then must give as complete an answer as possible to the examining committee. He is graded on his examinations in the way used throughout the school system: "5" is excellent, "1" is failing. Grades are the only measure of performance although Soviet educators are not wholly satisfied with this system. As Professor K. Topshieva, Dean of the University of Moscow Faculty of Chemistry, put it,

It is sometimes very hard to grade answers given in examinations and to evaluate them correctly. Departments and professors give much thought to the subject. Generally speaking, answers deserve the mark of "5" only if the student knows material in addition to the answers called for by the questions.

In this connection, she continued, it is very important for the students to do a great deal of laboratory work; it helps them get better marks because they understand the material more thoroughly.

If a student fails to pass one or two examinations, he can try again after the vacation. Should he fail in three or more courses he is asked to leave the University. Mr. Nekrasov put it this way:

> We usually advise such a student to go to work for a few years, especially if he failed through laziness, indiscipline, or other such reasons. After this period he may come back. However, there is nothing to prevent his applying to another higher educational establishment in the country.

Much effort is expended to prevent a student from failing and he is helped by the professors as well as by his fellow students. When asked about the number of failures among students, Professor Topshieva replied,

> Ninety-six per cent of our students pass their examinations and finish the course. Of these, 70 per cent get excellent marks or good marks; only 50 or 60 students in the whole department — out of a total number of 1500 — get unsatisfactory marks. Some of these students pass their examinations on the second try. About 10 to 15 per cent of the students drop out each year for various reasons. Most drop-outs occur in the first year.

Practical work in the student's special field is also stressed and, according to Soviet educators, will be increasingly stressed. In the Faculty of Chemistry students have seven weeks of practical work during the fourth year in addition to laboratory work at the University. They are sent to various chemical plants according to their own wishes and those of the administration and may not stay in Moscow but be sent to other parts of the country. The University plans the students' work jointly with the plant leaders. The great majority of students are attached to engineers or laboratory workers as assistants. In the chemistry curriculum 2100 hours are spent on laboratory and practical work.

The program of studies outlined above is more or less the same for all faculties. Within a department students are arranged in groups of twenty-two to twenty-five. Each group is assigned one professor, one assistant, and one instructor. In this way each student becomes well known to his teachers and can get individual attention. This system also permits the professor to keep a thorough record of the student's academic achievement. Both the academic and the "social" record are considered when job assignments are made.

The Diploma Project. Special mention must be made of the diploma project, a distinctive feature of Soviet higher education. This is a piece of independent and original research that every student must complete before he can graduate. The theme for the project must be approved by the chief of the department where the student is enrolled. The student then works under the direction and with the advice of his scientific adviser.

According to Professor Topshieva, great care is exercised that the choice be realistic:

> Sometimes the student will pick a theme that is entirely new and original; this may prove to be a risk for the student, as his research may not yield positive results and he will have to defend what he has done.

Before a student undertakes a piece of research for his diploma project, he must do some special practical background work that will be the foundation for his thesis and will prove that he is well enough grounded in the special field to go on with the proposed diploma work. When he has decided on the theme and has the background for it, he writes a literary outline to show that he understands the basis of the subject. Then he begins a period of about eight months of practical work. During this time he makes informal periodic reports to his adviser on his progress. The reports are made orally and are very important for the student, as the adviser may give valuable advice at this time.

When the thesis is written, the student delivers it to the University, together with accounts of his experiments and the literature he used. The dean of the faculty then fixes a date for the defense of the thesis. One member of the Comparative Education Society was given a description of this defense, which almost amounts actually to a defense of a doctoral dissertation. According to this source the defense is a public affair and takes place in a gala atmosphere. The date is announced ahead of time in the newspapers as well as at the University. A commission is named to examine the thesis, and it is before this commission that the student must appear. An opponent is designated whose duty it is to read the thesis and to expound his objections. On the day of his defense the student reports to the commission for about twenty minutes, telling about the aim of the thesis and the results obtained. The commission pays special attention to the way the student presents his work. When he has finished his presentation, the official opponent takes the floor and gives his estimate of the work and his criticisms. The student must then defend his work. After this the student's supervisor gives his evaluation of the work and of the student's achievement. Then the floor is thrown open to comments and questions by the audience. The student has the right to say the final word. At the end the commission decides in a closed session whether to accept or reject the thesis. If a diploma project is good enough, it may be published in a scientific journal.

In view of the large numbers of graduates each year, the load of oral examinations thus conducted must be truly formidable. Even more elaborate proceedings take place on the occasion of the defense required for graduate degrees. Relatively few students are recommended for graduate work, which is not, as in the United States, a qualification for an increasing number of the professions but rather a highly specialized preparation for university teaching and research. The two graduate degrees in the Soviet Union are the degree of *Kandidat Nauk*, which involves the defense of yet another thesis and at least three more years of study, and the highest academic degree, that of Doctor of Sciences, which requires several more years of active work and implies original contributions to the area of specialization. Degrees of Doctor of Sciences are awarded comparatively rarely and are a very high distinction indeed. The degree of *Kandidat* is probably higher than the American master's degree but lower than the American doctorate. It carries a great deal of prestige, and academic persons possessing it were introduced to the visitors with the title *Kandidat Nauk* preceding their name. Persons studying for the degree of *Kandidat* and Doctor do so at the universities or in research institutions not devoted to the function of teaching. For instance, the staff of the Sector for the Study of Contemporary Education Abroad, attached to the Academy of Peda-gogical Sciences, includes several aspirants and *Kandidats*. [4]

Job Assignments.   Plants and enterprises send lists of their labor requirements to the various ministries. The ministries in turn send these to the universities and institutes. About three months before graduation, job opportunities in the various fields are posted in the universities and institutions of higher learning, and students may apply for the position of their choice. Actual assignments are made by a state commission, which includes in its membership officials from the universities as well as officials from the ministry. Prorector Ivanov of Moscow University explained that

> The state commission tries to take everything into consideration when making the assignments. We take into consideration the stu-dent's record, his ability and his preferences. We think about his health and marital status. If the student is married, we try to get him a job which will not separate him from his wife; thus a man married to a major in forestry will be sent to a country district where his wife will also find work.

When such job assignments are made, the student is bound to accept. On being asked whether a student could refuse to go where he is sent, Ivanov replied that the commission was so careful to take the student's best interest into consideration that he hardly ever found reason to complain about the assignment or to refuse to go. When pressed on this issue, Mr. Ivanov replied smilingly:

> We always hear from Western observers how we force our students to go where they do not want to go. These writers always pick jobs in Siberia as horrible examples of assignments which the students do not like; why, Siberia is a very well-developed place now and has a lot of cultural facilities, besides having the most healthful climate in the world. Anybody would be glad to go there!

The question of whether the student had the right to refuse to go where he was sent remained unanswered. The implication was clear, however, that refusals were not possible unless there was a cogent reason which the commission had overlooked. Mr. Ivanov did admit that reasons of health could influence the commission to reconsider an assignment.

The years of study are years of hard and concentrated work for the Soviet student. As Deputy Minister Gerashenko put it,

> While the student is at a higher education institution he must study, study, and again study. The state is spending a great deal of money on him and he should realize this. When he is older and has achieved something, then he can rest.

This does not mean, however, that there is no time for recreation. Circles flourish in the universities as they do in the schools. They are part relaxation, part research work in the student's field. According to one student at the University of Moscow, each person is required to join at least one such circle. He may join more if he has the time. Moscow University has a beautiful auditorium that is used for student performances of plays and operas. The state also organizes summer vacation camps, trips, and hikes, as well as sports competitions and games. The role of the Komsomol organization in student life is considerable. It will be described in a subsequent chapter.

Institutes

Institutes of higher learning are organized on much the same principles as the universities but are usually limited to one broad specialty.

The Polytechnical Institute in Kiev admits students from the ten-year schools and the best graduates from the technikums. Each applicant must pass five admission examinations: in mathematics (written and oral), physics, a foreign language, Russian, and Ukrainian. "Our admission standards are very high. Only those who make the highest marks are admitted," maintained the director of the Institute. He explained further that the highest possible mark in the entrance examinations is 25; this represents a mark of 5 in each examination. Only those candidates who achieve a mark of 23 in the entrance examinations are admitted. The director stated proudly that because of these high admission standards the Institute has an insignificant number of failures and drop-outs; in the year 1957–1958 there were only thirty-two failures.

The Institute is divided into ten faculties, which train specialists in various fields. Four of these faculties are electrical engineering, mining, metallurgy, and chemical technology. Each faculty offers a five-year course of study, during which students leave the campus of the Institute for three periods of work in industry. After the last period of practical work, the student starts work on his diploma thesis, which takes about sixteen or seventeen weeks to prepare. When he has defended this before a commission, he takes a last examination before a state commission made up of faculty and industry specialists. If he successfully passes it he is graduated and recommended for a job by his faculty. Job assignments are handled in the same way as in the university, and a graduate must be kept in his first job for at least three years. He cannot be dismissed from it unless a job of equal standing is found for him, nor can he leave at will.

The Kiev Institute has an enrollment of 8000 regular, 1100 evening and 3500 correspondence students. "We graduated 1570 engineers in 1958 and we plan to graduate 2000 in 1959," stated the director. In general, the institutes are much smaller than the universities.

Students' stipends range from 300 to 600 rubles monthly, depending on the year of study and the student's marks. Students also are housed very cheaply in hostels and receive free medical care in the clinic and hospital attached to the Institute. When they graduate and start on the first job their starting salary is about 980 rubles a month, except for graduates of the Mining Engineering Faculty, who receive 1200 rubles a month.

The Kiev Institute has a staff of 700, of whom seven are members of the Academy of Sciences. There are 40 professors and 180 docents as staff. Faculty members must work six hours a day, six days a week, and a professor lectures about 500 hours a year on an average. But here too, as at the University of Moscow, the visitors were told by the director, "We require faculty members to do independent research, and the ones who are more talented for research have their lecture loads lightened." A professor is paid extra for the research work he does, sometimes up to 50 per cent of his base salary. Especially talented students may work with the professors in research projects that may be suggested or requested by industry or may be the original idea of the Institute members.

For relaxation the students themselves have built a summer camp on the banks of the Dnieper with materials supplied by the Institute. There are also many clubs and circles. Each faculty has its own wall newspaper and the Institute has an over-all newspaper.

Komsomol influence on the students in the Institute is just as strong as in the universities. The Komsomol keeps records of the students and watches over the achievement of the individual student. On this point the director of the Institute said:

> If a student fails, he is lazy or undisciplined. We screen our applicants so carefully before admitting them that the cause of failure cannot be that the lecture is too difficult for them. If a student fails consistently, the Komsomol leaders must see whether they can bring the student up to standard again.

He went on to say that professors also help the slow student, so that many failures are avoided and there are very few drop-outs.

Medical Academies

Medical academies differ slightly from the institutes and deserve, therefore, to be treated separately. Medical training takes place on two different levels. First, undergraduates are trained in a medical academy or, less often, in the medical faculty of a university; then they may attend postgraduate institutions to improve their qualifications as doctors. In a meeting in the Ministry of Health of the R.S.F.S.R. it was stated that there were at the present time eighty medical academies, four medical faculties within universities, and eleven institutes for the improvement of the qualifications of doctors. Second, there are medical technikums for the training of *feldshers,* a form of second-level medical practitioners, nurses, and medical technicians. Enrollment in the various medical institutions varies from 200 to 600 per class.

In the academies the curriculum for each faculty is constant throughout the U.S.S.R. and is laid down by the ministries of health under the supervision of the U.S.S.R. Ministry of Higher Education. The latter regulates details of the subject matter for each year, examination schedules, and hours for lectures, laboratory and clinical work, and seminars. An applicant to a medical academy applies for admission to a specific faculty. Each faculty has its own examinations for admission; thus transfers from one faculty to another after admission are most unusual. Medical academies admit graduates directly from the ten-year school, although preference is given, as in other institutions of higher education, to those graduates who have worked for two years. In fact, admission of ten-year-school graduates now seems to be discouraged. The director of the Medical Academy at Kiev said, "We feel that the age of seventeen is too young to enter a medical academy. The student should be more mature than the average graduate of the ten-year school is."

Entrance examinations are competitive and given in four subjects: Russian, chemistry, physics, and a foreign language. In the Ukraine a fifth subject is added: Ukrainian. The sole criterion for admission is performance in these examinations, though formerly gold medal holders from the ten-year school were admitted without examinations and silver medal holders had to pass only one examination, in chemistry; this practice has been discontinued because it was found that "medal holders from the ten-year schools do not always make the best medical students." Since 1944 medical academies have offered a six-year course. This is longer than most training in higher education in the Soviet Union, but precedents exist in all school systems. As an official at the R.S.F.S.R. Ministry of Health explained, "The development of medical sciences called for the introduction of new subjects and increased time was considered necessary for each subject, both in theory and in practical work."

The first two years of the program consist of purely theoretical courses. In the third year, theoretical work is continued with additional courses in general therapy and basic general surgery. The fourth, fifth, and sixth are practical clinical years. There is no definite internship. However, the sixth year entails some practical experience and bears some similarity to the American internship. The curriculum of medical institutes and faculties at universities also includes the compulsory courses in Marxism-Leninism, political economy, and dialectical materialism.

At graduation each year, representatives from various republics and regions come to the medical academies to interview students. The representatives describe their locales and the graduate may choose, within certain limits, where he will spend the three years of required practice. Student achievement and family situations are considered in placements.

Exceptional students who aspire to scientific research may go on to postgraduate study. There are two postgraduate degrees for a doctor in the Soviet Union and they are the same as for other postgraduate students: the degree of *Kandidat,* which entails a further three years of training and the defense of a dissertation, and the degree of Doctor of Sciences. The number who hold these degrees is small. Most doctors practice with merely a medical diploma as their qualification. A doctor who wishes to specialize may take a two-year course of training in a given specialty and receive the degree of Ordinator.

The Soviet Union has a special feature of medical training in its institutes for the improvement of physicians. These provide by far the greatest number of highly qualified specialists, but the quality of specialty training so achieved is reported to be uneven. Training may begin when the required three years of practice after graduation from a medical academy have been completed. The doctor then specializes in a given field while attending an institute. He alternates this training with practice and must return every three to five years for another period of training to improve his skill and knowledge of the field. Each period of training takes about five to six months.

One of the main defects of medical education in the Soviet Union is the separation of scientific research institutes from large medical centers and other scientific research institutes of allied subjects in medicine. This retards the full development of the specialty field. Cross-fertilization from one field to another does not occur so readily as it might if the specialties were not separated from one another.[5]

Academy of Sciences

One of the most striking features of higher education in the Soviet Union is the Academy of Sciences,[6] which organizes, coordinates, and supervises research for the whole country.

The Academy of Sciences was founded in St. Petersburg in 1725, during the reign of Peter the Great. It is now situated in Moscow. The constituent republics of the Union have academies of sciences of their own, while the autonomous republics have only "sectors" of the Academy. The Academy is divided into various departments, according to the various sciences. The term "science" covers not only the natural sciences but also what the Soviets call the "humanities," that is, the social sciences.

Members of the Academy carry on fundamental research but engage in no applied research. There is, however, some connection with industry through the Academy's various branches in other cities and regions and through the universities. The Academy of Sciences in Moscow has a close connection with the University of Moscow; some of its members are also professors in the University, and advanced University students use laboratory facilities of the Academy to prepare their diploma projects. The Academy also supervises and directs the work of approximately 200 scientific institutes.

Membership in the Academy is a coveted honor and the highest reward that a scientist in the Soviet Union can receive. Foreigners also may be elected to membership. An interview with one of the members of the Academy elicited the following information:

> Of the 500 members of the Academy, about 80 are foreigners at present. Of all the 500, 180 are full members, the others are corresponding members. There is a very strong competition for membership and there are usually about twelve candidates for one vacancy.

Election to membership is by secret ballot and is for life. Candidates for membership may be proposed by any scientific association. Membership in the Academy of Sciences represents the apex in a carefully graduated and highly selective system of higher education which has always represented and increasingly constitutes the road to success in the Soviet Union.[7]

Higher Education in the Future

A word should be said on the position of higher education in the recent reorganization of the educational system.

According to new regulations of admission, 80 per cent of students in higher educational establishments in the 1959–1960 school year were to be chosen from applicants who have spent a period of not less than two years in production work. These applicants must not only pass entrance examinations but also present a *kharakteristika,* that is, a recommendation from one of the "public organizations." This means that the factory trade-union committees, Komsomol committees, and Party committees will decide who should go to higher educational establishments and who should not. The organizations are urged to consider the applicant's general attitude toward society as well as his aptitude for study. Henceforth, also, admissions commissions at universities and institutes will have additional members from Komsomol, trade union, and Party organs. Preference in admissions will be given to applicants who are working in a field related to the proposed field of study. Twenty per cent of students will still be admitted directly from the ten-year schools, being picked from among the best graduates.

Every student during his course of study is expected to work part of the time. During this period he will carry on his studies in the evening and correspondence divisions of his institute or university. Accordingly, these divisions, and especially the correspondence divisions, will be greatly expanded and improved.

Admissions examinations to all divisions of higher learning are to be reorganized and divided into general subjects and those subjects indispensable to the specialty of the institute or faculty giving the examination. Thus, future students must show an aptitude for their chosen field. This step was taken to prevent students from simply applying to whatever higher educational establishments happened to have vacancies, a practice which the high rewards placed on higher education in the Soviet Union greatly encouraged.[8]

It is, of course, too early to evaluate the impact of the new regulations on the quality of higher education. Judging from the protests of scholars and professors against the work provisions,[9] some educators in the Soviet Union seem to fear that the quality of training will deteriorate under the new system. Time will tell how strictly the new regulations are implemented and how they affect the system of higher education.[10]

12

TEACHER EDUCATION

Teachers in the Soviet Union receive different kinds of training according to the kind of school in which they will teach. Thus, kindergarten and primary-school teachers are trained in one type of institution, secondary-school teachers in another. In addition, teachers already working in the school system have opportunities to improve their qualifications and to broaden their knowledge. They can also get help in solving special pedagogical problems encountered in their teaching. As is the case in all other countries, university teachers do not receive special pedagogical training.

General Characteristics

Primary-school and kindergarten teachers were formerly trained in pedagogical technikums, which offered a four-year course to graduates of the seven-year schools. A 1954 reform converted these technikums into pedagogical schools (*pedagogicheskie uchilishcha*) admitting only graduates from the ten-year schools. Consequently, the course has been cut from four years to two.

The conversion of the pedagogical technikums into pedagogical schools is still in progress.

Even the pedagogical schools are viewed as temporary institutions. As soon as material conditions permit, all teachers, kindergarten and primary-school as well as secondary-school teachers, are to be trained at pedagogical institutes or at universities.

The training of secondary-school teachers formerly took place on two different levels. Teachers of the *first three grades* of the secondary school were trained at *teachers' institutes,* which admitted graduates from the ten-year schools and offered a two-year course covering two closely related subjects and some teaching methods. Graduates had a training roughly equivalent to the first two years of a pedagogical institute and were qualified to teach only their two subjects. Teachers of the *last three grades* of the secondary school were trained in *pedagogical institutes* in a four-year course for graduates of the ten-year schools.

This system was reorganized in 1952–1953, when it was decided to abolish the teachers' institutes and to train all secondary-school teachers in pedagogical institutes. By 1958 only two teachers' institutes reportedly survived in the Soviet Union, one in Riga, the other in Central Asia. It will not be long before these also disappear, if they have not already done so by the time the present report is published.

A further reform, in 1956, lengthened the course of study at the pedagogical institutes to five years, in order to give their students the same period of training as those in the universities and technical institutes were receiving. All students in pedagogical institutes are now trained for five years, except for those enrolled in the preschool faculties, who still take only a four-year course.

To recapitulate: at the present time, almost all primary-school and kindergarten teachers are trained in pedagogical schools in a two-year course. Secondary-school teachers are trained in pedagogical institutes in a five-year course. Both the pedagogical schools and the pedagogical institutes admit graduates from the ten-year schools only.

Graduates of the universities can also be directed into teaching in the secondary schools. Such teachers will have little or no training in teaching methods, depending upon whether their university does or does not maintain a professorship of pedagogy. Graduates of any faculty are free to enter the teaching field if they desire, even if they did not plan to do so originally and did not receive any pedagogical training. The counteradvantage, according to Mr. Nekrasov, official in charge of the curriculum for the natural sciences faculties at the University of Moscow, is that they will be very well grounded in their special fields. "Methods-of-teaching courses are not necessary in the secondary grades; it will be enough if the teacher knows his subject well. Practice will teach him how to teach."

As might be expected, opinions on the importance of methodology courses differ in the Soviet Union no less than in other countries. Although officials at the Universities of Moscow and Kiev maintained that university graduates make the best teachers because they are well grounded in their subject matter, Professor Ogorodnikov, head of the Department of Pedagogy at the Moscow Pedagogical Institute, complained that authorities outside the department are slow to see the importance of courses in pedagogy for the students. Other persons consulted maintained that the training of teachers in the university differed only in insignificant ways from that in the pedagogical institute and that graduates from either institution did equally well as teachers. Present indications are that the Soviet authorities will heed all these views and continue to run varied pedagogical programs.

Administratively, teacher-training institutions are responsible to the Ministry of Higher Education as well as to the ministry of education in each republic. The ministries of education finance and maintain their own teacher-training institutions, but the curriculum is prescribed by the Ministry of Higher Education. Teacher training in universities is controlled in a similar fashion by the Ministry of Higher Education.

The Pedagogical Schools

Although pedagogical schools are eventually to be replaced by special faculties in pedagogical institutes, there are still two of these schools in existence in the capital of the U.S.S.R., and the R.S.F.S.R. reportedly still had 150 such schools in the year 1958–1959.

As indicated, these schools admit graduates from the ten-year schools, by competitive entrance examination, and train them for two years as kindergarten and primary-school teachers. In Moscow the schools are housed in buildings identical with those serving ten-year schools. Members of the Comparative Education Society had no opportunity to visit such schools outside the capital.

Pedagogical School No. 2 in Moscow had an enrollment of 540 students for 1958–1959. All but seven were girls. The vice-director reported that this was about normal for Moscow, although in the national schools the proportion of male teachers for the primary grades runs to about 40 or 50 per cent. The school operates as a day school, drawing most of its students from Moscow and training them for Moscow schools. It is divided into two faculties, the preschool faculty and the primary faculty. Students within each faculty are grouped into classes.

The vice-director informed the visitors that at present there were only ten pedagogical institutes in the R.S.F.S.R. Thus, the burden of training primary school teachers will, he anticipated, continue to fall to the pedagogical schools for the time being, a job for which they are inadequately equipped. As he said,

> It is clear that a two-year course is not enough for training teachers. All teachers should be trained for four years. But it will take about ten years to accomplish the transition to pedagogical institutes for training all teachers, and, until then, two-year pedagogical schools will continue to exist.

One may expect, therefore, continued pressure for transformation of the pedagogical schools into pedagogical institutes in the foreseeable future.

Students in this pedagogical school are taught one of three foreign languages — French, German, or English. They take some courses in psychology, pedagogy, history of pedagogy, and methods of teaching various subjects; they have classes in physical culture, drawing, and music. Practice teaching starts in the first year. A primary school is attached to the institution and students start their practice by observing the teaching there. Later, they go to a regular school, where teachers demonstrate the teaching techniques they have developed. The notes taken in these meetings are later discussed with the instructors in the pedagogical school.

Students do active practice teaching in all subjects, including agricultural practice, since they are to teach all subjects. In the second year students actually teach lessons at the school attached to their own and at neighboring schools. In April of the second year they work for three weeks as regular teachers under the direction of the teachers of the neighboring school.

Students at the pedagogical school receive stipends of 180 rubles for the first year, 200 rubles for the second. They may also earn extra income during the summer by working in Pioneer camps or in kindergartens.

Pedagogical Institutes

Pedagogical institutes are to become the basic form of teacher training. With the exception of the universities, whose graduates may choose to go into the teaching field, they are to be the only teacher-training institutions of the future. As higher educational institutions, pedagogical institutes have the same entrance requirements as the universities and institutes examined in Chapter 11. Candidates for admission must be graduates of the ten-year school and preference is given, as usual, to applicants with two years of work experience. Each of the various faculties admits applicants after competitive entrance examinations. As the director of the Leningrad Pedagogical Institute explained,

> Each faculty makes up its own examinations through an examinations committee composed of fifteen members. Two of these are the actual "examiners." In the event of disagreement on results of the examination, the director of the committee decides.

The director further stated that all applicants must take a written examination in the Russian language. All other examinations, except the one in mathematics, are oral. These examinations are highly competitive, and of the number of applicants — usually about 300 — who take them, only about one-third pass. A candidate who fails the examination cannot apply elsewhere until the next year, since all entrance examinations are given at the same time, in the fall.

Pedagogical institutes also have evening and correspondence divisions. The Institute in Leningrad reported 5500 students enrolled in regular classes, 1500 in evening classes, and 7000 in correspondence courses. The Pedagogical Institute in Kiev had 1400 enrolled in its daytime program, as against 2000 in correspondence courses. The Pedagogical Institute in Tashkent reported 7800 enrolled in correspondence courses, as against 2000 in evening classes. According to the director of the Tashkent Institute, "Most of the evening- and correspondence-course students are teachers who want to improve their qualifications while they are working. They are mostly preschool or primary-school teachers who want to qualify for work in secondary schools." The correspondence division had grown so rapidly, he added, that an independent correspondence institute was planned for the next year.

Pedagogical institutes are divided into subject-matter faculties. There are, for example, the faculty of geography and biology, the faculty of mathematics and physics, the faculty of philology, and the faculty of the natural sciences. There are also faculties of preschool training and faculties of defectology, which prepare teachers for work with the handicapped.[1]

Curricula. Only the programs observed by the members of the Comparative Education Society will be presented here.[2]

Students of the preschool faculty in a pedagogical institute are trained to be teachers in pedagogical schools rather than kindergarten teachers. They take courses in the following:

psychology	physical culture
general pedagogy	foreign language (in a national
history of pedagogy	republic, the national lan-
physiology of the preschool	guage will be added)
and school child	children's literature
preschool pedagogy	methods of teaching
hygiene	nature study
kindergarten songs and music	art education

In addition, they must take courses in practical work, such as preparing materials for children's play and games, making toys and equipment, and courses in organization and administration of schools. Like all other students in the Soviet Union, they must take the prescribed number of political courses.

A certain amount of practical work is required. It is of three kinds. The students are attached to a professor who goes with them to the kindergartens and discusses what they have observed. During the second year the students spend six weeks in actual practice teaching in a kindergarten. In the fourth year they spend a month and a half in a pedagogical school learning the administrative duties of the director there. In some pedagogical institutes still another type of practical work is undertaken by students of the preschool faculty. According to the head of the preschool faculty of the Lenin Pedagogical Institute in Moscow, "In the fourth year a professor goes with six or eight students to the country for six weeks of work. Students thus learn the work in rural conditions. The Institute finances this activity." In other pedagogical institutes this type of practical work was not mentioned by officials of the preschool faculties; however, one official in the Gorki Pedagogical Institute in Kiev told a visitor that students were sent to the rural areas to learn the duties of an inspector of kindergartens. Students are required to keep diaries of their observation in kindergartens. "We do not study any special characteristics of the children, but rather make a study of their all-round development."

Pedagogical institutes have divisions for training teachers of primary-grade teachers in pedagogical schools. The Gorki Pedagogical Institute in Kiev had such a department, but no data were available as to how this program differed from the training in the preschool faculty. Officials confined themselves to the statement that future teachers of primary-school teachers must take courses in methods of teaching every subject of primary school.

In the courses of study in the other faculties of a pedagogical institute students receive intensive training in two specialized subjects, which are usually related in some way. The vice-director of the Lenin Pedagogical Institute in Moscow formulated the aims of his curriculum:

> The problem used to be for pedagogical institutes to prepare students well in at least two subjects. Now, our main problem is to prepare them well in more than two subjects, if possible, and also to give them such practical training as will qualify them to teach the new polytechnic subjects.

Accordingly, new subjects have been introduced. Students of

mathematics and physics now take courses in radiotechnics and electrotechnics, and practical work in school workshops, and so forth. Biology and chemistry students take courses in the elements of agriculture, and specialization will be in this as well as in chemistry. Physics majors have a second specialty, called "basis of industry," which is one of the new polytechnical subjects in school.

Students also do some practical work during their course of study. Those in the physics and mathematics faculties are employed for a time in plants or factories, while students in the biology and chemistry faculties work on collective farms. The vice-director, in explaining the new program, felt that only practice will teach students the skills needed to teach polytechnical subjects in secondary schools. "From now on, teachers will know how to do what they teach. They will be educated in practical work, as well as in theory. Teachers will be able to draw on their own experience instead of referring to textbooks."

Apart from courses in their special fields, students take a certain number of pedagogical and general courses, as well as physical culture. General courses consist of lectures in Marxism-Leninism, dialectical materialism, and political economy. Physical culture embodies the usual indoor and outdoor activities and is taught for its own sake rather than for learning of teaching methods. Finally, there is a certain amount of training in pedagogical subjects. All students take courses in general pedagogy, psychology, the history of pedagogy, school hygiene, and methods of teaching their special subject. These last are given by professors in the student's own faculty rather than by the pedagogy specialists of the department of pedagogy. A member of the faculty of geography in the Lenin Pedagogical Institute in Moscow said, "In our faculty, we spend about 70 per cent of the student's time in the Institute on the training in his special subjects, only about 30 per cent on pedagogy and methods courses." He added that out of about 4200 total hours of study, about 300 were spent in pedagogy and methods, about 400 in social science courses, and the rest in the student's special fields.

Every student takes some seminar work, the number of seminars required depending on the faculty in which he is enrolled. He also takes two or three elective courses (how many are required again depends on the faculty) in teaching school circles, in amateur sports and art circles, in the use of visual aids in schools, and so forth.

As in the universities, yearly papers (*kursovye raboty*) and control work (*zachety*) are required. Each student must also pass, in addition to the examinations in the pedagogical institute, four state examinations. One of these is in the history of the Communist Party, while the other three vary according to the special field. Two of these are obligatory, but the student can pick his subject in the fourth.

Practice Teaching. The time devoted to practice teaching varies with the different faculties from sixteen to nineteen weeks throughout the five-year course. If the period is to be nineteen weeks, the student starts his practice teaching in the third year; if less, it starts in the fourth year. Students are divided into small groups, from twelve to fifteen in each group, with faculty members in charge. Practice teaching starts with "passive practice" — observation of a teacher at work. The faculty member accompanies his group and discusses the significance of what was seen in the classroom. Fourth-year students start giving lessons themselves in the schools, prepared with the help of the faculty adviser and later evaluated by him as well as by other students in the group. In the fifth year students prepare the lessons on their own and teach independently. The first and last two lessons that they give in this period are discussed and analyzed by the supervisor. Also this year students visit the families of the children whom they teach in school. "When practice teaching starts, students generally show greater enthusiasm and interest than before," reported a faculty member of the English Department of the Lenin Pedagogical Institute in Moscow.

A part of pedagogical practice consists of working in a Pioneer camp in the summer. This is required of all students in the "humanities" for three weeks at the end of the third year, but not of students in the natural-science faculties, since they have a great deal of other practical work to complete.

Besides practice teaching, students must take certain practical work in their special fields: laboratory work in the institute for natural-science majors, language practice for foreign-language majors, and so on. Students in the English Department of the Lenin Pedagogical Institute were observed working with a tape recorder to learn pronunciation and idiomatic speech. A faculty member informed visitors during this session that eight hours a week of such practice was required in the first year, ten hours in the second year, and ten hours in the third year; no figures were given for the last two years.

At the end of the five-year course the graduate is qualified to teach two or three subjects in the secondary schools.

Job Assignments. About three months before graduation, regions and districts send their requirements to the Ministry of Higher Education, which posts the lists in the pedagogical institutes. Prospective graduates may then apply for the job of their choice. As in the universities and institutes, records are kept of the students' academic and social progress, and those with the best records are given preference.

Graduates may return for advice and consultation at the end of their first year of teaching. Their faculty holds itself available for this purpose though, according to Ivan Ogorodnikov, head of the Department of Pedagogy at the Lenin Pedagogical Institute in Moscow, the problems that arise are usually general rather than specific. "The greatest problem of young teachers is understanding the goals of education and the aim of discipline. Understanding their subject matter is the problem second in importance."

Pedagogical institutes also serve as centers of training for postgraduate students working toward the higher degrees. The Pedagogical Institute in Leningrad had 250 postgraduate students working, for the most part, toward the degree of *Kandidat.* Such students aim to become faculty members in pedagogical institutes.

Pedagogical institutes, like all others, have their own circles and clubs. The director of the Institute in Kiev stressed that such amateur activity stimulated the student's interest and ambition and encouraged original efforts in special fields. She told of city, regional, and republic competitions in certain fields between such student clubs. The best works resulting from these extracurricular activities are often published by the pedagogical institutes.

Institutes for Teacher Improvement

Institutes for teacher improvement are one of the most interesting and significant features of teacher training in the Soviet Union.

The first institute for teacher improvement was established in Moscow, in 1938, by the presidium of the city soviet, with the approval of the Ministry (then Commissariat) of Education of the R.S.F.S.R. There is now one such institute in every *raion* in Moscow, in addition to the central institute. Other institutes were established in other parts of the republic and the union and today number one hundred.

These institutes exist to help the teacher with his current problems, to give him a better knowledge of his subject, and to keep him abreast of the latest developments in his field and in teaching methods generally. The advice and information they offer is free, and participation is open to any teacher who feels in need of their services.

The Moscow Institute for Teacher Improvement is housed in a five-story building situated in the middle of a group of small wooden houses of a kind that belongs to the Moscow of the Middle Ages. The auditorium is on the top floor, and lower floors are taken up by "cabinets," that is, the rooms of the various departments. Besides serving the 30,000 teachers of the city of Moscow, the Institute is available to teachers from outside the city who may come to it during the school holidays for advice and help. The director stated:

> Our activities have three different aspects. We give courses to teachers in subject matter; we help the teacher in his practical work in the schools; and we try to keep the teacher up-to-date with the latest and best experience.

The Institute is thus an excellent means of enabling teachers to keep up with the latest advances of their profession.

The Institute is divided into nineteen departments, including:

study and publication of the best teaching experiences	extracurricular activities
elementary teaching	work in orphanages
teaching of the various school subjects	physical culture
	polytechnical training
department of pedagogy	film library for school films
	library

There are also laboratories for teachers of the sciences, a laboratory for driver education, and workshops for the polytechnical subjects.

HIGHER EDUCATION

Institutions of higher learning include the universities, technical institutes, medical institutes, conservatories of music, institutes of fine arts, pedagogical institutes, and many other specialized establishments. Over-all control is vested in the U.S.S.R. Ministry of Higher Education, with the fifteen Republic Ministries of Higher Education supervising the various institutions in each republic.

High on the Lenin Hills, overlooking the city, towers Moscow State University, commonly known as the University of Moscow. This building houses the scientific faculties, a library, and dormitories. The humanities departments are still in downtown Moscow.

Students work in a chemistry laboratory at Yakutsk University.

Students of the department of humanities at Yakutsk University in the reading hall of the University library

Institute students gather during a midmorning breakfast break.

A typical university
library reading room

Students at a Moscow pedagogical school
specialize as elementary-school music teachers.

PARA-SCHOOL EDUCATION

Every aspect of the child's life in the Soviet Union is part of his education and of a co-ordinated system. In forming the Soviet man, education in the family, Octobrists, Pioneers, Komsomol, circles, and camps is as important as, if not more important than, formal education. Equally significant are leisure-time reading, radio, television, theater, and museums. Almost all children become Octobrists at the age of seven and Pioneers at the age of nine. Not all children become Komsomols because the Lenin Young Communist League is much more exclusive than the Pioneers and the Octobrists.

Students listen attentively at a Pioneer meeting.

In each school there is a room reserved for the Pioneers and at least one full-time leader is in charge.

Above: Each city has a Pioneer Palace, like this one in Leningrad, to sponsor circles and parties. Below: Leningrad's Pioneer Palace is a former royal palace.

All Pioneer activities are supervised by the All-Union Lenin Young Communist League. This young Komsomol is a camp counselor.

Above: Pioneer circle activities are designed for free periods during the regular school schedule, before and after school, and vacation periods. Below: Three little girls rest between activities at a Pioneer summer camp in a suburb of Moscow.

Above: Soviet boys and girls enjoy informal group singing. The accordion is a popular instrument at summer camps. At right: Each child is initiated into the Pioneers by taking an oath to be true to the principles of Lenin, to study diligently, and to become a worthy citizen.

Play equipment at a Pioneer Camp is similar to that of camps in other countries. The seesaw and volleyball are popular activities.

Above: School, university, and trade union sports clubs are organized into societies. In August over 4500 finalists gather at the Central Stadium in Moscow to compete in an All-Union Summer Sportskaid sponsored by the Trade Unions. Below: Nearly all of the 100,300 seats in the Lenin Central Stadium are filled for the Sportskaid. After a full parade, individual clubs give demonstrations.

The Institute offers long-term courses, which meet throughout the months of the school year, and short-term courses on special subjects and problems. These courses consist of lectures and seminars, and students may be taken to a school where an outstanding teacher works to observe the best or most up-to-date methods. New developments in science and pedagogy influence the work of the Institute. Thus, when the new polytechnical subjects were introduced in the schools, the Institute had to add the teaching of these subjects to its curriculum: "When the Sputnik went up, we had to introduce new courses in our Institute, as the teachers were suddenly flooded with questions about it which they could not answer." Apparently Soviet pedagogy was, like its American counterpart, caught by surprise by the spectacular technological advances of 1957.

Teachers at the Institute also work in the city schools for twelve hours a week. Schedules are so arranged that all teachers can come to the Institute while they are working. If a teacher's schedule is too crowded to allow him to come when he feels the need, it is lightened to permit him to do so.

Attendance at the Institute is free and quite voluntary. There are no credits or degrees from completion of the courses. It is only the professional desire to improve his methods and to increase his knowledge that brings the teacher to the Institute. The director said that 5000 teachers are helped annually. "When the Ministry wanted to state that it was the teacher's duty to improve his qualifications, the Union asked it to omit this sentence, so that there would be no pressure on the teacher, and still many teachers attend."

Recently the great stress has been on practice, as evidenced in the field of science teaching, polytechnical training, and foreign-language teaching. Previously children were only taught the laws of science; now they must be able to apply these laws to practical situations. Previously children received only academic training; now "we want them to learn other skills also." All this has influenced teacher training.

The Foreign-Language Department of the Institute had just acquired a tape recorder and the head of the department was eager to have American voices recorded for the teachers to study and imitate. Teachers practice speaking the foreign language that they teach, and often evenings are arranged in which the conversation is in the language studied.

In the Physics and Chemistry departments, equipment set up on a series of tables demonstrated various principles of science. The displays were arranged according to grade levels. Each one included a set of directions, listing the exact equipment needed, explaining the principle that was to be demonstrated, and giving instructions for presentation. The walls were covered with charts and diagrams. Wherever the work of a particular class was displayed, the picture of the teacher responsible for it was given a prominent place and her name was mentioned.

The Biology Department contained a great many plants and specimens of all kinds. Teachers who work in this room often make their own samples out of papier-mâché and take them back to their schools for use in the classrooms.

The film library had films intended for various grade levels in history and in moral education. Teachers view these films and are taught how to use them. Some are silent films in which the teacher has to supply the explanations.

The library of the Institute reportedly contains 200,000 volumes and pamphlets. Every August there are special readings and exhibitions where teachers report on their significant experiences and successes.

All in all, the Moscow Institute for Teacher Improvement provides an impressive opportunity for in-service training of Soviet pedagogues. In addition to central stations of this type, there are "methodological cabinets" in the various administrative districts, as reported by Chairman Petrokeevich of the Leningrad city department of education:

> Each district of the city has its own "cabinet" for teachers interested in improving their teaching methods and in exchanging their experiences. New teachers are encouraged to attend these meetings so as to develop their teaching methods. The city board of education also holds special seminars for district chairmen, for inspectors, and for directors of schools.

Teachers in Schools

A word must be added about teachers in school situations. In elementary schools there is a great demand for better-qualified staffs. In the opinion of some informants, this demand will not abate until elementary-school teachers get better pay. Secondary-school teachers receive extra pay for correcting papers, for example, while primary-school teachers do not. An official of the Trade Union of Educational, Cultural and Research Workers told one of the visitors: "We want to achieve the situation in which primary-school teachers are treated the same way as secondary-school teachers. They should have the same pay rates and the same opportunities for improving their qualifications." [3] Chairman Grivkov of the Presidium of the Union expressed similar sentiments: "Primary-school teachers, especially in the rural areas, must have more prestige. We arrange special teachers' days when representatives of the local soviets and party committees come to honor the teacher."

In secondary schools each teacher is a specialist in a certain subject area and hence is in a stronger position. The basic work load is eighteen hours of teaching a week, as against twenty-four hours for the primary-school teacher. Furthermore, there appears to be more self-help and cohesion among teachers at this level. The leading teachers in each field help their colleagues improve their methods. In School No. 150 in Tashkent, for instance, teachers attend each other's classes and discuss each other's methods. In other schools various other practices help give all teachers the benefit of the experience of the best teachers. The director of School No. 153 in Leningrad said his school insists on cooperation: "We require our teachers to attend orientation sessions with the older teachers. The oldest and best teachers in each field help the younger and less experienced ones." If the older teachers do not give such help to newcomers, they may be severly censured. According to the editor of the *Uchitelskaia Gazeta,* Mme. Parfenova,

> We recently discussed a case in the *Gazette* where a young and inexperienced teacher did not succeed in her work very well. The blame attached to the group of older colleagues in her school, who should have helped her instead of leaving her to work out her problems by herself.

She added that the pedagogical council of that school was critized in the newspaper for not helping the new teachers. [4]

Class Leaders. In the secondary schools, teachers impressed the visitors as having a high sense of duty. Each class has a class leader, a teacher who is responsible for the whole class. Since different subjects are taught by different teachers, the class leader is the only one concerned with the class as a group, as a "collective," and with each individual in it. The director of School No. 717 in Moscow pointed out that no special preparation or training is needed for this job. "One must merely be a good and experienced teacher." A class leader at a meeting in Moscow was asked whether she had a family of her own. She replied, "I have no children of my own, but I would have no time for my own family anyway. I have forty-two children to be a mother to in school." The task is a demanding one. The class leader is expected to know each pupil and to guide the class as a whole. She is expected to visit the pupils in their home and talk with the parents, especially if there is some problem with the child. She is also expected to work with the Pioneer leaders of the school on the Pioneer projects.[5]

Class leaders receive an additional 75 rubles a month. Teachers of Russian, foreign languages, and mathematics earn an additional 60 rubles a month for correcting papers. Teachers who direct laboratory work earn 50 to 150 rubles a month extra and those in language schools get an additional 15 per cent of the basic salary. Special-school teachers also receive more than ordinary teachers. The director of School No. 717 in Moscow is paid 2000 rubles a month. There are provisions for teachers to receive up to 80 per cent of their salary during maternity and sick leave. If a teacher falls ill and there are no substitutes, the other teachers fill in as best they can.

In addition to receiving better salaries, the teachers in secondary schools are more often rewarded by special titles for outstanding work. Several teachers interviewed had been awarded the title of "Meritorious Teacher of the Soviet Union." "In the classes of our 'meritorious teachers' no pupil receives less than a mark of '4,' and many receive only marks of '5,'" visitors were informed in School No. 20 in Tashkent. It is not clear whether the high marks of pupils are a criterion for awarding the title or are simply a result of the excellence of the teaching.

A great deal is done to increase the prestige of the teacher and respect for his profession, especially in the big cities. Visitors attended a gathering in a Leningrad park at the beginning of the school year where education officials and representatives of the parents' organizations joined in praising the work of the Soviet teacher and extolling the dignity and stature of the teaching profession. American educators had the unusual experience of hearing speeches along these lines:

> Who has made it possible for us to produce the Sputnik? Who has made it possible for us to achieve so much in the building of communism? Only the teacher has made it possible and it is to the teacher that we confide our most treasured possession of them all — the younger generation.

13

THE EDUCATIONAL, CULTURAL
AND RESEARCH WORKERS'
TRADE UNION

All trades and professions are
fully organized into unions in the U.S.S.R. Approximately 90 per
cent of the workers are members of labor organizations, which are
controlled by the government. Although the Soviet Union is a
state of, by, and for the workers, administrators in all industries
and professions are appointed by the government, and it is they
who decide the major matters of hours of work, rates of pay,
norms of output, and hiring and firing. The Soviet worker does
not have the privilege of striking or of collective bargaining with
his employer.

All this is due to the Communist Party claim that the Soviet
government is the workers' government and that therefore the
workers need not be safeguarded against exploitation. In the
words of Article 126 of the Constitution of 1936,

> Citizens of the U.S.S.R. are guaranteed the right to unite in . . .
> trade unions . . . and the most active and politically conscious citizens
> in the ranks of the working class, working peasants, and working
> intelligentsia voluntarily unite in the Communist Party of the Soviet

Union, which is the vanguard of the working people in their struggle to build communist society and is the leading core of all organizations of the working people, both public and state.[1]

It is clear that there is a close link between the unions and the Communist Party.

Function of the Labor Trade Union in the Soviet Union

The labor union's basic function is as an instrument of "pressure and control" on behalf of the government. It is expected to

... transmit the demands of the state for increased production, assure the satisfaction of minimum welfare needs, absorb and deflect dissatisfactions, and rally, insofar as possible, the workers to the support of the regime.[2]

More specifically,

Unions share responsibility with management for increasing labor productivity, reducing production costs, imparting new technical processes, and enforcing strict discipline. Serving as an important agency of welfare administration, they manage social insurance, sponsor cultural and athletic activities and look after workers' housing and their general labor safety.[3]

A well-known expert on Soviet government offers another viewpoint on the function of the trade union:

The Soviet trade unions are an instrument of state policy, rather than a pressure group through which interested citizens may formulate a program beneficial to their special interests and press for its adoption over programs presented by similarly organized associations of citizens with other interests. An instrument which has become, in democratic countries, a vehicle for expressing the will of an important segment of the population has been subjected in the USSR, together with other popular institutions, to control at vital points.[4]

The relationship between the trade union and the Party is precisely defined. The interests of the government and those of the worker are considered identical. Consequently, the trade union does not have the function, as it does in other countries, of protecting the workers against exploitation by management or by government. What the union can do is protect the worker against abuses that come up now and then in administration. It can also use its status to obtain better welfare provisions for its members. In general, however, the role of the union in fulfilling the fundamental aims of the state cannot be overemphasized. One writer has stated it as follows:

> Maintenance of democratic forms here (union officials are supposedly elected on a democratic basis, but most often are party appointees), as in other aspects of Soviet life, provides the regime with a lever for manipulating the citizen. At union meetings, conferences, congresses, as well as in the press, workers are encouraged to criticize the actions of union functionaries in regard to housing and other welfare responsibilities, and so are provided partial outlets for their grievances. Further, by means of periodic meetings and conferences devoted to problems of production, Soviet unions attempt to involve the mass of workers in the goals of the state.[5]

The Educational Trade Union

With this general background, we may turn to the Trade Union of Employees of Educational, Higher Educational, and Research Establishments of the U.S.S.R., to use its full name. A teachers' union existed in Russia even before the Revolution. Originally organized in 1907, the Trade Union of Teachers was re-established in 1918 under Communist auspices. In its early history, it also included higher educational and scientific workers in its membership, but later the two professional groups parted company. According to the official government report, it was not until 1957 that "the two trade unions of educational workers and of higher school and scientific workers merged to form a single trade union of educational, higher school and scientific workers."[6] When the Union was first established, it had 70,000 members, and in 1953 it had more than 1,700,000;[7] in 1958, owing to the merger, its membership exceeded 4,000,000. Furthermore, its geographic scope is now coterminous with that of the country, whereas a few years ago it was confined to the R.S.F.S.R.

Membership in the Union, according to its president, Ivan Grivkov, is voluntary and without distinction as to religion, race, sex, or nationality. Other sources say that it is absolutely and without exception compulsory. The Union is, however, a "nonparty organization." [8] About 98 per cent of the educational workers join immediately upon assuming their duties. The remaining persons take some time but eventually join. The dues are one-half of one per cent of the salary.

Grivkov, who personally directed the administration of the program of school visitation by the Comparative Education Society in the Soviet Union, began his educational career in 1925 in a village school. After two years of service as a primary teacher he went on to teach in a seven-year school, then directed a pedagogical technikum for ten years and administered various schools for nine more. He thus had had experience in different types and levels of educational service before being appointed head of the Union.

Principles of Organization. This Union shares with all other Soviet trade unions two basic principles of organization. The first is the industrial principle, under which all employees in education, on every level from preschool through university, are members — principals, teachers, librarians, clerks, other non-instructional personnel in school administration, janitors, cleaners, furnace tenders, and so forth. In Grivkov's own words, "all workers without exception employed in the particular institution" are members of the Union.[9]

The second basic principle of Union organization is democratic centralism. This means that:

> . . . every lower trade union body is subordinate to the higher body, the branch committee being subordinate to the district committee, the district committee to the regional, and so one. The union's leading body is the central committee, whose decisions are binding on all members and organizations of the particular trade union.[10]

In other types of society, democratic centralism is usually identified as hierarchy. The president of the Central Committee on the U.S.S.R. level, which stands over the central committees of the educational workers' unions of all the republics, is a man with considerable power and privilege. This fact was demonstrated time and again, both in talk and in action, during the visit of the Comparative Education Society.

The fundamental unit of the Union is the branch committee,

which is elected by all members working at a single institution. In rural areas particularly, where less than fifteen members are employed in a school, it is necessary to combine several schools to form a local branch committee. The branch committees are elected by secret ballot for a term of one year; the elected officials on the district, region, and republic levels serve two-year terms. The Central Committee is chosen biennially at a congress of the Union.

Each branch committee appoints an inspector of labor protection, who makes certain that the school administration observes the proper rules of health and hygiene and provides proper working conditions for the membership.

The actual work of the Union is carried on by commissions organized on the branch, district, and regional levels. They are concerned with organization, production, housing and welfare, cultural activities, labor protection, and social insurance. Each commission consists of from three to five members. The commission on production is responsible for making the experience of the best teachers available to all, and especially to the younger teachers.[11]

According to Grivkov, about 20 per cent of the Union members belong to the Communist Party. No one is eligible to teach history, for instance, unless he has a Party card. Moreover, 200 Union members are also members of the Supreme Soviet.

It is interesting to consider the figures on the Party membership of teachers. As noted before, the 1959 population in the Soviet Union was 208,826,000. At the Twenty-First Congress of the Communist Party in January, 1959, an announcement was made that there were 7,622,356 Party members and 616,775 candidates, or a total membership of 8,239,131.[12] This would mean that about 3.09 per cent of the Soviet people belong to the Communist Party.

Assuming that Grivkov's estimate that 20 per cent of his Union members are Party members is accurate, we see that Soviet educational functionaries provide almost seven times as many Party adherents as does the population at large. Also significant is the fact that the 800,000 educational members of the Communist Party comprise 10 per cent of the entire membership. Taking for granted that a Party member must be obedient and loyal to retain his status, it is obvious that the educational and research workers form a powerful ideological element in the U.S.S.R.

Activities. The Union participates actively in the preparation of laws concerning working conditions and salaries of educational employees and in the enforcement of such laws. Representatives of the Union also take part in the deliberations leading to governmental policy decisions relating to education and science. The American visitors were told that the 200 educational members of the Supreme Soviet generally see to it that the interests and needs of the Union are made known to the government. Grivkov cited Khrushchev as saying that no question concerning the trades and professions can be decided without prior consultation with the affected unions.

The Union's welfare projects include financial aid to needy teachers, in the form of either a grant or a long-term loan for the purchase of clothing or furniture or for other purposes; a social-insurance fund for sick teachers, which furnishes them with a sum equaling their average pay and which is obtained for a 6 per cent salary tax paid to the Union by the educational institutions and organizations; benefits (from the social-insurance fund) to temporarily disabled educational workers; a life pension of 40 per cent to every teacher with twenty-five years of service, regardless of whether he continues to teach or not; payments, also from the social-insurance fund, to pensioners who continue to teach after retirement; government-operated free hostels for aged teachers; free health and vacation centers for Union members and their families, paid for out of the social-insurance fund; and layettes for members giving birth to children. Its recreational facilities include gymnasiums, stadiums, swimming pools, excursion and tourist bases, pools for boating, and clubs. The Trade Union organizes libraries, mobile libraries, lectures, professional conferences, dramatic and musical activities, and cultural excursions and tours. The main teachers' houses in Leningrad and Moscow were visited by the Comparative Education Society members, who were quite impressed by the variety of social, recreational, and cultural activities available to the Union membership.

Rural teachers are given special consideration. A monthly Rural Teachers' Day enables the rural members to visit towns and attend lectures, dramatic productions, the cinema, or amateur theatrical performances by teachers' groups. Attendance at these Teachers' Days is almost compulsory.

The Union also looks after the interests of the children of its members by organizing after-school artistic and technical circles or clubs, children's parties and theatrical entertainment, and so forth. It maintains many children's summer camps, thus enabling the educational workers to provide their children with a much needed change of environment.

Teachers are encouraged by the Union to be active in community cultural work. Many serve as speakers, lecturers, and directors of general educational clubs.[13]

Mr. Grivkov's answers to the questions asked by the American visitors at the special conference arranged to discuss the Union are instructive. According to him, the Union can bring about changes in school administrative practice. Thus, the director of a school who unjustly dismisses a Union member may be investigated, punished, or even dismissed by the Union, and its decision permits no appeal. If a teacher was justly dismissed, the Union committee will apologize to the director of the school for not having disciplined the teacher early enough to avoid dismissal. Any disciplinary action by a school administrator is subject to the approval of the Union, whose decision is final.

In August, 1958, the Union was trying to bring about a reform in the teachers' pension plan. As of that date, men retired on a pension at the age of sixty and women at fifty-five. The new plan would lower the retirement ages to fifty-five and fifty respectively, as is the case in certain other professions, such as heavy industry. Grivkov stated that this problem was being considered by a government committee and he felt that a new law would be passed before the end of 1958.

Another campaign is in behalf of better living conditions for rural teachers. In the near future, Grivkov said, it is expected that they will receive apartments with utilities, near the school. The government had agreed to the Union's proposal and a law was in the making. Especially emphatic about what the Union was doing for the improvement of the social, cultural, and professional status of the rural educational workers, Grivkov even referred to the need for more opportunities for young men and women teachers to meet for possible future matrimony.

The Union's commissions on labor protection enforce the regulations of school operation, heating, and lighting; the various labor laws; and the safety rules in scientific laboratories. The commissions on social welfare are concerned with teacher housing, relief for sick teachers, and the teachers' material conditions. They help allocate any new apartments that are assigned by the government for the use of the educational workers. The commissions on children encourage young persons to undertake teaching careers, maintain summer camps for the members' children, and organize extracurricular summer activities for children. These commissions are usually organized by the teachers' clubs or houses, of which there are 1200 in the U.S.S.R. Altogether, 976,000 educational workers, or nearly one-fourth of the Union membership, participate in the work of the children's commissions.

In answer to another question, Mr. Grivkov stated that the Union did not possess a special code of ethics, since the standard of behavior of the teacher was identical to that of all other citizens. The teacher, accordingly, must be a lover of labor and of his people, a friend and collaborator of his colleagues, a worker in the interest of strengthening Soviet society, and an individual willing to submit to self-criticism and to criticism by others. At Union meetings a member may be criticized for immorality, for his behavior in family life, and for excessive drinking. The Union feels obliged to supervise moral behavior inasmuch as it is necessary to keep the teacher on a high professional plane if he is to be in charge of the character formation of children and youth.

The Union also operates a Sports Society for its membership, since physical culture is regarded as very important for well-rounded development. According to its director, more than 600,000 educational workers belong to the amateur sports clubs, which are organized into area and republic councils. A Central Sports Council coordinates the activities of all sports clubs. The Sports Society also sponsors children's sports clubs under the direction of qualified teachers. Some one million pupils and students took part in the Sports Society's programs in 1958. Sports activities for children and youth are not as a rule connected with the schools; however, each higher educational institution operates a sports club within the framework of the Union's Sports Society.

The Comparative Education Society witnessed a festival organized by the Sports Society on August 24, 1958, at the Lenin Stadium in Moscow. The athletic, acrobatic, and marching activities by children, youth, and teachers were spectacular, although to some members the entire program, including the massing of banners and slogans, was reminiscent of the sports activities of Nazi youth in Hitler's era. In any event, it was difficult not to agree with the director of the Sports Society when he remarked that his organization was one of the major athletic associations in the U.S.S.R.

Uchitelskaia Gazeta

Members of the Comparative Education Society visited the editorial offices of *Uchitelskaia Gazeta* (*Teachers' Gazette*) and conferred with the editor and her staff. This newspaper is the joint organ of the Ministry of Education of the R.S.F.S.R. and of the Central Committee of the Trade Union of Educational, Cultural, and Research Workers of the U.S.S.R. Founded in 1924, it appears in four-page issues each Tuesday, Thursday, and Saturday throughout the year and has a subscription roll of 600,000.

Uchitelskaia Gazeta, which reaches all corners of the Soviet Union, reflects all aspects of educational life in the country, from the pre-schools through the higher educational institutions and the research institutes. The responsibility for giving adequate space to each type of school activity is a heavy one, according to the editor, Nadezhda M. Parfenova, who admitted that the newspaper was not satisfying all the elements in the Soviet school system in this regard.

Uchitelskaia Gazeta is directed by an editor, a deputy editor, a chief secretary, and a deputy chief secretary. The various editorial departments are devoted to the school, pedagogical science, higher schools, children's homes, bibliography, Union affairs, foreign affairs, and letters from readers. Correspondents in each of the republics send in reports about school developments in their region.

Every issue carries on the masthead the traditional Communist imperative, "Workers of all countries, unite!" Photographs appear as a rule on each page and the articles are of varying length. Special features are designed to reach different types of readers.

Contents. Uchitelskaia Gazeta for July 25, 1957, contains reports from the Ukraine, Byelorussia, Georgia, the Kirghiz S.S.R.

and the Moldavian S.S.R. One article is I. Grivkov's review of the fifty years' history of the educational workers' union. On the last page are advertisements inviting qualified persons to submit applications for departmental chairmanships, professorships, and docentships in four pedagogical institutes, one electrotechnical institute, and the Kirghiz State University. In addition, there is a problem in checkers, a listing of the contents of the three leading Soviet educational periodicals (*Sovetskaia Pedagogika, Narodnoe Obrazovanie,* and *Nachalnaia Shkola*), and a book review. Finally, there is a summary of the opinions of a British educator on the Soviet schools.

About one-third of page 4 of the issue of May 6, 1958, is devoted to announcements of available positions in higher educational institutions. In addition, there are congratulatory telegrams on the occasion of the May 1 holiday from the editors of pedagogical journals in China, Korea, and Rumania. One article summarizes a *Time* magazine piece on the "crimes" of American teachers, while another discusses the culture and art of the Arab countries.

The June 10, 1958, issue includes a poem, "Alpinist," advertisements of vacancies, an advertisement announcing three dictionaries useful to "literary workers" and teachers of Russian, and a review of a recent movie. The issue of June 12, 1958, features an article on the didactic views of S.T. Shatsky. That of August 19, 1958, advertises new books of general interest and the recent publications of the Academy of Pedagogical Sciences. S. Shapovalenko discusses "The Aims of the Chemistry Course in Secondary Schools" on August 21, 1958. In the same issue is an article by an instructor of education at the University of Chile, an obituary of Academician N. A. Petrov, and a brief account of the arrival in Moscow several days earlier of the members of the Comparative Education Society.

Uchitelskaia Gazeta of August 28, 1958, contains, among other things, some Lenin documents relating to education, a report of an "interesting experiment" concerning the training of six-year-olds, current developments in physics, and a chess problem. The September 1, 1958, issue, which is devoted to the opening of the new school year, features a long poem, greetings by Czech, East German, and Rumanian educators, and a message from the officers of the Comparative Education Society.

Editorial Policy. At the conference with the American educators Mme. Parfenova supplied considerable information concerning the workings of *Uchitelskaia Gazeta.* Its major functions, she said, were to help bring the school closer to life and to equip the children and youth with the scientific and practical knowledge necessary for life. It is very difficult to achieve a correct balance in the curriculum. The success of Sputnik has made pupils and students interested in studying science to such an extent that the teachers of the humanities and the social sciences have begun to complain of the decline of interest in their fields. The newspaper seeks to improve this situation through articles, reports, and other kinds of writing.

The staff of *Uchitelskaia Gazeta* are constantly analyzing and criticizing what they have done. A staff meeting is held every two weeks at which the recent issues are given careful scrutiny. There is a spirit of willingness to improve on the part of all members of the staff.

Editorial policy, Mme. Parfenova stressed, is not founded upon armchair experiences. Many of the staff members travel in order to observe school conditions at first hand. They are alert to suggestions and reports concerning successful experiments in their specialties. For example, when the chief of the school department of the *Teachers' Gazette* learned of a particular school in Kazan that was successfully relating the school to life by developing initiative in the pupils, he sent several journalists to visit the classrooms, talk with the pupils and teachers, and attempt to evaluate the methods. They also attended a teachers' conference in Kazan where they heard the experimenting teachers give an account of their program. All the details appeared shortly afterward in the *Gazette,* thus enabling the teaching profession of the entire country to become acquainted with a promising new procedure of bridging school and life.

Moreover, editorial policy is based upon the policies and directives of the Ministry of Education of the R.S.F.S.R. and of the Central Committee of the Party as well as those of the educational workers' union. The experiences of the staff supplement the official view and together these represent the editorial policy of the teachers' own journal.

The *Teachers' Gazette* helps teachers in many ways. In 1957, for example, a young fourth-grade teacher in her first year of service wrote a letter asking for help with a boy who was not interested in his studies, the only such pupil in her class. The boy, it seems, enjoyed horses and reading books on the fine arts but loathed the school textbooks. The editor published the letter and invited teachers all over the country to offer suggestions. A total of 150 letters were received. Many were published, and all were sent to the inquiring teacher. At a Rural Teachers' Day devoted to this problem, the young teacher obtained additional help from the experienced teachers of her own and neighboring villages. The collective advice boiled down to this: the teacher should start with the pupil's natural interest and gradually widen its scope to include other kinds of books.

The newspaper receives, on the average, 10,000 letters each month or 100,000 per school year. Obviously only a few can be published. The staff chooses those that are likely to be of the greatest interest and significance for the practical work of the teachers.

Nearly every head of a department in the *Gazette* has had training and experience in pedagogy or journalism or both. For example, the head of the department of pedagogical sciences has served as director of an institute for the improvement of the qualifications of teachers and as assistant head of education on the regional level. He also holds the degree of Doctor of Pedagogical Sciences and has had training in journalism. The head of the department of foreign affairs is a 1929 graduate of a pedagogical institute with a specialty in German, French, and English. After several years of experience as an interpreter he entered the field of journalism.

The editor, a specialist in history, is a graduate of the University of Moscow. She has worked on all levels of education — as teacher, school director, school inspector, and head of the school division of the Ministry of Education of the R.S.F.S.R. She has never had any training or experience in journalism, but she likes the field and is determined to study it. Because the newspaper operates, as do all other Soviet institutions and organizations, on the collective principle, the experiences of all the workers are pooled to further the collective aims of Soviet society and education. This fact is symbolized by the photographic presence in the editorial offices of Lenin and Stalin.

The issue of September 11, 1958, gives the prices of an introductory subscription: twelve months — 46 rubles, 80 kopecks; six months — 23 rubles, 40 kopecks; three months — 11 rubles, 70 kopecks. Each number of the *Uchitelskaia Gazeta* costs 30 kopecks. It is interesting to note that *Pravda, Izvestiia,* and *Sovetskaia Rossiia* cost only 20 kopecks when they appear in four-page issues, although a six-page number of these national newspapers sells for 30 kopecks. The price of the four-page issue of *Literaturnaia Gazeta,* the organ of the board of directors of the Writers' Union of the U.S.S.R., is 40 kopecks.

The *Gazette* devoted some space in a number of issues to the Comparative Education Society during its visit in the Soviet Union. Several American educators were interviewed and quoted and photographs of some were printed. A reporter of the *Gazette* met the incoming Americans at the airport and traveled with them almost every day.

Uchitelskaia Gazeta resembles no other educational periodical known to the writer in any country. We do not have in the United States even a weekly educational newspaper, let alone one that appears three times a week. In terms of content, it resembles an issue of the *Times Educational Supplement,* which is published in England once a week with book reviews, articles, foreign school news, letters to the editor, educational and book advertisements, photographs, and other features; but the latter exceeds the total size of an issue of the *Gazette* by three times.

Such, then, is the official journalistic educational venture of the Trade Union of Educational, Cultural, and Research Workers.[14] A statement in the official Soviet report on education in 1957–1958 serves as a fitting conclusion to the description of the activities of that Union:

> As the functions and rights of the trade unions have been extended during the past year, the new trade union has come to do more to settle problems of labour and to exercise a more exacting supervision of adherence to labour legislation and public control over labour legislation. It has also become more active in improving the standard of living of its membership and raising the level of its cultural and educational work.[15]

14

THE ACADEMY OF PEDAGOGICAL
SCIENCES IN MOSCOW

A truly unique institution in Soviet education is the Academy of Pedagogical Sciences of the R.S.F.S.R. It has high prestige and influence, and its name arises in any discussion of educational problems.

Origin and Membership

The *Akademiia Pedagogicheskikh Nauk R.S.F.S.R.*, abbreviated to A.P.N., was founded on October 6, 1943, in the midst of World War II, by the Soviet of People's Commissars of the R.S.F.S.R.[1] This action showed clearly "the great attention and the deep concern by the Communist Party and the Soviet Government for the development of pedagogical sciences."[2] The first President was Academician V. P. Potemkin, Doctor of Historical Science and winner of the Stalin Prize. Upon his death, in 1946, Vice-President I. A. Kairov was elected; in 1950 and in 1955 he was re-elected.

In 1944, the Academy had a roster of thirteen full members and thirteen corresponding members.[3] By 1946 membership had increased to 31 and 41, respectively.[4] As of March, 1957, there were 32 full members and 53 corresponding members, of whom 19 were specialists in the theory and history of pedagogy, 15 in psychology, 48 in the methodology of the basic disciplines, and three in physiological growth. In 1950 the Academy elected as corresponding members 11 teachers on the basis of their work in educational research.[5] The current strength, as given by Professor Anatoli A. Smirnov on August 22, 1958, is 100 — 35 full members and 65 corresponding members.

A word on the qualifications of the A.P.N. leaders is in order. President Ivan A. Kairov became a full Academy member in 1943. He joined the Communist Party in 1917, concentrated on Party work from 1933 to 1938, was elected deputy to the U.S.S.R. Supreme Soviet in 1950 and 1954, and has been active in many ways in Party work. His professional career was originally in the field of agricultural education but was later identified with the general field of education and teacher training. After receiving the degree of Doctor of Pedagogical Sciences in 1935, Kairov served as head of the Department of Pedagogy at the Lenin Pedagogical Institute in Moscow. His highest administrative position was that of Minister of Education of the R.S.F.S.R., a post he held from 1949 to 1957. He is the author of *Pedagogika* and other educational textbooks. He received the Order of Lenin for his work.[6] It is interesting to note that he has never been a teacher but always an administrator of teacher education. One may also recall that he was active in the pedology purge and in destroying the remnants of progressive education.

The First Vice-President is Professor Nikolai K. Goncharov, known to American educators as the co-author of a textbook on the principles of education, which has been translated in part as *I Want To Be Like Stalin*.[7] He is the editor of *Sovetskaia Pedagogika*, the organ of the A.P.N., which is proof of the influential position he holds among Soviet educators.

Professor Anatoli A. Smirnov, Second Vice-President, is a Doctor of Pedagogical Sciences who specialized in psychology. He became director of the Institute of Psychology of the A.P.N. in 1944 and has held that position ever since. His election to the Presidium of the A.P.N. is recent. Smirnov, who met with the Comparative Education Society on August 22, 1958, is professor of psychology at the University of Moscow, has been editor of *Voprosy Psikhologii* since 1955, and is co-author of the textbook *Psikhologiia*, author of twenty volumes on general, child, and educational psychology, and winner of the Ushinski Medal.[8]

The Academy is under the direction of a presidium consisting of the three officers and four additional members. Two leaders of the Comparative Education Society met with Aleksei A. Leontiev, presidium member, Doctor of Pedagogical Sciences and professor of psychology at the University of Moscow. Professor Leontiev has traveled abroad and speaks French fluently. He has published an important monograph, *The Development of Memory* (1931), and various other studies. Some of his work has appeared in America in the *Journal of Genetic Psychology*.[9]

Another member of the presidium, Aleksei I. Markushevich, also met with members of the Comparative Education Society. Markushevich, until recently Second Vice-President of the Academy, is now First Deputy Minister of Education of the R.S.F.S.R. He is a Doctor of Mathematical Sciences, has been a professor of mathematics at the University of Moscow since 1944, and is author of *The Theory of Analytic Functions*. His membership in the Communist Party dates from 1951.[10] Both Markushevich and Smirnov were members of a Soviet educational delegation that visited schools in the United States in December, 1958.

The Secretary of the Academy, Mikhail A. Melnikov, was elected to his present position in 1957. He coordinates the entire work of the Academy. He is the author of numerous monographs and textbooks and was rewarded for his achievements with the Order of Lenin and other medals.[11]

Election of new members takes place by secret ballot of all members after the publication of the list of candidates in the newspapers. A candidate may be nominated by a higher educational institution or by an individual educator. As noted on an earlier page, members may be drawn from the teaching ranks, although the majority of members have never taught.

The director of an institute in the Academy receives 5500 rubles a month, a deputy director 5000 rubles. The head of a department is paid 4300 rubles, a senior scientific worker 3500 rubles. Any full member of the Academy receives a monthly payment of 3500 rubles, while a corresponding member's payment is 1750. The Academy salaries supplement what these people earn in their regular positions. The scientific workers are full-time employees of the Academy.

Organization

The fundamental aims of the Academy are as follows:

> . . . the scientific analysis of the problems of general and special pedagogy, the history of pedagogy, problems of aesthetic and physical education, psychology, and school hygiene; methods of teaching educational subjects in the school of general education; the promotion of training of scientific personnel for pedagogical sciences and promotion of the development of the people's education and dissemination of pedagogical knowledge among the people.[12]

There are two distinct activities of the Academy: one, in the province of ideology, politics, and dogmatic polemics; the other, in that of educational research, defined in terms of pedology, psychology, sociology, and some of the related social sciences.

The Academy of Pedagogical Sciences consists basically of eight institutes (seven in Moscow, and one general-purpose institute in Leningrad) in which research projects are carried out.[13] It also operates the State Library of the People's Education in the Name of K. D. Ushinski, the Scientific-Pedagogical Archives, the Museum for the People's Education, and the Museum of Toys. In addition, it maintains a press and publishes a variety of periodicals, books, and pamphlets.

Theory and History of Pedagogy. The Scientific-Research Institute of the Theory and History of Pedagogy was directed by Professor Nikolai A. Petrov until his death, on August 18, 1958. The new director, who met with the Comparative Education Society, is A. M. Arseniev, former Minister of Education of the R.S.F.S.R. The Institute of the Theory and History of Pedagogy is concerned with preschool education, didactics, school administration, principles of education in the school and at home, moral and aesthetic education, physical and polytechnical education, general history of education and of the Soviet Union, history of the education of the nationalities in the U.S.S.R., and comparative education. Its actual work is organized in the form of projects, with teams of specialists engaged on specific subtopics contributing to a collective result.

During the year 1958 Institute personnel worked on twenty topics. One of these, on the history of progressive educational ideas in Germany, England, and France in the nineteenth century, was under the supervision of the educational historian, Academician N. A. Konstantinov, Chairman of the Department of Pedagogy at the University of Moscow. This subject was divided into three parts: the pedagogical ideas of the German labor movement in the 1830's; the pedagogical ideas of the English labor movement in the 1840's; and the struggle for the democratization of the French schools from 1850 to 1870. Other historical projects deal with Krupskaya and Ushinski.[14]

Professor Vladimir A. Veikshan, director of the comparative education section of the Institute, told the Comparative Education Society that the study of this field is in its infancy in the U.S.S.R. His staff studies the educational developments in such countries as England, France, and the United States. He maintained that "Dewey is studied very deeply in the U.S.S.R.," but could cite for support only a book by Komarovskova that was published in 1926 and the more recent denunciatory work by V. S. Shevkin, *The Pedagogy of J. Dewey in the Service of Contemporary American Reaction,* published in 1952. Veikshan showed considerable interest in American educational theory, particularly in the anti-Dewey trends.

Psychology. The Scientific-Research Institute of Psychology, directed by Second Vice-President Smirnov, deals with general, educational, child, and special psychology, as well as with the history of psychology. Fourteen problems are being studied at present, among them the processes of perception, thinking, and speech, the means of studying the personality of a child in a boarding school, and the psychology of polytechnical training.[15]

At a conference with the Comparative Education Society, members of the Institute of Psychology, led by Professor Smirnov, discussed the research they were doing and showed their laboratory facilities in general and in preschool and educational psychology. One American psychologist, while observing the experimental apparatus for "a very elaborate electro-encephalogram investigation," asked the experimenter if he knew anything about work being done along these lines in the United States. The Soviet psychologist denied any knowledge, but "when quizzed about the

Alpha and Beta waves he immediately fell into the familiar lingo of persons who work with the EEG."

Since all research and thinking in Soviet psychology is founded upon Marxist-Leninist dialectical materialism and the work of Pavlov, outside of experiments with the conditioned reflex there is little or no interest on the part of the Institute of Psychology in foreign work of any sort. The history of psychology section conducts research on the evolution of Russian and Soviet psychology only. The American visitors inquired about their Soviet colleagues' knowledge of the researches of Freud, Moreno, Piaget, Gesell, Olson, and others. The replies were that their work was known but that it had no relevance to the situation in the Soviet Union. The Pavlovian and Marxist-Leninist orientation places real constraints on research in the Institute of Psychology. Soviet psychologists, of course, said that they looked upon these sources of their science as towers of strength and inspiration.

Methods of Teaching. The Scientific-Research Institute of the Methods of Teaching organizes research projects on the content and methods of teaching, methods of adult education, and development of suitable school equipment. Its members are concerned with research problems of many kinds, including an experiment in the teaching of the Constitution of the U.S.S.R. in grade ten, methods of teaching French vocabulary to eighth-grade students, the history of teaching foreign languages in secondary educational institutions in prerevolutionary Russia and the U.S.S.R., and methods of scientific research in the ways of teaching geography.[16]

Director Sergei G. Shapovalenko, Doctor of Pedagogical Sciences, has been a corresponding member of the Academy since 1946. He stressed the fact that his Institute is concerned with research on methods of teaching specific subjects by specialists in the various areas of subject matter, while the Institute of Theory and History treats the problems of general methodology.

The visual-aids section, naturally enough, prepares all kinds of instructional helps for specific subjects and tests them in experimental schools. It also seeks to develop the best school desks and chairs, as well as other school equipment.

Another section is concerned with the production of textbooks.

Members of this branch work on experimental textbooks, test them in experimental schools, and then study the reports by teachers and methodologists before they determine final form.

Nationality Schools. The Scientific-Research Institute of the Nationality Schools, directed by Academician E. I. Korenevskii, conducts inquiries on methods of teaching the languages of the different nationalities of the Soviet Union and methods of teaching the Russian language in the nationality schools. Of the four problem areas covered, one deals with the teaching of native languages, the rest with the teaching of Russian. The projects on native-language teaching concern the Mordovian, Buryat-Mongolian, Komi, and Abkhazian Autonomous Soviet Socialist Republics and the Khakassian Autonomous Region.[17] This Institute prepares textbooks and minimum bilingual word lists for the acquisition of vocabulary in the nationality schools.

Artistic Education. The Scientific-Research Institute of Artistic Education studies problems relating to aesthetic training of pre-school children and to training in all forms of artistic expression — drawing, music, literature — of children in the general education schools. In addition, it devotes time to problems of artistic education out of school. The ten topics of current research include musical education in schools and its role in well-rounded educational development, aesthetic education in boarding schools, and the system of aesthetic education in kindergartens.[18] Workers in the Institute pay much attention to methods of teaching and they prepare textbooks and other instructional aids. Moreover, they help teachers of the aesthetic subjects both in the schools and in the Institute. As explained by the assistant director, Professor S. N. Pavlova, the term "artistic" applies mainly to appearance, while "aesthetic" refers to the ability to perceive nature through the arts and to the development of artistic interests.

Physical Education and School Hygiene. The Scientific-Research Institute of Physical Education and School Hygiene, under the direction of A. A. Markosian, is concerned with the theory and methods of physical education of preschool and school children, improvement of pupil health, home and school hygiene in relation to children, and the design and organization of school buildings from the health standpoint. Educators, physicians, teachers, and parents benefit from its work. Among the ten topic areas of current research are the hygiene of polytechnical training and the hygiene of the physical education of pupils.[19] Institute studies are yielding suggestions on the length of lessons and of homework, the regulation of children's sleep, and the spacing of labor and study.

Defectology. The Scientific-Research Institute of Defectology deals with research on methods of teaching preschool and school children who are deaf, dumb, blind, or mentally retarded. Directed by A. I. Dyachkov, its members work in twenty-one research areas.[20] Although the psychologists here do not make use of mental tests, they do show a series of pictures graded in difficulty to a child under study and score his "responses."

Activities and Publications

The Academy maintains a number of experimental schools for testing new methods, textbooks, visual aids, and school furniture and equipment. Another distinctive activity is the series of pedagogical lectures on readings (*Pedagogicheskie Chteniia*) held every second year in all areas of the country, culminating in the biennial conference of the Academy in Moscow. Lecture topics are proposed by the Academy and submitted by educational scientists, inspectors, and administrators, workers in Komsomol, Pioneer, and other paraschool institutions, teachers and professors, and parents. The writers of the best papers are rewarded by prizes, testimonials, and publication. The pedagogical lectures help to disseminate the latest findings in educational practice and science.[21]

The State Library for the People's Education in the Name of K. D. Ushinski, the largest pedagogical library in the U.S.S.R., now has close to one million volumes. The collections include Russian and Soviet educational writings, Marxist-Leninist classics, and foreign pedagogical literature. It is directed by N. A. Sundakov, who has a staff of fifty, including twelve bibliographical specialists.[22] Personal observation revealed that the Ushinski Library's material on foreign education, that is, on French, British, and American school systems, are far from complete or current. However, library personnel are making an effort to improve their collections, since much of the research by the Academy workers depends on the literature available in this institution. Since the library possessed only 600,000 volumes in 1949, it is obvious that it is expanding rapidly.[23]

The museums and the archives operated by the Academy also help in the collection and dissemination of educational information, past and present. The collection is of great value to the research workers of the Academy and of considerable interest to other educators and to the public.[24]

The publishing activities of the Academy help further its influence on education in the U.S.S.R., especially through three periodicals, *Sovetskaia Pedagogika, Voprosy Psikhologii,* and *Sem'ia i Shkola.* It is important to note that directors and deans of the various research institutions also control the publications — a very powerful censorship factor.

Soviet Pedagogy. This monthly journal is now in the twenty-third year of publication. The September, 1958, issue, which appeared during the American visit, came out in 50,700 copies. Edited by Vice-President Goncharov of the Academy, this periodical publishes articles on pedagogical theory and practice, history of pedagogy, the education of teachers, foreign education, news and reports of Academy research, discussion and debate, and critical reviews of current educational literature. The last issue in 1956 carried a review of I. L. Kandel's *The New Era in Education,*[25] by M. S. Bernshtein. That writer had published essays in 1948–1949 on "Reactionary Conceptions of Contemporary American Pedagogical Philosophy (Neo-Thomism, Neo-Aristotelianism, and Personalism)," "Reactionary Elements in the Experimentalism of Professor Kilpatrick," and "The Reactionary Conception of American Pedagogical Philosophy (Neo-Realism)," and was also the author of a review article, "The Latest Revelation in American Philosophy of Education," in a 1957 issue.[26] In the issue commemorating the fortieth anniversary of the Revolution, V. A. Veikshan contributed an article on "Foreign Pedagogues and Public Figures on Schools in the USSR." Among the foreigners quoted were George S. Counts, Stuart Symington, William Benton, Sir Ronald Gould, and J. D. Bernal.[27] Professor Veikshan devoted eight double-columned, closely printed pages in the August, 1958, number to a critical analysis of *Education in the USSR*, a bulletin issued by the United States Office of Education the previous fall. His contribution, which included a résumé of the visit by the delegation headed by Commissioner Lawrence G. Derthick of the United States Office of Education, was entitled "In a Distorted Mirror." [28] Interestingly, an English translation of this journal began publication in November, 1958, under the title *Soviet Education.*

Problems of Psychology. This journal, edited by Second Vice-President Smirnov, appears six times a year and has a circulation of 5600 (July-August, 1958). The articles comprise reports on research in general, educational, and child psychology, reports on the status of psychology in foreign countries, an index of current Soviet psychological literature, reports on the teaching of psychology, and discussions and news of interest to professional psychologists. The section on foreign psychology in one issue includes an annotated bibliography on international congresses and conferences and on conventions of various foreign psychological associations during 1954–1957.[29] The table of contents appears in English on the last page of each issue.

Family and School. This monthly is addressed to a popular audience. Its circulation increased from 50,000 in 1946 to 300,000 in 1956.[30]

Other Educational Journals

The following is the list of subject magazines published in the Soviet Union:

Biologia v Shkole (Biology in School)
Fizika v Shkole (Physics in School)
Geografia v Shkole (Geography in School)
Inostrannye Iazyki v Shkole (Foreign Languages in School)
Khimiia v Shkole (Chemistry in School)
Literatura v Shkole (Literature in School)
Matematika v Shkole (Mathematics in School)
Politekhnicheskoe Obuchenie (Polytechnical Education)
Prepodavanie Istorii v Shkole (History Instruction in School)

Professionalno-Tekhnicheskoe Obrazovanie (Professional-Technical Education)

Ruskii Iazyk v Natsionalnoi Shkole (Teaching Russian in Nationality Schools)

Ruskii Iazyk v Shkole (Russian in School)

Srednee Spetsialnoe Obrazovanie (Middle School Specialty Education)

To this impressive wealth of educational publication the Academy contributes in several areas.

Short reports on research are published four times a year in *Doklady Akademii Pedagogicheskikh Nauk RSFSR,* which appears in 1000 copies. Edited by B. G. Ananer and A. R. Luria, this publication contains articles on polytechnical education, principles and problems of education, psychology and physiology, school hygiene, and defectology. An English table of contents follows the Russian listing.

The Academy also publishes periodically a volume of *News,* which is another outlet for research workers. A recent issue was edited by Director A. A. Markosian of the Institute of Physical Education and School Hygiene. *The Yearbook of Pedagogical Lectures* contains abstracts of the prize-winning educational essays submitted by teachers and others, and three papers of greater length by such prominent educators as V. A. Veikshan.

The Academy has published an impressive number of books, all of which are issued under the imprint of its press, Izdatelstvo Akademii Pedagogicheskikh Nauk RSFSR. The list covers a wide variety of subjects. In methodology, there are volumes on elementary foreign-language teaching, German-language teaching, three grade-four subjects, polytechnical training, and teacher improvement; also on principles of education, educational textbooks for prospective and in-service teachers, detailed descriptions of education in the U.S.S.R., and school administration. In educational theory, the Academy issued K. D. Ushinski's works in eleven volumes and A. S. Makarenko's in eight; several volumes of the selected educational writings of A. N. Hertzen, V. G. Belinsky, N. G. Chernishevsky, N. A. Dobroliubov, L. N. Tolstoi, N. K. Krupskaya, M. N. Kalinin, and A. S. Makarenko. In recent years, it has collected the pedagogical works of Marx-Engels and Lenin. The field of educational history is taken care of with general textbooks for teachers and other works.

Abstracts. Not much has been printed as yet on the systems of education in foreign countries, the only work known to the writer being a volume published in 1957 on the school system of the People's China. An attempt is being made by Academy specialists, however, to keep up to date with what is written abroad on educational matters. At infrequent intervals abstracts of *Pedagogy and the People's Education in Foreign Countries,* now under the editorship of V. A. Veikshan and V. A. Grachev, appear. The first number, dated 1955, contained summaries of eighty-four articles, representing journals in Bulgaria, East and West Germany, Poland, England, France, Italy, Czechoslovakia, Hungary, and the United States. Some of the abstracts dealt with the activities of international educational organizations. The subject matter covered history of pedagogy, general foundations of pedagogy, theory of education, problems of didactics, special methods, psychology, organization of the people's education, and problems of the teacher. The second issue, published in 1957, contained 105 abstracts taken from British, Bulgarian, Vietnamese, East and West German, Indian, Italian, Polish, Rumanian, American, French, Czechoslovakian, and Yugoslavian journals. Thirty-three entries summarized articles in educational periodicals published in the United States.

There are three points of interest in connection with this publication. In the first place, its circulation rose from 600 to 6000 in two years, indicating the need for it among Soviet educators. Secondly, its scope and size are extremely limited. We need only to compare it to the abstracting journals published by the Institute of Scientific Information of the Academy of Sciences of the U.S.S.R. (*Akademiia Nauk SSSR*). The smallest of the thirteen journals prepared by the Academy of Sciences is the one on physics and geophysics; a monthly, it consists of forty pages more than the educational abstract journal and sums up scientific writings in several languages, including Japanese and Finnish. Finally, the second number of the educational abstracts added a section on teaching polytechnical training, reflecting the rising interest in this form of teaching.

Bibliographical Sources. The Ushinski Library prepares three series of bibliographical compilations for the use of teachers and educators. *Novye Knigi* is a monthly list of recent books acquired by the library in the fields of pedagogy, child and adolescent literature, linguistics, the natural and the social sciences, the arts, mathematics, psychology, philosophy, and Communist lore (Marxism-Leninism, atheism, the Communist Party, and so forth).

Literatura po Pedagogicheskim Naukam is a quarterly listing of books and articles restricted to the field of pedagogy. More than twenty major branches of the subject, such as psychology, methodology, administration, higher education, teacher training, school systems in the Iron Curtain block and in other foreign countries, boarding schools, and bibliography, are represented. This compilation is very valuable to anyone desiring to have the fullest and latest information on what is taking place in all phases of Soviet education. An author index makes rapid reference possible.

The third bibliographical source is another quarterly, *Novye Knigi po Pedagogike i Narodnomu Obrazovaniiu Zarubezhnykh Stran* (*New Books on Pedagogy and the People's Education in Foreign Countries*), summarizing in each issue some 250 to 300 books printed abroad on such topics as educational history, general and educational psychology, administration, preschool education, and the like.[31] The Soviet educator can keep himself informed of the most recent sources of knowledge about education in various parts of the world. Like the *Novye Knigi,* this publication is free and widely distributed.

Projected Reference Works. The need for substantial reference works in education was realized early in the history of the Academy. In 1949 an article stated that the Academy "is preparing for publication a *Short Pedagogical Encyclopedia* and a *Children's Encyclopedia.*"[32] But in 1958 the Academy could announce only that the first two volumes of the latter would come off the press during the year,[33] in spite of Kairov's prediction in 1949 that the ten-volume project would be completed in the course of the next few years.[34] The chief editor of the *Children's Encyclopedia* is Professor A. I. Markushevich. A. G. Kalashnikov and D. A. Epstein, two of the editors of Volume III, were also co-editors of the first Soviet educational encyclopedia, which appeared in the 1930's.

In 1957 Kairov announced the resumption of work on the *Pedagogical Encyclopedia,*[35] but the 1958 program of publications of the Academy did not mention this project at all. Probably more time will elapse before work is begun once more.

Kairov also announced that the compilation of a *Pedagogical Dictionary* would be concluded in 1958. The editorship of this volume is in the hands of a six-man collegium headed by Kairov, Goncharov, and Smirnov.[36]

In summing up, it is appropriate to quote the *Bolshaia Sovetskaia Entsiklopediia* on the significance of the Academy: "By concentrating its work on the problem of Communist education, by the methods of research, by the scope of its activities and budget, the APN, RSFSR is the only very advanced and powerful scientific-pedagogical institution in the world."[37]

Although we can admire this unequaled educational research organization, it is necessary to remember the important role played by the Academy in furthering the objectives of the Communist Party in the Soviet Union.

PART
THREE

PART

THREE

15

EDUCATION OF THE
HANDICAPPED

Of the special areas in Soviet education that cannot be fitted easily into a general description, the training of handicapped children deserves first appraisal. Although schools for the handicapped have existed in Russia since tsarist times, this field has received much less attention than has general education. Only in recent times has improvement been made and research intensified on methods and means of helping the handicapped child. Research and pilot programs have led to improved techniques and expanded facilities, although much work is still neccessary to bring the program up to date.

The Defectives in the Society

The aim of education of the handicapped in the Soviet Union is to help the children become, as far as possible, productive members of society. Schools for the physically handicapped, as well as schools and institutions for the mentally retarded and the mentally ill, have vocational courses and provide their graduates with jobs in industry and agriculture. Some of them follow their pupils' careers for a time after graduation. Thus, the most advanced schools for the blind give the pupils shop experiences and prepare them for job placement as vocational schools for the blind in the United States do. Schools for the mentally retarded stress preparation for an active and useful life; and schools for the deaf and hard of hearing give their pupils manual training and some job preparation.

There is a sharp contrast to this attitude in the social life of handicapped people. Handicapped children are kept apart, not only from normal children, but also from other categories of the handicapped. Blind children are kept with the blind, deaf children with the deaf, and so forth, in schools, in summer camps, in recreation, and in all social activities connected with school life. This isolation continues through life. Both the deaf and the blind have their own All-Union Society, which not only provides job opportunities but also takes care of social life. It may thus easily happen that a deaf person will marry a deaf person, as most of his acquaintances and social life are derived from the activities of the All-Union Society for the Deaf. The same is true for the blind. This creates the possibility of deafness or blindness in the children of such marriages, but such a possibility is disregarded because of the Soviet views on heredity.

Administration of Special Education

Special education is organized on three levels, according to the nature of the disability. The ministry of education in each republic controls the schools for immediately trainable children. These include schools for the blind, the deaf, the partially blind, and the partially deaf. Here also belong schools for children in delicate health and children with illnesses such as rheumatic ailments and tuberculosis. These are the "Forest Schools," where children follow the program of the regular schools at a slower pace and receive medical care. Schools for mentally retarded children who can be educated also fall in this category, as do the schools for emotionally disturbed children.

Schools for the partially trainable are controlled by the republic ministries of health and take care of cripples and victims of congenital diseases. The ministries of health also control hospitals and institutions for psychotics and other serious mental cases. In these institutions an attempt is made to educate the children as much as possible according to the regular school curriculum.

Nontrainable cases are the responsibility of the ministries of public insurance. It is not easy to visit the institutions in this category.

Research for the whole field of the education and care of the physically and mentally handicapped is carried on by the Institute of Defectology of the Academy of Pedagogical Sciences. It has branches in major cities and is aided by defectology faculties, which train teachers for the special schools, in the various pedagogical institutes.

The Institute of Defectology, working with the Ministry of Education of the R.S.F.S.R., prepares programs and curricula for the special schools and writes the textbooks for the handicapped. In the schools attached to it new methods can be introduced and experiments carried on. Results of the research are valid for the whole Soviet Union.

This chapter will deal only with the schools and institutions for the trainable and partially trainable. While evaluating figures and statistics from Soviet sources the reader should keep in mind that the program for the handicapped is comparatively new in the Soviet Union and figures may not include the many handicapped persons who have not yet been reached by the available services.

Education of the Mentally Retarded

Mentally retarded children are, by Soviet definition, children who have suffered some form of brain damage. The prominent Soviet psychologist A. R. Luria put it this way:

> Only when, either at the pre-natal stage or at an early age, a child has suffered serious brain disease which profoundly disturbs his further development and makes him defective intellectually, may we speak of intellectual backwardness of a kind which makes the child's education in the common school impossible and calls for his transference to an auxiliary school.[1]

Children are referred to special schools after careful observation in nursery school or kindergarten. No standardized tests are used to determine their condition, but individual tests for each child may be devised. The study of one child may extend over a period of six months to a year.

The Institute of Defectology makes an elaborate case history of each child referred to it, including a medical report, a pedagogical history, and a study of the child's speech development. There is an attempt to relate the study of the child's mental development to his health, his work and his play; and emotional as well as mental development is considered.

Tests used here also are not standardized. One of the tests consists of a series of pictures of moving objects but including a picture of an object that does not move, and the child is asked to identify that one. In another instance, the child is asked the significance of three pictures, each showing something from the animal, mineral, and vegetable categories. He is also confronted with a series of pictures that, if placed in the right sequence, tell a story. There are no particular norms for these pictures according to either the level of educational training or any level of mental ability that can be related to the age of the child. Other pictures, containing outline drawings of common objects, are marked over with all sorts of lines designed to confuse the youngster as to the actual form of the picture. The ability to perceive the outlined object tells something about the child's perceptive ability, but again, no age or achievement norms are admitted. This procedure is comparable to a standard testing device used in the United States to identify or diagnose, among other things, perceptive disturbances resulting from brain damage.[2]

Auxiliary schools for the mentally retarded are seven-, eight-, or nine-year schools. They offer vocational training, general knowledge, or whatever the children can absorb. The children are also given special labor exercises. Mentally retarded boys are taught woodworking and construction; girls are trained in textile work. Psychologists and physiologists are included in the staffs of these schools and there is a speech correctionist in every school.

Description of a School. In the Rossilimo School for retarded orphan girls in Moscow the course takes seven years. The program corresponds to about the first four years in a regular school, but special textbooks are used. Pupils are taught singing, drawing, and handicrafts. More manual work is introduced than in the regular schools, and physical training is emphasized. According to the director,

> The aim of the school is to make the pupils self-sustaining. The
> girls are taught sewing and also learn gardening. Some have to go

to the country for their practical experience, and the girls seem to be better gardeners than dressmakers.

If a pupil is not self-supporting at the end of seven years in school, she may stay for another year or even two. Most of the girls are sixteen or seventeen when they leave, but they may stay until they are eighteen. Visitors were told that some other schools of this type now have an eight-year program and teach more labor.

Most graduates of this school go to work in the dressmaking industry. After a girl takes a job she remains under the supervision of the school for two years. The trade unions and the Komsomol organization also help supervise her. The pupils return to the orphanage for visits, and the teachers visit the girls at work.

The school has a Pioneer organization, to which all the eligible children belong; it is self-governing, like any normal Pioneer organization. The children elect their leaders and their representatives on the various committees.

The object of the school is to train the girls to be polite, modest, and well disciplined. Pupils who are particularly well behaved have their names and pictures put on the bulletin board. Each class has five honor girls who are so distinguished. Each girl also receives a star every fortnight she improves. Graduates may stay on to help the other girls and are sometimes allowed to work independently without supervision.

A few short visits to classrooms yielded the following observations: A first-year class had ten pupils; the girls were reading the names of their classmates on the materials they were distributing for a drawing lesson. A fifth-year Russian-language class was trying to make sentences about a picture. A seventh-year mathematics class had thirteen pupils, all very small for their age, who were doing work in the multiplication of one-place numbers. The school has a gymnasium with climbing apparatus and other equipment for Swedish gymnastics. There is also a small library and reading room. The sewing room is equipped with both electric and treadle machines. The girls' rooms were bare, but clean and adequate. A doctor comes to school for about five hours every day and takes care of all the pupils' health problems.

During the visit to this school, as well as in other interviews on the subject of retarded children, Soviet experts insisted that some form of brain damage was the only possible cause for mental retardation.

Even when the record of the child showed no history of a brain injury, the Soviet doctors and educators maintained that it must be present in some form. Something possibly wrong with either one of the parents could have been transmitted to the child. Or brain injury could have occurred previous to birth in the mother's womb. The resulting condition of limited intelligence could be permanent but it could not be a result of inheritance of innate ability.

Treatment of the Mentally Ill

The treatment of mentally disturbed children in the Soviet Union is under the control of the ministry of health of each republic. At the Research Institute of Psychiatry the director reported that dispensaries are provided for such children where they can go once or twice a week and where various treatments are used. Therapists — Soviet experts use this term to denote general practitioners and physicians — go to schools and visit the homes of emotionally disturbed children. In conversations with the parents they try to learn about the child's symptoms and the reasons for the emotional imbalance, hoping to improve the home situation and thus the child's state of health. For example, if the child does not sleep well he receives medication, and his parents are given a daily regimen for him to follow. There are also summer camps for neurotic children. And, finally, the ministries of education have special "Forest Schools," where such children may be sent for a period of one to three months.

As the Soviet psychologists do not divide the mental from the somatic state, every child with an emotional problem is first given a thorough physical examination. If none of the above-mentioned measures helps (including the Forest School) the child is then placed in a hospital.

Soviet psychologists feel that the most frequent cause of neurosis is an organic or infectious disease, although sometimes the neurosis can be caused by adverse family conditions, such as when parents do not live together harmoniously. The therapeutic measures taken depend obviously on the nature of the disease. It is not considered correct, pedagogically, to pay too much attention to the child and his attitude, although counseling is sometimes part of his therapy.

Speaking to the child correctly and rationally may do some good but cannot be the only treatment.

Neurosis is classified into several types, as in the United States. If a patient is not better in a month or so, he is always hospitalized, but time is not the only measure in treatment. Projective techniques, such as the Rorschach method, are almost never used. The Soviets rely a great deal on a technique called electrosleep in dealing with children who have emotional problems. A treatment lasts from twenty minutes to two hours, and it consists of the use of a machine that produces a very light electric current transmitted to the scalp by means of several small electrodes placed on the head. Various kinds of neurosis are treated by this method, but it is not used with psychotic patients.

Psychotics are treated by a process called "labor therapy," which is similar to occupational therapy, and also by the use of insulin shots and drugs. Electroshock is used very little. Restraint or shackles of various types are reportedly applied sometimes, but the Soviets prefer to use tranquilizing drugs. Visitors were told again and again that the Pavlovian theory is the basis for all therapeutic techniques in the Soviet Union.

The Psychological Hospital for Children and Youth in Moscow is divided into three kinds of institutional setups. There is a hospital for children of preschool and school age; a polyclinic, where consultations are given but the patient does not stay; and a section for children of preschool age with speech defects. Children may be referred to this hospital by pediatric therapists or doctors in the schools if the latter feel, in the course of their examination, that referral is necessary for diagnostic purposes. In diagnosis, the hospital therapist always consults the school authorities, the family, and the child, and also observes behavior to a considerable extent. Every phase of the child's life is taken into consideration before the final decision is made. Special teachers are employed in this hospital, as in all children's hospitals, so that children can pursue the same lessons as their schoolmates in the regular schools. There is a considerable effort to return the children to school without loss of time. This hospital has also a research laboratory on reflexes. It is located here because these children are very young and cannot be taken into the regular laboratories.

There are two psychiatrists in each of the eighteen administrative districts into which Moscow is divided. One of these works in a child polyclinic with various other specialists, another in an outpatient clinic dealing with both children and adults in each particular district.

The largest mental hospital in Moscow is the Kashenko Hospital. It has 2400 beds and a staff of 2207: 160 doctors of all kinds, 628 trained nurses, 1092 ward attendants, and 281 other employees. The annual budget is 33 million rubles, about 14,000 rubles per hospital bed. Patients here come from eleven of Moscow's eighteen districts. Each district has a dispensary for neurotics, which is similar to an outpatient clinic.

The hospital specializes in the treatment of the seriously ill — schizophrenics, epileptics, manic-depressives, paranoids, and all types of psychotics. It has departments for men, women, and children. Violent and nonviolent patients are placed in separate wards. Insulin shock and drugs are the chief type of therapy; surgery is used very little. Tranquilizing drugs take the place of shackles. Freudian concepts are definitely rejected by the Soviet psychiatrists, but observers felt that many of the therapeutic techniques were similar to those used in America. Physiotherapy and labor therapy also play an important part in treatment. When a patient feels better he is sent to a sanatorium, which seems to be a midway point on the road to recovery.

The children's department of the Kashenko Hospital has facilities to care for 200 boys and 200 girls. Drugs are used heavily with violent patients. Even here, in a hospital dealing with the seriously ill and the psychotic, regular school classes continue. The children have many activities. Dances and concerts for parents and other patients are arranged, so that shyness is reduced and the patients keep active. There is a garden with birds and animals for schizophrenic children where the child can work. Each child has a piece of land to cultivate and care for. Other occupational therapy is also available.

Soviet doctors questioned at this hospital agreed that the cause of schizophrenia is unknown or at least not definitely known at present. They also agreed that heredity is a factor, as in epilepsy, although in the former environmental factors are perhaps stronger. Since World War II there may be some syphilis and thus a very small incidence of paresis, but officials at the hospital maintained that there is no such disease as general paresis in the country, because there is no syphilis (except for infections from abroad). The impact of political beliefs upon theories in biology and defectology reveals itself in a fascinating way in comments such as these.

Education of the Deaf and the Hard of Hearing

The Institute of Defectology has a Department for the Deaf, which is divided into a number of subdepartments: one covering the theory of teaching the deaf, one for the teaching of the partially deaf, a phonetics and acoustics laboratory, a department for the psychology of the deaf, and an experimental laboratory. It is the responsibility of these departments and of the Institute as a whole to develop methods of teaching, to write textbooks, and to plan the curriculum for the special schools.

Research departments follow something of this procedure: The departments are given problems to work out in cooperation with the schools. Teachers are expected to participate in some form of scientific research with the help of experts from the Institute. Such experimental work is checked by observation, not by tests that would allow for statistical discrimination of their validity and reliability, as is the case in the United States. It is common practice for each school to publish the best research done by its teachers. Visitors were given one such book, autographed with some pride by the author, director of School No. 337 in Moscow.

In the Soviet Union there are special schools for deaf-mutes, mentally retarded deaf-mutes, congenitally hard of hearing who can speak, hard of hearing who have speech difficulty, children who have become hard of hearing or deaf, the blind, and the partially blind. This classification is not always adhered to exactly, however. In all schools children receive normal teaching as well as special work in overcoming their disabilities. The Ministry of Education defines programs that incorporate the recommendations of the Institute of Defectology. As an official of the Institute stated, "There is a high degree of cooperation between all establishments concerned with our research. This makes it possible for ideas to be put into practice quickly."

There is no special theory about the reason for deafness in the

Soviet Union. It is mostly ascribed to various nonhereditary diseases. The director of School No. 337 in Moscow, for instance, claimed that meningitis is a frequent cause of deafness. "Out of our school population, about 37 per cent of the children had this disease." There is no adequate way of explaining the cause of deafness in the other 63 per cent.

According to Mme. Andreeva, chief of the Faculty of Defectology at the Pedagogical Institute in Leningrad, there are 270 schools for the deaf in the U.S.S.R. Seventy are boarding schools. There are also schools for adults and for the hard of hearing. The R.S.F.S.R. has forty special kindergartens for the deaf. Teachers of handicapped children are trained at pedagogical institutes by special faculties.

Classification of children with hearing losses is comparable to that in the United States. First are those born deaf or with deafness acquired before three years of age and without speech or language. Second are those with acquired deafness after three years of age and with some speech and language. Children who cannot hear vowel sounds are classified as deaf, while those who can are classified as partially hearing. The partially hearing are divided into those who have severe losses and poor speech and those with less severe losses and fair-to-good speech. Another descriptive classification relates to distance of hearing. In School No. 337, a school for the partially hearing, 500 children were reported to hear at one and one-half meters, 100 at three meters, and 25 at two meters. The volume of voice or tone was not given. The measurable loss by audiometric examination for classification purposes was not ascertained, but audiometers (somewhat crude) were used and otologists as well as pediatricians were full-time staff members. Children received audiometric examinations at least twice a year.

There are special nurseries for deaf children from one to three years of age and kindergartens for those from three to seven years of age. After that, the children are ready for special elementary schools. The standard pattern in schools for the deaf provides for nine years as the equivalent of the traditional seven-year secondary school. There are also complete twelve-year secondary schools. After finishing the work in these schools the child may go on to a technical school or register for the competitive entrance examination to a university.

The only real link between nurseries and kindergartens and the school programs noted in the Soviet Union was in the area of the deaf and partially hearing. Teachers of the deaf visited the special kindergartens for children with hearing losses to evaluate their readiness to enter the special schools. While the child is in the special kindergarten his parents are instructed in methods of teaching. Guidebooks and lesson plans to be used in home instruction are published by the Academy of Pedagogical Sciences. Only those children considered ready for the rigorous demands of the formal educational programs are accepted at seven years of age for the first grade. Some go to regular schools; some, with impaired speech, to special schools. Others are placed in a readiness class and a few are retained in the special kindergarten for a year or more. The program for all schools for the deaf is identical and is based on the one prepared by the Academy of Pedagogical Science.

Higher educational facilities are open to physically handicapped students, but they get no special privileges except a double stipend and special interpreters for spelling and singing. Most of those who enter higher educational establishments go to technical schools. Some go to a university, but none is found in faculties of pedagogy, medicine, or engineering.

Teaching Methods. In the kindergartens children are taught by the oral method. Some instruments are used for articulation and there is experimentation with motion pictures. Primitive signs are taught only to help children learn to speak. Finger spelling is now being introduced in the kindergarten in place of signs so that the whole word can be spelled. Children are taught to read by the whole method. Lip reading is started in the first year; the children learn letters by analyzing words. Special instruments for manipulating the speech organs as an aid in articulation are used throughout the U.S.S.R.

A School for the Hard of Hearing. The largest school for the hard of hearing is School No. 337 in Moscow.[3] This is almost entirely for hard-of-hearing children; there are only 75 deaf children in over 600 pupils. The director has been a teacher of the deaf for twenty-six years and organized the school. He is himself deaf and an expert speech reader.

The school has ten grades. The primary grades take five years;

grades five, six, and seven take four years; grades eight, nine, and ten take three years. Textbooks are the same as those of the normal schools. The children range from age seven through nineteen. Five per cent had been deaf before three years of age, while the rest acquired deafness later. The school is open from eight-thirty to six o'clock. It operated on two shifts until November, 1958, when a new school accommodated half the pupils and eliminated the second shift. Every room in the new building is equipped with sound amplifiers. A special kindergarten for the deaf attached to this school is housed in a separate building and has 100 children aged three and a half to seven. Many more such kindergartens are planned, as the Russian home is not suitable for the education of the deaf.

Education at School No. 337 is based on the training of residual hearing and the development of vision. The method used is to stimulate the residual hearing and to teach lip reading. Teachers learn to speak clearly but not to exaggerate. Hearing aids are used and, although they are not up to the quality of those in the United States, they have been improved over the past ten years. Generally, there are ten to twelve pupils in the class and group hearing aids are used in the classroom.

Great attention is paid to the child's speech. There are three speech therapists on the staff of the school, two otolaryngologists and a pediatrician. Children have all their medical service at school, including ear, nose, and throat examinations.

The 100 teachers in the school are all graduates of the Department of Defectology of the Pedagogical Institute of Moscow. Fifty of them are recent graduates and gained their laboratory and student teaching experience in this same school, which is experimental and closely affiliated with the Institute of Defectology and the Faculty of Defectology of the Pedagogical Institute. Many student teachers were seen in the building. Teachers get 125 per cent of base salary for teaching handicapped pupils. Students planning to become teachers get 150 per cent of the ordinary stipend. The director claimed that as a result he could recruit highly qualified teachers and that there is no teacher shortage.

The school has two buses to transport children from their homes and to use on field trips. It also has its own summer camp, accommodating 380 pupils.

Much attention is paid to the polytechnical program. Girls are taught sewing, while boys are taught photography, woodworking, and metalworking. The connection between the school and plants and factories is stressed, and vocational preparation is designed to send pupils directly into the factories. In summer children quite often work on collective and state farms. An example of what is expected of the children is that the upper grades in this school helped to build the new school, each pupil working some three hours a week. After graduation pupils go into industry, some after seven grades of education, most after finishing ten years. Boys are directed into tool industries or farm work, girls into the textile industries. Those who finish up to nine years are allowed to take advanced courses. About two-thirds of the graduates have taken examinations for some form of higher education.

Communist ideology is taught in this school, as in every other in the U.S.S.R. There is a Pioneer organization and the usual round of meetings and activities. In a special seminar twice a week families with deaf children in grades one and two are taught how to use lip reading with their own children. Audiograms are made twice a year and a complete folder of the child's record in speech and hearing passes with him from class to class.

A School for Deaf-Mutes. School No. 2 in Moscow houses children who lost their hearing before they learned to speak, that is, before the age of three. Children at this school have very little hearing. There are seventy teachers and thirty-one classes, for 350 pupils. The program is planned for twelve years, during which the children get seven years of the ordinary school. After graduation they may go to one of the technical schools for additional courses or they go to work.

Most children come to school knowing a few words, as they have learned to speak and read lips at kindergartens. At the school they have special work on breathing, voice, and articulation. When the children learn to imitate, they are taught signs and finger spelling as an aid. Hearing aids are employed to help the rhythm in two of the elementary classes. Audiograms are made at the beginning and at the end of the school year. Lip reading is started in the first year as well as in kindergarten.

This school does not have special speech correctionists, but all teachers have some training, and speech and hearing experts visit the school to help. There are twenty-six student teachers and, to help the boarding students, several matrons and special nurses, most of whom have worked there for twenty years and are able to help with speech and lip reading.

In a second-grade mathematics class visited, the children were all completely deaf and had not been trained in kindergarten. Nevertheless, their speech was generally clear. In a second-grade language class the children were describing fruit and its properties. The speech of these children was only fair, but a person not ac-customed to the deaf could understand very well. The room was fitted with a group hearing aid, but it was not being used. Visitors were told that it was ordinarily used although the children were profoundly deaf.[4] At a seventh-grade Russian class in poetry, ques-tions and answers were used and the teacher used finger spelling to indicate word endings and grammatical structure, although every-thing else was oral. Visitors noticed some signing in the hall.

There are 200 boarding students at this school; other students, who are somewhat older, commute. The school has been working on a revised program to lower the period of study from twelve to eleven years. The year 1958 graduated two classes, one of which had completed eleven years, the other twelve years. Both had had seven years of regular work.

Neither this boarding school nor another day school for the deaf in Moscow, School No. 338, appears to have the progressive, experimental approach of School No. 337. Much more empha-sis is given to the manual method of communication, although the oral method is available. These schools remind one of our resi-dential deaf-schools of yesterday and the few remaining nonpro-gressive residential schools of today.

Special organizations, such as the All-Union Society for the Deaf, are engaged in finding vocational possibilities for the deaf and in providing a social life and arranging for summer camps, ballet schools, and amateur circles for school children.

Evaluation of the System. There are certain advantages offered by the system of education of the deaf in the U.S.S.R. Deafness in a child can be detected at a very early age and remedial work can be started almost at once. When the deafness is discovered at the nursery or kindergarten level, parents are required to get some educational training on the treatment of deaf children. The parents may be taught how to begin informal lip reading with the child; they keep in touch with the school and assist in training throughout the child's school career. It is also possible for the teachers of a regular school for the deaf to observe deaf children in nursery schools and kindergartens and have a chance to decide in which category a child should be placed and to which type of school he should be sent.

There is apparently ample supervision and ample opportunity for training. Nor is there any apparent problem in getting student teachers. The teachers are enthusiastic and the schools have a relaxed atmosphere, quite different from that in other schools in the U.S.S.R. Equipment and teaching aids are plentiful, and there are ample visual aids. Each of the boarding schools had a special cabinet and a library where aids and equipment were kept. We were told that there are frequent teachers' meetings at which various problems are discussed.

On the debit side of the Soviet system we must count the fact that, from the beginning, the child is placed in one of the categories, depending upon the amount of deafness and his skill in speaking. He has very little opportunity to change his status. A further disadvantage lies in the Soviet educational aim, which is to train the deaf child to become a productive worker rather than a fully developed person. Thirdly, the Russians segregate those who are handicapped so that the deaf child has little contact with and knowledge of the life of normal people.

But care for the deaf in the Soviet Union is still only nascent. It is significant that no deaf person encountered outside the schools — and a considerable number were observed — used any method of communication other than finger spelling and signing, although there were some slight attempts at reading the lips.

Education of the Blind

There are two types of schools for the blind in the Soviet Union, one for the totally blind and one for the partially seeing. Blindness is defined as inability to read the test chart from a distance of more than five feet. Thirty per cent of the students in the schools for the blind are totally blind.

Although the general practice in the U.S.S.R. is for the young child to go to nurseries and kindergartens while both parents work, in the case of the deaf or blind child it is recommended that he stay at home in the early years. The formal training of the blind begins, therefore, at the age of seven.

In the schools for the blind and partially seeing the child receives the regular ten-year program in eleven years, after which he can enter a university or any technical school except those that train for dangerous work. At higher educational establishments he is eligible for double the usual stipend and there are extra funds for readers.

Teachers of the blind are trained at pedagogical institutes by special faculties. However, there is no section on blindness at the Gorki Pedagogical Institute in Kiev because "Blindness is declining and all teachers for the Ukraine are trained in Moscow. Research done in Moscow is also available in Kiev, so we do not need a special faculty here."

The Herzen Pedagogical Institute in Leningrad does prepare teachers for the blind, who as student teachers do practice teaching at the school for the blind in Leningrad. Schools for the blind also exist in Odessa, Kharkov, Lvov, and Kiev, and four were reported in the republic of Uzbekistan. Teachers for the blind in Uzbekistan are trained in Moscow, although the local pedagogical institute offers some courses in special education. There are reported to be 500 pupils in schools for the blind in Uzbekistan, and 6000 in the U.S.S.R. These figures, it must be remembered, include only children enrolled in the special schools or in the clinics as patients and do not give the total of blind children in general.

Description of a School. The Leningrad School for the Blind, which members of the Comparative Education Society visited, has 210 pupils and is very overcrowded. A new building is going up within the year, which will have a kindergarten for blind children attached to it. This seems to be an innovation, as the only kindergarten for blind children now in existence is reported to be in Ufa. The school is a boarding school, but some partially blind children are allowed to live at home. About one-third of the pupils are totally blind. The major causes of loss of sight are injuries, mine explosions, meningitis, cataracts, brain tumors, tuberculosis of the eye, and accidents. The school doctor said that there had been some but not much retinal fibroplasia.

In addition to the regular ten-year school program, there are courses in cold-metal engineering, making musical instruments, textiles, needlework, and brushmaking. In the shops, where they work three or four hours a week, the children produce goods sold by trade unions. Twenty-five per cent of the proceeds are banked for the children and given to them at graduation. This cold-metal shop seemed amazing to a Western observer; here the children make cuticle shears, door keys, desk fastenings, and so forth — work that would not be done by the blind in the United States. Last year six graduates entered universities and institutes for higher education. A close connection of the school with industry is also stressed. "We teach our pupils specific skills for a particular factory and our graduates often go directly to work in such factories as semiskilled machine operators."

The visitors saw at least two blind teachers at this school and full-page braille slates. There were no clear type books, only braille. The school has a gymnasium and stresses physical culture. It offers track, skating, skiing, handball, and a wide range of gymnastics. Like any other, it has its Pioneer organization and its Pioneer room. The Pioneer leader was blind himself and a graduate of the school and of the Institute of Defectology in Leningrad. Instead of photographs of Lenin the school has many busts of the Communist leader.

Speech Correction

The Institute of Defectology carries on research in the area of speech pathology, helps to train therapists, and exercises general supervision over speech correction. It has an acoustics, psychological, physiological, and speech laboratory, and teamwork of specialists is greatly stressed. Assistant Director Morosova told visitors that the Institute works with aphasics and cleft-palate children. She also said, "We do not work with crippled children. These do not come under the jurisdiction of the Ministry of Education but under the Ministry of Health." Visitors were left to assume that orthopedic cases, such as cases of cerebral palsy, were meant to be in the latter category.

The following problems are studied and decisions regarding them made at the Institute of Defectology:

1. The examination of children and the decisions as to the program to be administered to them.

2. The development of special establishments, all of which come under the Ministry of Education.
3. The development of content of teaching and the preparation of textbooks.
4. The development of methods for teaching children with particular problems.

These tasks are complicated and demanding. The officials of the Institute repeatedly stressed the need for tight organization of resources as an indispensable condition of their work: "We can only succeed in the measure we do because the Institute consists of many specialists — medical personnel, psychologists, research workers, speech pathologists, and teachers — who all work together and pool their knowledge."

The Department of Logopedics, or speech disorders, has a special clinic to conduct experiments and decide on techniques and methods to be used with children who have speech problems. The Minister of Education of the R.S.F.S.R. uses the results of the experiments worked out in the Department of Logopedics in textbooks and manuals.

In the Institute of Defectology there are preschools and nurseries, as well as special elementary schools for handicapped children. For children with slight speech defects special teachers are employed in the regular schools. This means that the children can attend classes with non-speech-defective children and have supplementary speech-correction classes.

Outpatient clinics for speech-defective children were reported to exist in most cities, and faculties of defectology, including logopedics, in a number of pedagogical institutes. A special experimental school for fifty children with speech defects is maintained adjacent to the Institute during the school year. Also, according to the Institute, there is a logopedist in every school for children who need help in speech. These children are required to learn phonetics and have special help, which is given individually or in small groups. In the special schools, all of the teachers know phonetics.

Dr. Levina, in charge of speech correction at the Institute of Defectology in Moscow, mentioned the following research problems that were being investigated at the Institute: (1) methods of distinguishing between speech, hearing, aphasic, and mental retardation difficulties, and (2) difficulties of writing not due to paralysis. She felt that the latter was one of the main problems. Spelling is considered of great importance, as many speech-handicapped children are not able to write or speak correctly. The Institute is not concerned with agraphia as a result of brain injury but rather with the ability of children to hear sound sequences properly. As regards the investigation of writing disorders, Dr. Levina said that it was of prime importance to determine the cause. She tried to distinguish between the following, in determining which observation and puzzles were to be used: alalia and hearing problems, alalia and aphasia, and alalia and mental retardation.

One of the divisions of the Institute of Psychology is a laboratory on "thinking and speech." Here the professors had been studying the mechanisms of inner speech. The method of X-ray photography was used and the following conclusions were reached:

1. The speech mechanism involves more of the body than is usually considered.
2. The unit of speech is the syllable.
3. New ideas in breathing for speech have been reached.

The following ideas were given as developing from their research:

1. Speech is spoken on the outgoing breath stream.
2. There are three systems involved in the production of speech:
   a. the generator system, which is vocal
   b. the resonator system, which alters the tone of the sound
   c. the energy system, breathing

Much of this material has been in American textbooks on speech pathology and voice science for many years.

Several views on stammering were expressed by Soviet officials. The director of the laboratory felt that he had a new theory as to the cause and he had charts showing impulses coming from the brain down to the peripheral speech mechanism. He said that, since the brain controls the production of sounds when a person stammers, the reason a person stammers is that the connection between the brain and the "subcortex" has been broken. He added:

If the balance of control is re-established, stammering will disappear. The throat is controlled by the vagus nerve and the tongue by the cortex; therefore, to treat stammering, change the control of the sub-cortex to the cortex. Take the person's attention away from his stammering speech and build up a conditioned reflex. This will re-establish the connections and his fear of speech will disappear.

Many of these ideas have been so well known abroad that they hardly warrant the special recognition they are receiving in the U.S.S.R.

Dr. Kraevsky of the Department of Defectology of the Gorki Pedagogical Institute in Kiev felt that prophylactic programs for stammering were the best. If normal nonfluency is not allowed to develop into a full-blown stammer, the child has a better chance to develop normal speech. This can be done, according to Dr. Kraevsky, by putting him on silence for two or three weeks. If the stammer develops from shock, the use of sleep and silence is recommended. A didactical method of going from the easy to the complicated in seven different steps is used in the Ukraine to treat stammering. These steps are as follows:

1. Reading and speaking with the teacher. Then the teacher stops and the child continues alone.
2. Reflected speech: the teacher speaks and the child repeats.
3. The child tells a story from a well-known picture and answers questions of the teacher.
4. The child creates the story alone with the teacher asking questions.
5. The child creates a story from a strange picture and answers the teacher's questions.
6. The child creates a story from an unknown picture without questions.
7. Free speech: the child answers questions and carries on a conversation.

Phrasing exercises and psychotherapy are also used. In addition, Professor Kraevsky felt that good results were achieved when the child was motivated to overcome his stammering and assumed some responsibility for the cure.

According to this informant, stammering falls into one of three categories:

1. Vocal stammering — in which special exercises for the voice are given.
2. Breathing stammering — in which basic therapy is worked on and diaphragmatic breathing has to be taught.

3. Articulation stammering — in which tongue and lip gymnastics are taught.

When asked about cleft palate, Dr. Kraevsky reported that there was one cleft-palate child born in the U.S.S.R. in every four or five thousand births. This response indicates that the data might be insufficient. In the United States, where most states have a law that children born with a cleft palate or cleft lip must be reported at birth, the proportion is one in every 700 to 750 births. Further, in the U.S.S.R. surgery on the lips and nose of cleft-palate cases is performed during the first and second year of life, but surgery on the palate is deferred until about the sixteenth year. This necessitates the use of prosthetic appliances and speech therapy adapted to the use of the prosthesis throughout most of the school life of the child. The Soviets also seemed gravely concerned with the number of deaths of infants with cleft palates.

Demonstration of Cases. In addition to discussing theory, members of the Comparative Education Society attended demonstration of cases. In Kiev as well as in Moscow speech-correction procedures with pupils in the special schools were observed. Therapy was demonstrated in one of the schools in Kiev, but no regular speech-correction classes were visited.

Dr. Kraevsky showed the visitors several of his cases. One was a nine-year-old deaf girl who hadn't spoken until two years before, when she started therapy with the professor. Her speech was good but had the typical hollow quality of a deaf person's speech. She was able to read well and was successfully carrying on schoolwork in regular classes.[5] An eight-year-old girl with a hearing problem and the resultant speech defect was also seen. It appeared that her main difficulty was in the vestibular chain, as she became dizzy when whirled around. To improve her speech, she was doing work to help her balance. She was not considered to have so severe a hearing problem as the first girl. This seemed logical as her voice quality was very good.

A seventeen-year-old girl, postencephalitic with cranial nerve damage, had had no control over her drooling. Under treatment she improved, but her face was rather expressionless and she had a great deal of difficulty in moving her tongue and lips. An excessive amount of nasality was present in her voice and she was emotional and tense during the interview. Visitors were told that sucking, chewing, and swallowing exercises had been used at first. During the therapy administered, she made her hands into fists and energetically pushed down with her arms as she spoke in order to make her speech more precise.

A ten-year-old boy who stammered as a result of being frightened during a thunderstorm three years previously was diagnosed as having the articulatory form of stammering. He was receiving therapy somewhat analogous to our linking and phrasing work.

Dr. Kraevsky had a small box of articles that he used to test the speech of the children. He felt that the analytical-synthetic method is best for articulatory cases, meaning the separating of words into syllables so that the component parts are understood, then putting them together again so the child is aware of the whole word. The kinesthetic method, whereby the child is made aware of the feel of the different sounds, was also used.

The visitors were informed that last year in Kiev only 74 out of 16,000 school children had speech problems. These figures are perhaps so low because they may exclude all children in the segregated special schools. A partial explanation also may be in the phonetic nature of the Russian and Ukrainian languages, or in the fact that remedial service does not yet extend to the more remote rural areas.

In Moscow two boys from the special school attached to the Institute of Defectology were brought over to the director's office for demonstration purposes. Here the director, Dr. Levina, believed strongly in the use of zonds,[6] which she felt could cure the articulation mistakes of a child in two days. Both boys used in the demonstration were assumed to have good mental ability. One was aphasic and the other had difficulty in spelling; since he didn't pronounce words correctly, he misspelled them in writing. (Russian is a phonetic language and is spelled the way it is pronounced.) Overcoming the problem of misspelling is one of the researches being carried out at the Institute. The aphasic child was said to have normal intelligence because he could assemble a puzzle. This was another example of the use of selected segments of standardized intelligence tests. Why a test segment was considered valid while an entire test was not was never made clear.

Speech therapists were observed in several schools for the deaf and partially hearing. One school for 600 partially hearing children employed three speech correctionists. It was also reported that with children having speech problems resulting from auditory defects, male therapists were preferred; for children with less severe losses, female therapists were used. In subsequent visits to schools for the deaf and partially hearing this distinction was not noted. All therapists observed were women.

The Department of Defectology in the Gorki Pedagogical Institute in Kiev offers a five-year course for logopedicians. Eighty hours are offered in course work and sixty hours are devoted to laboratory and practice work each semester. Specific areas of study are anatomy and psychology, technique of speech (articulation of sounds), logopedics, organic defects of speech, articulation disorders, psychopathology, and acoustic causation.

Workers in logopedics are a dedicated and enthusiastic group in the U.S.S.R., as in the United States. However, care of the handicapped has been so long neglected in the U.S.S.R. that work in this field has not progressed so far as it has in the United States.

16

EDUCATION OF THE GIFTED

A survey of provisions for the treatment of the handicapped in an educational system always raises the question of opportunities for the talented. Information about the attention and lack of attention accorded to gifted children in the Soviet Union has already been included in several chapters. The aim of the present chapter is to consolidate and expand upon this information.

Historical Development

A brief review of the historical facts relevant to the education of the talented will be useful. Gifted children, defined as those with a high intelligence quotient or unusual aptitude, received varied attention before and after the Revolution of 1917. The Russian public school before the Revolution had a "multi-track" system, patterned after that in western European schools. The schools thus developed in Russia were designed for an upper 7 per cent of the school population pursuing a Gymnasium education in preparation for certain professions and academic careers. The remaining percentage received, if any, an education insufficient to raise the country above backwardness and illiteracy. This arrangement resulted in a selectivity of children to reinforce and revitalize the existing class structure and to assist the authorities in the promotion of talent indispensable for the formation of an intelligentsia. Hence, the upper 7 per cent of the school population under the tsars possibly included those who might have been called talented or gifted in terms of intelligence and achievement without being inclusive of all gifted children because of the limited access to the Gymnasium education. Since this group was recruited mainly from the nobility, representing also the intelligentsia, it included few of the gifted and talented children of the peasants. These people, by and large, had only limited access to an education preparing for a professional career. An exception was made for a singular proficiency in the dance, a talent that was emphatically recognized in whatever social group it could be found. The famous Russian ballet school, as a result, made its debut long before the Russian Revolution but did not enjoy a high social prestige until much later.

The multi-track school was completely abandoned with the Russian Revolution. In its place, there was introduced a universal school accessible to all children without distinction as to sex, class, religion, race, or nationality. The only acceptable educational system within Marxist-Leninist ideology was one that would provide mass education for all children. Nevertheless, selectivity on the basis of ability and talent was neither given up nor disregarded. On the contrary, the search for intelligence and talent among the "toiling masses" became a new objective. For one thing, the ballet school, admitting selected talented children at an early age, was continued.

The new unified labor schools, established after 1918, recognized ability levels, and "students were organized in coeducational groups classified according to ages and levels of achievement." [1] Standardized psychometric, intelligence, and aptitude testing devices were known but were used in Russia to a very limited extent. The scientific objectivity of these devices had definite appeal to the pedologists of that period as a contrast to the more subjective, class-determined selectivity employed by the Gymnasiums of tsarist times. Marxist-Leninist ideology was compatible with the evidence that intellectual superiority could be objectively identified among the children of peasants and workers.

Since the unified labor schools eliminated disciplinary actions, textbooks, compulsory homework, and examinations of any kind, and introduced self-management by children from age thirteen on, this system wound up in chaotic confusion by 1930. Thus the pioneering effort to introduce ability grouping came to an end and with it any trace of a concept that would recognize innate or genetic individual differences. The pedology practiced in Russia after 1918 was drastically censored and condemned in 1934 because of its aim "to prove special giftedness and a special right to life of the exploiting classes and of 'superior races' while on the other hand [rationalizing] the physical and spiritual doom of the working classes and 'inferior races.'" Objective standardized testing techniques have been excluded from the educational scene ever since. Model schools, of the type developed until 1937, were discontinued because they were detrimental to the principle of uniform standards throughout the total Soviet educational system. Administrative devices tolerating individual differences and frequent acceleration or segregation of superior students were ruled out within the school system.

The Gifted in the Regular Classroom. The traditional system of promotion by class, examinations, and grading was reinstated with the Party decree of 1934. All students were to be instructed from identical textbooks and were to meet the same requirements universally and collectively complied with by the whole nation. This decree ushered in uncompromising rigidity in the curriculum, with detailed instructions as to content and an exacting timetable for the completion of subject matter. Obviously there was no room for teaching procedures that recognized the needs of superior children in a regular class. Ability grouping within the class or acceleration of superior students became objectionable.

This stand against the provision for gifted children in the regular classroom is implied, even within the Academy of Pedagogical Sciences, in Professor Anatoli Smirnov's statement that if needs cannot be satisfied in the classroom the gifted child can go ahead and work elsewhere. He can develop according to his capacities in the amateur circles of the Pioneer palaces, trade union circles, and extracurricular circles in the schools, where his talents and interests will be furthered by work outside of the school curriculum.

Grade-skipping by superior students was considered inadvisable because the children carried such a heavy academic load that if a pupil did particularly well in one subject the chances were he would not do so well in others. Consequently, he would not have much extra time available for special work in his field of high achievement since he would of necessity have to work longer on his homework in those subjects in which he did not excel.

In sum, differentiation in teaching to allow for the heterogeneous nature of student ability in a class is not now practiced. Any sort of ability grouping within a class would direct attention to the fact that children are born with individual differences in ability. Communist ideology does not acknowledge innate superior talent. Only environmental factors, such as poor teaching in school or lack of industry on the part of the child, are presumed to cause ability differences.

For the same reason, standardized tests are not used to identify ability. Professor Smirnov stated that they do not and will not identify gifted pupils for innate abilities. Soviet educators resort to other methods, such as competitions and contests, which seem to accord more with their ideological pronouncements. If a student prevails in contests a number of times and works himself up through competitions he is then considered obviously gifted. Examinations, particularly oral examinations that subjectively measure achievement and performance, are generally used. No evidence objectively arrived at concerning potential giftedness in the individual is permitted to be considered. Consequently, it is to be assumed that with the absence of standardized identifying tests children of undeveloped and undetected giftedness may become a total loss to the Russian society. Further, in view of the Soviet refusal to expand the number of university places and thus to accommodate all available academic talent, a great number of people of known ability are also frustrated.[2]

The organization of the curriculum as it stands does not permit any versatility, flexibility, or differentiation adapted to the intellectually gifted. The superior student has to do precisely the same work that is required of the lowest student in his class. The prevailing principle is "one kind of education for all." Formal education for the academically gifted means acquiring the minimum general information and helping weaker students to overcome their difficulties by serving as their model and tutor.

Soviet educators do recognize those children who show outstanding ability in the expressive arts. The term "talent" is generally used in relation to superior abilities in mechanical aptitude, dramatics, crafts, and skills of various kinds. Although the ten-year school itself does little to nurture intellectual giftedness, a great deal is done for the gifted and the talented outside the school.

It was pointed out to Russian educators that the concept of equal innate abilities and the practice of making elaborate provisions for gifted and talented children in the expressive arts are perplexingly paradoxical. The Russians countered with the reply that theoretically any child can be taught to draw, dance, or play music efficiently if given sufficient time. Special schools are established for gifted children because they need less time to acquire proficiency than others. Thus a random selection of children for the gifted-child schools would seem to be justified. However, this is not the actual case. On the contrary, an extensive system covering the whole nation is set up for the purpose of discovering, motivating and developing giftedness and talent. The Soviet educators explain such inconsistency by the rationalization within the scope of their political theory that special talents must be identified and encouraged but not recognized as innate endowments.

Talented children are taken care of in two large categories. One category represents the special schools for the gifted in art, music, and the dance. These schools are under the supervision of the ministries of culture, while the regular schools are under the supervision of the ministries of education, although there is collaboration between the ministries regarding the academic curriculum.

The other category typifies a vast network of "circles," which are made available for all children, including those showing talent or considerable ability and interest in a great variety of activities. They compare with the extracurricular activities organized by schools or with clubs in the United States.

Special Schools for Gifted Children

Music Education. The musical education of Russian youth is provided by part-time and full-time special music schools. There are also special music boarding schools, of which a few, connected with orphanages, were visited.

Children attending part-time special music schools are not unusually gifted but have some ability, show an interest, and are referred to the school by their parents or teachers. They may participate if their academic school record is satisfactory. Selection or admission is not based on examination or independent investigation. Instruction is free of charge; however, parents can arrange for additional private lessons and pay for them. Students of the ten-year school attend these special schools outside regular school hours. One music teacher of a ten-year school stated that 30 to 40 per cent of each class attend such special schools, receiving lessons in music six to eight hours every week, either in the morning or afternoon, depending upon the time the student has free for this work.

At the part-time special music school the students may take individual and/or group lessons in singing. A student may also take instrumental lessons on some native musical instrument or on the conventional band and orchestral instruments. These lessons are free once the student has been accepted. Students can participate in the choruses and orchestras when school musical programs are presented. The general plan is to have a part-time music school in each urban school district.

Full-time special music schools are for the "highly gifted" and combine the regular school program with instruction in music. There are two of these schools in Moscow, the Central Musical School, which has existed for twenty-five years, and the Gnessin Music Pedagogical Institute. The Conservatory of Moscow guides the Central Musical School, and its graduates expect to be professional "performers." Students of the Gnessin Institute look forward to careers as special music teachers. There are five such music schools in the Soviet Union. They are coeducational and enroll an equal number of boys and girls.

Children enter the first grade at the age of seven. Because of the combination curriculum, the Central Musical School is an eleven-year school. It takes forty to fifty new students each year, but not all who apply are accepted. In September, 1958, out of 250 children admitted for entrance examination only forty were accepted. Recruitment and selection of talented children is nationwide. Announcements for application to these schools is made through national magazines and local newspapers, and over the radio. Parents hear about the school and bring their children to take the entrance examinations. Other children may be referred to "Central" from district music schools or orphanages for the musically talented. As a part of the entrance examination the applicants are asked to sing a song, to repeat a musical phrase from memory, and to repeat various rhythmic patterns.

The enrollment of the Central Musical School as of September, 1958, was approximately 300 students. The 136 teachers belong to the Trade Union of Educational, Cultural, and Research Workers. A few of the teachers may give lessons at the Conservatory of Moscow, but the large majority work only at "Central." The school's budget is two million rubles annually. There is no connection between this school and the circles except that students of the school sometimes give concerts at Pioneer palaces or other youth functions.

Since 75 per cent of the graduates enter the Conservatory, an institution of higher education, the chief aim of Central Musical School is to prepare students to pass the entrance examinations at the Conservatory. The school is not for "vocal specialty." On completion of the eleven-year curriculum students with special vocal ability may enter a vocal school. It is claimed that the drop-out is low.

Group lessons at this school are conducted in rhythms, solfeggio, theory, musical literature, and harmony. All instrumental lessons are individual. The curriculum provides for:

> rhythms, first through fifth grade
> solfeggio, first through eleventh grade
> musical literature, sixth through eleventh grade
> theory of music, seventh grade
> harmony, eighth through eleventh grade

There is a chorus and an orchestra of approximately seventy students. At graduation, each student gives a forty-minute recital before the graduating class.

The following observations were made during a visit to a fifth-grade class in solfeggio: The teacher played the first phrase of a two-phrase musical sentence and the class wrote the music in their music notebooks. They sang their written melodies as a check against the original, then wrote the second phrase to complete

SPECIAL EDUCATION

There are educational provisions for the gifted, the deaf and hard of hearing, the blind, the mentally retarded, and the crippled. The Institute of Defectology of the Academy of Pedagogical Sciences and the faculties of defectology in various pedagogical institutes have undertaken major research and experimental programs which have contributed significantly to the expansion and improvement of educational facilities for exceptional children.

Deaf children in this second-grade class are observed by student teachers. Classes are smaller than those with children of normal hearing.

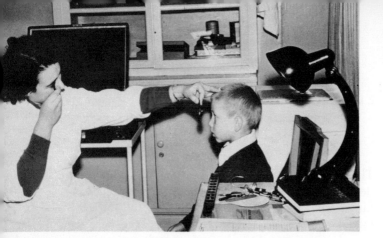

Above: All children in Soviet schools receive an ophthalmological examination by a physician who is a full-time member of the school staff. Below: These partially sighted children have tilt-top desks which hold large-type books similar to those used in the United States.

Boarding School

Children in boarding schools take turns in kitchen duty. There are opportunities for going home on weekends and during vacation periods.

Chicken with rice is a popular dinner.

The regular schools, compulsory for all Soviet children, make few provisions for individual differences. Communist ideology does not permit acknowledgment of innate superior talent, and ability grouping within a grade or acceleration of superior students is not permitted. However, the needs of the gifted are met in amateur circles of the Pioneer Palaces, Pioneer school troops, trade unions, and Pioneer summer camps. Students with artistic talent are recommended for special schools of music, art, and ballet which are under the supervision of the Ministry of Culture.

An orphanage in Leningrad for musically talented children features an excellent orchestra.

At left: This talented child takes her piano lesson. Below: An extremely talented xylophonist

A musically talented child recites a poem with dramatic expression.

An eleventh-year class in portrait painting in a school for young artists

Above: Sculpturing is emphasized in the schools for those talented in art. Below: Exhibits of students' work are found in all schools for the gifted in art.

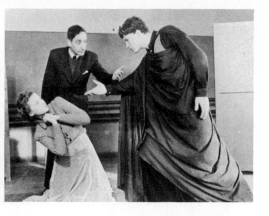

Above: Students and teacher of the Moscow Ballet School during a lesson in dramatic art. Only a few of the many hundreds who seek a place in this school are accepted. At right: A thirteen-year-old boy receiving his daily training at the Moscow Ballet School. He is in his third year of this all-day, year-round school. Below: Student ballerinas in the Moscow Ballet School

A very expressive recitation by a junior-school student at the Pioneer Palace in Leningrad. The poetry circle is one of the most popular of the many club activities.

Members of a music circle entertain fellow students in Tashkent.

the sentence and, using the sol-fa syllables, sang the whole melody. One boy had written an exact duplication of the composer's music.

The third type of music school is a boarding music school, usually for orphaned boys and girls seven to seventeen years of age who are selected because of their musical aptitude. In these coeducational schools the children receive the regular ten-year schooling along with the additional music training.

One example of such a school is the Leningrad Orphanage for Musically Talented Children, which gives instruction in classical, semiclassical, and folk music. A band of approximately thirty boys and girls gives frequent concerts. Solo presentations are given on the xylophone, cello, flute, clarinet, trumpet, and violin. Instruction is also given for small ensembles of instruments and in folk music and dance, with original costumes. Another example of this kind of school is an orphanage for musically talented children in Tashkent, Uzbekistan, which was established after World War II for children evacuated from western Russia. The director stated that the seventy-two girls and fifty-three boys in the school were selected by a special committee.

Besides the regular ten-year program, the curriculum of these schools provides for special courses in music, dancing, and painting. The teachers of these classes are specialists in their own art media. Many graduates of such schools are now famous in the various art fields.

Art Education. There are about fifty art schools across the nation for children with higher than average aptitude to receive instruction after school hours.

Five special full-time art schools, in Moscow, Leningrad, Kiev, Kazan, and Riga, take care of the highly gifted in art. The Moscow Art School has been in operation for twenty years and is considered the best. This coeducational school has 306 pupils, from grades five through eleven, of whom fifty are boarders. It is compulsory for the children to wear uniforms except in the upper grades. The ratio of boys and girls has remained the same through the years — 70 per cent boys and 30 per cent girls.

The selection of gifted pupils in art is very complicated. Competitions are announced nationally, as they are for the special full-time music schools. In the Fall of 1958 the Moscow Art School had 1500 applicants and admitted only 250 for examination, of whom fifty finally were accepted into the school. Admission is determined by a commission consisting of the director, the assistant director, fifteen artists, one representative from the Art Institute and one from the Academy of Art. The examinations take ten days and are in drawing, painting, and composition. Candidates must have satisfactory marks in academic subjects, but exceptions are made if unusual talent is indicated with a less commensurate academic record. Attendance is free of charge; parents of boarders pay for food if they can afford it. The director confirmed that generally children with the highest artistic talent have also the best academic records. Of thirty children starting in grade five, about five drop out and go back to the regular school. Practically all graduates continue training at the Art Academy. The majority become free-lance professional artists.

This school teaches the full academic curriculum of a regular ten-year school in addition to special art classes, so that the work load is very heavy. The students formerly had classes for eight periods of fifty minutes each a day, six days a week. The load has recently been reduced to six hour classes a day, but the pupils have the same amount of academic work as before. In addition to their academic work they must also do homework in art.

Contests are conducted within the school for the best homework record, the best drawing, and the best painting. The children are supposed to have sketching albums so that they can make sketches wherever they go. They also participate in national and international exhibitions of children's art. At the exhibition of 1958 in India the Moscow Art School won five prizes and one first prize. The director claimed that all students are members of the Pioneer organization, but they do not participate so much in Pioneer activities as do children of other schools. Nor do they have a polytechnical program except for making their own picture frames.

A number of the instructors are former students of the Moscow Art School who completed their training at the Art Academy. Other artists teach at the Art School as well as at the Academy. Teachers have the rank of professor and have had training at the Art Academy.

The Moscow Art School has its own summer camp. For the twenty-six days the children are there they work for three hours every day in their artistic specialty and play for the rest of the day.

Visits to the classes furnished the following observations: A group of eleven seventh-graders, each with an easel, were doing pencil drawings of a chair lying on the floor. The curtains were drawn, and the room was poorly lighted with electric light. In another seventh grade fourteen boys and girls were drawing with pencil two stools lying on the floor side by side and partly covered by a piece of cloth. All of the drawings looked exactly alike; they were virtually photographic copies of the objects. The stated purpose was to teach exact perspective. The eighth and ninth grades also did portrait work with pencil. Anatomic foundations of a portrait are studied by drawing first a human skull, then the plaster cast of a head showing muscle structure, and last the head of a live model. All three drawings are made on one sheet of paper for comparisons.

There were three live models in another class of fourteen pupils. In the eleventh grade boys and girls learn to compose a pencil drawing of a nude model. Each student applies himself for seven years almost exclusively to pencil drawing and only in the last grade paints in oil. Most drawings and paintings are portraits. The only other medium for art work is clay or plaster of Paris for making sculptures. Only thirty pupils in the whole school did sculpture.

The quality of work was excellent. The likeness of the portraits was striking. However, there was no room left for an original or individual interpretation of a subject. High technical skill was obvious, but creativity was absent. The training may be described as purely representative art without imagination. The concept of art is based on "realism." Art training demands obedience to precisely prescribed forms of art expression and consists of an accumulation of standardized techniques of portraiture. It is painstaking, mechanical reproduction without even a subtle reflection of the artist's personality. The limitation of materials used and the insistence on meticulous accuracy and a high degree of perfection make the work appear somehow monotonous, undramatic, and lacking in vividness. The teaching methods seem to smother any flight of fancy, any extravagance. The children are required to produce precise likenesses because, as professionals, their main income will come from painting portraits of Lenin, Marx, Khrushchev, and other leaders for Soviet classrooms and public buildings. In effect, these schools are commercial art schools with exclusive emphasis on skill. Abstract art is given no consideration. The director of this school, as well as the director of the Institute for Art and Esthetic Education, confirmed the fact that these pupils and the people in general would not understand abstract art and therefore it is neither discussed nor encouraged.

Education in the Dance. There are sixteen ballet schools in the Soviet Union, with the most important in Moscow, Leningrad, Tashkent, Molotov, Minsk, and Kiev. The Soviet training in ballet, renowned throughout the world, is a classic example of Soviet attitudes toward training of talent. It is plainly conceived of as a specialization in established knowledge, rather than as a means of creating new knowledge. The Soviet educators claim that creativity comes later and thrives best if built upon solid mastery of all the known facets of a specialty.

Though no ballet school was visited by the members of the Comparative Education Society, a description of the Leningrad Ballet School is included here for the sake of completeness.[3] The school is housed in the same square yellow building in the theater district of Leningrad that it has occupied since before the Revolution. Considering that this is the school that graduated Nijinsky and Pavlova, its entrance is not imposing; a simple placard identifies the building. There are 350 pupils, roughly one-third boys and two-thirds girls (girls "wear out" more quickly, one is told), selected at the rate of sixty a year from some 2000 applicants. A substantial number drop out, some because they develop wrong body proportions. The children are selected from among those who apply; only rarely is there talent scouting. The rule is that each year forty Leningrad children and twenty from other localities or republics are admitted. Sixty per cent of all pupils are said to be from the working class, the remainder from the intelligentsia. Occasionally, able pupils are transferred from other schools for two years of study and receive the Leningrad diploma.

Children are admitted at the age of ten and pursue a nine-year course of study, graduating with the diploma of *Artist Baleta*. The curriculum comprises four cycles: general education, professional ballet education, musical education, and practice on the theater stage. In their professional training children take two hours a day in classical dance and, twice a week, two hours in folk dance, two hours in historical dance, and two hours in stage practice. The course of studies is three years longer than in general schools and does not include polytechnization or Pioneer activities.

Pupil presentations revealed an extremely high level of precision, emphasis on perfection of movement, teamwork, and timing, but no opportunity for individual self-expression. The dedication and anxiety to do well, especially in younger children, can be described only as frenetic. There is iron discipline, evident in curt, rasping commands of the teachers, but it is tempered by the tremendous pride and sense of common purpose shared by instructors and pupils.

Organization of Circles

Although the ten-year school, with its inflexible curriculum, has not proved to be satisfactorily challenging to the gifted, and although teaching methods in the regular classes do not sufficiently recognize ability differences, Soviet education has nevertheless developed in the circles a system that successfully identifies, for future careers, intellectual giftedness. It would be misleading to assume, however, that the circles are only for the gifted. They are not explicitly oriented toward the development of extraordinary talent. As far as the cities are concerned, they are organized for a majority of the child population. In concept, the circles are agencies of mass education and not a means of intellectual selection. Nevertheless, they do help in identifying and nurturing unusual talent.

Circles are extracurricular activities for children aged nine to eighteen. Although they are organized by schools, Pioneer palaces, trade unions, or factories, they are voluntary and free of charge. On the whole they might be compared with the extracurricular "clubs" in the schools in the United States, with the 4-H clubs or the Boy Scouts, or with those groups sponsored by the Y.M.C.A. In the category of circles belong also the stations for young technicians, "Know-Your-Home-Region-Better Hikers," "Natural Science Lovers," and so forth. The circles cover a great variety of activities: physics, music, dramatics, literature, astronomy, agriculture, radio, woodwork, gymnastics, electronics, and numerous others.

The circles, technical stations, and other extracurricular activities seem to act as an antidote to the rather drab, rigid, formal teaching situation in the school. Here the children can develop more independent initiative, individual aptitude and ingenuity, and special ability, and apply their imagination. Gifted-child education is given considerably more recognition outside of the schools than the examination of the formal educational program would seem to indicate. It has to be kept in mind, however, that most circle work is done as a collective. Unsupervised individual spontaneity of the talented is absent in the U.S.S.R.

The circles have made very respectable contributions to science and to the quality of pupil research because of the scope of their interests, the high level of instruction, and the leadership given to them. It is in this way that they stimulate outstanding talent. The work of certain circles and technical stations, when examined at close quarters, leaves no doubt that they serve to provide a specialized outlet for ability not permitted in schools by the official theory.

A visit to an electronics club of tenth-graders in Moscow revealed a closed-circuit television station, complete with camera, transmitters, and screen, all in one room. Another circle, the Natural Science Lovers, at the Ozerskaya School in the Moscow Region, produced a valuable hybrid melon. The experimental work of this circle is said to have initiated the introduction of advanced agrotechniques and new crops into wide-scale practice in the Soviet Union.

The Biological Experiment Station for Young Naturalists, located near Kiev, is a combination of a serious research station and an extracurricular center for children from the ten-year schools. The scientific staff, permanently placed at the station, has conferences with directors of schools and Pioneer leaders in Kiev. The station publishes not only literature for science clubs in schools but the results of scientific work. Its notable feature is that children here carry out experiments in connection with the over-all program of the station. Some fifty-five circles come here from Kiev twice a week. Children participate in planning the research projects and have some real responsibility, apparently, for projects of their own. Many scientists in the Ukraine got their start at this station, where their work led them further to professional careers. They began as "young naturalists." A special variety of tomato, called "Young Naturalist," presumably a hybrid, has been developed here by the students.

The leadership given to these activities seems to be of the highest caliber. Scientists and university teachers work with the circles and technical stations and give direction to their projects. Moreover, certain circles in science and engineering with high-ability children in their membership are directly affiliated with departments of the University of Moscow.

Russian circles also make an impressive contribution to the education of intellectually gifted children and facilitate their identification by a nation-wide program of contests and competitions. In fact, the circles have in this way taken a central position in the education of the gifted. When Professor Smirnov stated that children who work themselves up through competitions must be gifted, he obviously referred to the contests by which the circles offer a challenge to gifted children, who can then be easily identified by their achievements.

As an example, we may cite the "Mathematics Olympic Games." These are public contests on a city-wide, regional, and national scale. An account of one such was given by Professor Smirnov:

> In 1957–1958 the Moscow University organized a Mathematics Olympics. The Olympics was attended by pupils of the ninth and tenth grades. The questions and problems were those concerned with mathematics in the secondary-school program. If the student does well, he is identified as a gifted pupil.

Children from each unit compete by solving difficult mathematical formulas. The winner in the region competes for the city or *oblast'* contest; the *oblast'* winner competes at the republic level; the republic winners compete in the All-Union meeting.

Identification of the gifted is very efficiently enhanced by this elaborate system of competitions between circles, technical centers, and schools. Motivation is strong since the winners are formally honored with medals, announcements over the radio and television, praise in newspapers, and exhibition of their work, as, for instance, in the recent display, the All-Union Exhibition of Children's Technical Ingenuity, in Moscow.

New Trends in Education for the Gifted

The fall of 1958 brought school reform proposals of prodigious magnitude. Some of these affect the education of the gifted and talented. It is hard to imagine that the reforms are exclusively a consequence of academic maladjustment of the educational system. They are, rather, an outcome of essentially political and economic considerations. We get this cue from the widespread discussions of Khrushchev's reform proposals in the Soviet press.

Khrushchev himself made several suggestions regarding the education of the gifted in his September, 1958, memorandum, as follows:

> The new system of public education must provide appropriate secondary schools for particularly gifted children who, at an early age, clearly show an obvious aptitude for mathematics, music and arts. These schools should be *an exception* where these children receive the kind of higher school. We need this to enable our State to properly develop and use the talents from among the people. . . . It may be found expedient to pick from among capable pupils at the existing schools particularly gifted children showing, for instance, an aptitude for physics, mathematics, biology, drafting, etc., and have them concentrated in certain schools.[4]

It would be of some value to present the pro and con arguments in greater detail, if in selected form, because these throw some light on the trends in education in the Soviet Union.

On the one hand, Khrushchev's proposed special schools pleased those scientists and educators who were concerned with the standards of education and with recruitment and training of the intellectually superior children. On the other hand, Communist politicians seemed to insist on the "no exception" feature and felt supported by Khrushchev, who made this point very emphatic when he stated in another place in the memorandum, "I repeat that there must be no exceptions in this matter [i.e., work at fifteen instead of a continuous secondary education], regardless

of the standing of the parents in society and the posts they hold."
This insistence on equality was motivated by a real underlying
fear of the emergence of a privileged intellectual class which
might threaten a departure from the Leninist concept of equal
innate ability and "one education for all."

It is because of strong feelings on both sides of the fence that
we have witnessed what amounts to a public dispute in the
daily press. Only a few articles need to be mentioned here by way
of substantiation. Voices of scientists, concerned with the build-up
of a reservoir of superior ability and giftedness, were heard protest-
ing in principle against work at fifteen. Academician N. N.
Semenov argued that enrollment in higher educational institutions should be *directly from the secondary schools* because
"an interruption of studies at an early age *is bad* for the development of scientific creativity." [5] Semenov pointed out that the new
school reform would send children to work precisely at the age
when they begin to enjoy creativeness in science:

> Here we must pose the problem of how to recognize scientific
> giftedness. This is much harder to recognize than artistic giftedness.
> In the first place, it can be recognized only much later, when the child
> is 12–16. (This is not true for mathematics, which can be identified
> earlier.) At this age the child begins to enjoy all kinds of experiments
> and begins to show some creativeness in science. Such a type of gifted-
> ness has nothing to do with the sum of knowledge the child possesses.
> The sum of knowledge depends on the quality of the school, the home
> environment, etc. Giftedness is recognized by the quality of creative
> activity which the child shows, and has nothing to do with these
> conditions.

He countered the arguments of the politicians that special education of the gifted is undemocratic, as follows:

> It must not be thought that giftedness in science or non-giftedness
> divides people into categories of one kind or another. It is in no way
> different from a gift for language or even a gift for organization and
> we mention it here merely because the development of science is so
> important in our epoch.

Semenov also suggested an elaborate system for the identification of the gifted:

It is vitally necessary to pick out the gifted in the secondary eight-year school. This will become possible in the older classes of the eight-year school and must be done by the following means:

We must organize scientific circles better.

We must make sure that these circles have all the equipment they need.

We must organize the "sponsoring" of schools by enterprises more actively.

Thus the sponsors, the school, the pedagogical council in the schools, the Komsomol organization, all must try to sort out the gifted children who will then be sent to special secondary schools after they have finished the eight-year school. I think that about 5–8 per cent of all those finishing the eight-year school might be sent to special secondary schools, naturally independent of the influence or position of parents.

This identification should be followed by further screening of the gifted in senior secondary schools:

In these schools a second sifting out of the gifted will be made for the enrollment of students in universities and higher educational institutions. About one-fourth of the pupils of the schools will be taken into universities and institutions. This will amount to about 2–3 per cent of all children finishing the eight-year school. The special secondary schools should be sponsored by the research institutes and the nearest universities. This will make the choice of the gifted students easier. It will be done by the school and social organizations [Komsomol] with the advice of the institute or university.

Semenov's argument was supported by other authorities. In the November 19, 1958, issue of *Pravda* an article by two members of the Academy of Sciences, I. Zeldovich and A. Sakharov, stated, "Natural science-mathematics schools are needed," and claimed that people gifted in science usually perform best in their early twenties. These writers suggested that special two-year schools be established for children gifted in mathematics or science, where they would go after the eight-year school. They would then enter a university at the age of sixteen or seventeen.

The *Uchitelskaia Gazeta* of October 9, 1958, carried an article, "An Affair of National Concern," by V. Kuroyedov, secretary of the regional committee of the Party, Sverdlovsk region. In a long argument devoted to all aspects of the reform, he discussed both sides of the question of gifted-child education and came out in favor of special schools for the gifted. However, he suggested no ways of identifying talent.

More moderate but similar proposals were made on November 21, 1958, when *Pravda* published an article by N. Goncharov, Vice-President of the Academy of Pedagogical Sciences, and A. Leontiev, member of the presidium, entitled "Differential Teaching in the Second Stage of Secondary Education." They postulated that after the eight-year school should come schools with special emphasis on physics, chemistry, or other sciences. One of these sciences should be stressed in each type of school, with the accent on its *practical* application. General education and polytechnic subjects should be the same for all these schools. Thus, the all-around development of the personality would be assured and at the same time special talents would be furthered, without an undesirable classification of children into gifted and non-gifted. "Graduates of these schools will be qualified, skilled special workers and they can also enter universities or institutes."

On December 20, 1958, the *Uchitelskaia Gazeta* carried an article, "Develop the Talents of *All* Children," by N. Levitov, Doctor of Pedagogical Sciences. He advanced the same proposal as Goncharov and Leontiev, but he cautioned, "We must not identify good marks with special talent. There must be better ways to pick out the gifted, and we will find them."

The controversy on gifted children was carried on from another, more uncompromising, point of view in *Pravda*, November 25, 1958, by Academician M. Lavrentiev, writing on "Are Schools for the 'Specially Gifted' Necessary?":

> No, they are not. The ways of picking out the gifted are too uncertain. Science does not need early training, like ballet or music. We must build creative interest in science in all children by better publications for children, etc. Mass competitions held by such publications will bring out the really gifted. For instance, A. Luzin, an academician and great mathematician, now deceased, got "2" in mathematics in school. Thus good marks do not signify talent; we must bring out the talent by other means. Besides, all classification of children is bad and in our society we should make no distinction between intellectual and manual labor.

This view was supported by a letter in *Pravda*, December 13, 1958, from P. Litvinenko, worker-metallurgist, who maintained that work in production will develop, not stifle, talents. Such also was the tenor of a letter by a corresponding member of the Academy of Science, I. Eichfeld, in *Pravda*, December 22, 1958. "Children's talents must be recognized and developed through circle work as early as possible," he said, "without disturbing the design of the general reform." Others also opposed the proposals of separation of the gifted.

It seems that the politicians won in the struggle over gifted-child education. On December 25, 1958, the school reform law was passed by the Supreme Soviet. It follows very closely the thesis of the Central Committee of the Communist Party elaborated in November, 1958, with some exceptions. One of these is that there is no reference to special schools for gifted children in science, mathematics, and physics. The special schools for the gifted in music and art are so well entrenched in their tradition that they remain unaffected by the school reform.

17

EDUCATION OUTSIDE
THE SCHOOL

The establishment of socialism in Soviet society supposedly eliminated the contradictions between the interests of the individual and the interests of society. All Soviet citizens, we are told, now have a common point of view, and the most progressive philosophy possible:

> Under the Soviet power the successful combination of family and school conditions, of social influences and self-education, forms a single internally connected and consistent system of convictions, attachments, needs, and interests, which is characteristic of the best representatives of our society. . . . As a matter of course, they [the individuals of Soviet society] are unified in their social structure, in the system of consistent upbringing, and in the system of actively acquired basic principles which regulate their relations and their actions.[1]

If every member of society is to be imbued with the same set of convictions and opinions and with the same set of reactions to the surrounding world, it is very evident that education cannot confine itself to the transmission of knowledge in the schools. All influences on the growing child can and must be coordinated.

379

Thus, in the Soviet Union, every aspect of the child's life — from his family life through his school activities and the organization of his leisure — is a planned part of his education and part of a coordinated system. The all-pervading influence of this ideology allows only for the approved set of opinions, from political ideas to art appreciation and amusements. All organized activities of children are aimed at inculcating the official set of opinions and tastes and at producing the ideal Soviet citizen, who will do freely and on his own initiative what is expected of him by the state. The present chapter discusses the contribution of activities outside the school to the formation of the Soviet child.

The Family

The first and most important influence in a child's life is the family. In Soviet society the family is now an integral part of socialist organization.

> The Soviet family is the primary cell of socialist society. The interests of the Soviet family and of all socialist society are identical. The Soviet family is the natural, friendly labor collective, whose basic life content is joyful toil for the good of the Motherland. In the family children grow and are brought up as the future builders of Communist society.[2]

It is obvious that for this upbringing education in the family must be consistent with education in the kindergartens and schools and with the over-all educational goals of the socialist society.

In spite of the difficulty of attaining a unified education in each individual family, considerable effort is made to teach parents how to bring up their children and what goals to aim for in their education. Work with parents is organized and coordinated by a subdivision of the Institute of the Theory and History of Pedagogy, the Sector on Education of Children in the Family. It does research on work with the family, publishes literature for parents, helps the school in its work with parents, and helps parents solve problems in upbringing. Mme. Markova, head of the Section on Preschool Children, described the work as follows:

> We try to teach parents how to bring up their children; we try to answer their questions and we try to find solutions for their problems.

However, we can only advise and teach; if parents do not listen, we are powerless to act. Who can interfere in family life!

The Sector is divided into four sections, one for preschool children, one for primary-school children, one for younger secondary-school children, and one for older secondary-school children.

The work with the parents consists mostly of lectures to the parents' committees, given in the schools themselves or at workers' clubs and in the Red Corners of factories and plants. Sometimes the lectures are broadcast to the workers of a plant during their lunch hour. If a lecture concerns the preschool child — parents of several kindergartens often combine to ask for a lecturer at their place of work — the parents of children who are not yet in kindergarten are invited to attend. The Academy of Pedagogical Sciences publishes a list of topics for such lectures:

The Role of the Family in the Communist Upbringing of Children.
Personal Example and the Authority of the Parents.
Education of Small Children in the Family and How to Prepare Them for School.
How to Help Children Study Well.
Moral Education of Children in the Family.
Atheist Education in the Family.
Physical Education of Children in the Family.
Artistic Education of Children in the Family.
The School, the Pioneer and Komsomol Organizations, and the Family.[3]

There is, in addition, "mass" work with parents. Publications, mostly in the form of pamphlets on particular problems, are written in a simple, semifictional style. The head of the division for younger secondary-school children told of a book she had written, a fictionalized account of her own experience with her young son during the war, when the child's father was at the front and she alone was responsible for his upbringing.

Nation-wide radio programs on problems of family education are also prepared. Topics for the lectures broadcast on these programs may be suggested by parents themselves who write and ask for advice. In the national republics the lectures are given in the native language, so as to reach the maximum number of people. At the beginning of each school year a series of lectures and programs is given to familiarize parents with the work of the school. The sector also publishes articles on child education in magazines for women, and once every two years the Academy of Pedagogical Sciences holds "pedagogical readings," where teachers, directors, and parents report on their experiences. Three years ago the Sector on Education of Children in the Family organized a permanent seminar for parents, the "active" parents. It is a three-year course and meets once a month in the evenings. In 1957–1958, 40 per cent of the students were fathers. At the end of three years the parent receives a diploma. Besides regular students, "listeners," that is, parents who are interested in only one particular problem and do not wish to take the whole course and receive a diploma, are admitted. Lectures are given by professors and experts in the various fields. As the seminar in Moscow proved to be a great success, similar seminars are now being organized elsewhere.

The program of work for the seminar is as follows:

First Year: Questions of general principle and practical day-to-day problems are discussed. Often these subjects are brought up by the parents themselves. Other parents will recount their experiences on this point and the resulting discussion is often very animated and serves to stimulate the parents' interest. Some topics discussed in the first year are how to help children succeed in school, the duties of a parents' committee, how much should children be supervised, health questions, etc.

Second Year: The content of education in the family is discussed, and age characteristics of children are studied. During this year parents may form their opinions on problems of education by discussing publications on certain topics. Mme. Markova reported that second-year students had just read a forthcoming publication of the Sector in manuscript and had made some helpful suggestions and corrections. "They can be quite severe critics," she said.

Third Year: In this year the parents hear lectures on psychology and physiology and the ideas of Pavlov on the types of higher nervous activity. Development of character attributes is studied. Parents may also help the experts in some research project. In 1957–1958 third-year students helped the Sector in a project on how to keep contact between the family and the teachers of circles.

Satisfying as the work of these seminars may be, the experts in the Sector are under no illusions as to the difficulties they face.

They freely admit that much remains to be done in educating the family in the correct ways of rearing the new generation:

> One of our greatest problems is to make the parents understand the importance of bringing children up to love and respect labor. The parents had to work so hard themselves that they want to spare the children now that life is becoming easier. They still think that childhood is merely a time to be happy. We try to teach them that it is also a time to learn the duties and responsibilities one will be faced with in life.

Mme. Markova added a story of a father who wanted to pay the school to free his daughter from the duty of cleaning the classroom, as he did not want her to touch "dirty mops." The workers of the Sector see their most important problem in breaking down such attitudes.

The Sector has comparatively little contact with the "ordinary" parent. This is where the parents' committees in kindergartens and schools come in. It is the duty of the parents' committee, for example, to "mobilize public opinion" against the parent whose child is failing and to try to shame him into watching over his child's work.[4] Parents' committees seem to have a considerable amount of authority and function as an arm of the school. "It would never occur to any parent to refuse to appear if summoned before the presidium of the parents' committee," said the chairman of such a committee in School No. 151 in Moscow.

Teachers in the schools also do their share of parent education. As Mme. Markova put it,

> This should be done tactfully, since the school does not wish to discourage the parents from coming to meetings. Thus, the teacher is told to find something good to say even about the worst child, so that the parents will not hear only unfavorable things.

Teachers are expected to visit the children's homes and acquaint themselves with the family background of each child. Finally, the teacher may arrange for special parents' meetings on particular problems.

An interesting experiment of one teacher was reported to visitors: The children were told to write essays on the topic "How I Behave at Home." When the essays were all in — and they were reportedly written with astonishing honesty — the teacher called a meeting of parents and children and discussed the essays with them. The result was that the children begged to be allowed to repeat the experiment when they had had time to improve their behavior.

"Active" parents may help to organize the children's leisure. For this purpose parents' committees are formed in the big apartment houses and may include public-spirited citizens who are not parents. Two per cent of the rent paid by the tenants is set aside for these committees, which set up circle activities for the children. Visitors heard of one retired ballerina in an apartment house in Moscow who organized a dancing class for the children; in Leningrad a sailor got a group of boys together and built a boat with them which is now the property of the Pioneer palace of the city and is used by all children. In another apartment house in Moscow parents made a workshop in the basement where the children repaired household utensils for the tenants free of charge. Such committees, with the help of the neighboring school, also arrange for "summer camps" in the yards of the apartment houses for children who cannot get away to the country for the summer. It should be stated, however, that all parent activities are so far on a relatively small scale.

Extracurricular Activities

The main work of organizing numerous extracurricular activities is done by schools and Pioneer establishments. Amateur circles, already referred to in the preceding chapter, direct the children's leisure activity into useful channels and enrich the school program. Curricula are crowded, and there is little time during classroom instruction for arousing the children's interest and for making the material come alive for them. Special interests and abilities are developed and discovered, therefore, in the circles or clubs. "We try to make the school come to life here," said the director of the Leningrad Pioneer Palace.

Circles are organized on every conceivable subject and activity and children are free to join if their marks in school are not too low. There are "shopwork" circles, "skilled hands" circles, sports circles, photography circles, circles on painting, music, drama, and dancing, and "subject" circles. Circles may meet in the schools or in the various institutions for children, the Pioneer palaces and houses, the children's sections of Houses of Culture, trade-union clubs, and so forth. They may be taught by the teachers of the school, by special teachers, and by Pioneer leaders. Some-times children who have shown a particular proficiency in a sub-ject may help the teacher.

The number of circles is startling. In 1956 there were 2382 Pioneer houses and palaces, 258 centers for young technicians, and 214 centers for young natural-science lovers.[5] It is reported that there are 2400 circles of young naturalists in various phases of biology in the Ukraine republic alone. This is only one branch of the circles, in which 600,000 pupils are said to be involved. Nevertheless, the network of circles will have to be considerably expanded if they are to serve as a general extracurricular agency and reach all pupils.

Palaces. A visit to the Pioneer Palace in Leningrad gives a sample of circle activities. The Palace (in large cities there is one central Pioneer palace for the whole city, and a Pioneer house in each district) is genuinely a palace, a building that housed members of the tsar's family in imperial days. After the Revolution it was turned into a museum and finally, in the thirties, was turned over to the Pioneer organization. The build-ing is well kept up. The large rooms still have their chandeliers and the windows their brocade draperies. The period furniture, though covered with slip covers, is hardly what one would expect to find in a house devoted to the leisure activities of school chil-dren. Two thousand children are said to pass through here each day. The Palace is crowded with children even before formal circle work starts in the third week of September. Two hundred and thirty-five teachers help with activities, which include every conceivable circle subject. The Palace serves exclusively members of the Pioneer organization and attendance is free of charge. It operates on a government budget of seven million rubles a year.

Visitors are eagerly greeted by children picked for the honored job of welcoming guests. The latter are taken by the hand, shown over the Palace, and often, at the end, presented with the red Pioneer scarves of their small guides. The showpiece of the Palace is the planetarium, which takes space-minded children on a "rocket ride" for a close-up view of the planets. The Pushkin Room is a small room used for literature meetings. The walls have paintings of scenes from Pushkin's works. The room is matched by the adjoining Gorki Room, which has paintings from Gorki's best-known works. Workshops are equipped for wood-working, machine work, and electrical work, and the children proudly show the radio and television sets that their comrades have built. For recreation, there are chess tables and tables with different games. It is easy to believe that children spend many happy and profitable hours here.

Circles and Stations. School children who are interested in the natural sciences can join the groups of Young Biologists or Young Naturalists which are widely distributed throughout the Soviet Union. These circles do the serious scientific work described in the preceding chapter. By way of leisure-time activities they also observe various festivals and special days during the year. In March they celebrate the festival of the "Meeting of the Birds," where the children make birdhouses and take them to the woods to meet the birds migrating north. Every August there are mass meetings of the young biologists where experiences are exchanged and the children report on their work. Visitors to a naturalist station are particularly impressed by the extremely specialized nature of the work and by the seriousness with which it is carried on.

Circles in the schools may be less elaborate than the activities discussed above, but they serve the same purpose of deepening and broadening the knowledge acquired during school hours and of directing child activity into useful and purposeful channels. The history circle, for example, may ask its members to do research on a certain topic and to report on it to the group as a whole, or the group may undertake a project such as building models of medieval cities or castles. The geography circle may make maps and visual aids. Visitors in one school were shown primitive but serviceable measuring instruments made by the children of the fourth- and fifth-grade circles. The foreign-language circle may study songs and poems in the language of its choice. Again, physics and chemistry circles may plan interesting experiments that cannot be done in school time. "Technical" circles will build radio sets for the school or for other institutions. The list of activities is almost endless. Finally, there are the sports and physical-education circles and the "excursion-tourism" stations, which are spreading throughout the country.

Circle activities are not confined to Pioneer palaces and general schools. Universities and institutions of higher learning also organize the students' leisure in clubs of all descriptions. The University of Moscow has a little theater where drama and music circles put on plays and operas. The director of the Gorki Pedagogical Institute of Kiev reported that her students have many drama and music circles, as well as foreign-language circles, which organize social evenings and give performances for other students.

"Subject" circles in these institutions may enter competitions and present reports, which may be sent on to city-wide and republic-wide competitions. The best of the reports are published by the universities or institutes. The vacations of the students are also provided for, as the government allows some money for excursions, trips, and other activities. Boris Gerashenko, Deputy Minister of Higher Education of the U.S.S.R., stated the official policy as follows: "Our students must be all-around developed people; their inner culture is developed by music, art, and literature circle activities, and the physical development is taken care of in physical education groups." A part of this development of all sides of the personality is the training of the student to serve the society in all fields. Thus, students who go to help bring in the harvest in the virgin-land areas are furthering their education. Mr. Gerashenko explained this in what appears to be a rather sweeping generalization:

> Our students do such work gladly and voluntarily. We educate our students to feel themselves the masters of their own land; they must learn to be at home in the field. We educate people to contribute to all and thus make love possible; and without love, life is a very narrow corridor.

It is clear that circle activities are not merely a leisure-time entertainment for school pupils and students. They serve a serious purpose in the scheme of education and character formation in the Soviet Union.

Camps. Circle activities cease in the summer months when the schools are closed. In this period school children may go to the Pioneer camps. These are not reserved for the members of the Pioneer organization exclusively; they range from elaborate institutions in beautiful surroundings, like the famous "Artek" camp on the shores of the Black Sea, to organized activities and day-long excursions into the country arranged by the apartment house parents' committees in cooperation with the staff of the neighborhood school. The most usual version of a Pioneer camp is one in the country where children go to spend a period of some weeks in the summer. Some of these camps are maintained by trade unions for the children of their members.

One such camp is run by the Trade Union of Educational, Cultural, and Research Workers for the children of employees of the Academy of Sciences. Situated about thirty-five miles outside of Moscow in the heart of a wooded area, it accommodates 450 children at one time and is run in shifts of twenty-six days, three shifts to the summer. Parents pay about 30 per cent of the total cost of keeping their child in camp — about 360 rubles — and the rest of the cost is borne by the Trade Union. Ten per cent of the children come completely free of charge. Campers do not have to be members of the Pioneer organization and, indeed, as they range in age from seven to fifteen, some of them are too young to belong. The director of the camp reported that Pioneers did not even get preferred treatment in admissions. "We can accommodate every child whose parents wish him to come. This year we did not have to refuse a single application." It is unlikely that this is generally true.

The camp consists of small, one-story wooden houses scattered through the grounds. These cabins house the dormitories, the mess hall, the washing facilities, shop activities, and the Pioneer room. The equipment is simple but adequate and the cabins are kept scrupulously clean. The grounds have several playing fields and are dotted with the statues of Pioneer girls and boys. At the entrance to the main part of the camp is a large white statue of Stalin. Signboards with various slogans are set about the grounds. One such board bears the following inspirational poem:

> For you there will be no obstacles;
> What you want to be, you will be;

> As the years fly by, all dreams will become reality.
> Our golden childhood was given to us by October.
> We will build the world of Communism;
> This is what we are growing up for.

Activities are much the same as they would be in any camp. After flag-raising, breakfast, and cleaning chores, group activities are in order. One group will go swimming in the nearby river, another will go mushrooming or berrying in the woods, another will take a hike. The main meal of the day is followed by a rest period, when the younger children sleep and the older ones rest. After this the children get a snack and then play games or engage in shop activities. From time to time there are competitions and campfire festivals in the evenings.

The camp is staffed by eighty adults. Children are divided into thirteen Pioneer and four Octobrist groups; the camp forms a temporary brigade for the duration of the shift. Each detachment and group is led by two adults, a "pedagogue" and a Pioneer leader. Pioneer leaders are mostly students from pedagogical institutes, whose curriculum demands a period of practical work in a Pioneer camp. The children have self-government through an elected brigade council which plans the work and the program for each week. Non-Pioneers can attend the meetings and listen in, but they cannot vote.

Some of the activities in the camp are similar to circle work during the school year. For example, the camp has an experimental garden where children can raise fruits and vegetables. Those who join this activity can take home the seeds of the plants they have raised. The biology teacher in charge of the garden reported that it was very popular with the children:

> It is very good for the children from the big city to learn a little bit about nature and agricultural work. Most of the children get this opportunity only during their camp period, as they all come from Moscow in this camp.

The aim of the camp, said its director, is to give the children a good rest and to make them happy and healthy. She reported with pride that most children put on weight during their stay in camp and return to the city well rested.

Children's Railroads. Another type of extracurricular activity is represented by the children's railroads. There are thirty of these in the Soviet Union and they give children serious instruction on how to operate a real railroad.

The Kiev streetcar takes the visitor to the gaily painted main gate of the railroad. This is the main station but not the only one. The railroad has fourteen kilometers of track and three stations. The rolling stock consists of a diesel engine, a steam engine with tender, and three passenger cars, small replicas of the real thing. There are also a signal system and all other appurtenances of a real railroad. Children of Kiev enroll through their schools; they are admitted only upon the school's recommendation and are eligible when they reach the fifth grade.

Usually the school will recommend a pupil only if his marks in school are satisfactory; however, in some cases work on the railroad has helped a child to do better. The director of the railroad, a woman engineer, reported that sometimes the teacher of a difficult pupil hardly recognized his problem child after a period of work in the railroad circle. The railroad is open only in spring, summer, and fall. In the winter, children enroll in circles in school and learn the theoretical part of their work. Practical work starts in May. During the spring and fall seasons, the railroad operates every Saturday from three to six and every Sunday from eleven to six; one shift works Saturdays, three shifts on Sundays. In summer, when the schools are closed, the railroad is open twice a week, three hours each time. The program enrolls 800 children in all, while one shift consists of forty-five children.

The railroad was originally meant for pupils of the railroad schools, but it now admits other children as well. Participants start by learning the easy jobs — monitoring railroad crossings and being on duty on the station platforms — and work their way up to the most difficult positions — engine drivers, radio operators, and so forth. They also do the necessary upkeep and repair work under the supervision of teachers and adult supervisors, who are all trained engineers. According to the director of the railroad,

> Children take their duties on the railroad very seriously and work in this circle many years. Work in this circle is a part of the children's polytechnic education and also teaches them to take on responsible jobs.

The best workers are rewarded by trips to other children's railroads. There are specialized railroad circles in the schools where children can learn more about their jobs if they so desire.

Recently steamship circles have been started on the same principle, and a group in Leningrad *oblast'* had organized a children's machine tractor station which worked to help nearby collective farms.[6]

Youth Organizations

Extracurricular activities in the Soviet Union are very closely interwoven with the various youth organizations. These organizations are an important factor in the achievement of a consistent and unified education. They exist not only to aid the work of the school and to insure better scholastic achievement but also to train the children in Communist morality, to teach them various skills, and to order their leisure and amusements. Finally, they develop the civic virtues of the future "builders of the Communist society" that fit them to work with independence and initiative to carry out the demands of their world.

Octobrists. Children of the primary grades are grouped in an organization called the "Octobrists." This grouping disappeared for a period and was reintroduced only recently, when the eighth Plenum of the Central Committee of the Komsomol decided, in November, 1957, to experiment with fixing the age for admission to the Pioneer organization at ten years instead of nine. At that time it became necessary to organize the younger children in some way to prepare them for entry into the Pioneer organization.

The Octobrists are a very loose and informal organization of young children. There are few rules, no firm admission procedure, and no definite tasks. Octobrists are distinguished by little red stars worn on their school uniforms, and a child can become an Octobrist when he behaves and studies well. However, teachers are admonished not to use the title of Octobrist as a means of reward for good pupils or to withhold the title as a threat for unsatisfactory pupils. Teachers are expected to use Octobrist groups to instill elementary concepts of self-organization. Thus, Octobrists will be taught to prepare for a school holiday by themselves, to plan the enactment of a fairy tale, to organize to keep their classroom clean, and so forth.[7] Elementary concepts of Communist morality are embodied in Octobrist slogans, such as "Only those who love labor can be called Octobrists." As Octobrists approach the age of ten, the teacher and the sponsoring Pioneer detachment from a higher class in the school are expected to instill in them a desire to join the Pioneer organization. They learn about the deeds of the Pioneers, they are taught the rules and the "solemn promise" of the Pioneers, and they are impressed with the honor and joy of being a Pioneer.

Pioneers. The Lenin Pioneer organization is the first serious youth organization. It is:

> . . . a mass political children's organization which . . . brings up children in the spirit of love and devotion to the Motherland, friendship between nations and proletarian internationalism; it draws Pioneers and school children into public life, develops in them a conscientious attitude towards study discipline, love of work, and curiosity; it brings up children to be all-around developed individuals, conscientious, healthy, courageous, full of the joy of life and unafraid of difficulties, future builders of Communism. . . .[8]

It should be noted that the Pioneers are described as a "mass" organization and that they are expected to draw other school children into their work. Far from being an exclusive group, like the Communist Party, the children's organization is expected to involve as many children as it can bring into its ranks. Great efforts are expended to make membership in the organization as attractive as possible, to make nonmembers feel that they would like to join. The line between members and nonmembers does not seem to be too fine; nonmembers are often allowed and even urged to participate.

Although the Pioneer organization was originally based on the factory or plant where children were working, since the reforms of the thirties it has been centered around the school. Each school has its Pioneer brigade (*druzhina*), which is subdivided into detachments, usually comprising the Pioneers of one class. The detachments can be subdivided into links (*zveno*) if there are enough members. The links are formed by the children themselves and are based on special friendships. Each brigade is led by a brigade council, and a brigade council chairman, both elected by the Pioneers of the whole school. Each detachment has its detachment council and chairman, elected by the detachment, and the links are led by link leaders.

Council members and chairmen should be elected from among children who have shown themselves to be "activists," and serious discussions of the elections are led by the senior Pioneer leader.[9] The brigade council organizes and plans Pioneer work for the whole school under the guidance of the senior Pioneer leader. He or she is an adult, a Komsomol recommended by the district Komsomol committee. Senior Pioneer leaders are professionals, trained for the job in pedagogical schools or in training courses and special seminars. Every school is supposed to have a senior Pioneer leader, who is a full-time paid member of the staff. In practice, however, senior Pioneer leaders are not always available and the turnover seems to be great. Many senior Pioneer leaders prefer to go on with their training and become regular teachers. If no senior Pioneer leader is available, a teacher may have to take over his duties.

Pioneer detachments also have Komsomol leaders, picked, until recently, from the senior pupils of the school who were members of the Komsomol organization. The school Komsomol committee made the choice and the district committee confirmed it. However, the Thirteenth Komsomol Congress decided that, in line with the current insistence on the importance of polytechnical education, it would be better to have the detachment leaders come from the Komsomol organization of the sponsoring plant. They can be helped by the senior pupils of the school. Visitors to School No. 29 in Leningrad were told that the Pioneer detachments of this school draw their leaders from the Komsomol organization of the sponsoring plant. The plant also advises the two senior leaders in their work and stresses the polytechnical education of the children.

Admission to the Pioneer organization is a solemn affair. When a child has reached the required age and wishes to join, he announces his intention to the detachment council. If there is no detachment in his class, he goes to the brigade council. The applicant is discussed by the council. All new candidates are usually admitted at one time in a ceremony that takes place at a school assembly or at a special occasion arranged by the Pioneer organization of the school. Thus, children of the Pioneer organization of School No. 57 in Kiev arranged to have their new members admitted at a ceremony at the famous plant "Arsenal," on the occasion of an excursion devoted to the slogan, "Labor is a matter of honor, heroism, and glory." Whenever the ceremony takes place, the Pioneers line up in formation and the candidates for admission line up to face them. The "solemn promise" is then recited by the candidates, and the Pioneer leader ties the symbolic three-cornered red scarf around their necks. The scarf symbolizes the unity of Pioneers, Komsomols, and Communists. The Pioneer pin is fastened on their breasts and in some cases the new Pioneers advance one by one to kneel and kiss the flag of the brigade.[10]

Pioneer activities are manifold. Besides the circle and summer activities discussed above, Pioneers are expected to train for the achievement tests of the organizations BGTO (Be Prepared for Labor and Defense) and BGSO (Be Prepared for Sanitary Medical Defense), both paramilitary activities. Pioneers also are expected as a matter of course to be good pupils and to help others who may have difficulties with their studies. They are expected to behave in an exemplary manner at home, in school, and in public; one of their slogans is "A Pioneer is an example to all children."

Pioneers also participate in socially useful work. This may consist of collecting scrap metal needed by factories, in helping bring in the harvest, or in building radio sets for old people. Pioneers may be called upon to read to the sick, to help their parents with the housework, to build things for their school, and to help in projects planned for the good of their whole community or even the whole republic. Aleksei Markushevich, Deputy Minister of Education of the R.S.F.S.R., has defined these goals as follows: "We want our children to become the 'doers' in society. They must be able to live the life of the whole community; they must see where help is necessary and act." An official publication spelled it out more explicitly:

> The acquired knowledge must be practically applied in life, in labor for the good of the community. Communist consciousness makes sense only and has real strength only when it is expressed in practical communist deeds, in communist toil. And what is communist toil?

Communist toil, said V. I. Lenin, is unpaid labor for the good of the community, labor performed not for the fulfilment of some definite duty, but voluntary labor, labor performed from the habit of toiling, for the common good, labor as the need of the living organism.[11]

Another important aspect of the Pioneer organization is the development of civic virtues and of the ability to organize for the fulfillment of certain duties and plans. The brigade council organizes Pioneer work for the school, while the detachment council does the same for the detachment. The senior Pioneer leaders only guide and advise; the main work is done by the children themselves, independently. Complaints abound in the literature on the Pioneer organization that the independence and initiative of the children is not developed enough and that teachers and Pioneer leaders try to dominate the councils with their advice and suggestions. On the other hand, complaints are also heard that all the work of the organization is done only by a handful of "activists" and that the other Pioneers rest content with their title of membership in the organization without ever doing any work for it as a true Pioneer should. To improve this situation reforms were adopted in July, 1958, by the Plenum of the Central Committee of the Komsomol. If he is to remain in the organization, the Pioneer will henceforth be required to take three "steps." [12] Each "step" involves the completion of a certain number of definite duties, which the regional and local councils of the Pioneer organization can vary according to local conditions. The Pioneer will carry a book in which are noted the tasks completed, and he cannot advance to the next stage if he does not comply with the regulations. These reforms are meant to "activate" each individual Pioneer and will serve to teach him some desirable skills and attitudes. It would be a mistake, we are told, to think that they will lead to dangerous tendencies toward "individualism" and "Boyscoutism." Indeed, individualism is the last thing Party leaders want! [13] Since many of the tasks must be fulfilled by the group and emphasis is on collective work and achievement, the collective nature of the work in the organization will be preserved. The reforms merely aim at greater activity for the rank and file of the Pioneers; and they strive to assure that every member will acquire a minimum number of skills and work habits.

An examination of the tasks that the Pioneer must fulfill gives a very good picture of the over-all aims of the organization. First there are the patriotic tasks: A Pioneer must know the hymn of the Soviet Union and his republic; he must know the name and history of the hero or heroine after which his detachment or brigade is named; and he must know the names of the local heroes and their histories. The next set of tasks is work for the good of the community: A Pioneer must make something for his classroom and for his school, in collaboration with his link; he must learn to help his parents at home; he must make something for his home; he must plant trees or flowers and care for them. Another set of tasks concerns his physical development: He must learn to swim, to jump, to run; he must go on marches; he must learn to play games; in every "step" he must accomplish a more difficult feat of "tourism," from day-long excursions to excursions of several days. In the course of these excursions he must learn to read a compass, to build fires, and to cook at them. He must also improve his knowledge: He should tell his link about an interesting play or movie he has seen, or an interesting book he has read; he should strive to be named "Pioneer instructor" in one of the circles he attends. Finally, he has to learn to sing and do group dances with his group. These tasks become progressively more difficult as the Pioneers advance into the higher stages. The last step adds the task of learning about the Komsomol.

The Komsomol. When a child reaches the age of fifteen he becomes eligible for membership in the Komsomol organization. It is a much more serious step to join the Komsomol than to join the Pioneer organization. Although still a "mass" and non-Party organization, the Komsomol is the "reserve and aid of the Communist Party" and has serious duties to fulfill. A candidate for membership must have the recommendations of two members of the Komsomol of at least one year's standing or the recommendation of one Party member. The sponsors are held responsible for their recommendation. The candidate, if he is a Pioneer, can substitute the recommendation of his brigade council for one recommendation of a Komsomol.

The Komsomol has no symbolic rites of admission, and the new member does not pronounce a "promise" or oath. The charter of the organization lists his rights and duties; the list of duties is the longer one and includes, among others, the following:

To improve his knowledge of technology and of his special field constantly.

To help put into practice the policies of the Communist Party.

To explain the policies of the party to the "broad masses of young people."

To study Marxism-Leninism attentively.

To set an example in labor discipline.

To take good care of public property.

To develop criticism and self-criticism.

To study military science and be ready to defend the Motherland and give his life if need be.

To work actively in the Komsomol organization.

To keep state secrets.

His rights include participation in the discussion of all questions of the work of the Komsomol organization; a vote in the election of representatives to the organs of the organization; election to the various organs; criticism of all persons and organs of the Komsomol; attendance when he is discussed by his fellow members; and access to all committees all the way up to the Central Committee.[14]

The Komsomol is modeled after the Communist party. The basic unit is the primary organization, which exists in schools, universities, plants, collective farms, and offices. This can have a membership of from three to a hundred persons. Primary organizations are led by secretaries. The work of the Komsomol at the district level is done by a committee which elects a bureau and one or more secretaries. Regions and republics have their committees and elect their bureaus and secretaries. The highest organ of the Komsomol is the Congress, which elects a Central Committee to carry on the work in the intervals between Congress meetings. As in the Party, the important man in the Komsomol at each level is the secretary. At the levels above the primary organization the secretary is a full-time worker and, starting at the district level, the secretaries must be Party members or candidates for Party membership. The Central Komsomol Committee has its publishing house, Molodaia Gvardiia, which issues books for young people as well as newspapers and magazines for children, students, and Komsomol members — *Pioner, Pionerskaia Pravda, Komsomolskaia Pravda,* and *Molodoi Kommunist.*

At the level of the secondary school the duties and the work of the Komsomol organization are much like those of the Pioneers. In accordance with the children's age level the work becomes progressively more responsible and the demands become more stringent. The sharp difference between demands on a Pioneer and demands on a Komsomol is illustrated by the statement of the director of Boarding School No. 12 in Moscow. He reported that of all children in his school eligible for membership in the Pioneer organization, only four were not members; of all children eligible for membership in the Komsomol, only 30 per cent were members. "They feel that they are not yet ready to join. They are preparing themselves and when they feel that they are ready, they will apply; they will not apply until they feel themselves worthy of the honor of membership."

It is in the institutions of higher learning that the influence of the Komsomol organization becomes important and strongly felt. Khrushchev defined the role of the Komsomol in Soviet society as follows:

> Public organizations, including the Komsomol, must play an ever greater part in the struggle with failings and vices and for the affirmation of the new in our life. It is not right to bring matters to such a point that state organs must handle everything. . . . We say that under Communism the state will wither away. Which organs then will remain? The public organizations! Whether they will be called Komsomol or trade union or otherwise, it will be the public organizations through which society will regulate its relations. . . .[15]

It is among students that the educational role of the Komsomol becomes really apparent. Here it is important not only to train young people in the virtues of a Communist society but also to keep the new intelligentsia in tune with the regime.

In universities and institutes the primary organization is established within each faculty, and students are grouped in Komsomol organizations according to their specialties. A Komsomol committee is elected for the whole institution and its representatives sit on every administrative committee, from the committee allotting housing space to the one deciding stipends. A Komsomol representative keeps a record of each student while the professors and teachers keep a record of his academic achievement. If the "social" record of the student is not satisfactory he may be deprived of his stipend on the recommendation of the Komsomol. If the record of his social behavior is not good, his career may be hampered. When job assignments are considered, the Komsomol record of the student is weighed with his academic record. As Mme. K. Topshieva, Dean of the Faculty of Chemistry at the University of Moscow, informed visitors,

> If a student is doing well in his studies and is not recommended by the Komsomol for his social behavior, he may not get the more interesting jobs; he may be sent to a plant, where he will have to work in a large group and learn collective behavior this way.

Komsomol control of student behavior goes so far that one student reported to visitors that she moved out of the university dormitory because she did not like the constant interference with her privacy.

The Komsomol also organizes "socially useful" activities. When students were needed on the virgin lands to bring in the harvest the young people traveled to the east on Komsomol *putevkas,* travel permits issued by the organization. Although, officially, students volunteer for such work, one student succinctly stated, "You go if the Komsomol secretary tells you that you had better go." The Komsomol organization also has a hand in organizing the extracurricular and vacation activities of the students, and it helps arrange the sports festivals and holiday celebrations. Indeed, if Soviet fiction is to be believed, the Komsomols even have an influence on what and how a professor teaches.[16]

Apart from learning the proper spirit and attitudes themselves, Komsomol as well as Pioneer members play a leading part in building up the proper "public opinion" in the institutions where they work. This is done partly by organizing wall newspapers in schools, universities, and factories which criticize, satirize, or praise, as the case may be, the pupils, students, or workers leading the "broad masses" in order to condemn or encourage certain practices or deeds.

Cultural Influences

In a Communist society all spheres of activity are mobilized to achieve the desired objectives of the system. Thus, in the Soviet Union it is not only school and youth organizations that contribute to organized education; every field of activity plays its part in the upbringing of the child and the forming of public opinion.

Books. Reading matter for young people is supplied by the Children's Publishing House, established by decree of the Central Committee of the Communist Party in 1933. Here, books for children that attempt to develop their appreciation of literature and of art, and to widen their knowledge of all subjects, are published. The publishing house is under the Ministry of Education of the R.S.F.S.R. Mme. Maksimova, manager of the House of Children's Books, a part of the Children's Publishing House, explained that "the problems of publishing children's books are considered to be problems in pedagogy and character development, as well as problems in artistic education."

The publishing house is proud of the fact that the quantity of books published has risen enormously since the Revolution. Where there were seven million books for children in 1917, 170 million were published in 1957. The growing number of libraries insure distribution in all the republics and many books are published in the national languages.

The publishing house serves children from three to seventeen years of age. Classics of literature are published, Russian and foreign, as well as the folk literature of all countries. The best contemporary works are put out too. The smallest children can start with picture books, books on their immediate environment, and the simplest animal stories. The child's education is begun by emphasizing such books as *What Does My Father Do?* and *Gromov, the Builder,* which are meant to inculcate respect for the various professions.

When the child gets older he is offered fairy tales and stories by classic writers. The children of the elementary grades can read Pushkin's and Tolstoi's fairy tales as well as Andersen's stories. Books by the well-known Russian children's writers Gaidar and Marshak are published. Older children can read the Russian classics and also Mark Twain, Jack London, Dickens, Jules Verne, Hugo, Defoe, Swift, James Fenimore Cooper, Hemingway, Longfellow, and many more foreign authors. The list includes authors from all countries — Japanese, Indian, and Argentine, as well as French, English and American.

Books are published acquainting children with various branches of science. For younger children there are works on nature study, history, and zoology, and for older children books on cybernetics, automation, and atomic energy (its peaceful uses only).

When a new book on a certain subject is needed, the publishing house runs a competition among authors. A commission of teachers and pedagogues decides on the entries and winning authors get substantial bonuses.

The Children's Publishing House is also considered a laboratory for finding out what children like to read. The publishers receive many letters from children praising or criticizing the books and asking for more books on certain subjects. Criticism is also invited from adults — teachers and parents — and manuscripts are often discussed by them before publication.

The publishing house has a library for adults interested in children's books and a reading room for children. Here children can read what they wish and also participate in circle activities. Mme. Maksimova pulled out a folder of "letters" written by the geography circles and explained them as follows:

> Children traveled to the U.S.A. in a submarine from here. They picked the country they would like to visit and the means of transportation themselves and they wrote "letters" to their friends about what they saw.

Children did much better in geography in school after participating in these circles, she reported.

Radio. Radio programs for children serve the cause of the correct upbringing and education of the younger generation. The state committee for radio broadcasting has a special section for children's programs, staffed by seventy-five people. The same institution exists in each national republic. The editor-in-chief of the children's section of Radio Moscow told visitors that "the principal aim of children's programs is to develop humanism and patriotism and to help them in their school work." The central board for children's broadcasts has several sections, divided according to the age groups aimed at. There are special programs for every age from preschool to senior school children.

Preschool children are said to enjoy a program called "Will You Guess It?" which involves the identification of characters from various stories. They also seem to favor a program telling them about school and the work they will soon be doing there.

For older children there is a program organized around the lives of great authors, which is designed to help them with their work in literature in school. Plays studied in school are frequently dramatized on the radio, and a program called "Literary Post" answers children's questions about literature.

For older school pupils there are programs acquainting them with the latest developments in science as far as the children can understand them. There is a special program for young naturalists and one for children interested in art. The latter describes the various art museums in the world.

A program on youth problems at home and in foreign countries is called "Children's Gazette." There are also programs discussing vocational choices and one, "Sincere Talks," gives the children an opportunity to exchange ideas on social issues.

Radio programs are evaluated on the basis of letters received from the listeners by the station. Permanent correspondents of the radio station are posted in different cities of the Union and send information on the problems and needs of children in their area.

Museums. In Moscow's museums — as in the museums of all other cities of the Union — children can study the past of their country and the correct trends of present art. In the Kremlin Museum the pomp and circumstance of imperial times have been carefully preserved. The Museum of the Revolution tells the story of the revolutions of the twentieth century. History is edited to eliminate the role of the revolutionaries now discredited and to emphasize the role of Stalin, who is still to be seen at Lenin's elbow in most writings and paintings. The Museum of Lenin preserves mementos of the great hero of the Soviet Union. Not the least of these reminders of the past is the Mausoleum on Red Square, where long lines form every day to view the bodies of

Lenin and Stalin. The Tretiakov Gallery, devoted to Russian painting, extols the virtues of socialist realism in art as well as the outstanding qualities of the Soviet people on its canvases.

Theaters. Evening entertainment is part of the children's and adult education in a totalitarian state. The great classic plays are beautifully produced in the theaters, insofar as they do not conflict with the prevailing philosophy. The Moscow Art Theatre is justly famous for its productions of the plays of Chekhov. The contemporary theater is in a more difficult situation. Audiences are not undemanding, but the crop of new plays is not always satisfactory.

The theatrical season 1958–1959, for example, saw the opening of a new play by the well-known Soviet author Leonov, *The Golden Chariot.* The plot is summarized here, since it is typical of the kind of philosophy of life considered worth inculcating in audiences in the Soviet Union. The hero is a man who was prevented in prerevolutionary times from marrying the girl of his choice by her father, who felt that the suitor was too poor. "Go forth and make your fortune," he told the suitor, "and then come back in a golden chariot for her." The hero goes forth and truly makes his fortune, Soviet style — he comes back as a member of the Academy of Sciences. In the meantime, however, he has married and has a grown son — also a scientist — and she has married and has a grown daughter and a position as secretary of the local Soviet executive committee. It is too late for the original pair, but the son and daughter fall in love. At the same time the daughter is loved silently by her childhood sweetheart, a soldier who has come back from the war blinded. He always wanted to be an astronomer, but now he must give up this dream. The daughter now has to choose between the golden chariot — the scientist offers to take her to the Pamir mountains and show her the complexities of geology — and the poor suitor. . . . Needless to say, after some hesitation she chooses the hard life at the side of the war hero.

It is interesting to note that the audience did not like this play, although the acting was excellent. They hardly clapped at all and a woman apologized to foreign visitors for such a boring play and recommended the Chekhov performances at the Moscow Art

Theatre for true entertainment. One wonders how successful indoctrination by entertainment can be.

The charming puppet theater in Moscow keeps alive the works of the Soviet humorists and satirists Ilf and Petrov, brilliantly performed and highly entertaining. Visitors saw an excellent performance of their story *Twelve Chairs* with none of its satiric content omitted.

In the fall of 1958 posters in Moscow were announcing the imminent opening of *All My Sons,* by Arthur Miller. It is evident that this play is acceptable to the Soviets as proof of the general decadence of capitalist society.

The one overwhelming impression that a Western visitor carries away from Soviet society is of a deadening uniformity. However well organized the children's activities, however well equipped the circles, however beautifully executed and illustrated the children's books, however well produced and well acted the plays, the all-pervading influence of the official ideology is inescapable and produces an impression of unbroken monotony. The whole of Soviet cultural life is indeed like the "narrow corridor" mentioned by a Soviet official — a narrow corridor that leads straight to one exit only, with no possibility of deviation on the way. It is hard for a Westerner to believe that youth would be satisfied with such a straight and narrow path, wherever it purported to lead. Frequent complaints about "capitalist survivals in the consciousness of youth" in the Soviet press lead one to believe that some young people are showing at last some impatience. How strong and widespread this impatience may be is, of course, a matter for conjecture.

CHARACTER AND MORAL
EDUCATION IN A
COLLECTIVIST SOCIETY

Members of the Comparative Education Society, in discussions with Soviet educators, often implied that there could be no morality in a Communist state. This the Soviet educators vehemently denied, and for support they quoted Lenin:

> Is there such a thing as Communist ethics? Is there such a thing as Communist morality? Of course, there is. It is often made to appear that we have no ethics of our own; and very often the bourgeoisie accuse us Communists of repudiating all ethics. . . . We say that our morality is entirely subordinated to the interests of the class struggle of the proletariat. We say: Morality is what serves to destroy the old exploiting society and to unite all the tools around the proletariat, which is creating a new, Communist society.[1]

With morality placed in a context such as this, communication between Communist and non-Communist educators naturally encountered semantic difficulties. Most members of the Comparative Education Society approached the subject of moral values as apologists for Christianity or other varieties of theism. They were

405

met head-on by Soviet educators and teachers who were apologists for dialectical materialism. When the former examined and weighed the authority underlying Communist morality, they found it wanting. When the latter examined and weighed the theistically oriented morality, they found it laughable.

It was quite evident, however, in the contacts with the research staffs of the institutes of the Academy of Pedagogical Sciences and in talks with the Soviet teachers and educators that one of their major professional concerns is the moral growth of their young people. Teachers on all grade levels assured the American observers that they are endeavoring to build into the minds and hearts of their students basic loyalties, qualities of character, and world views. Like their counterparts in America, they are teaching their children to be honest, kind, truthful, and trustworthy. Members of the visiting group judged these intentions noble but most thought they ran counter to the professed assumptions of the teachers. The Judeo-Christian ideals were judged noble by the Communists but, in their judgment, contradicted the whole capitalistic system. They kept daring the Americans to demonstrate a higher morality than theirs. They asked many questions that were difficult to answer: Why does America have the highest crime rate of any country in the world? If the United States is a democratic nation, why does it have such severe problems of racism? Why is there so much juvenile delinquency? Why does a Christian nation tolerate slum conditions?

In formulating answers to these questions the American visitors all too frequently treated the subject of morality in a polemic fashion rather than in terms of a disinterested attempt to arrive at an objective description of the Soviet moral system. In short, the problem faced was how could the observers, the majority of whom were committed to the thesis that religion and morality are inseparable, evaluate a moral system resting on the assumption that a genuine morality can be expressed only in and through society?

Sources of Soviet Morality

As long as the ethical discussions with Soviet educators were in broad terms, the mutual generalizations had much in common. When dealing with specifics and the realm of affectivity the observers soon discovered not only that they held different philosophical views but that the two educational systems produced different kinds of men, with different styles of interior life. Many felt that the gulfs of division were almost unbridgeable. In fact, the differences were so great at times that instead of creating understanding they resulted in alienation. As a result, the problem of moral unity in relation to the cultural pluralism of the world society took on a new challenge and seriousness for all members of the Comparative Education Society.

Philosophical-Scientific Basis. Communist morality is rooted in a materialistic concept of the universe. This concept, called dialectical materialism, assumes that all facts about men's minds and wills and the course of human history are causally dependent upon physical processes or even reducible to them. Matter is prime, and although it may change its form, it is everlasting. All forces operate within nature; there are no forces other than those of this world.

This concept of the universe is used as a frame of reference for critical analysis of other moral concepts and institutions. Aleksei Markushevich, Deputy Minister of Education of the R.S.F.S.R., was asked, "Are moral values developed out of social conditions alone?" This was his answer: "We Soviet scientists believe that all values originate in and out of social conditions. The supernatural is not needed. All is based on the materialistic dialectic."

A. M. Arseniev, Director of the Institute of the Theory and History of Pedagogy of the Academy of Pedagogical Sciences, made this reply to the same question:

> As to the source of morality, we believe that the source of all ideas is in life itself. Somewhere in the Bering Straits the custom was to take the old people to an island and to let them die there. This was necessary because of the shortage of food on the island. In most societies such deeds would be declared immoral. So there is moral development on various levels.

Hence, morality is naturalistic and materialistic. Man is merely a product of nature and is bound only by the laws of nature that can be discovered in the universe. On this point, Arseniev commented, "Nature existed before the nature of people. Man appeared only at certain stages of the development of nature. We believe that nature existed before man."

There is, therefore, an objective world independent of man, the knower, but man is governed by this world through a cause-and-effect chain.

When asked if Soviet moral theory could be equated with materialistic determination, Markushevich answered,

> Yes, but it is only part of it and not the whole of it. Under this theory, human behavior is said to be dependent upon and determined by antecedent events of a natural order. This is not fatalism.

This kind of philosophical discussion led the American observers to inquire into the nature of the Marxian theory of moral knowledge. Arseniev once again was the spokesman on this point:

> Under our theory of reflection, ideas or knowledge reflect the objective world. Mind does not give birth to ideas. In the foundation of the nervous system of man is a reflective state of conditioning. Some say that this theory is that of mirror reflection, namely, static and passive. We do not agree with such an interpretation. We believe in dialectical reflection. Dialectical reflection has two characteristics: a constant state of flux or change, and activity. . . . This latter point emphasizes that this is not passive reflection but that, in reflecting the outer world, the brain creates.

Markushevich held that acts of choice arise out of a set of conditions. Moral conduct is the product of specific causes with man participating in the processes of nature. Man can, therefore, be a passive effect or an active causal factor. These were Markushevich's words on this subject:

> Man possesses the ability to select from among several alternatives, each of which has antecedent causal connections. For every act of man, there is a natural cause. Consequently, high moral conduct demands knowledge of one's environment.

Arseniev described in detail the Marxian system of morality, which to a large extent emphasizes conformity to the laws of nature and the laws of society, and particularly to the great laws of evolution. As he stated it,

Moral truth is everything that is carefully reflected. This is absolute and it is possible to secure it. Absolute truth exists but this absolute truth has no limits. When we talked about theory of knowledge, we said that all knowledge is reflected. If the human mind is able to reflect the phenomena of nature, we believe the human mind can reflect properly the phenomena of morality.

At the same time, we believe that all human knowledge is relative. Once upon a time the elementary particle of material stuff was considered to be a molecule. So all materials were said to consist of molecules. This is true and absolute. Substances do consist of molecules but then we discovered more elementary particles called atoms. Yes, the atom is an absolute truth, not the final and whole truth. So we are moving into new moral concepts. The human mind is capable of properly reflecting the phenomena of society. This development is eternal. Knowledge accumulates and, when we reach a certain point, we realize there is something unstable and we move beyond it for still greater truth. . . . It is possible that we may move beyond communism to still greater truth.

Thus, evolution is the great lawgiver.

Through the use of the empirical method, within a frame of reference of Engels-Marx-Lenin, the Soviet theory claims that man can discover truths that are basic to Communist morality. Man, then, must put himself in line with the collectivistic-socialistic tendencies, conform his conduct to them, and, insofar as he is able, cooperate with them and hasten the achievement of the Party's goal. The basic truths must be known by the teacher and taught by the instructor on each grade level. For example, the Soviet history teacher must explain the conditions of the rise of moral belief from primitive to modern forms. This is to show that morality was not implanted in man from the beginning by God but is one of the forms of human social consciousness, arising out of certain definite circumstances of the social condition. This theory is consistent with the words of Friedrich Engels:

> We therefore reject every attempt to impose on us any moral dogma whatever as an eternal, ultimate, and forever immutable moral law on the pretext that the moral world too has its permanent principles which transcend history and the differences between nations.[2]

Engels was referring to eternal and immutable principles grounded in supernatural or metaphysical sources as well as in a decadent capitalistic system. When the natural world is viewed by the naturalistic-collectivist mind, however, entirely different insights into truth can be secured. The ethical system, therefore, is objectively relative to the given economic and social structure and reflects the interests of the dominant class. All of the Soviet educators agreed with the following concept of the Soviet value theory:

> Our theory of value is called in our philosophy the cultural inheritance of attitudes. Our problem is that of showing the attitude of one generation toward another generation, the attitude of the present generation to the past generation, and one historic epic to another historic epic. We believe that ours is the most advanced economic society in terms of inheritance. So we educate our children in and to this advanced system.

Political Basis. The Soviet system has built an almost blind loyalty to the Party and its hierarchy. "The leaders know best. We trust and respect them." This the visitors heard over and over again. Lenin attached special importance to education in Communist morality; hence, great importance is attached to it by the educators. The names, writings, and slogans of Engels, Marx, and Lenin and others of the past and present Party leadership were constantly referred to with the greatest reverence. These men embodied all that was wise and good. Thus, the moral principles that are accepted as wise, right, and necessary by the Party have to be accepted by the people. Hence the authority of the state and the Party is basic to the ethical system.

The cultivation of patriotism is one of the most important responsibilities of the moral educator in the Soviet Union. One of the teachers phrased it in this way: "We desire future citizens of the Soviet state who will act from a sense of public duty and will possess a feeling of responsibility before the Motherland." Another teacher of a primary school outlined her responsibility in developing a feeling of patriotism as follows:

> We start with the little things in the daily life of children to build a national pride and a national self-consciousness. Love for one's Motherland starts with love for one's parents and friends, one's native town.

Everywhere in the schools visitors were confronted with pictures and statues of Marx, Engels, Lenin and other political leaders, together with their sayings and their slogans. Their names are invoked at every assembly of students and adults. In this way, children are taught that their individual interests and welfare are inseparable from the interests of their government. Morality in this context means conformity to the will of the leaders.

No agencies in the Soviet Union assume greater responsibility for the moral upbringing of children and youth than do the youth organizations, already discussed in Chapter 17. Upon becoming members of these groups, children take a solemn pledge to be true to the precepts of Lenin, and to live and study in a way that will make them worthy citizens of the Motherland.

One of the chief duties of the Young Pioneer organization, for example, is to watch over and direct the behavior of students in and out of school. Members are asked to account for the ways in which they fulfill their sacred tasks and moral obligations. Pressures are put upon each individual to serve as a personal example in study and in conduct. Those who fail in their duties are privately and publicly censured.

Economic Nature. Morality in a Communist state must also be viewed in terms of the struggle of the working class to develop a new society and, along with it, a new morality.

As pictured by the Soviets, the new morality requires a society in which there is no exploitation of man by man. Boris Gerashenko, Deputy Minister of Higher Education, briefly referred to the economic basis of the Soviet ethical system as follows:

> We educate so that our young people can combine their individual interests with social interests. All that the individual produces belongs to society but society rewards him individually for his work. Our economic system tries to induce our young people to live peacefully, not to rob, not to make enemies, and not to be proud.

It is true that in 1917 classes were officially abolished in the U.S.S.R. Over the years, however, there has developed social and economic stratification along with a prestige and status system. As a result, a group of managers, bureaucrats, and intelligentsia has imposed its moral prejudices upon the masses just as the older classes did. There are many evidences that the Soviets are confronted with the dilemma of the role of the intelligentsia in the new society. Arseniev touched upon this:

> We believe in education for the working class. Intelligence plays a very important role in our society. Workers cannot determine their role by themselves. An intelligentsia must help them. In the U.S.S.R. we believe in the working class but we cannot underestimate the role of the intelligentsia. This is why we here in the U.S.S.R. think of scientific socialism being led by the intelligentsia, and the practical labor by the worker.

The moral man is expected to have a Communist attitude toward ownership of property, namely, that it must be used solely for the welfare of the toiling masses. It is the duty of every citizen to safeguard and to strengthen public, socialist property as the sacred and inviolable foundation of the Soviet system. Equally important is the Communist attitude toward labor, as Khrushchev brought out:

> It must be constantly inculcated in the youth that the chief thing for society is that by which society lives, i.e., productive labor, because only it creates material values. Work is a vital necessity for every Soviet man.
>
> Any work at a factory, or collective farm, an industrial establishment, a state farm, a machine and tractor station, a repair technical service station, or an office — any honest, useful work for society — is sacred work and necessary for every person who lives and enjoys the benefits of society. The chief task of our schools must become that of preparing our growing generation for life, for useful work, inculcating in our youth a deep respect for the principles of a socialist society.[3]

The development of good work habits is viewed as basic to moral education. Laziness is not tolerated. Everyone is expected to work and to assume responsibilities. Khrushchev dealt with the growing disdain of many Soviet citizens for manual labor in his September speech:

> . . . All school graduates shall be placed in production and no one shall skip it. In the first place it will be democratic, since there will be more equal conditions for all citizens. Neither the standing of parents nor their positions will relieve anyone whatever from productive labor.[4]

Lack of a Religious Influence. Individual Soviet citizens may accept a morality rooted in belief in a supernatural power, but it is officially discouraged. Throughout the Soviet Union the American observers visited Jewish synagogues, Moslem mosques, and Roman Catholic, Russian Orthodox, Baptist, and Seventh-Day Adventist churches. They appeared to be well attended. It is clear, however, that the state uses its resources to undermine theistic sources and sanctions. Through a campaign of scientific-atheistic propaganda and teachings a definite war is waged in all schools against religion. Pupils are instructed in the natural origin of morality and its historically changing aspects. In the Museum of the History of Religious Cults in Leningrad, for example, where children are taken on field trips, there are displays of the inhumanity and excesses of interreligious fighting, witch-burning, religious proselytizing, and the Inquisition. Any dependence of a Soviet citizen on God is looked upon officially as a barrier to knowing the true source of morality. This is one of the reasons for the nonexistence of group instruction in religion for children.

Markushevich was asked, "What moral qualities are sought in Soviet schools and in what are they rooted?" He answered this question by referring to his experiences at the Geneva Conference on Education, which he attended in the summer of 1958, as follows:

> A representative from the Vatican said that without religion there could be no moral education. I differed with him. The Vatican representative said our points of emphasis in moral education were the same as those of the Commandments.
>
> We in Soviet education pay much attention to moral education and the family stresses it. It is not just verbal. First, it is the education of behavior. Second, it is the education of the inner life.

Markushevich agreed that bourgeois and Christian morality contains certain permanent elements no different from those of a classless morality, but he argued that kindliness in itself is not a virtue, but becomes one only when it is harnessed to the proletarian cause.

Nature of Morality

Social Aspects. Since right conduct traditionally has meant obedience to an established authority or adherence to a common standard, it is not surprising to find that morality in the U.S.S.R. can be largely reduced to rigid conformity to a set of customs, laws, rules, and codes of various kinds. The authoritarian, here as elsewhere, is in control of morality. Over the years, the Party has selected those convictions and standards judged basic to a Communist society and spelled them out for common acceptance. It was quite obvious that Soviet educators do not suffer from the extreme fragmentation that is a phenomenon of the cultural pluralism of the United States. Hence, they maintain that many of their moral decisions are easily made because there is no question in most situations as to what is the right course of conduct.

One of the interpreters unconsciously provided insights into the ethical system of the U.S.S.R. After several seminar sessions at the Academy of Pedagogical Sciences spent probing for a description of the Soviet moral system, a student working toward the degree of *Kandidat* in law impatiently interrupted a translation with these words: "I don't know what you people are talking about. What is moral behavior? Behavior is either legal or illegal." At another time this same interpreter, still confused by all the talk about moral education, made this observation: "Moral education and character education? Isn't moral education more closely connected with religion than is character education?" In a social sense, then, Soviet educators tend to use "morality" to mean behavior that has become customary because of the approval of the state. Given a set of behavioral norms, the Soviet citizen seemed to ask himself how far he could go without being punished for violating the norm. Indeed, this appeared to be the essence of their moral dilemma.

Several of the bureaus of the institutes of the Academy of Pedagogical Sciences were studying the social nature of the moral upbringing of children. Researchers were seeking specific ways and means of influencing behavior at each grade level. The assumption under which they were operating was that moral character is learned in a variety of ways at various levels of growth.

They discovered, first, that Soviet children, like any youngsters, at times exhibit impulsive behavior. Consequently, training in conscious discipline is given very high priority in moral education. From early years children are trained so that the discipline remains as a permanent possession. Discipline in this sense means a conscious inner control that enables the individual to live up to the accepted standards which have priority over the impulses of the individual. This was illustrated by the words of one of the Soviet teachers: "A morally educated individual is one who subordinates his own desires and interests to the services of his motherland." Hence, early moral training in the Soviet schools emphasizes teaching the child to inhibit or to control his impulses.

A second kind of learning is that of mastering and obeying rules, laws, codes, and principles, all of which help establish habits and develop traits. This is a more positive approach to moral conduct than the "Don't" of the earlier stage. Early childhood is considered especially important because basic habits and the socialist mind are formed during this period. A definite number of moral habits are fully formed as early as the first grade. These are set down in the "Rules for Pupils." [5]

These rules are very specific. Each one is aimed at eliciting highly specific habits of disciplined behavior. Not only are these principles taught in the same graded and systematic manner as school subjects but they are introduced and enforced in the daily life of the school. This is not a question of constant supervision or of repressive regulation of the children at every step. It is the establishment and maintenance of a cultural core that insures normal work procedures and discipline. The aim is to develop habits that will enable children to act quickly and accurately in familiar situations, to make habitual numerous actions, attitudes, and ways of thinking.

All of these rules must be cultivated in the school, in the family, in the collective, and in the Pioneer organization. Not only is the child taught the rules but he is also taught why they must be obeyed. Some of the teachers admitted that there are many instances in which pupils are unable, because of immaturity, to understand a given moral requirement. The teachers, unable to wait for these young students to grow up and to understand, merely demand conformity to the rules. Under such circumstances categorical obedience is expected. Failure to comply brings unpleasant and severe consequences to the student. Nadezhda Parfenova, editor of *Uchitelskaia Gazeta,* was critical of this practice, which she thought was more widespread than necessary. "It happens that too many of our teachers order children instead of developing in them the abilities to assume responsibilities in the collective without bringing pressure to bear."

The third type of moral learning is the overcoming of self-centeredness. Some children are inclined from the first to share their possessions with their comrades, but others take advantage of these few and exploit them for their own selfish purposes. Such children learn to conform outwardly but they still regard themselves as the center of interest and concern. Hence, they often do things that are against the rules if they think they can get away with them. There is a need, therefore, to internalize the moral voice of the home, the school, and the state.

Nicholai Petukhov, Chairman of the Department of Pedagogics in the Herzen Pedagogical Institute of Leningrad, is a specialist in moral education. In answer to the question "What is morality in the U.S.S.R.?" he made the following statement:

> Morality is a category of social conscience that is built within a student. The Communist state has very definite moral rules defining the kinds of attitudes and behaviors students should exhibit in matters involving labor, property, human relations, and the role of the state. Morality is a condition of moral feeling and a set of moral habits as they apply in the areas of patriotism, internationalism, collectivism, and humanitarianism. Conformity to the basic moral rules and truths as defined by the Party is synonymous with morality in the U.S.S.R. These rules are not moral absolutes but are common interests as defined by the Party. They are the bases for criticizing all other moral systems.

Under this concept of morality, the Soviet teacher attempts to develop in children good motives and not just good behavior. The aim is the formation of a consciousness of duty toward the state. For example, the "Rules for Pupils" begin with the words, "It is the *duty* of every school child." At times Soviet educators seemed to be quoting Immanuel Kant in explaining how to develop a voice of obligation and a sense of right. One of the teachers of the fourth grade explained how she hoped to form a sense of duty. "I believe that practice in fulfilling one's obligations is fundamental to developing a sense of duty and responsibility. This is why we assign children definite tasks and check to see that they are done." A teacher of history in one of the ten-year schools explained that his subject was an excellent source for many concrete examples of consciousness of duty. He stressed personal biographies to illustrate how individuals with a sense of duty were successful in reaching goals that were almost unattainable. In the pedagogical institutes we heard again and again that the teacher must set the example by having a responsible attitude toward his own work and being conscientious in his own undertakings.

So the Soviet teacher aims to develop a morality that is an expression of an inward sense of duty or a conscience, one that will, as a result of acting, bring a feeling of either contentment or dissatisfaction, praise or blame, fulfillment or remorse. To this end the Institute of Psychology in the Academy of Pedagogical Sciences is experimenting to learn more about how to train the emotions of an individual to approve some actions and to disapprove others.

A fourth kind of learning is the cultivation of an ideal Communist self. One Pioneer leader expressed it this way:

> During the years in a child's life under supervision of the Pioneers, together with independence in action, a new factor in the development of his personality, which is called self-training, appears. Children begin to want to work for their own growth and development.

To this end, teachers strive to build within the child a private opinion of what he really is and what he hopes to and can become in terms of the ideal Communist self. This, they hope, will challenge his aspirations and guide him through childhood and adolescence to ever higher moral behavior. "We teach children to be honest because they are active builders of a Communist society. This becomes a dominating ideal or idea which should absorb the whole child."

A final kind of moral learning is the development of an understanding of the hierarchy of values, so that when one value conflicts with another the child knows which is the more important. A naïve view of the Soviet Union pictures every citizen operating on the level of social conformity, automatically adjusting himself to the demands of social relationships as defined by the state. Certainly this looms large in the U.S.S.R., and well-defined relationships no doubt are for the most part the determining factors in outward behavior of children. Life in the U.S.S.R., however, is too complex and behavioral situations are much too complicated for the state to provide complete guidance for all moral decisions. There are, obviously, some situations where relationships are not defined by the state and where the individual has to think and to judge for himself.

That the Soviets have failed to develop a rational and reflective morality was evident to all members of the Comparative Education Society. The kind of moral development in which men formulate moral judgments on the basis of a critical examination of principles, free access to all data, and an open and critical analysis of facts in their relation to human life was virtually nonexistent. In the United States, we believe that a complete morality is reached only when the individual understands alternatives, chooses freely, and devotes himself to the fulfillment of a particular choice, although the degree to which customs, laws, and social pressures determine our conduct is probably greater than is generally admitted. Most members of the Comparative Education Society agreed, however, that the pressures to conform are very much greater in the U.S.S.R. and there is extremely limited opportunity and encouragement to analyze critically one's basic moral commitments.

Collective Orientation.   The American visitors thought that the Soviets had interpreted existence and the universe in a way that lessened the meaning and value of life and man's sense of dignity and worth. They were assured by the teachers and educators whom they met that this was not the case. Many educators insisted that communism provides goals and a zest for living that the capitalistic countries are failing to give. Not many hours in the U.S.S.R. were needed, however, to observe how the collective, as a means to individual growth and development, had replaced to a certain degree man's individual freedom and responsibility. It was obvious that the individual man is forced to determine his role and meaning in life within and through the collective. All Soviet educators stressed the role of the collective in the moral upbringing of children. Thus, Markushevich said,

> The basic idea in moral education is to develop in them the ideal of society or the collective. . . . It is important that children learn to subject their egoistic tendencies and feelings to the discipline of the collective.

Mme. Zoya Malkova of the Sector for Comparative Education in the Institute of the Theory and History of Pedagogy was even more emphatic in believing that morality demands collective orientation:

> The creation of a closely knit children's collective is one of the most important means for the development of moral character. The collective grows out of feelings of comradeship and friendship among the children. It is expected that all pupils in the class will become comrades but friendship is a more intimate relationship, implying common interests and understandings.

For a more detailed explanation of a collective observers were usually referred to N. K. Goncharov and B. P. Yesipov, whose definition is as follows:

> By the term "collective" we do not mean a mere gathering of people but an organization of people having a definite goal. It is an organization in which certain obligations are established and in which there are those designated and fully empowered to lead. There are concrete tasks upon the basis of which the organization is formed and firmly welded together. . . . The collective removes the individualistic, small-property-holder psychology and creates the psychology of a collectivist, who is conscious of being a member of the socialist society.[6]

A. S. Makarenko, the most frequently cited educator on the subject of Soviet morality, was especially praised for his thoughts on the role of the collective in moral upbringing of children. He regarded groups as collectives only if the members are aware of their common tasks, conscious of their mutuality of interests, devoted to common purposes, and dedicated to working together toward a general good. He believed that from very early life this spirit of comradeship and collectivism has to be consciously developed.

Professor Ivan Ogorodnikov, Chairman of the Department of Pedagogy in the Lenin State Pedagogical Institute in Moscow, elaborated upon the contribution of Makarenko to school practice and collective work:

> We still accept Makarenko's concept of collective work in certain aspects of school life but it is impossible to carry it out in all school

work. Some undertakings demand individual work. It is necessary to combine with care collective and individual work. When each member can find his place and his contribution in group work, there can be a collective. The collective does exert a disciplinary effect on students in terms of misbehaving in class, lagging behind in class, and preparing homework. In the collective individual problems may be discussed.

It was evident in talks with professional educators that, with the renewed emphasis upon the collective in Soviet schools, one of the real problems is to determine which phases of individual growth would be best achieved in and which would be best achieved out of the collective. Again and again one heard that "in the Soviet state there are no contradictions between individuality and society." Most of the teachers maintained that it is only through the collective that moral abilities of individuals are developed. For this reason they place great stress upon a consciousness of the interdependence and unity of the individual and society. One teacher put it this way: "Our task in the school is to educate each individual child but this is to be reached as each child is educated in the spirit of collectivism." Mme. Malkova phrased it more strongly: "The individual must not stand against the state and what the state stands for. There is a point at which he must conform to the collective good."

Mikhail Melnikov, secretary of the presidium of the Academy of Pedagogical Sciences, made the following statement:

> We believe that all of the multi-potentials of the individual should be developed. The test of all Soviet education is in the development of all of the personal features of a human being. This can be done best in a collective group. All features of a human being arise out of social relations. Hence, individuality develops only in society. The teacher has the responsibility for developing the collective sense of each pupil. We think that, if the collective is correctly understood, it does not prevent the development of the individual.

Mme. Malkova was likewise insistent that the individual has a greater opportunity to develop and to express himself today in the U.S.S.R.:

> It is the job of the individual to be a fighter for what is right. Now it is more possible for the individual to do this, to fight for what is right

and to push it through to the top. This has not been true in the past. There was too much to be done. There was no time for individual differences of this sort.

Now we can disagree more and we have more opportunity to fight for what is right. It is important to develop each person to become a leader — not one, but all.

As observers moved from school to school they noticed that each teacher had organized a class collective with monitors. In School No. 35 in Moscow, for example, in each room two children with red bands were serving as monitors. Each monitor appeared to know his responsibilities: cleaning the blackboards, checking attendance, watering plants, lining up fellow pupils, checking neatness of notebooks, and caring for school property. One had a red cross on his band. He checked on the grooming of his fellow students. There were usually a number of assistant monitors.

In School No. 51 in Kiev the class was organized into units, each row serving as a unit. A monitor supervised each unit and once a week the monitors met to plan their duties for the coming week. Once a month the units met as a class to evaluate the performance of monitorial duties and class order. Discipline was discussed and ways to improve it were suggested. Pupils who needed assistance in their studies were named and volunteers to help them were secured. The director of the school appointed a grade supervisor for each grade from among the more experienced teachers. The main function of this person was to organize a friendly and well-operating collective.

There is a degree of competition within and between collectives that serves to awaken student initiative and independence. Competition between class collectives, instead of negating individual competition between members, actually organizes them for it. Each person in the class collective, entering into the larger competition between collectives, thereby assumes responsibilities. The success of the entire collective depends upon the success of each individual pupil within it. Hence, the collective has a positive moral effect upon its members. If an unorganized, undisciplined pupil comes into it, he soon finds himself compelled to carry out the requirements of the collective. This, the teachers reported, is a wonderful way to develop moral maturity.

The work of each class collective is monitored and inspected by the larger school collective and an authorized body of the whole supervises and notes how well the members of the entire collective fulfill their responsibilities. This body rewards the class collective that wins the competition, and the latter rewards its most active members.

Each individual or group project completed has to be reported to the collective. The child is first supposed to arrive at an objective appraisal of his own and then to submit it to the critical examination of his fellow students. This criticism is considered to be a factor of no little importance in the formation of student character. The teachers contend that the pupils gradually learn to accept it as a form of comradely help without bearing the critic a grudge.

Within this context, therefore, the moral Soviet man is one who accepts and conforms his conduct to the same set of ethical convictions and standards as do his fellow Soviets. He is one who does his best for the common or collective good. Traditional moral traits assume a distinctive quality and meaning in this collective orientation. Honesty, for example, does not mean honesty only for one's own good but for the good of the entire group or collective. An essential trait in Communist morality, therefore, is a dedication to the larger collective.

Psychological Implications. The Soviet concept of human nature is that man is born neither good nor evil but rather with possibilities for both good and evil. Man's original nature includes many unorganized responses, which through maturation and learning take on a definite moral pattern. Anatoli Smirnov, Director of the Institute of Psychology, summarized his views in this way:

> The most important point of the theory of the development of the child is to know by what factors the psychic development is determined. The main principle is to know that the decisive role in the psychic development of a human being is played by the conditions of his life, which is always the life of the society and is not determined by the natural biological inclinations of men, but by the historical conditions of the material life of the society.
>
> It is not by the mere fact of their existence that the condition of life may determine the psychic development. . . . Man is not a passive object determined by the surrounding world. Man can create and does create the conditions of his life. . . . Education, home upbringing, and the conditions of life play the largest part in the moral development of

the child. . . . The conditions of life existing at a given moment, as well as the natural differences in the nervous systems, do not predetermine the psychic development. . . . The psychic processes depend upon what is done, the purpose, the character, and the structure of the activity.

Smirnov's views were explained more fully by the emphasis Soviet psychologists placed on the concept of the "second signal system." This, they said, is the notion that individuals can react to or stimulate themselves by symbols and ideas. In education it means that a greater responsibility is placed on the individual "will" and that character change can be achieved without a change in the social milieu.

Arseniev dealt with the materialistic and Marxian theory of the nature of the individual:

> Variety of the world is not limited. A law of nature is that complicated types are more varied than simple types. Alongside of variety, however, there are common features. . . . We believe that no matter how much multiplicity there is, there are common laws under which this society lives. Accordingly, we recognize each personality as an individual, developing in his own way, but ruled by laws of society. Man must study these laws and live by these laws.

Soviet psychologists recognize that the Soviet man has physical cravings and often acts on impulse. They have studied the conflict that takes place, that is, between selfish and altruistic impulses. The moral aim of Soviet education is to modify impulses so that they will harmonize with the welfare of the total group. It was maintained that sharing, self-sacrifice, and friendliness are as basic to human nature as selfishness and hostility. The decisive factor is how the child is brought up. Man can be made into a self-seeking or an altruistic person. A child raised in a society that emphasized cooperation, sharing, and friendliness would display different character qualities from those shown by one who saw only selfishness, hate, and hostility. Observation, however, indicated that Soviet subjects were not always characterized by friendliness and self-sacrifice. The question might well be raised: What are the factors of alienation of an individual from society and how are they related to the personality traits frequently displayed by Soviet subjects?

The devotion to Pavlov as official Communist theoretician was in evidence at the Institute of Psychology. Almost all of the discussions here centered on the conditioned reflex. The Department of Child Psychology maintains a special laboratory for the study of moral education, where three major questions are being studied:

1. What are the formative features of a school child on each grade level?
2. What enters into the formation of moral behavior?
3. How can a child's moral behavior be influenced during his play?

When asked how the characteristics of children were being studied, Melnikov answered,

> By observations in real life and in the environment. These are being made and recorded on students and adults on various levels. School children are being observed but not under laboratory conditions. The use of laboratory methods is being explored but not yet applied to children.

The visitors were given a much more detailed description of the researches under way and the methods being utilized, as follows:

> We observe children at play. One way is to have them play freely and observe them under these conditions. Another way is to let them act out such roles as doctors, policemen, etc. The child is assuming the role of a doctor and thus reveals his concept of that profession.
>
> We are studying the motives of our pupils which lead them to study better. Among these are social motives. Why do some students study to advance our country and others do not? What forms the collective sense of our children? What enters into the motives of children? Specifically, we are studying how to develop conscientiousness in our children and how to get our children to appreciate certain ideas and behavior rather than others.
>
> We also know that adults and children often know what to do but that they behave in other ways. So we are studying moral acts themselves. The psychologist assists the teachers in securing these data. This institute is going to make a study to compare the moral act with moral consciousness. There are many connections between conscience and moral behavior. This is often different at different levels of behavior, so we are studying this at varying age levels.

The Moral Climate

Visitors from capitalist countries are seldom invited into Soviet homes since in the past such visits have been officially discouraged. A few members of the Comparative Education Society received invitations. They reported living quarters in the cities to be somewhat similar to apartment living in New York City but with much smaller room space per person.

A few visitors became acquainted with a young Komsomol, a graduate of the Pedagogical Institute of Foreign Languages, who lived in an apartment house with her father, stepmother, and a brother. Her father was a building engineer and a member of the Party. Both mother and father worked all day and often attended meetings in the evening. The brother was in the ninth year of the secondary school. This girl reported that there was little or no home life as we know it in the United States and that she had little in common with her family. When she was not reading in her bedroom, she preferred to attend a ballet or the theater with her girl friends. There was television at home but she seldom watched it. Such home tasks as cooking, sewing, and keeping house had little appeal for her. Although a member of the Komsomol, she was not very active in it.

The tendency is, it seems, to de-emphasize family life and to substitute for it collective experiences outside the home. Such an approach is bound to produce youth disorganization. It was impossible to secure statistics on juvenile delinquency; however, Markushevich did admit to the existence of delinquent behavior:

> Children are taught not to commit immoral deeds. Of course, there are cases of immoral acts in the U.S.S.R. We have moral defects or delinquents. The public is usually indignant when an immoral act is made known. We as a people discuss this publicly. Newspapers of the Pioneers and Komsomols take this up in public discussion.

One of the best insights into youth problems, therefore, is supplied by *Komsomolskaia Pravda,* organ of the Communist Youth League. The editorials and the letters to the editor are good sources of information concerning the moral conditions of the home and the community. Here one can read, directly and indirectly, about cases of juvenile theft, reckless driving, drunkenness, orgies, and the like. The *Komsomolskaia Pravda* from time to time directs its criticism toward some of the children of high-ranking army and navy officers, top government officials, important factory managers, and leading intellectuals, known as the "jet set" and the *stiliagi.*

The "jet set" are children of the very top families, a much smaller group than the *stiliagi.* Since the income tax takes only a small proportion of the earnings of these families, great fortunes can be accumulated. Many parents lavish their wealth upon their children, who often take no active part in politics but pursue instead their own pleasures. However, the Russian educators maintained defensively that they are quite loyal to the political and economic system that supports them.

The *stiliagi,* or "style chasers," are often called the "center boys" in Moscow because they frequent the center of town where the tourists are housed. They let their hair grow long, wear narrow-legged trousers, and imitate other Western fads. They engage in little or no productive work. Here is ample evidence that the authority and pressures of the Komsomols are often to no avail. It is frequently suggested that these youths ought to be sent to the virgin lands to work. Several of the republics actually have passed laws permitting communities to exile such "parasites."

The *stiliagi* are frequently the children of the newly rich of the middle class. The parents want to give their children all of the advantages they did not have in their youth. They often attempt to keep them from serving in the armed forces, to have them avoid any unpleasant job assignments to the virgin lands, and to insure their good grades in school by means of special tutors. In most instances these children, too, take little interest in youth organizations and in politics.

Khrushchev recognized the existence of these privileged groups and the pressures they can exert:

> It will be noted that the practice, which prevailed until recently, of providing college-entry privileges for persons who finished school with a gold or silver medal had aggravated the situation still further. Some parents who wanted their children to get medals brought great pressure to bear upon teachers.
>
> . . . Frequently it is not enough to pass the examinations to enter college. Great influence of the parents also plays a part here. With

good reason, one rather widely hears youth entering college saying that after they themselves pass the contest, a contest among the parents begins — and it often decides the whole matter.[7]

The Revolution is now forty years old. Young people no longer share the early Bolshevik fervor. The passionate enthusiasm to make money and accumulate consumer goods has, it seems, replaced the enthusiasm to destroy the wealthy.

The Party has succeeded in imposing an outward conformity which has certainly eliminated the temptations and challenges found in a pluralistic society. No private-interest groups or private enterprises can be organized spontaneously and freely by youth or for youth. The Party or its agencies organize and direct all clubs, societies, entertainment, and work. The constant calls to support a cause or to give oneself to a newly organized activity often, therefore, fall on deaf ears.

On the whole, however, the great majority of the Soviet youth have an aura of seriousness about life and work that is not found in other countries. For the most part they exhibit an incredible dedication to their studies and their work as well as to the need to achieve ever greater results and ever loftier goals in their lives.

The Soviet School and Moral Education

From the days of its origin, the Soviet school has emphasized moral training. Although many programs for the inculcation of character had been elaborated and tested over the years, the Soviet educators interviewed were still far from satisfied with the outcome. The Institute of Pedagogy and the Institute of Theory and History of the Academy of Pedagogical Sciences of the R.S.F.S.R. were both studying the continuing problems of moral education. The latest of the detailed programs, drafted by the Bureau of Moral Education of the Institute of the Theory and History of Pedagogy, was under discussion while the American observers were in Moscow. Its aim was to help each student form a scientific outlook on life and to train him in the spirit of Communist morality. The qualities and virtues considered basic to this morality were stated in broad terms and then analyzed into more specific behaviors. For each grade level various activities and tasks were suggested, selected in terms of interests and needs of the children being taught and classified under four headings: class and school activities, extracurricular activities, Pioneer and Komsomol activities, and home activities.

The proposal pointed out that character traits could not always be built in a logical order. Honesty, for example, could not be built one year, courage the next. These traits often appear simultaneously and at different age levels. The development of particular traits, therefore, is closely related to the larger process of the formation of moral qualities.

The purpose of this well-defined list and sequence was to coordinate the efforts of the subject teachers, class advisers, Pioneer and Komsomol leaders, parents, and lay persons. It also set a standard so that by the time the child reached the fifth grade he would presumably have acquired certain minimum general and specific moral qualities and behavior outcomes.

Beginnings of Communist Character. The following outline represents the primary-school program proposed by the Academy:

I. Elementary ideas of good and bad.
   A. To differentiate between good and bad actions.
   B. To behave well.
      1. To love all useful work, especially manual work.
      2. To carry out properly all duties.
      3. To study diligently.
      4. To be orderly and obey all rules.
      5. To help fellow comrades and younger children.
      6. To be truthful, brave, and kind.
      7. To take good care of one's health.
      8. To know that breaking rules is bad.
      9. To obey the teacher and parents.
     10. To follow the example of the best pupils.
     11. To follow the rules of the Octobrists and the laws of the Young Pioneers.
II. Love of Motherland.
   A. To respect the work of adults for the common good and the welfare of the family.
      1. To bring adults joy through one's success in study and in behavior.
   B. To love one's school.
      1. To develop the ability to study well.

2. To respect the teacher.

C. To love one's native locale.

D. To take an interest in the heroic past and present of our Motherland.

   1. To have a warm love for V. I. Lenin.

   2. To have a feeling of gratitude to the Communist Party and the Soviet Government.

E. To have a feeling of friendship for the children of all nations.

F. To hate instigators of wars.

G. To have a desire to be good Octobrists or Pioneers.

III. Industriousness and frugality.

   A. To respect all socially useful labor, especially manual labor.

   B. To have habits of self-service and assistance to the family.

   C. To desire to work for the social good.

      1. To make useful things.

      2. To take care of "green friends," birds, and animals.

   D. To have good work habits.

   E. To respect property.

IV. Truthfulness, honesty, modesty, and kindness.

   A. To speak the truth.

   B. To carry out promises.

   C. To avoid boasting about successes.

   D. To recognize mistakes and to avoid them in the future.

   E. To apologize if you are wrong.

   F. To fulfill honorable duties.

V. Friendship and comradeship.

   A. To have friends and comrades among the students.

   B. To give help to a comrade.

   C. To be able to plan work together.

   D. To respect the monitors and to obey their orders.

   E. To obey the decisions of the collectives.

VI. Discipline.

   A. To carry out assignments.

   B. To obey "The Rules for Pupils" and to understand the reasons for them.

   C. To obey these rules without being reminded of them.

VII. Love of studies and conscientiousness.

   A. To be curious, listen attentively, read, observe, work, study, and create.

   B. To carry out all requirements and teachers' instructions with a degree of independence.

   C. To apply the acquired knowledge to life and to share it with others.

VIII. Good social conduct in the school, at home, in the streets, and in public places.

A. To be orderly, neat, and well-groomed.

B. To be polite.

1. To use common forms of politeness, such as "Good morning," "Please," "Thank you," and so forth.

2. To look affable during conversations and not interrupt each other.

C. To behave properly at home.

1. To leave and to enter the home quietly and without banging doors.

2. To ask permission to take something or permission to leave the house.

D. To conduct oneself properly in the streets and in public places.

1. To obey the rules of conduct in movies, dining rooms, libraries, and so forth.

a. To be on time.

b. To wipe footwear at the entrance.

c. Not to run around.

d. Not to break in line.

e. Not to speak loudly.

2. To prevent comrades from committing bad actions.

There followed a very detailed listing of experiences and activities for each grade level which might be used to secure the desired outcomes. For the guidance of the class leader, these activities were classified under nine headings, and these in turn were organized in terms of the class, the total school life, the extracurricular activities, the home and the youth organizations. The headings are as follows:

1. Preparation for the school year.
2. First days of the class.
3. Cooperation with the home.
4. Cooperation with the Pioneers.
5. Personal example of the teacher.
6. Common welfare.
7. Celebration of certain days.
8. Themes, storytelling, reading, dramas.
9. Preparation for the summer.

Teachers were to be expected to make actual lesson plans setting forth the desired moral outcomes and the content, experiences, and activities utilized. They were to try to achieve understanding of the local conditions of the community as well as the peculiar needs of the school and the individual pupils in the class by collecting comprehensive data on the home life of the pupils, the level of their upbringing, and their individual traits. The activities were to be stated as concrete tasks for the class as a whole or for individual students. The teacher was also to be encouraged to develop a plan of cooperation with the parents and the leaders of the youth organization. Finally, the teacher was to develop for each pupil a program of extracurricular activities that would affect moral outcomes. These would consist of such activities as home study, individual and group reading, collective work, meetings, walks, excursions, amateur circles, and theater and television performances.

As the program was carried out by the teachers they were to record personal observations of students and to gather observations of other teachers, parents, and youth leaders. The final evaluations of the students would then be recorded in the class books and in the students' journals, to be sent home each quarter to the parents. Wherever possible, they would systematically record in their own educational diaries the basic changes they noticed in the conduct of each student.

Fundamentals of Communist Character. The same general program was outlined for the junior school, grades five through eight. New expectations and tasks were spelled out in terms of the new life activities and demands upon adolescents. Several instructors and a class leader now replaced the one teacher of the primary school. Working together, they were to strengthen and reinforce what had been achieved in character growth through the first four grades and to develop new ideas, attitudes, habits, and skills of a moral nature. A sampling of the general and specific outcomes desired for these grade levels is given here:

I. Soviet patriotism and a feeling of friendship among peoples.
   A. To love one's own locale.
   B. To respect the historic revolutionary and other monuments.

C. To love the homeland, the Communist Party, and the Leninist Komsomol.

D. To understand the superiority of the Soviet system over the bourgeois system.

E. To work for the good of the native land.

F. To love and to respect soldiers of the Soviet Army.

G. To take a lively interest in the activities of the Communist Party, Soviet Government, Pioneers, and Komsomols.

H. To participate actively in the Lenin Pioneer organization and to strive to become a member of the Komsomol.

I. To take an interest in the life and culture of the people of other lands.

J. To love children of workers all over the world.

II. Realization of social duty.

A. To understand and do one's duty to the school and the student collective.

B. To value the honor of one's school and the Pioneers.

C. To be honest in sports.

D. To know Lenin's precepts to youth.

E. To love work for the common welfare.

III. Discipline, persistence, and endurance.

A. To obey the "Rules for Pupils" and the Laws of Young Pioneers.

B. To fulfill conscientiously all assignments.

C. To be demanding of oneself and to be punctual.

D. To overcome difficulties.

E. To distinguish between caution and cowardliness, between boldness and recklessness.

IV. Friendship and comradeship.

A. To help a comrade in misfortune.

B. To tell a comrade tactfully the truth to his face and to help him find the right solution.

C. To fight any manifestation of egoism.

D. To respect the collective body's public opinion.

V. Attentive and thoughtful attitude toward people.

A. To show gratitude and love toward one's parents and teachers.

B. To be courteous to all adults.

C. To do good turns.

VI. Truthfulness, honesty, and modesty.

A. To speak the truth.

B. To have a proper attitude toward criticism on the part of one's comrades.

C. To be able to withstand bad influences — profanity, gambling,

rowdyism, drinking, idleness, excessive fondness of motion pictures and football.
   D. To serve fellow students and the collective.
   E. Not to boast or to brag about the position of one's parents.
   F. Not to attract attention to oneself by loud clothing and by accentuated manners.
VII. Responsible attitude toward study and labor.
   A. To aspire to acquire lasting knowledge and skills.
   B. To aspire to become a diligent student.
   C. To have good work habits.
   D. To apply knowledge and skills to life and labor for the common welfare.
   E. To show a concern for the study achievements of the whole class and the intermediate grades.

There followed a long listing of experiences and activities that might be used to secure these outcomes. At the junior-school level, much of the moral development was to be achieved through a deeper understanding of the Soviet social-political life, mastery of appropriate subject content, fulfillment of the Pioneer degree requirements, and socially useful labor in the home, school, and community.

Detailed instructions were to be given to the class leaders on how they could plan the moral education program for each class, covering a period of eighteen months, including the summer vacation. Definite tasks or activities were suggested for each grade level, listed under school activities or extracurricular activities.

The class leaders were advised to discuss the plan with the class or its self-government organ. The older children in the seventh grade were to participate in drawing up the program. Before the beginning of the school year, the class leaders would meet each new pupil under their care, discuss each pupil with the teachers who had taught him personally, study the data collected, and visit homes with the former class leader. On the eve of the school year, they were to schedule a general meeting with their pupils. Permanent seats would be assigned and monitors and attendants elected and instructed even before school got under way.

The teachers of all subjects would be informed about the general programs of the class leaders and each teacher would be asked to relate his teaching to it. Parents were to be informed of their responsibilities.

This intermediate grade program was completed by a detailed outline of the methods by which the class leaders, the teachers, the parents, and the youth leaders could secure the desired moral attitudes and habits.

The Basis of a Scientific World Outlook.   The program for the senior classes embraces not only all of the moral outcomes of the earlier grades but many new ones because of the more active part these children take in productive labor and in society and political life. The sensation of first love often manifests itself during this period. Adolescents take a more active interest and role in household affairs. They now may pass from the Pioneers to the Young Communist League and receive their passports. Hence, circumstances place on them greater civic and moral responsibilities for all their acts. They begin to assume some responsibility for the moral upbringing of the younger children. Along with this comes preparation for more independent action and the status of citizenship. The character outcomes to be developed in senior students were outlined in detail but only those significant for moral education are listed here:

I. Understanding of the general concepts of world outlook and morality.
   A. Understanding of dialectical materialism as the only scientific and revolutionary system.
   B. Understanding of the importance of Marxism-Leninism as the ideological weapon of the working people.
   C. Understanding of the role of V. I. Lenin in bringing about the Great October Socialist Revolution.
   D. Capacity for giving all one's knowledge and force for the common cause.
   E. Readiness to respond to every call of the Communist Party.
      1. To overcome all difficulties and obstacles on the path to the great goal.
      2. To fight staunchly to make the policy of the Party a reality.
      3. To remain always true to Communist views.
      4. To convince others of their correctness.
      5. To conduct oneself always as befits a citizen of the U.S.S.R.
   F. To fulfill unswervingly the decisions of the Young Communist League for the observation of the norms of Y.C.L. life.

       1. To maintain high principles and not to allow divergencies between word and deed.

       2. To participate actively in the Y.C.L.

       3. To discover shortcomings in work through criticism and self-criticism.

    G. To strive constantly to raise one's theoretical and ideological level.

       1. To maintain an irreconcilable attitude toward bourgeois ideology and morality that are hostile to us.

    H. To understand morals as a form of social consciousness.

       1. To understand the connection between morals and other forms of social consciousness.

       2. To understand concepts of the moral Soviet man.

II. Understanding of the meaning of Soviet patriotism and proletarian internationalism.

    A. To understand the advantages and superiority of the socialist system over the capitalist system.

    B. To have pride in one's Soviet fatherland and in its science, culture, and art.

    C. To have knowledge of the heroic past.

    D. To conduct oneself in the spirit of revolutionary and labor traditions of the Soviet people.

    E. To hate local nationalism and have feelings of friendship for the peoples among the many nationalities that make up the U.S.S.R.

III. Communist attitude toward labor and socialist property.

    A. To understand the role of labor as a high obligation and a matter of honor for every Soviet person.

    B. To combine collective and individual labor.

    C. To have an irreconcilable attitude toward loafers, slackers, thieves, and those who would damage public property.

IV. Understanding of the essential meaning of collectivism.

    A. To place social interest above personal satisfaction.

    B. To be loyal to the Young Communist League and the collective of pupils.

    C. To understand the basis for an ideological and spiritual community of comrades.

    D. To maintain friendly relations between boys and girls.

    E. To maintain an intolerant attitude toward individualists and egoists who devote their lives to narrowly personal interests.

    F. To be loyal to one's principles.

    G. To fulfill one's social duty, maintain personal dignity, and have pride in one's collective.

H. To guard one's honor and to fight for it.

I. To be morally responsible for one's behavior to the collective and to society.

V. Understanding of social humanism.

    A. To have concern and respect for comrades, elders, and parents.

    B. To be modest in one's relation with people.

    C. To be intolerant of all forms of humiliation and insults to a person and toward indifference to people.

    D. To be intolerant toward abnormal and amoral acts, hooliganism, drunkenness, toadyism, bureaucracy, rudeness, and all evidences of disrespect, boasting, haughtiness, and other violations of the norms of socialist humanism.

    E. To hate the enemies of peace, democracy, and socialism.

    F. To be intolerant of the racist theories of the superiorities of one race over others and of one people over others.

VI. Internalized character traits.

    A. To be ready to make the principles of Communist morality over into one's behavior and activities.

    B. To be independent, decisive, and staunch in making decisions and in achieving goals.

    C. To maintain a negative attitude toward lack of spirit, cowardice, and stubbornness.

    D. To be restrained, tolerant, and patient.

    E. To master one's moods and control one's behavior.

    F. To use self-education as a means of developing character traits.

VII. Understanding of the social meaning of education.

    A. To gain knowledge for active participation in the building of Communist society.

        1. To understand the need for highly educated people.

        2. To recognize the need for a responsible attitude toward general and polytechnical education.

        3. To learn about all that is new and advanced in the fields of science, technology, literature, and art.

        4. To choose an occupation on the basis of the country's needs and on the basis of personal inclinations and capabilities.

        5. To show stauchness and initiative in studies.

        6. To be intolerant of a dishonest approach to studies.

    B. To constantly raise one's standards of mental work.

VIII. Mastery of the rules of the socialist community and standards of behavior.

A. To be guided by the norms and rules of the socialist community.
B. Not to violate Soviet laws and to keep others from violating them.
C. To eliminate shortcomings in behavior of one's comrades.
D. To maintain a human attitude toward one's fellows.
E. To aid those in need.
F. To be intolerant toward uncomradely attitudes toward women.
G. To have a correct concept of the mutual relations between adults, among young people, boys and girls, and among the members of the family.
H. To use good manners everywhere.

Activities and methods for use in the classes and at home were suggested under six headings: social and political work, studies, socially useful work, rules of the socialist community and standards of personal behavior, artistic work, and physical culture and sports.

As in the previous stages, the unity of the program was stressed. The school, the youth organizations, the family, and the public were to work together to bring the best influences to bear upon the collective and individual pupils. Although types of activities that could be used in the majority of school situations were suggested, the plan encouraged the school to supplement or replace them with others more appropriate to the specific features of the geographical region. Debates, political circles, literary evenings, and lectures were not suggested for wide use in the junior period but were to be especially encouraged for senior students.

Each student in a pedagogical institute was required to take a course in theory of moral education. This course consisted of lectures and practical work at schools. Students made reports on their observations of the ethical behavior of ten-year-school pupils in classes, as well as in Pioneer activities and meetings. In answer to the question "What are the problems in teaching this course?" Professor Petukhov made this observation:

> The theory is easy to get over to the students but how to direct behavior and develop skills is a greater problem. However, we do not encounter serious discipline problems in our schools.

General Methods in Moral Education

As the members of the Comparative Education Society moved from school to school, they recorded observations of the general methods used in the classrooms of the ten-year schools and in life situations to guide and direct moral behavior.

Slogans. In spite of Makarenko's warning that "lecturing and exhortation are the least effective means for exerting influence," Soviet educators made wide use of slogans. Sentiments from the writings of Lenin, Makarenko, and Gorki appeared on banners and blackboards and walls, over doorways, and in auditoriums. Lenin's "Study, study, study!" is a good example of a much repeated but hardly inspiring slogan.

Ethical Conversations. The use of ethical conversations was directed at forming moral conscience. The Institute of Psychology of the Academy of Pedagogical Sciences was studying ways and means to organize these conversations so as to give them a significant impact on children. Here is how one teacher described what she believed her colleagues were doing:

> One example is the explanation of school rules. Our schools have special rules for school behavior. Our teachers organize many group and individual conversations on these rules. Teachers explain school rules to children of the first grade. The children of the seventh, eighth, and ninth grades enter into conversations on problems in literature relative to moral content, heroes, and acts of bravery. We also organize literary conversations and debates where children from different grades hear and explore problems gathered from books.

At the Institute of Psychology, studies seeking to determine how moral consciousness is developed in children place much stress upon moral conversations. These are designed to discover what children think about their moral obligations, honesty, and truthfulness. Another experimental approach is to read or tell short stories to children. Good and bad behavior is depicted and children are asked to express their opinions as to why some acts are bad and others are good.

Subject-Matter Teaching of Morality. Each teacher of the Soviet school is instructed to utilize his classroom teaching to develop character and moral traits. Literature offers many opportunities, as Markushevich pointed out: "We expose our children to the best examples of literature of all nations, drawn from life and experience, to influence their moral growth." Reading of the great Soviet masterpieces, such as Makarenko's *Flags on the Tower*, is encouraged because of the imprint such works leave on youngsters' minds. Stories, tales, fables, children's newspapers, and periodicals are widely utilized in the primary school. Both the *Pionerskaia Pravda* and the *Komsomolskaia Pravda* stress content that is intended for moral education purposes.

In many classes poems written by students are posted for all to read or to memorize. In School No. 29 in Leningrad the following poem was recited in the first grade to teach children respect for the toil of others:

> Things do not grow by themselves;
> To make them, toil is necessary.
> So be careful of all the things in school:
> Books, pens, desks, windows, and walls.
> Do not break, tear, or dirty them.

At an evening party honoring the teachers of Leningrad at the beginning of the school year, the following poem was written by a student and recited in recognition of the contribution of the Soviet teachers to the advancement of the nation:

> If we only study well
> Every one of us can realize his dream for the future.
> Some will go to the virgin lands,
> Some will be construction workers,
> Some will be chauffeurs.
> For everyone who studies well
> His dream will come true,
> If only there is no more war.

Mme. Shatskaia, Director of the Institute of Art Education, was high in her praise of singing and dancing to develop joy of life and also a feeling of love and friendship for other nations. Folk dancing and the study of folk music are especially encouraged for this purpose.

Physical education is inseparably connected with moral education. Mass physical culture and sports in the schools and in all other educational establishments are aimed at moral fitness. Considerable attention is devoted to extraclass and extraschool physical education as worthwhile leisure-time activities.

History, of course, is a marvelous vehicle for acquainting children with the great moral deeds of Soviet historical figures. The children, for example, are taken each year to the graves of the Komsomols who died in World War II. Many case studies of heroic children taken directly from life as well as literary works, folklore, history, and biography are used for the purpose of arousing the emotions and inner feelings of the child.

Teacher's Criticism. Soviet teachers assured us that admonition in the presence of comrades evokes shame in a child. If skillfully and tactfully employed, they consider it an extremely effective method in moral education. They did say, however, that admonition should at times be given in private. A class leader in one of the Leningrad schools had this to say to one of our seminar participants:

> I meet with my group at least once a day. If any of my children behave badly, I take it up with them at this time. If there is a behavior problem and if taking it up with the pupil privately or in front of the class does not help, I talk to the director of the school. We may decide to bring the pupil's behavior before the parents' committee. If this fails to bring improvement, we might place the child in another school, where he does not have friends and thus is not so brave. There are some children who are hard to handle. You talk to them but it has little or no effect. They are very brave and they won't listen.

The teacher is directed to criticize different moral opinions and the bases for them. His responsibility is to throw scientific light upon them and to be critical of their false sanctions. But the visitors were told that there is some opposition to pointing out and discussing false opinions and sanctions in the classroom since so many of the students might not be aware of them.

Teacher's Example. The Soviet teacher is constantly being reminded that he is the ever-present model of behavior for children to emulate. Although in the early years of a child's life the influence of teacher example is much more informal, the process of imitation might be made more and more conscious and purposeful as the child grows older. Selective imitation would enable him to know what to follow consciously and what to refuse to imitate. Hence, the teacher must deliberately set an example of the habits he wants the pupils to acquire. Again and again teachers are told that a moral truth has great power for children simply because it is uttered by some adult close to them.

Several teachers quoted the great Soviet educator Kalinin on the significance of the authority of the teacher, as follows:

> It can be safely said that if a teacher enjoys great authority some people will bear traces of his influence throughout their lives. That is why it is important for the teacher to look to himself, to be aware that his conduct and his actions are subject to a stricter control than those of any other person on earth.[8]

Class Supervision. In setting the example, the teacher must be firm and consistent. He is told that it is wrong for a teacher to punish a pupil for delinquency at one time and to ignore an infraction of the rules another time. Moral demands upon children are to be made in a decisive form and are to be carried out. The teachers must be careful not to contradict each other as well as to avoid contradictions between word and deed, both in small and in large things. The entire community can furnish examples. Each school, for instance, has public patrons, retired people of ability who live in the area and are willing to give their time and services to the school.

The teachers were of the opinion that children ought to finish whatever they start, in spite of difficulties and disappointments. The belief was that overcoming difficulties on the job strengthens the will power of the students.

Khrushchev stressed the need for greater supervision from society as a whole:

> We come across people who maliciously violate the rules of our socialist community. It is impossible to put an end to these ugly manifestations merely by administrative measures, without participation by the masses themselves. In this matter, public opinion has a great role to play. It is necessary to create such an atmosphere that people violating standards of conduct, the principles of Soviet morality, should feel that their actions are condemned by the whole society.[9]

Professor Petukhov made some observations on the close supervision of the community over the children:

> We use parents' committees. They help to organize different out-of-school activities. They serve as resource persons in classes and circles. They act as leaders.
>
> Children are not permitted to go to the movies after 8:00 P.M. until they are sixteen years of age unless they are accompanied by parents. There are some theaters that will not permit children at all. The law also provides for a curfew here in Leningrad. Children under sixteen years are not to be on the streets after 10:00 P.M. Cigarettes, liquor, and matches are not sold to children under sixteen years of age.

Supervision goes beyond that of the teacher and community to that of the collective itself. One of our participants submitted this report on his visit to a Pioneer camp:

> A group of boys were asked if they would have their picture taken. They were interested, and a small boy was in front. He was pulled to the back by a bigger boy. When the person who was taking the picture asked if the little one couldn't stand in front, the older boy first of all buttoned up the young one's shirt and neatened him up, then let him come to the front. This is rather typical of the care of older children for the young and of the importance of having the group look well. Therefore, someone took the initiative to see that each child looked well. This concern for helping the one who is not particularly in step and getting him up to the standard of others was frequently mentioned when discussing Pioneer work or work with groups of youth of different types.

Love and Persuasion. Members of the Comparative Education Society were told that Communist morality has a genuine concern for the individual and his development. Teachers are told to show love and concern for their pupils, to develop an understanding of each child through a study of his behavior in and out of school. This was described to us, however, as a disciplined love. Far too many children, it was said, are indulged by their parents. The teacher is to advise the parents to correct this condition. If the parents are indifferent to the child or neglect him, the teacher is under instruction to do something about this condition.

One teacher described how she tried to make the children doers of good deeds for others:

We have children assist families in need and we have them engage in activities and projects which will contribute something to the improvement of the school or town. The aim is to take on the large ideals of communism and be dedicated to them.

The Soviets make great use of the methods of direct and indirect persuasion. If a child fails to conform to given rules, he is forced to observe them. One teacher said, "Some children promise to improve and do not improve. It is necessary to keep after them and to help them improve." Another teacher spoke out concerning the use of this method: "The child must develop an understanding of himself, admit his faults and mistakes, show a desire to improve, and put forth effort to alter his conduct." What they were saying was that the authority of the teacher should not rest upon excessive kindness or fear of punishment but upon a sense of love and gratitude.

The use of fear is deplored by most of the teachers. "Authority of the teacher should not be built upon fear of the instructor or fear of severe punishment," said one. Makarenko called this authority by suppression. It is not advocated because, they said, it leads to deceit and lies.

At the Institute of Psychology it was noted that pupils often refrain from violating regulations for four reasons:

1. Fear of displeasing adults or teachers.
2. Fear of disapproval on the part of the collective.
3. Fear of reproaches of his own conscience.
4. Fear of unpleasant experiences of shame.

The ultimate goal is to get the child to act on the basis of his inner feeling and not external pressures. This kind of self-discipline is nurtured in the daily life of the school.

Discipline and Habit. Obviously, habit formation receives as much stress in the U.S.S.R. as it does in other nations. Teachers are instructed so to direct their teaching that good habits will be developed in the course of the day and those running counter to the norms of Communist morality will be discouraged. The draft plans for moral education emphasized that discipline is best achieved in a classroom where instruction is correctly organized. "A well-planned recitation sets good habits of punctuality, order, and efficiency." Teachers are expected to be strict and create conditions for good work habits.

Labor. A number of teachers complained that too many parents think childhood is just a time for play and fun. This is especially true of parents who have had a very hard life themselves and now want to make life easier for their children. One teacher in Leningrad made the following comment:

> Parents must be taught that it is important to teach children love of toil from the earliest age on. Some children have very good work habits. They know how to do all kinds of work but they will do it only for themselves or their own family. They must be taught that the family is good but one must think of society also. In labor, also, children must be taught the collective good.

Dean Topshieva of the University of Moscow told us how the method of labor is used to discipline immature and wayward students:

> There are two types of students who are of concern to us. The first type cannot behave properly because they are immature. These are admonished, restricted, and urged to do better. The professor pretends to be very severe but still he gives the student every opportunity to become mature.
>
> The second type is not due to immaturity but to the type of mind the student has. This is the uncooperative student. Since there is not much we can do with this type, they are sent to labor where there are many workers. Sometimes this helps them. As a rule, they are assigned to less interesting work. Sometimes they are given jobs for which they are qualified. The object is to cure them of their bad behavior, to make them see the error of their ways.

One of the professors of psychology at the University of Kiev explained how he engaged in research on moral learning by setting up a natural experiment. It consisted of assigning a child a moral task, that is, a task involving obligations of group members to each other, such as being a class leader or helping the poor students. The psychologist observed how the students did their tasks and what organizational possibilities were involved. He tried to determine the attitude of the child and how the child related to his duties. He also tried to determine which factors facilitated the task being done and which factors were barriers to its fulfillment.

Makarenko was quoted again and again to the effect that labor is basic to moral development.

Films. At the Moscow Institute for the Improvement of Teachers, members of the Comparative Education Society were shown three films that had been made for moral education in the classroom.

> Vasia, a little boy, brought home a dog, Sharik, and begged his mother to let him keep it. The mother agreed, if the boy would promise to take good care of the pet himself. He promised but soon he forgot about it. The dog was not fed regularly, he was not washed or brushed, and he was never taken for a walk. One day the dog found the door to the apartment open and he ran away. When Vasia came home, Sharik was gone.
>
> While running the streets, Sharik was knocked down by a car. Another boy, Petia, picked him up and, as his owner could not be found, took him home and nursed him back to health. He found another name for the dog and the two became the best of friends. He took care of the dog and always took him for walks.
>
> On one of these walks they met Vasia, who recognized the dog as his old pet. The two boys argued about whose dog it was and finally agreed to let the dog decide who his master should be. The dog would belong to the boy to whom he ran when he was called. He ran to Petia. Petia was most happy but he decided that it was only fair to let Vasia share the dog. The film ended with the two boys shaking hands and deciding to be firm friends.

A second film, *The Find,* told of an old lady receiving a letter from her son with a money order in it. The story went as follows:

> She cashed the order and put the bulging purse in her pocket. Then she walked home. On the way she got tired and sat down on a park bench. It was hot, so she pulled out her handkerchief to wipe her face. The purse fell out unnoticed. She got up and walked away.
>
> Two boys, playing ball, found the purse. They hurried after her to return it but the traffic light was against them. When they were permitted to cross the street, the old lady had disappeared. The two boys decided to take the purse to the police station. While the boys were explaining their story, the old lady entered, very upset. The police officer returned her purse and, when she tried to embrace the

boys, they were much embarrassed. They only did their duty. The film ended as they stood at attention and gave the Pioneer salute and slogan, "Always ready!"

There was never any indication that the boys were tempted to keep the money. Nor were they tempted to cross the street against the light in order to reach the old lady. This film was obviously designed to develop a formal morality of habit and duty.

The True Friend, for second- and third-graders, was about a dog who was saved from drowning by a boy. The children in it were very happy and very considerate of each other. The boy, for example, remembered that his sister had forgotten to take her doll when she went out to play and took it to her. Later the dog saved the boy's sister from being bitten by a snake.

All three films provided moralizing in an obvious but pleasant way. The children were loving and most protective toward each other. In each instance, nature or outer conditions imposed a punishment for nonconformity to the moral principle.

Punishments. The main kinds of punishment are set by the ministries of education. "Many parents," said Professor Petukhov, "still believe in corporal punishment and they have to be convinced this is harmful and only makes the child sly and deceitful. It is not used because it is not a means of educating the child."

Only the most frequently mentioned punishments are given here. Corporal punishment is not among them.

First, Professor Petukhov stressed natural consequences as a means of punishment:

> For example, a child's toys were in disorder. The mother asked the child to put them in order. The child refused. The mother put them in order and refused to give them to the child even though he cried. We got this idea from Rousseau and Spencer.

Secondly, the teacher may use reproof, either in private or in front of the entire class. First a warning is given the child and an entry made in his diary. If the bad behavior is continued, a more severe punishment is inflicted, such as asking the child to leave the room or assigning him to detention after class. Misbehavior may be publicly announced in an assembly or on a wall newspaper. The whole class may discuss it, or the director or grade supervisor may censure a student in private. Unfavorable criticism by the grade counselor for slipshod work calls for its being done over again. If other children are involved, the guilty one has to ask the pardon of his comrades for the harm he has done them. Reprimand may be before the entire class in the form of a written order by the director of the school. "We do not approve of a blackboard list of delinquents," said one teacher. "This is a mockery of a child's personality." The director may, however, have a reprimand of a student read to the class.

Starting with the third grade, there is a class council. If a child fails to conform, the class council may vote to ostracize him. If poor conduct continues, the council may go with a three-member parent council team to the home of the child, and even go so far as to appeal to the father's union. Another example was given: If a student receives bad marks in his school work, he is denied participation in the extracurricular work of the Pioneers.

The discussion of conduct problems can be taken to the pedagogical council of the school. Any decision of the council takes effect only after the approval of the director. The grade supervisor grades the child on his behavior at the end of each quarter. The highest mark is "5." Minor violations in conduct result in a "4." A student who receives a "4" in one quarter must raise it to a "5" in the next quarter or be subject to a discussion before the pedagogical council as to whether the grade should be lowered to "3." Serious violations in conduct bring a "3." It is a final warning that expulsion from school is the next step. If there is no improvement in the conduct grade in the next quarter, the pedagogical council deliberates over the expulsion of the student. If the council decides that he should be dismissed, the grade is lowered to a "2" and a request is formally made to the local board of education to have the pupil expelled. Expulsion is voted only after all other measures have been tried and have failed. The purpose of expulsion is primarily to protect the other children in school.

Professor Petukhov revealed that there are detention homes for delinquents who cannot be influenced by any other means. Two of these are in Leningrad. If parents are financially able, they pay for the child's keep.

Rewards. The main forms of rewards are fixed by the ministries of education and classified under four major headings:

Praise by the teacher or by the director. This can be written or oral praise in private or before the whole class.

Written or oral appreciation or praise announced to the entire class or to a general assembly. The whole school may be gathered for a special program during which the announcement is made with trumpet and drum.

Prizes. A traveling pennant is often awarded at an assembly and is displayed in the room for a stated period of time. Free movie tickets and badges of honor are often used.

Testimonials. A ceremonial parade by the children is often arranged in front of the entire student body. A written testimonial of character is issued to each child with a conduct mark of "5" for the year. A written testimonial is frequently published in the wall newspaper citing those with good conduct records.

Summary

One could not visit the schools of the Soviet Union and talk with the students and teachers without realizing that a great struggle is under way to win the minds and loyalties of the children and youth of the U.S.S.R. for their country and the Communist experiment. Outwardly there appears to be widespread optimism. There is faith in science and confidence that the empirical method will be able to solve most of the great social, economic, and moral problems in the not-too-distant future. The certainty of progress under communism and the great hopes for the future make for a patriotism or nationalism that is everywhere in evidence.

The impression members of the Comparative Education Society received unmistakably was that the Soviets are firmly convinced that as more and more knowledge and technical skill are achieved, the good life will be in the possession of every Soviet citizen. In short, under dialectical materialism and the leadership of the Party, education, science, hard labor, and time will certainly bring into being in the U.S.S.R. a new morality and spirituality grounded in collectivism and with it happiness and freedom from exploitation.

What were the final reactions of the American educators to this Soviet dream? There were many differences of opinion, but those who had seriously studied ethical systems as they operate in other cultures and in other eras of history would probably agree on four generalizations:

1. When custom is made the basis for morality, the individual tends to become submerged in society. The moral man must frequently challenge the customary morality to secure wider and deeper moral insights. This he cannot do when morality means conformity to the mores.

2. If law is made the moral standard, moral judgment becomes the exclusive right of legislators and courts. Obviously there are good laws and bad laws, but who is to say and how is one to say which is good and which is bad? And who is to watch the watchers?

3. To internalize feelings and make these the moral standard is not sufficient. Conscience is a social product. A moral nation must have conscientious individuals. But this in itself is not a guarantee of a moral people.

4. Only when morality is raised to the level of free inquiry and free discussion, and man has the power to choose betwen alternative courses of action, can moral judgment free itself from conformity to prejudice, bigotry, and propaganda.

To equate morality with unquestioned obedience to a code of conduct determined by a totalitarian authority is to endanger the whole of moral life and the whole essence of humanity. One cannot aspire to scale the heights of human excellence by means that are subhuman in character. Observations of this danger in the Soviet Union alerted the visiting Americans to their obligation to maintain alive, dynamic, and bright the alternative pattern of social living. Free men must be adequately and intelligently informed of alternative choices before them and of the restrictions, both conscious and unconscious, under which they may be laboring. In response to Soviet methods, we must struggle, if we are to have a dynamic morality, to widen the area of calm search for and discussions of ever new ethical principles, without any limit as to range of the moral precepts to be considered. Only thus can we hope to meet the Soviet challenge in education and show the world the way to solutions combining concern for the welfare of every man with the spontaneity that comes from a mind and heart unbounded in freedom of inquiry.

NOTES

CHAPTER 1

This chapter was written by George Z. F. Bereday.

1. See, for example, one of the following comparisons:
   A. McAndrew, "Are Soviet Schools Better Than Ours?," *The Reporter*, February 20, 1958; G. Fisher, "Soviet and American Education, Mistaken Envy," *The Progressive*, March, 1958; N. DeWitt, "Soviet Science Education and Its Challenge," *Mathematics Teacher*, February, 1958; G. Z. F. Bereday, "American and Soviet Scientific Potential," *Social Problems*, January, 1957; H. Chauncey, "Some Comparative Checkpoints between American and Soviet Secondary Education," *Comparative Education Review*, February, 1959; R. J. Havighurst, "Is Russia Really Outproducing Us in Scientists?," *School and Society*, April 26, 1958.

2. How much or how little of the original Marxist design remained when communism was grafted to the Russian government is a matter for dispute. The subject is treated at length in Chapters 3 and 4. See also G. S. Counts, *The Challenge of Soviet Education* (New York: McGraw-Hill Book Company, 1957), p. 330.

3. See G. Z. F. Bereday, "A Comparative Look at English, French, and Soviet Education," *Current History*, September, 1958.

4. See "The Content of Education," in G. Z. F. Bereday and J. A. Lauwerys (eds.), *The Secondary School Curriculum* (Yonkers-on-Hudson: World Book Company, 1959), pp. 25–32.

5. Recent sources discussing the new Soviet school reforms include:
   A. Boiter, "Khrushchev School Reform," *Comparative Education Review*, February, 1959; N. DeWitt, "Khrushchev at the Helm, Upheaval in Education," *Problems of Communism*, January-February, 1959; G. Kline, "Russia's Lagging School System," *New Leader*, March 16, 1959; C. Arnold Anderson, "Educational Dilemmas in the USSR," *The School Review*, Spring, 1959; G. Z. F. Bereday and R. V. Rapacz, "Khrushchev's Proposals for Soviet Education," *Teachers College Record*, December, 1958; G. S. Counts, *Khrushchev and the Central Committee Speak on Education* (Pittsburgh: University of Pittsburgh Press, 1959).

6. Figures are taken from *Kulturnoe Stroitelstvo SSSR* (Moscow, 1956) and M. M. Deineko, *40 Let Narodnogo Obrazovaniia* (Moscow, 1957); a later source, *Kulturnoe Stroitelstvo SSSR* (Moscow, 1957), was advertised as published by *Sovietskie Knigi* but seems never to have reached this coun-

try and is now reported from Moscow to be out of print. See also *Public Education in the Soviet Union: Report for 1957–1958* (Geneva: Twenty-First International Conference on Education, 1958).

7. Deineko, *op. cit.*, p. 13.

8. Nicholas DeWitt, "Basic Comparative Data on Soviet and American Education," *Comparative Education Review*, June, 1958.

9. I. Z. Kaganovich, *Ocherk Razvitiia Statistiki Shkolnogo Obrazovaniia v SSSR* (Moscow, 1957), p. 88.

10. *Ibid.*

11. George Z. F. Bereday, "Recent Developments in the Soviet Schools," Part II, *Comparative Education Review*, October, 1957.

12. From personal conversation. See also *Soviet Commitment to Education, Report of the First Cultural Mission to the USSR* (Washington: Government Printing Office, 1959).

13. N. S. Khrushchev, "Memorandum," *Pravda*, September 21, 1958, p. 3.

14. *Zakon Ob Ukreplenii Sviazi s Zhyzniiu i o Dalneishem Razvitii Sistemy Narodnogo Obrazovaniia v SSSR* (Moscow, 1958), p. 13.

15. See "Class Tensions in Soviet Education," in George Z. F. Bereday and Jaan Pennar (eds.), *The Politics of Soviet Education* (New York: Frederick A. Praeger, 1960).

16. See G. Z. F. Bereday, "Education and Values Since 1917," in C. Black (ed.), *The Transformation of Russian Society since 1861* (Cambridge: Harvard University Press, 1960).

CHAPTER 2

This chapter was written by William W. Brickman.

1. William H. E. Johnson, "Recent American Interest in Soviet Education," *Teachers College Record*, May, 1958, p. 474.

2. B. P. Yesipov and N. K. Goncharov, *Pädagogik* (Berlin: Volk und Wissen Verlag, 1948), p. 459. The original was not available to the writer.

3. *Ibid.*, p. 462.

4. N. K. Gudzy, *History of Early Russian Literature* (New York: The Macmillan Company, 1949), p. 344.

5. Yesipov and Goncharov, *loc. cit.*

6. Gudzy, *op. cit.*, p. 347.

7. *Russia at the Close of the Sixteenth Century: Comprising the Treatise "Of the Russe Common Wealth," by Dr. Giles Fletcher* (London: Hakluyt Society, 1856), p. 63.

8. *Ibid.*, p. 112.

9. Raymond Beazley, Nevill Forbes, and G. A. Birkett, *Russia from the Varangians to the Bolsheviks* (Oxford: The Clarendon Press, 1918), p. 191.

10. V. O. Kluchevsky, *A History of Russia* (London: J. M. Dent & Sons, 1913), Vol. III, p. 279.

11. S. Konovalov, "Anglo-Russian Relations, 1620–4," in S. Konovalov (ed.), *Oxford Slavonic Papers* (Oxford: The Clarendon Press, 1953), Vol. IV, p. 104. Original letter in the Public Record Office, London.

12. *Ibid.*

13. *Ibid.*, p. 106. Original letter in the Public Record Office, London.

14. *Ibid.*, p. 81.

15. *Ibid.*, p. 110. Original memorandum in the Public Record Office, London.

16. S. Konovalov, "Twenty Royal Russian Letters (1626–34)," *ibid.*, Vol. III, pp. 119–121. The Russian texts of Michael's two letters to Charles are on pp. 133–134 and pp. 137–138.

17. John E. Sandys, *A History of Classical Scholarship* (New York: Hafner Publishing Company, 1958), Vol. III, p. 384.

18. William H. E. Johnson, *Russia's Educational Heritage* (Pittsburgh: Carnegie Press, 1950), pp. 11, 17–21. The Russian text of the rules is given in V. Z. Smirnov (ed.), *Khrestomatiia po istorii Pedagogiki* (Moscow: Uchpedgiz, 1957), pp. 133–137.

19. Kluchevsky, *op. cit.*, p. 330.

20. Michael T. Florinsky, *Russia: A History and Interpretation* (New York: The Macmillan Company, 1953), Vol. I, p. 299.

21. Kluchevsky, *op. cit.*, p. 291.

22. *Ibid.*, p. 283.

23. Florinsky, *loc. cit.*

24. Quoted in Stuart R. Tompkins, *The Russian Mind from Peter the Great through the Enlightenment* (Norman: University of Oklahoma Press, 1953), p. 31.

25. Quoted in Kluchevsky, *op. cit.*, p. 373.

26. Nicholas Hans, "The Moscow School of Mathematics and Navigation (1701)," *Slavonic and East European Review*, June, 1951, p. 532.

27. John Perry, "The State of Russia under the Present Tsar," in Peter Putnam (ed.), *Seven Britons in Imperial Russia (1698–1812)* (Princeton: Princeton University Press, 1952), pp. 33–36.

28. Daniel B. Leary, *Education and Autocracy in Russia from the Origins to the Bolsheviki* (Buffalo: University of Buffalo Press, 1919), p. 38.

29. For the educational provisions of these Instructions (*Nakaz*), see W. F. Reddaway (ed.), *Documents of Catherine the Great* (Cambridge: Harvard University Press, 1931), pp. 215–217, 219, 255, 271–273, 293–294.

30. For Diderot's plan, see Gabriel Compayré, *Histoire critique des doctrines de l'éducation en France depuis le seizième siècle* (Paris: Hachette, 1879), Vol. II, pp. 195–201, 206–219.

31. The 113 articles are given in the original Russian in Smirnov, *op. cit.*, pp. 144–159.

32. See Nicholas Hans, *History of Russian Educational Policy (1701–1917)* (London: P. S. King & Sons, 1931), pp. 26–30.

33. Florinsky, *op. cit.*, p. 601.

34. Leary, *op. cit.*, p. 44.

35. Florinsky, *op. cit.*, p. 602.

36. Hans, *History of Russian Educational Policy* (*1701–1917*), p. 33.

37. Beazley, Forbes, and Birkett, *op. cit.*, p. 351.

38. Tompkins, *op. cit.*, p. 82.

39. Leonard Froese, *Ideengeschichtliche Triebkräfte der russischen und sowjetischen Pädagogik* (Heidelberg: Quelle und Meyer, 1956), p. 24, note.

40. Hans, *History of Russian Educational Policy* (*1701–1917*), p. 45.

41. For an excellent historical survey of this Institute, see Johnson, *Russia's Educational Heritage*, pp. 109–133.

42. Marc Raeff, *Michael Speransky: Statesman of Imperial Russia, 1772–1839* (The Hague: Martinus Nijhoff, 1957), p. 61.

43. Tompkins, *op. cit.*, p. 88.

44. Raeff, *op. cit.*, p. 255.

45. Hans Kohn, *Basic History of Modern Russia* (Princeton: D. Van Nostrand Company, 1957), p. 12.

46. Quoted in Hans, *History of Russian Educational Policy* (*1701–1917*), p. 66.

47. *Ibid.*, p. 68.

48. Quoted in Florinsky, *op. cit.*, Vol. II, p. 797.

49. Quoted in Beazley, Forbes, and Birkett, *op. cit.*, p. 405.

50. Quoted in Froese, *op. cit.*, p. 28.

51. Beazley, Forbes, and Birkett, *loc. cit.*

52. Nicholas V. Riasanovsky, *Russia and the West in the Teaching of the Slavophiles* (Cambridge: Harvard University Press, 1952), pp. 30–31.

53. *Ibid.*, p. 145.

54. Leary, *op. cit.*, pp. 74–75.

55. Florinsky, *op. cit.*, Vol. II, p. 1033.

56. Beazley, Forbes, and Birkett, *op. cit.*, p. 446.

57. *Ibid.*, pp. 469, 471, 473; see also Florinsky, *op. cit.*, Vol. II, p. 1034.

58. Florinsky, *op. cit.*, Vol. II, p. 1036.

59. Hans, *History of Russian Educational Policy* (*1701–1917*), pp. 123–128.

60. *Ibid.*, p. 116.

61. Florinsky, *op. cit.*, Vol. II, pp. 1048–1049.

62. For a good survey of Russian educational thought of the eighteenth and nineteenth centuries, see Johnson, *Russia's Educational Heritage*, pp. 226–249.

63. I. T. Ogorodnikov and P. N. Schimbirjew, *Lehrbuch der Pädagogik* (Berlin: Volk und Wissen Verlag, 1950), pp. 41–42. The Russian copy was not available to the writer.

64. Yesipov and Goncharov, *op. cit.*, p. 493.

65. I. V. Chuvashev, "Velikii Russkii Pedagog K. D. Ushinskii," in M. F.

Shabaieva (ed.), *Istoriia Pedagogiki* (Moscow: Uchpedgiz, 1955), pp. 120-121. The translations are by the present writer.

66. George S. Counts, *The Challenge of Soviet Education* (New York: Mc-Graw-Hill Book Company, 1957), p. 20.

67. See V. A. Veikshan, "Lev Tolstoi kak pedagog," in L. N. Tolstoi, *Pedago-gicheskie Sochineniia*, 2nd ed. (Moscow: Uchpedgiz, 1953), pp. 21-22. Dr. Veikshan also edited the volume. The school building, as well as Tolstoi's home, his estate, and his grave were visited by the Comparative Education Society on August 29, 1958, under the guidance of Dr. Veikshan, who is the foremost Soviet authority on Tolstoi's educational ideas and work.

68. Hans Kohn (ed.), *The Mind of Modern Russia* (New Brunswick: Rutgers University Press, 1955), p. 27.

69. Hans, *History of Russian Educational Policy (1701–1917)*, p. 163.

70. *Ibid.*, p. 193.

71. Florinsky, *op. cit.*, Vol. II, p. 1233.

72. *Ibid.*, pp. 1234–1235.

73. Hans, *History of Russian Educational Policy (1701–1917)*, p. 221.

74. Florinsky, *op. cit.*, Vol. II, p. 1235. Florinsky cites these figures but does not mention their source. For a detailed breakdown of the census figures see C. Arnold Anderson, "A Footnote to the Social History of Modern Russia: The Literacy and Educational Census of 1897," *Genus*, December, 1956, pp. 1–18. According to Anderson, "only a third of a century after the emancipation of the serfs," there were clear signs that "more demo-cratic policies of education had reached a period of accelerating growth."

75. P. Ignatiev, "Education," in P. Malevsky-Malevitch (ed.), *Russia: U.S.S.R.* (New York: Payson, 1933), p. 663.

76. *Ibid.*, p. 662.

77. *Ibid.*, pp. 662–663.

78. Florinsky, *op. cit.*, Vol. II, p. 1256.

79. Hans, *History of Russian Educational Policy (1701–1917)*, p. 222.

CHAPTER 3

This chapter was written by William W. Brickman.

1. The document is in *Education and Art in Soviet Russia* (New York: Social-ist Publication Society, n.d.), pp. 9–10.

2. The document is in Theresa Bach, "Educational Changes in Russia," *Bulletin No. 37*, U.S. Bureau of Education (Washington: Government Printing Office, 1919), pp. 9–10.

3. *Decrees and Constitution of Soviet Russia* (New York: The Nation, n.d.), p. 7.

4. Ruth Widmayer, "The Evolution of Soviet Educational Policy," *Harvard Educational Review*, Summer, 1954, p. 159.

5. Scott Nearing, *Education in Soviet Russia* (New York: International Publishers, 1926), p. 8.

6. Quoted in Daniel B. Leary, *Education and Autocracy in Russia from the Origins to the Bolsheviki* (Buffalo: University of Buffalo Press, 1919), pp. 113–114.

7. *Ibid.*, p. 114.

8. *Loc. cit.*

9. *Loc. cit.*

10. *Education and Art in Soviet Russia*, p. 27.

11. Samuel N. Harper, "Documents on the Government of the Soviet Union," in William E. Rappard *et al.*, *Source Book on European Governments* (Princeton: D. Van Nostrand Company, 1937), pp. v20–v21.

12. William H. E. Johnson, *Russia's Educational Heritage* (Pittsburgh: Carnegie Press, 1950), pp. 250–251.

13. C. Arnold Anderson, "A Footnote to the Social History of Modern Russia: The Literacy and Educational Census of 1897," *Genus*, December, 1956, pp. 1–18.

14. Thomas Woody, *New Minds: New Men?* (New York: The Macmillan Company, 1932), pp. 47–48.

15. Lucy L. W. Wilson, *The New Schools of New Russia* (New York: Vanguard Press, 1928), p. 13.

16. Sergius Hessen and Nikolaus Hans, *Fünfzehn Jahre des Sowjetschulwesens* (Langensalza: Beltz, 1933), p. 190.

17. Luigi Volpicelli, *Storia della Scuola Sovietica* (Brescia: La Scuola, 1951), p. 29.

18. Nearing, *loc. cit.*; Hessen and Hans, *op. cit.*, p. 83; William W. Brickman, "John Dewey's Foreign Reputation as an Educator," *School and Society*, October 22, 1949, pp. 260, 264.

19. Nearing, *loc. cit.*

20. Hessen and Hans, *op. cit.*, p. 227.

21. Karl Marx, *Capital, The Communist Manifesto, and Other Writings* (New York: Modern Library, 1932), p. 343.

22. The German text of the resolution, which includes the term *polytechnische Erziehung*, is given in S. M. Shabalov, *Politekhnicheskoe obuchenie* (Moscow: Izdatelstvo Akademii Pedagogicheskikh Nauk RSFSR, 1956), pp. 47–48.

23. Quoted in D. Ryazanoff, "Explanatory Notes" to Karl Marx and Friedrich Engels, *The Communist Manifesto* (London: Martin Lawrence, 1930), pp. 190–191.

24. Karl Marx, *Capital* (New York: Modern Library, 1906), pp. 529–530.

25. Maurice J. Shore, *Soviet Education: Its Psychology and Philosophy* (New York: Philosophical Library, 1947), p. 145. The third point of the plan of Lenin calls for "the fulfillment of free and compulsory general and polytechnical . . . education" of children of both sexes up to the age of six-

teen. For the text, see V. I. Lenin, *O narodnom obrazovanii* (Moscow: Izdatelstvo Akademii Pedagogicheskikh Nauk RSFSR, 1957), pp. 290–291.

26. George S. Counts, *The Challenge of Soviet Education* (New York: Mc-Graw-Hill Book Company, 1957), p. 60.

27. N. K. Krupskaya, *Izbrannye pedagogicheskie proizvedeniia* (Moscow: Izdatelstvo Akademii Pedagogicheskikh Nauk RSFSR, 1955), pp. 40, 152.

28. *Ibid.*, pp. 205–206.

29. Quoted in Samuel N. Harper, *Civic Training in Soviet Russia* (Chicago: University of Chicago Press, 1929), p. 44.

30. *Ibid.*, p. 42.

31. *Ibid.*, pp. 65–66; Hessen and Hans, *op. cit.*, pp. 101–102.

32. Harper, *op. cit.*, p. 66.

33. Georg von Rauch, *Geschichte des bolschewistischen Russland* (Wiesbaden: Rheinische Verlags-Anstalt, 1955), p. 197. Georg von Rauch, *A History of Soviet Russia* (New York: Frederick A. Praeger, 1957), p. 144. The English translation omits part of the sentence.

34. M. M. Deineko, *40 Let Narodnogo Obrazovaniia v SSSR* (Moscow: Uchpedgiz, 1957), p. 213.

35. Quoted in Beatrice King, *Changing Man: The Education System of the U.S.S.R.* (New York: The Viking Press, 1937), p. 33.

36. Quoted in Albert P. Pinkevitch, *The New Education in the Soviet Republic* (New York: John Day Company, 1929), p. 375.

37. Lenin, *op. cit.*, p. 397. The translation is by the present writer.

38. Deineko, *op. cit.*, pp. 213–214. According to Counts, *op. cit.*, p. 181, the age range is eighteen to fifty, but another Soviet authority has it as eight to fifty. See E. N. Medinsky, *Prosveshchenie v SSSR* (Moscow: Uchpedgiz, 1955), p. 107. Counts cites A. M. Ivanova's book on the liquidation of illiteracy as his authority. The original text of the decree was not available to the present writer.

39. Deineko, *op. cit.*, p. 214.

40. Counts, *op. cit.*, p. 182.

41. Deineko, *op. cit.*, p. 216.

42. M. P. Kim, *40 Let Sovetskoi Kultury* (Moscow: Gosudarstvennoe Izdatelstvo Politicheskoi Literatury, 1957), p. 119.

43. Pinkevitch, *op. cit.*, p. 380.

44. Hessen and Hans, *op. cit.*, pp. 67–68; see also pp. 69–70.

45. George S. Counts, "Education in Soviet Russia," in Stuart Chase, Robert Dunn, and Rexford Guy Tugwell (eds.), *Soviet Russia in the Second Decade* (New York: John Day Company, 1928), p. 280.

46. M. I. Kalinin, *O vospitanii i obuchenii* (Moscow: Uchpedgiz, 1957), p. 11. The translation is by the present writer.

47. Hessen and Hans, *op. cit.*, p. 213.

48. Medinsky, *op. cit.*, p. 13.

49. Von Rauch, *op. cit.*, p. 194.

50. *Ibid.*, p. 195.

458 *Chapter 3 · Notes*

51. Volkskommissariat für Bildungswesen R.S.F.S.R., *Die Volksbildung in der russischen sozialistischen föderativen Sowjetrepublik*, 2nd ed. (Moscow: Staatsverlag, 1928), p. 10.

52. Eugène Dévaud, *La pédagogie scolaire en Russie soviétique* (Paris: Desclée de Brouwer, 1932), p. 190. For the entire syllabus, see pp. 189–191.

53. Samuel N. Harper, *Making Bolsheviks* (Chicago: University of Chicago Press, 1931), p. 37.

54. Harper, *Civic Training in Soviet Russia*, p. 207.

55. N. Klepinin, "Religion," in P. Malevsky-Malevitch (ed.), *Russia: U.S.S.R.* (New York: Payson, 1933), p. 637.

56. *Ibid.*, pp. 638–639.

57. Paul B. Anderson, *People, Church and State in Modern Russia* (New York: The Macmillan Company, 1944), pp. 114–116.

58. N. S. Timasheff, *Religion in Soviet Russia (1917–1942)* (New York: Sheed and Ward, 1942), pp. 95–111.

59. Nicholas S. Timasheff, *The Great Retreat: The Growth and Decline of Communism in Russia* (New York: E. P. Dutton and Company, 1946), pp. 228–240.

60. Ivan D. London and Nikolai P. Poltoratzky, "Contemporary Religious Sentiment in the Soviet Union," *Psychological Reports*, Monograph Supplement 3, 1957, p. 117.

61. *Ibid.*, p. 128.

62. Pinkevitch, *op. cit.*, p. 28.

63. Counts, "Education in Soviet Russia," in Chase *et al., op. cit.*, pp. 268–269.

64. Harper, *Civic Training in Soviet Russia*, p. 255.

65. Paul Blonsky, "Russia," in I. L. Kandel (ed.), *Educational Yearbook of the International Institute of Teachers College, Columbia University, 1927* (New York: Teachers College, Columbia University, 1928), p. 324.

66. Both quoted in Shore, *op. cit.*, p. 176.

67. Pinkevitch, *op. cit.*, p. 7.

68. Blonsky, in Kandel, *op. cit.*, p. 332.

69. R. A. Bauer, *The New Man in Soviet Psychology* (Cambridge: Harvard University Press, 1952), p. 65.

70. Counts, *The Challenge of Soviet Education*, p. 66.

71. An interesting reference to Shatsky and Blonsky is found in N. A. Konstaninow, *30 Jahre Sowjetpädagogik* (Berlin: Volk und Wissen Verlag, 1948), p. 3. Both are criticized by this writer, a member of the Academy of Pedagogical Sciences, as "powerfully influenced by the bourgeois pedagogy of Western Europe and America," as having no prerevolutionary consciousness of "the close connection between school reform and the radical social transformation of Russia and with the Socialist Revolution," and as "mostly dependent upon capitalistic ideologies." The original article appeared in *Sovetskaia Pedagogika*, No. 2, 1948.

72. Counts, *The Challenge of Soviet Education*, p. 61.

73. Bauer, *op. cit.*, pp. 52, 59–60.

74. G. Schoenchen, *The Activity School* (New York: Longmans, Green and Company, 1940), p. 88. See also p. 56.

75. Anna L. Strong, "Education in Modern Russia," *Progressive Education*, October–November–December, 1924, p. 158.

76. Jawaharlal Nehru, *Soviet Russia* (Bombay: Chetana, 1929), p. 85.

77. Counts, "Education in Soviet Russia," in Chase *et al.*, *op. cit.*, p. 302.

78. Carleton Washburne, "The Common Schools of the R.S.F.S.R.," in Chase *et al.*, *op. cit.*, p. 306.

79. *Ibid.*, p. 319.

80. *Ibid.*, p. 323.

81. Carleton Washburne, "The Good and Bad in Russian Education," *New Era*, January, 1928, p. 12.

82. John Dewey, *Impressions of Soviet Russia* (New York: New Republic, 1929), p. 54.

83. *Ibid.*, p. 76.

84. *Ibid.*, p. 86.

85. *Ibid.*, pp. 105–106.

86. *Ibid.*, p. 106.

87. *Ibid.*, pp. 106–107.

88. *Ibid.*, pp. 107–108.

89. *Ibid.*, pp. 128–129.

90. Pinkevitch, *op. cit.*, p. 163.

91. *Ibid.*, p. 177.

92. W. W. Brickman, *loc. cit.*

93. Quoted in Martin Levit, "Soviet Version of John Dewey and Pragmatism," *History of Education Journal*, Summer, 1953, p. 137. See also pp. 136–138.

94. "Diui (Dewey), Dzhon," *Bolshaia Sovetskaia Entsiklopediia*, 2nd ed., 1952, Vol. 15, p. 343.

95. *Ibid.*, p. 344. For a translation of the full article, see Levit, *op. cit.*, pp. 138–139.

96. Levit, *op. cit.*, pp. 139–140.

97. V. S. Shevkin, *Pedagogika D. Diui na sluzhbe sovremennoi amerikanskoi reaktsii* (Moscow: Uchpedgiz, 1952), p. 135. The translation is by the present writer. A large portion of this book has been translated into German: W. S. Schewkin, *Die Pädagogik J. Deweys* (Berlin: Volk und Wissen Verlag, 1955).

98. Shevkin, *op. cit.*, p. 142.

99. Corliss Lamont, *Soviet Civilization* (New York: Philosophical Library, 1952), p. 226.

100. Nicholas Hans and Sergius Hessen, *Educational Policy in Soviet Russia* (London: P. S. King & Sons, 1930), p. 203.

101. All quotations are from *Constitution (Fundamental Law) of the Union of Soviet Socialist Republics* (Moscow: Foreign Languages Publishing House, 1956), pp. 99–102.

102. See *History of the Communist Party of the Soviet Union (Bolsheviks): Short Course* (Moscow: Foreign Languages Publishing House, 1951), pp. 165–206. This entire paragraph is based on von Rauch, *op. cit.*, pp. 340–341.

103. The full text of the resolution is given in V. Z. Smirnov (ed.), *Khrestomatiia po istorii Pedagogiki* (Moscow: Uchpedgiz, 1957), pp. 449–457.

104. A. Pinkevitch, *Science and Education in the U.S.S.R.* (London: Victor Gollancz, 1935), p. 40.

105. For the full Russian text, see V. Z. Smirnov, *op. cit.*, pp. 457–464. The English translation is quoted in I. L. Kandel, "The Educational Merry-go-round in Soviet Russia," *Kadelpian Review*, May, 1935, pp. 328–330.

106. Quoted in Michael Demiashkevich, *An Introduction to the Philosophy of Education* (New York: American Book Company, 1935), p. 185.

107. The English text of this decree is given *ibid.*, pp. 186–188.

108. *Ibid.*, p. 188.

109. The English translations of the two decrees are reprinted in Kandel, *op. cit.*, pp. 332–333.

110. A. Gilenson, "The Teachers of the USSR Fifteen Years after the October Revolution," *Soviet Culture Review* (Moscow: Voks, 1932), Nos. 7–9, p. 41.

111. The original Russian text is given in Smirnov, *op. cit.*, pp. 464–468.

112. *Ibid.*, pp. 468–472.

113. Bauer, *op. cit.*, pp. 123–127.

114. Smirnov, *op. cit.*, p. 494. See also N. A. Konstantinov and V. Z. Smirnov, *Istoriia Pedagogiki* (Moscow: Uchpedgiz, 1955), pp. 215–222.

115. Pinkevitch, *Science and Education in the U.S.S.R.*, pp. 40–41.

116. Nina M. Sorochenko, "Pre-School Education in the USSR," in George L. Kline (ed.), *Soviet Education* (New York: Columbia University Press, 1957), p. 6.

117. *Ibid.*, p. 12.

118. Joseph Stalin, "The Political and Social Doctrine of Communism," *International Conciliation*, December, 1934, p. 424. See also p. 423.

119. Volpicelli, *op. cit.*, pp. 227–228.

120. Bauer, *op. cit.*, pp. 41–42.

121. Timasheff, *The Great Retreat*, pp. 321–322.

122. *Ibid.*, p. 196.

123. Bauer, *op. cit.*, p. 41.

124. Counts, *The Challenge of Soviet Education*, pp. 151–152.

125. A. V. Shestakov (ed.), *A Short History of the U.S.S.R.* (Moscow: Co-operative Publishing Society of Foreign Workers in the U.S.S.R., 1938), pp. 246–247.

126. A. M. Pankratova (ed.), *Istoriia SSSR*, 2nd ed. (Moscow: Uchpedgiz, 1941), Vol. III, pp. 13, 140, 277, 333.

127. E. F. Bushtueva, *English: Uchebnik angliiskogo iazyka, Third Year* (Moscow: Uchpedgiz, 1936), p. 36.

128. E. F. Bushtueva, *English: Uchebnik angliiskogo iazyka, Fourth Year* (Moscow: Uchpedgiz, 1937), p. 29.

129. André Gide, *Retour de l'U.S.S.R.* (n.p.: Gallimard, 1950), pp. 46–47.

130. See Conway Zirkle (ed.), *Death of a Science in Russia* (Philadelphia: University of Pennsylvania Press, 1949). This book contains a full documentary history of the controversy over genetics.

131. On the activities and influences of Zhdanov, see von Rauch, *op. cit.*, pp. 532–541.

132. On the glorification of Stalin, see B. P. Yesipov and N. K. Goncharov, *"I Want To Be Like Stalin,"* translated by George S. Counts and Nucia P. Lodge (New York: John Day Company, 1947). This is a portion of the 1946 edition of the authors' *Pedagogika.* See also G. M. Alexandrov *et. al., Joseph Stalin: A Short Biography* (Moscow: Foreign Languages Publishing House, 1950), especially pp. 200–207. The Stalinization of culture is treated competently in George S. Counts and Nucia P. Lodge, *The Country of the Blind: The Soviet System of Mind Control* (Boston: Houghton Mifflin Company, 1949); and more recently in the comprehensive survey edited by Walter Z. Laqueur and George Lichtheim, *The Soviet Cultural Scene: 1956–1957* (New York: Frederick A. Praeger, 1958). On cultural developments from the Soviet standpoint, see *Decisions of the Central Committee, C.P.S.U. (B) on Literature and Art (1946–1948)* (Moscow: Foreign Languages Publishing House, 1951), and A. F. Ioffe *et al.,* "Twenty-Five Years of Soviet Culture," *Science and Society,* Summer, 1943, pp. 193–250.

133. N. S. Khrushchev, *Forty Years of the Great October Revolution* (Moscow: Foreign Languages Publishing House, 1957), p. 33.

134. *Ibid.,* p. 30.

135. N. S. Khrushchev, "Targets of the Seven-Year Plan for Soviet Economy: 1959–1965," *Soviet Booklet No. 43* (London: Soviet Booklets, 1958), pp. 7–8.

136. For a recent survey of the various aspects of Soviet culture, see Laqueur and Lichtheim, *op. cit.*

CHAPTER 4

This chapter was written by William W. Brickman.

1. E. N. Medinsky, "Soviet Education in Wartime," in G. B. Jeffery, chairman, *The Year Book of Education: 1948* (London: Evans, 1948), pp. 435–437.

2. Nikolay Ivanov, "The Training of Soviet Engineers," in George L. Kline (ed.), *Soviet Education* (New York: Columbia University Press, 1957), p. 170.

3. *Ibid.*, p. 438.

4. Quoted in George S. Counts, *The Challenge of Soviet Education* (New York: McGraw-Hill Book Company, 1957), p. 262.

5. Medinsky, *op. cit.*, p. 439.

6. Quoted in Counts, *op. cit.*, p. 80.

7. Medinsky, *op. cit.*, p. 438.

8. The original text of the "Rules for Pupils" was published in *Sovetskaia Pedagogika*, October, 1943, p. 2, and in several later sources. It is reproduced in Chapter 7, Note 14.

9. Medinsky, "The U.S.S.R.," in Jeffery, *op. cit.*, pp. 412–413; Counts, *op. cit.*, pp. 72–73.

10. Medinsky, "The U.S.S.R.," p. 401.

11. *Ibid.*, p. 405.

12. Counts, *op. cit.*, pp. 280–282.

13. E. N. Medinsky, *Public Education in the U.S.S.R.* (Moscow: Foreign Languages Publishing House, 1950), p. 6.

14. A. M. Pankratova (ed.), *A History of the U.S.S.R.* (Moscow: Foreign Languages Publishing House, 1948), Part II, p. 293.

15. *Ibid.*, Part III, p. 422.

16. I. I. Godlinnik and M. D. Kuznets, *English: Uchebnik angliiskogo iazyka dlia 6-go klassa semiletnei i srednei shkoli* (Moscow: Uchpedgiz, 1951), p. 57.

17. *Ibid.*, p. 59.

18. "Asiatic Republics of the Soviet Union," in G. B. Jeffery, chairman, *The Year Book of Education: 1949* (London: Evans, 1949), pp. 380–411.

19. William O. Douglas, *Russian Journey* (Garden City, N.Y.: Doubleday & Company, 1956), p. 222; see also pp. 219–221.

20. Central Statistical Board of the U.S.S.R. Council of Ministers, *Cultural Progress in the U.S.S.R.: Statistical Returns* (Moscow: Foreign Languages Publishing House, 1958), pp. 12–13; and *Forty Years of Soviet Power in Facts and Figures* (Moscow: Foreign Languages Publishing House, 1958), p. 249.

21. Central Statistical Board of the U.S.S.R. Council of Ministers, *Cultural Progress in the U.S.S.R.: Statistical Returns*, pp. 78–79.

22. Central Statistical Board of the U.S.S.R. Council of Ministers, *Forty Years of Soviet Power in Facts and Figures*, p. 249.

23. Eighteenth International Conference on Education, *Public Education in the Soviet Union: Report for 1954–1955* (Geneva: International Bureau of Education, 1955), p. 23.

24. See for example, I. A. Nelidova and L. R. Todd, *English: Uchebnik angliiskogo iazyka dlia 8-go klassa srednei shkoly* (Moscow: Uchpedgiz, 1955), pp. 11–12; I. V. Belova and L. R. Todd, *English: Uchebnik angliiskogo iazyka dlia 8-go klassa srednei shkoly* (Moscow: Uchpedgiz, 1956), pp. 7–9.

25. I. Lazarévitch and N. Lazarévitch, *L'école soviétique (enseignements primaires et secondaires)* (Paris: Les Îles d'Or, 1954), *passim;* and Ivan D.

London, "Evaluation of Some Current Literature about Soviet Education," in William W. Brickman (ed.), "Teaching about Soviet Education," *School and Society,* November 8, 1958, Special Supplement, pp. 9–15.

26. L. V. Dubrovina, "Union of Soviet Socialist Republics: Educational Progress in 1955–1956," *International Yearbook of Education: Vol. XVIII, 1956* (Geneva: International Bureau of Education, 1956), p. 377.

27. *Ibid.,* p. 380.

28. I. Iliouchine, "Byelorussia: Educational Progress in 1955–1956," and P. Mirgorodsky, "Ukraine: Educational Progress in 1955–1956," *International Yearbook of Education: Vol. XVIII, 1956* (Geneva: International Bureau of Education, 1956), pp. 91–98, 359–365.

29. N. S. Khrushchev, *Report of the Central Committee of the Communist Party of the Soviet Union to the 20th Party Congress* (Moscow: Foreign Languages Publishing House, 1956), pp. 95–99.

30. *Resolutions of the 20th Congress of the Communist Party of the Soviet Union* (Moscow: Foreign Languages Publishing House, 1956), pp. 19–20, 81–82.

31. Khrushchev, *op. cit.,* p. 138.

32. L. Labedz, "History between the Thaw and the Freeze," in W. L. Laqueur and G. Lichtheim (eds.), *The Soviet Cultural Scene: 1956–1957* (New York: Frederick A. Praeger, 1958), p. 144.

33. Counts, *op. cit.,* pp. 103, 205.

34. S. V. Utechin, "Current Problems of Soviet Secondary Education," *Soviet Survey,* February, 1957, p. 15. This article is reprinted as "Educational Problems," in Laqueur and Lichtheim, *op. cit.* See especially pp. 232–233.

35. *Ibid.,* p. 16.

36. A. M. Pankratova (ed.), *Istoriia SSR: Uchebnik dlia 10-go klassa srednei shkoly* (Moscow: Uchpedgiz, 1957).

37. Labedz, *op. cit.,* p. 145.

38. N. S. Khrushchev, *Forty Years of the Great October Socialist Revolution* (Moscow: Foreign Languages Publishing House, 1957), p. 33.

39. Utechin, *op. cit.,* p. 15.

40. Twenty-First International Conference on Education, *Public Education in the Soviet Union: Report for 1957–1958* (Geneva: International Bureau of Education, 1958), pp. 20–22.

41. Central Statistical Board of the U.S.S.R. Council of Ministers, *Cultural Progress in the U.S.S.R.: Statistical Returns,* pp. 210–211.

42. Central Statistical Board of the U.S.S.R. Council of Ministers, *Forty Years of Soviet Power in Facts and Figures,* p. 254.

43. *Public Education in the Soviet Union: Report for 1957–1958,* p. 23.

44. Nikita S. Khrushchev, "Educating Active and Conscious Builders of a Communist Society," *School and Society,* February 14, 1959, p. 66 (translated by Ina Schlesinger).

45. *Ibid.,* p. 67.

46. Vyacheslav Yelyutin, "Adapting Higher Schools to Contemporary Demands," *School and Society,* February 14, 1959, p. 68 (translated by Ina Schlesinger).

47. N. S. Khrushchev, "Strengthening the Ties of the School with Life, and Further Developing the System of Public Education," *Soviet Booklet No. 42* (London: Soviet News, 1958), pp. 3–4, 6–7, 11, 12. A partial translation is given as "School and Life," in *School and Society,* February 14, 1959, pp. 72–74 (translated by Ivan D. London).

48. N. S. Khrushchev, "Targets of the Seven-Year Plan for Soviet Economy: 1959–1965," *Soviet Booklet No. 43* (London: Soviet News, 1958), pp. 7–8.

49. *Ibid.,* pp. 68–69.

50. Albert Boiter, "The Khrushchev School Reform," *Comparative Education Review,* February, 1959, p. 8.

51. Central Committee of the Communist Party of the Soviet Union and the U.S.S.R. Council of Ministers, "Strengthening the Ties of School with Life, and Further Developing the System of Public Education," *Soviet Booklet No. 44* (London: Soviet News, 1958), p. 4. See also the penetrating commentary by Boiter, *op. cit.,* especially pp. 13–14.

52. Central Committee of the Communist Party, *op. cit.,* pp. 8–9.

53. *Ibid.,* p. 20.

54. *Ibid.,* p. 21.

55. *Ibid.,* pp. 22–23.

56. Max Frankel, "Party Confirms Khrushchev Role," *New York Times,* February 3, 1959.

57. L. Dubrovina, *Women's Right to Education in the Soviet Union* (Moscow: Foreign Languages Publishing House, 1956), p. 13.

58. For a clear and explicit exposition of this arrangement, see George Z. F. Bereday, "Changes in Soviet Educational Administration," *School and Society,* January 18, 1958, pp. 37–39.

59. *Public Education in the Soviet Union: Report for 1957–1958,* p. 20.

60. See, for example, Tsentralnoe Statisticheskoe Upravlenie, R.S.F.S.R., *Kulturnoe Stroitelstvo RSFSR: Statisticheskii Sbornik* (Moscow: Gosudarstvennoe Statisticheskoe Izdatelstvo, 1957), pp. 182–183.

61. *Public Education in the Soviet Union: Report for 1957–1958,* p. 21.

62. Nicholas DeWitt, *Soviet Professional Manpower: Its Education, Training, and Supply* (Washington: National Science Foundation, 1955), p. 197.

63. *Ibid.,* p. 198.

64. Division of International Education, U.S. Department of Health, Education, and Welfare, "Education in the USSR," *Bulletin No. 14* (Washington: Government Printing Office, 1957), p. 192.

CHAPTER 5

This chapter was written by Herbert C. Rudman. Notes were contributed by W. Benjamin, C. Bergeson, E. Dyer, M. Edman, L. Fox, G. Z. Gass, C. T. Goodwill, F. Horler, L. Lindberg, A. Lowe, S. Marquez, G. McConnell, D. Pages,

L. Pettit, C. Potter, G. H. Read, J. Roth, S. St. John, I. Schlesinger, C. Sorensen, A. Stegall, B. D. Stuart, K. Vickery, C. S. Williams, and F. Wirth.

1. Nicholas DeWitt, *Soviet Professional Manpower* (Washington: National Science Foundation, 1955), p. 23.

2. Division of International Education, U.S. Department of Health, Education, and Welfare, "Education in the USSR," *Bulletin No. 14* (Washington: Government Printing Office, 1957), p. 10.

3. George Z. F. Bereday, "Changes in Soviet Educational Administration," *School and Society,* January 18, 1958, pp. 37–39.

4. This table is adapted from *ibid.,* p. 37. The changes announced in June, 1959, transfer some of the functions of the Union Ministry of Higher Education to the republic level.

5. *Ibid.,* p. 38.

6. For a more detailed description of the work of the ministries of education see M. M. Deineko, *Forty Years of Public Education in the USSR* (Moscow: Foreign Languages Publishing House, 1957), pp. 14–21.

7. Bereday, *op. cit.,* p. 38.

8. The following description of the district and city boards of education is taken from an interview with Dimitri Petrokeevich, Chairman of the Educational Committee, Leningrad City Soviet of Workers' Deputies, September 6, 1958.

9. This fictional lecture is paraphrased from A. N. Volkovskii and M. P. Malyshev, *Shkolovedenie,* 1st ed. (Moskva: Akademiia Pedagogicheskikh Nauk RSFSR, 1952), p. 115. The remainder of the chapter relies heavily upon this source.

10. The basis for this fictionalized lecture was an interview with I. Grivkov, head of the Central Committee of the Trade Union of Educational, Cultural and Research Workers of the U.S.S.R., on August 27, 1958, in the Moscow offices of the Union.

11. The lecturer is referring to recent reforms in the educational system of the U.S.S.R. For a more detailed description of these, see Herbert C. Rudman, "De-emphasis of Academics in the USSR," *Elementary School Journal,* February, 1959, and "New Trends in Soviet Education," *Yearbook for 1958, American People's Encyclopedia.*

12. This fictionalized account is based upon interviews with Director Asimova, School No. 171, Leningrad, and Director Filatov, School No. 717, Moscow; and upon Volkovskii and Malyshev, *op. cit.,* pp. 107–115.

13. Volkovskii and Malyshev, *op. cit., passim;* and M. M. Deineko, *Spravochnik Directora Shkoly* (Moskva: Gosudarstvennoe Uchebno-Pedagogicheskoe Izdatelstvo Ministerstva Prosveshcheniia RSFSR, 1954), *passim.*

14. Volkovskii and Malyshev, *op. cit.,* 2nd ed., 1955, p. 114.

15. *Ibid.,* p. 114.

16. *Ibid.*

17. *Ibid.,* p. 116.

18. *Ibid.*, 1st ed., p. 111, points out that, among other concerns of the director who conducts a conference with a teacher, "It is important that the director remember . . . not to turn to trifles nor to lose his dignity [when conducting a conference]."

19. *Ibid.*, p. 114. Insertions in brackets are those of the translator.

20. See Chapter 17.

21. Deineko, *Forty Years of Public Education in the USSR*, p. 17.

22. Volkovskii and Malyshev, *op. cit.*, 1st ed., p. 114.

CHAPTER 6

This chapter was written by Ina Schlesinger, with the assistance of notes contributed by W. Barnett, C. Bergeson, R. Dunbar, E. Dyer, M. Edman, L. Fox, F. Horler, L. Lindberg, A. Lowe, G. McConnell, S. Marquez, D. Pages, C. Potter, A. Romney, J. Roth, A. Stegall, B. D. Stuart, and K. Vickery.

1. This and similar statements that appear throughout the book are from notes taken by members of the Comparative Education Society during interviews with the educators quoted.

2. M. M. Deineko, *40 Let Narodnogo Obrazovaniia* (Moscow: Uchpedgiz, 1957), p. 66.

3. A. M. Danev, *Narodnoe Obrazovanie, Osnovnye Postanovleniia, Prikazy i Instruktsii* (Moscow: Uchpedgiz, 1948), p. 272.

4. J. F. Cramer and G. S. Browne, *Contemporary Education* (New York: Harcourt, Brace & Company, 1956), p. 383.

5. See, for example, the discussion on teaching arithmetic in N. Talyzina, "Pervye Arifmeticheskie Poniatiia i Deistviia," *Sem'ia i Shkola*, March, 1959, pp. 16–17.

6. See Chapter 12.

7. Ministry of Education of the R.S.F.S.R., *Guide for Educators in Kindergartens* (Moscow: Uchpedgiz, 1954), p. 3.

8. *Ibid.*

9. The following readings represent a cross section of literature on preschool education available in the West:

   V. Fadiaevsky and P. S. Hill, *Nursery School and Parent Education in Soviet Russia* (New York: E. P. Dutton & Company, 1936). B. King, *Russia Goes to School* (London: Heinemann, 1948), Chap. IV. D. L. Meek, *Soviet Youth* (London: Routledge and Kegan Paul, 1948), Chap. I. M. M. Sorochenko, "Pre-school Education in the U.S.S.R.," in G. Kline (ed.), *Soviet Education* (New York: Columbia University Press, 1957), pp. 1–24. A. P. Usova, "L'educazione prescolastica nell' U.R.S.S.," in

L. Volpicelli (ed.), *La Scuola e la Pedagogia Sovietica; I Problemi della Pedagogia*, July–October, 1956.
See also one of the numerous discussions on how to improve rural preschool education, such as P. S. Golubkin, "Uluchshit' Rabotu Detskikh Sadov v Selskikh Natsionalnykh Raionakh," *Doshkolnoe Vospitanie*, March, 1959, pp. 71–72.

CHAPTER 7

This chapter was written by Ina Schlesinger, with the help of notes supplied by W. Barnett, W. Benjamin, C. Bergeson, R. Dunbar, E. Dyer, M. Edman, L. Fox, G. Z. Gass, G. T. Goodwill, F. Horler, M. Kelly, V. Kelly, L. Lindberg, A. Lowe, G. McConnell, S. Marquez, D. Pages, D. Partridge, C. Potter, G. Read, G. Roeper, A. Romney, J. Roth, C. Sorensen, A. Stegall, B. D. Stuart, K. Vickery, and C. S. Williams.

1. V. I. Lenin, "Sochineniia," as quoted in M. M. Deineko, *40 Let Narodnogo Obrazovaniia* (Moscow: Uchpedgiz, 1957), p. 79.

2. M. J. Shore, *Soviet Education: Its Psychology and Philosophy* (New York: Philosophical Library, 1947), pp. 128–130.

3. *Sobranie Uzakonenii*, 1918, Art. 812.

4. *Programma i Ustav RKP (b)* (Moscow: Gosizdat, 1919).

5. N. I. Boldyrev, *Direktivy VKP (b) i Postanovleniia Sovetskogo Pravitelstva o Narodnom Obrazovanii* (Moscow: Akademiia Pedagogicheskikh Nauk, 1947), Vol. 1, p. 128.

6. The most important recent instance is an article by the Minister of Education of the R.S.F.S.R., E. Afanasenko, "Nekotorye Zadachi Vseobshchego Obiazatelnogo Obucheniia Detei," *Narodnoe Obrazovanie*, January, 1959, p. 14.

7. Division of International Education, U.S. Department of Health, Education and Welfare, "Education in the USSR," *Bulletin No. 14* (Washington: Government Printing Office, 1954), p. 62.

8. Before 1944 the compulsory school age was eight.

9. For an English-language discussion of arithmetic instruction in Soviet primary schools, see John De Francis, "Beginnings of Mathematical Education in Russia," *The Arithmetic Teacher*, February, 1959, pp. 6–11, and 16.

10. This section was written by William W. Brickman and is based on notes of A. Lowe and H. S. Pryor.

11. S. P. Alekseev and V. G. Kartsov (eds.), *Istoriia SSSR* (Moscow: Uchpedgiz, 1957).

12. For a discussion on how to teach "labor" in the primary school, see I. G. Rozanov, "Nekotorye Voprosy Metodiki Urokov Ruchnogo Truda," *Nachal'naia Shkola*, 1958, No. 10.

13. "Uroki po Teme Sovietskaia Armiia," *Nachal'naia Shkola*, 1959, No. 2.

14. The original text of "Rules for Pupils" can be found in *Sovetskaia Pedagogika*, October, 1943, p. 2. The following is the text in English:

It is the duty of every school child:

1. To acquire knowledge persistently in order to become an educated and cultured citizen and to be of the greatest possible service to his country.

2. To study diligently, to be punctual in attendance, and not arrive late at classes.

3. To obey the instructions of the school director and the teachers without question.

4. To arrive at school with all the necessary textbooks and writing materials; to have everything ready for the lesson before the teacher arrives.

5. To come to school clean, well groomed, and neatly dressed.

6. To keep his place in the classroom clean and tidy.

7. To enter the classroom and take his place immediately after the bell rings; to enter and leave the classroom during the lesson only with the teacher's permission.

8. To sit upright during the lesson, not leaning on his elbows and not slouching; to listen attentively to the teacher's explanation and the other pupils' answers, and not to talk or let his attention stray to other things.

9. To rise when the teacher or the director enters or leaves the room.

10. To stand at attention when answering the teacher; to sit down only with the teacher's permission; to raise his hand if he wishes to answer or ask a question.

11. To take accurate notes in his assignment book of homework scheduled for the next lesson, and to show these notes to his parents, to do all the homework unaided.

12. To be respectful to the school director and teachers; when meeting them, to greet them with a polite bow; boys should also raise their hats.

13. To be polite to his elders, to behave modestly and respectfully in school, on the street, and in public places.

14. Not to use coarse expressions, not to smoke, not to gamble for money or for any other objects.

15. To protect school property; to be careful of his personal things and the belongings of his comrades.

16. To be attentive and considerate of old people, small children, and the weak and sick; to give them a seat on the trolley or make way for them on the street, being helpful to them in every way.

17. To obey his parents, to help them to take care of his small brothers and sisters.

18. To maintain cleanliness and order in rooms; to keep his clothes, shoes, and bed neat and tidy.

19. To carry his student's record book with him always, to guard it

carefully, never handing it over to anyone else, and to present it upon request of the teacher or the school director.

20. To cherish the honor of his school and class and defend it as his own.

15. For a discussion of these problems see G. Savonin, "Nachalnaia Shkola v Novoi Systeme Narodnogo Obrazovaniia," *Narodnoe Obrazovanie*, 1958, No. 12; and M. A. Zhidkoblinov, N. G. Viazmina, and A. E. Iagupova, "O Nachalnigkh Klassakh Shkol"; and N. I. Liakhov, "O Perestroike Pervogo Zvena Shkol," *Nachalnaia Shkola*, 1958, No. 12.

16. "Novyi Istoricheskii Etap v Zhizni Shkoly," *Nachalnaia Shkola*, 1959, No. 1. This article mentions a new curriculum for the primary grades, where the hours devoted to "labor" are doubled and the three special subjects in the fourth grade are abolished.

17. For a description of the house see L. Mosvina, "Dom Shkolnika," *Nachalnaia Shkola*, 1959, No. 2.

CHAPTER 8

This chapter was written by Ina Schlesinger, and includes manuscripts by William W. Brickman and Seymour St. John. Notes were contributed by A. Beeman, W. Benjamin, C. Bergeson, R. Dunbar, E. Dyer, U. Fleege, L. Fox, G. Z. Gass, F. Heisler, F. Horler, V. Kelley, L. Lindberg, A. Lowe, G. McConnell, S. Marquez, D. Pages, D. Partridge, C. Potter, H. Pryor, G. Read, A. Romney, J. Roth, C. Sorensen, A. Stegall, B. Stewart, B. D. Stuart, K. Vickery, C. S. Williams, and F. Wirth.

1. A. G. Korol, *Soviet Education for Science and Technology* (New York: John Wiley & Sons, 1957), p. 22.

2. *Ibid.*, p. 23.

3. M. M. Deineko, *40 Let Narodnogo Obrazovniia* (Moscow: Uchpedgiz, 1957), pp. 134–135.

4. *Ibid.*, p. 136.

5. *Programmy srednei shkoly na 1957–58 uchebnyi god: Istoriia drevnego mira, istoriia srednikh vekov* (Moscow: Uchpedgiz, 1957).

6. *Programmy srednei shkoly: Biologiia* (Moscow: Uchpedgiz, 1958).

7. *Programmy srednei shkoly na 1958–59 uchebnyi god: Fizika, Astronomiia* (Moscow: Uchpedgiz, 1958).

8. *Programmy srednei shkoly: Khimiia* (Moscow: Uchpedgiz, 1958).

9. *Programmy srednei shkoly na 1958–59 uchebnyi god: Inostrannye Iazyki, Angliiskii, Nemetskii, Frantsuskii* (Moscow: Uchpedgiz, 1958).

10. *Programmy srednei shkoly na 1958–59 uchebnyi god: Prakticheskie zaniatiia v uchebnykh masterskikh i na shkolnom uchebno-opytnom uchastke v V–VII klassakh* (Moscow: Uchpedgiz, 1958).

11. *Programmy srednei shkoly: Risovanie* (Moscow: Uchpedgiz, 1958).

12. *Programmy srednei shkoly: Penie, I–X klassy* (Moscow: Uchpedgiz, 1958).

13. *Programmy srednei shkoly: Fizicheskaia Kultura, I–X klassy* (Moscow: Uchpedgiz, 1958).

14. *Programmy srednei shkoly: Literatura, VIII–X klassy* (Moscow: Uchpedgiz, 1958).

15. *Programmy srednei shkoly: Matematika* (Moscow: Uchpedgiz, 1958).

16. *Programmy srednei shkoly: Biologiia*, p. 54. (Translated by W. W. Brickman.)

17. *Programmy srednei shkoly: Fizika, Astronomiia, loc. cit.*

18. *Programmy srednei shkoly: Khimiia, loc. cit.*

19. *Programmy srednei shkoly: Psikhologiia* (Moscow: Uchpedgiz, 1958), p. 6. (Translated by I. Schlesinger.)

20. *Programmy srednei shkoly na 1958–59 uchebnyi god: Istoriia SSSR, Novaia Istoriia* (Moscow: Uchpedgiz, 1958). (Translated by W. W. Brickman.)

21. *Ibid.*

22. *Ibid.*

23. *Programmy srednei shkoly: Geografiia.* See I. I. Mamaiev, *Ekonomicheskaia geografiia zarubezhnykh stran: Uchebnik dlia 8 klassa srednei shkoly* (Moscow: Uchpedgiz, 1958); I. I. Mamaiev, *Economic Geography of Foreign Countries: Textbook for the 8th Form of the Secondary School* (Leningrad: Uchpedgiz, 1957).

24. *Programmy srednei shkoly. . . : Inostrannye Iazyki. . . , loc. cit.*

25. I. V. Rakhmanov, *Metodika obucheniia nemetskomu iazyku* (Moscow: Izdatelstvo Akademiia Pedagogicheskikh Nauk RSFSR, 1956).

26. See, for example, E. V. Belova and L. R. Todd, *English: Uchebnik angliiskogo iazyka dlia 7-go klassa srednei shkoly* (Moscow: Uchpedgiz, 1955); and E. V. Belova and L. R. Todd, *English: Uchebnik angliiskogo iazyka dlia 9-go klassa srednei shkoly* (Moscow: Uchpedgiz, 1956).

27. *Programmy srednei shkoly: Penie.*

28. *Programmy srednei shkoly na 1958–59 uchebnyi god: Osnovy proizvodstva i proizvodstvennaia praktika v VII–X klassakh* (Moscow: Uchpedgiz, 1958).

29. *Programmy srednei shkoly: Fizicheskaia Kultura.*

30. Division of International Education, U.S. Department of Health, Education and Welfare, "Education in the USSR," *Bulletin No. 14* (Washington: Government Printing Office, 1957), pp. 79–81. See also N. DeWitt, *Soviet Professional Manpower: Its Education, Training, and Supply* (Washington: National Science Foundation, 1955), pp. 57–58.

31. See Chapter 7, Note 14.

CHAPTER 9

This chapter was written by William W. Brickman, with the assistance of notes contributed by J. Altena, A. Beeman, W. Benjamin, C. Bergeson, R. Dunbar, E. Dyer, M. Edman, G. Z. Gass, G. Goodwill, F. Horler, V. Kelley, F. Kring, L. Lindberg, R. Linskie, G. McConnell, S. Marquez, W. Nelson, D. Pages, C. Potter, G. Read, A. Romney, J. Roth, S. St. John, I. Schlesinger, C. Sorensen, A. Stegall, B. Stewart, K. Vickery, C. S. Williams, and F. Wirth.

1. For the teaching of science in Soviet schools, see Nicholas DeWitt, *Soviet Professional Manpower: Its Education, Training, and Supply* (Washington: National Science Foundation, 1955); and A. G. Korol, *Soviet Education for Science and Technology* (New York: John Wiley & Sons, 1958).
2. See William W. Brickman, "Truth about Russia's Schools," *New York Mirror*, April 14, 1958, and April 16, 1958.

CHAPTER 10

This chapter was written by Gerald H. Read, with the assistance of Richard V. Rapacz. Notes were contributed by J. Altena, A. Beeman, W. Benjamin, C. Bergeson, R. Dunbar, E. Dyer, M. Edman, L. Fox, G. Z. Gass, F. Horler, V. Kelley, L. Lindberg, A. Lowe, G. McConnell, S. Marquez, D. Pages, C. Potter, J. Roth, S. St. John, I. Schlesinger, C. Sorensen, A. Stegall, B. Stewart, B. D. Stuart, K. Vickery, C. S. Williams, and F. Wirth. In addition, Byron D. Stuart contributed advice in personal conferences.

1. M. Saburov, *Report of the Directives of the Nineteenth Party Congress relating to the Fifth Five-Year Plan for the Development of the USSR in 1951–1955* (Moscow: Foreign Languages Publishing House, 1952), p. 53.
2. N. S. Khrushchev, *Report of the Central Committee of the Communist Party of the Soviet Union to the Twentieth Party Congress* (Moscow: Foreign Languages Publishing House, 1956), p. 56.
3. Karl Marx, *Capital* (Moscow: Foreign Languages Publishing House, 1954), Book I, p. 482.
4. Nadezhda Krupskaya, *On Education* (Moscow: Foreign Languages Publishing House, 1957).
5. I. A. Kairov, "Nazrevshie Voprosy Narodnogo Obrazovaniia," *Pravda*, September 6, 1958, pp. 3–4.
6. N. S. Khrushchev, "Memorandum," *Pravda*, September 21, 1958, pp. 1–2.

7. *Ibid.*

8. *Ibid.*

9. *Ibid.*

10. Institute of the Theory and History of Pedagogy, Academy of Pedagogical Sciences of the R.S.F.S.R., *Pedagogy and Popular Education in Foreign Countries* (Moscow: Printing Office of the Academy of Pedagogical Sciences, 1957).

11. The data in the preceding paragraph were supplied by N. I. Kova, Assistant Chairman of the Department of Education, Kiev.

12. N. S. Khrushchev, *op. cit.*

13. *Ibid.*

14. For another analysis of polytechnization, see R. V. Rapacz, in George Z. F. Bereday and Jaan Pennar (eds.), *The Politics of Soviet Education* (New York: Frederick A. Praeger, 1960).

CHAPTER 11

This chapter was written by Ina Schlesinger, with the assistance of H. Gass. Notes were contributed by C. Bergeson, W. W. Brickman, E. Dyer, M. Edman, G. Z. Gass, G. Goodwill, F. Horler, V. Kelley, L. Lindberg, G. McConnell, L. Pettit, C. Potter, G. Read, J. Roth, S. St. John, C. Sorensen, A. Stegall, B. Stewart, J. Tarbell, K. Vickery, C. S. Williams, and F. Wirth.

1. Quoted in M. M. Deineko, *40 Let Narodnogo Obrazovaniia v SSSR* (Moscow: Uchpedgiz, 1957), p. 257.

2. *Pravda*, June 27, 1959.

3. For a general description of the University of Moscow, see Burton Rubin, "Moscow University — the Summit of Soviet Education," in G. Z. F. Bereday and Jaan Pennar (eds.), *The Politics of Soviet Education* (New York: Frederick A. Praeger, 1960), p. 218.

4. For further information on this topic, see V. A. Veikshan, "The Moscow Center in Comparative Education," *Comparative Education Review*, June, 1959, p. 3.

5. For further information on the training of doctors, see Mark G. Field, *Doctor and Patient in Soviet Russia* (Cambridge: Harvard University Press, 1957).

6. For a description of the Academy of Sciences, see also U.S. Office of Education, *Soviet Commitment to Education, Report of the First Official U.S. Education Mission to the USSR* (Washington: Government Printing Office, 1959).

7. Current Soviet thought on higher education can best be followed in

Vestnik Vysshei Shkoly, the journal of the Ministry of Higher Education of the U.S.S.R.

8. For a discussion of the new rules of admission, see "Novye Pravila dlia Postupaiushchikh v Zaochnye i Vechernie Vuzy," *Pravda,* April 5, 1959; and "Gotovitsia k Priemu v Vuzy," *Pravda,* April 8, 1959.

9. See Chapter 14.

10. For further discussion of higher education, see V. Yelyutin, *Higher Education in the U.S.S.R.* (New York: International Arts and Science Press, 1959); and E. H. Litchfield *et al., Report on Higher Education in the Soviet Union* (Pittsburgh: University of Pittsburgh Press, 1958).

CHAPTER 12

This chapter was written by Ina Schlesinger, with the assistance of notes contributed by J. Altena, A. Beeman, W. Benjamin, C. Bergeson, R. Dunbar, E. Dyer, M. Edman, U. Fleege, L. Fox, G. Z. Gass, G. Goodwill, F. Horler, M. Kelly, L. Lindberg, A. Lowe, G. McConnell, S. Marquez, D. Pages, D. Partridge, C. Potter, H. Pryor, G. Read, J. Roth, S. St. John, C. Sorensen, A. Stegall, B. Stewart, K. Vickery, C. S. Williams, and F. Wirth.

1. See Chapter 15.

2. All pedagogical institute programs are published in *Uchebnye Plany Pedagogicheskikh Institutov* (Moscow: Uchpedgiz, 1957) and are discussed in U.S. Office of Education, Division of International Education, *Soviet Commitment to Education, Report of the First Official U.S. Education Mission to the USSR* (Washington: Government Printing Office, 1959), and in N. Dodge, "Recent Changes in the Training of Soviet Secondary School Teachers," in G. Z. F. Bereday and J. Pennar (eds.), *The Politics of Soviet Education* (New York: Frederick A. Praeger, 1960), pp. 144–165. Further changes in these programs were contemplated in 1959.

3. N. I. Kova, Assistant Chairman of the Kiev Department of Education, gave the following monthly salary scale for primary-school teachers:

teachers without seniority	575 rubles
teachers with 5 to 9 years' seniority	635 rubles
teachers with 10 years' seniority	690 rubles
teachers with 25 years' seniority	759 rubles

Salaries for secondary-school teachers are as follows:

teachers of grades five through seven without seniority	690 rubles
teachers of grades five through seven with 5 to 9 years' seniority	735 rubles
teachers of grades five through seven with 10 years' seniority	795 rubles
teachers of grades five through seven with 25 years' seniority	895 rubles
teachers of grades eight through ten without seniority	710 rubles
teachers of grades eight through ten with 5 to 9 years' seniority	765 rubles

teachers of grades eight through ten with 10 years' seniority   850 rubles
teachers of grades eight through ten with 25 years' seniority   935 rubles

4. *Utchitelskaia Gazeta* is also an excellent source for tracing the dissatisfactions of teachers, now being expressed with considerable freedom. For a more detailed discussion of this newspaper, see Chapter 13.

5. Pioneer leaders in the schools are considered teachers and take an active interest in the profession. The director of a Kiev school reported that his two senior Pioneer leaders were members of the faculty council and attended its meetings.

CHAPTER 13

This chapter was written by William W. Brickman, with the assistance of notes contributed by C. Bergeson, F. Horler, A. Lean, and G. Read.

1. *Constitution (Fundamental Law) of the Union of Soviet Socialist Republics* (Moscow: Foreign Languages Publishing House, 1956), p. 103.

2. Thomas Fitzsimmons (ed.), *RSFSR: Russian Soviet Federated Socialist Republic* (New Haven: Human Relations Area Files, 1957), Vol. II, p. 338.

3. *Ibid.*, pp. 338–339.

4. John N. Hazard, *The Soviet System of Government* (Chicago: University of Chicago Press, 1957), p. 60.

5. Fitzsimmons, *op. cit.*, p. 339.

6. Twenty-First International Conference on Education, *Public Education in the Soviet Union: Report for 1957–1958* (Geneva: International Bureau of Education, 1958), p. 30.

7. I. I. Grivkov, "USSR: Professional Organizations," in Robert K. Hall, N. Hans, and J. A. Lauwerys (eds.), *The Year Book of Education: 1953* (Yonkers-on-Hudson: World Book Company, 1953), p. 413.

8. *Ibid.*, p. 414.

9. *Ibid.*

10. *Ibid.*

11. The preceding paragraphs are based on *ibid.*, pp. 413–415.

12. *Soviet Weekly,* February 5, 1959.

13. The preceding paragraphs are based on Grivkov, *op. cit.*, pp. 416–417.

14. For a discussion of several other educational publications, see Chapter 14.

15. Twenty-First International Conference on Education, *loc. cit.*

CHAPTER 14

This chapter was written by William W. Brickman, with the assistance of notes contributed by A. Beeman, E. Beeman, C. Bergeson, E. Dyer, L. Fox, A. Lowe, D. Partridge, C. Potter, J. Roth, and K. Vickery.

1. M. M. Deineko, *40 Let Narodnogo Obrazovaniia v SSSR* (Moscow: Uchpedgiz, 1957), p. 62.

2. E. N. Medinsky, *Narodnoe Obrazovanie v SSSR* (Moscow: Uchpedgiz, 1947), p. 225.

3. E. N. Medinsky, *Prosveshchenie v SSSR* (Moscow: Uchpedgiz, 1955), p. 201.

4. "Akademiia Pedagogicheskikh Nauk RSFSR (APN)," *Bolshaia Sovetskaia Entsiklopediia*, 2nd ed., Vol. I, p. 582.

5. I. A. Kairov *et al.* (eds.), *Narodnoe Obrazovanie v SSSR* (Moscow: Izdatelstvo Akademii Pedagogicheskikh Nauk RSFSR, 1957), pp. 461–462.

6. Institute for the Study of the USSR, *Biographical Directory of the USSR* (New York: Scarecrow Press, 1958), pp. 239–240.

7. George S. Counts and Nucia P. Lodge, *"I Want To Be Like Stalin"* (New York: John Day Company, 1947).

8. Institute for the Study of the USSR, *op. cit.*, p. 614.

9. Ivan D. London, "A Historical Survey of Psychology in the Soviet Union," *Psychological Bulletin*, July, 1949, pp. 250–251, 274–275.

10. Institute for the Study of the USSR, *op. cit.*, pp. 384–385.

11. *Ibid.*, p. 395.

12. Deineko, *loc. cit.*

13. For a brief description of the functions of the Academy of Pedagogical Sciences, see E. I. Monoszon, "Educational Information Services in the USSR," *Education Abstracts*, January, 1958, pp. 3–10; and *Das Erziehungswesen der Sowjet-Union* (Berlin: Material- und Nachrichten-Dienst ["Mund"] der Arbeitsgemeinschaft Deutscher Lehrerverbände, 1956), p. 56.

14. M. A. Melnikov, *Plan Nauchno-Issledovatelskikh Rabot Akademii Pedagogicheskikh Nauk RSFSR na 1958 God* (Moscow: Izdatelstvo Akademii Pedagogicheskikh Nauk RSFSR, 1958), pp. 28–29.

15. *Ibid.*, pp. 43–44, 49–51.

16. *Ibid.*, pp. 75–78.

17. *Ibid.*, pp. 103–104.

18. *Ibid.*, pp. 106, 111–112.

19. *Ibid.*, pp. 119, 123.

20. *Ibid.*, pp. 132, 137–138.

21. Monoszon, *op. cit.*, pp. 5–7.

22. *Ibid.*, p. 4.

23. "Akademiia Pedagogicheskikh Nauk RSFSR (APN)," *loc. cit.*

24. I. A. Kairov, *Akademiia Pedagogicheskikh Nauk RSFSR* (Moscow: Izdatelstvo Akademii Pedagogicheskikh Nauk RSFSR, 1957), p. 21. This is a reprint of a chapter of the same title in Kairov *et al.*, *op. cit.*, pp. 461–486. In this volume the author of the chapter is not identified.

25. Boston: Houghton Mifflin Company, 1955.

26. M. S. Bernshtein, "Noveishie Otkroveniia Amerikanskikh Filosofov Pedagogiki," *Sovetskaia Pedagogika*, August, 1957, pp. 134–144. See especially p. 143.

27. V. A. Veikshan, "Zarubezhnye Pedagogi i Obshchestvennye Deiateli o Shkole i Prosveshchenii v SSSR," *Sovetskaia Pedagogika*, November, 1957, pp. 139–149.

28. V. A. Veikshan, "V Krivom Zerkale," *Sovetskaia Pedagogika*, August, 1958, pp. 141–149.

29. "Khronika Nauchnykh Sobytii za Period 1947–1957 gg," *Voprosy Psikhologii*, May–June, 1958, pp. 151–160.

30. Kairov, *loc. cit.*

31. Monoszon, *op. cit.*, p. 9. No copy of this periodical was available to the writer.

32. "Akademiia Pedagogicheskikh Nauk RSFSR (APN)," p. 583.

33. Melnikov, *op. cit.*, p. 155.

34. Kairov, *op. cit.*, p. 27.

35. *Ibid.*

36. Melnikov, *op. cit.*, p. 156.

37. "Akademiia Pedagogicheskikh Nauk RSFSR (APN)," *loc. cit.*

CHAPTER 15

This chapter was prepared by Ina Schlesinger from manuscripts contributed by R. Clark, G. Z. Gass, F. Hunt, E. Klinkhart, F. Kring, and K. Vickery. Advice and notes were contributed by J. Tenny.

1. A. R. Luria, "Selection of Children for Special Schools," *New World Review*, June, 1958, p. 29.

2. See A. A. Strauss and L. E. Lehtiven, *Psychopathology and Education of Brain-Injured Children* (New York: Grune & Stratton, 1947).

3. For further discussion of this school, see L. G. Jones, "Education of the Deaf behind the Iron Curtain," *Volta Review*, Vol. 60, No. 65, 1958, p. 203.

4. Hearing aids developed in Leningrad are reportedly superior to those developed in other cities.

5. This was unique inasmuch as in this case deaf and partially hearing children were admitted to regular schools, an experiment reminiscent of integrated programs in the United States.

6. The Institute of Defectology of the Academy of Pedagogical Sciences uses zonds to help in speech correction. A zond is a wire apparatus that forces the tongue into a certain position for the production of a certain sound. A diagram of a zond, this one for the production of "sh," appears below:

Dr. Kraevsky, from Kiev, was unenthusiastic about zonds, however, and preferred to use his index finger. This is a good example of differences in practice.

CHAPTER 16

This chapter was written by George A. Roeper, with the assistance of notes contributed by U. Fleege, F. Horler, L. Lindberg, A. Lowe, G. McConnell, C. Potter, S. St. John, I. Schlesinger, C. Sorensen, and A. Stegall.

1. A. G. Korol, *Soviet Education for Science and Technology* (New York: John Wiley & Sons, 1958), p. 20.

2. See E. H. Litchfield *et al.*, *Report on Higher Education in the Soviet Union* (Pittsburgh: University of Pittsburgh Press, 1958).

3. Contributed by George Z. F. Bereday. See also U.S. Office of Education, *Soviet Commitment to Education, Report of the First Official U.S. Education Mission to the USSR* (Washington: Government Printing Office, 1959), pp. 66–67.

4. From N. S. Khrushchev's memorandum to the Presidium of the Communist Party, as released by the Embassy of the U.S.S.R. in Washington, D.C., on October 1, 1958.

5. "Zagliagubaia v Zavtrashnii Den," *Pravda*, October 17, 1958. Passages quoted are a paraphrase, not a direct translation.

CHAPTER 17

This chapter was written by Ina Schlesinger, with the assistance of notes contributed by A. Beeman, C. Bergeson, E. Dyer, U. Fleege, G. Z. Gass, G. Goodwill, G. McConnell, D. Partridge, C. Potter, G. Roeper, J. Roth, C. Sorensen, A. Stegall, B. Stewart, B. D. Stuart, K. Vickery, and C. S. Williams.

1. A. G. Kovalev and V. M. Miasishchev, "Psikhicheskie Osobennosti Cheloveka," *Kharakter* (Leningrad: University of Leningrad, 1957), Vol. I, p. 165.

2. L. I. Krasnogorskaia, *Rol Semii v Vospitanii Doshkolnika* (Moscow: Uchpedgiz, 1955), p. 9.

3. *Programma Lektora dlia Roditelei* (Moscow: Akademii Pedagogicheskikh Nauk, 1955).

4. For a discussion of this problem, see M. Dneprovskii, "Fabrika i Shkola," *Sem'ia i Shkola*, No. 8, 1953.

5. *Kulturnoe Straitelstvo SSSR*, 1957, p. 188.

6. See M. M. Deineko, *40 Let Narodnogo Obrazovania v SSSR* (Moscow: Uchpedgiz, 1957), p. 179.

7. For a discussion of the work of the Octobrists, see L. A. Vysotina, "Podgotovka Detei k Rabote v Pionerskoi Organizatsii," *Sovetskaia Pedagogika*, October, 1958.

8. *Bolshaia Sovetskaia Entsiklopediia*, 1955.

9. For a description of how such an election is handled, see *Sovet Druzhiny-Organizator Pionerskoi Raboti v Shkole* (Moscow: Akademiia Pedagogicheskikh Nauk, 1956), pp. 6ff.

10. The following is a free translation of some of the prescribed rituals in the Pioneer organization.

    The Solemn Promise of the Young Pioneer:
    I, a Young Pioneer of the Soviet Union, in the presence of my comrades solemnly promise to love my Soviet Motherland passionately, to live, learn, and struggle as the great Lenin bade us, as the Communist Party teaches us.

    The Pioneer Slogan:
    In the struggle for the cause of the Communist Party, be ready!

    Rules for the Pioneers:
    A Pioneer loves his Motherland and the Communist Party of the Soviet Union.
    A Pioneer prepares himself to enter the V.L.K.S.M.
    A Pioneer honors the memory of those who gave their lives in the struggle for freedom and for the prosperity of the Soviet Motherland.
    A Pioneer is friendly with the children of all the countries in the world.
    A Pioneer learns well.
    A Pioneer is polite and well-disciplined.
    A Pioneer loves labor and is careful of public property.
    A Pioneer is a good comrade; he cares for the young and helps the old.
    A Pioneer is brave and unafraid of difficulties.
    A Pioneer is honorable and values the honor of his detachment.
    A Pioneer hardens himself, goes to physical culture every day, and loves nature.

    The first of the three steps newly introduced:
    Know why we celebrate the great holidays: February 23, March 8, April 22, May 1–2, May 9, November 7–8, December 5.
    Learn the hymn of the U.S.S.R. and of your republic.
    Know the meaning of the Red Banner, the Pioneer scarf and pin, and the salute of the Young Pioneers.

Know the great deeds of the Pioneer organization and its heroes.

Know the heroes after whom your brigade, detachment, school, and street are named and the local heroes.

Know the song of the Young Pioneers.

Make a thing necessary for school work, together with your link.

With your link, make a thing necessary to the Pioneer room in your school.

Help your elders with the housework: set the table, wash the dishes, make something for your home.

Plant trees or flowers and care for them.

Care for useful birds, make birdfeeders and birdhouses.

Learn to distinguish poison mushrooms and berries from edible ones.

Learn to take care of your person: sew on buttons, darn your socks, make your own bed, wash yourself and your underwear.

Do your morning physical exercises.

Learn how to run quickly, throw a ball accurately, jump, ski, swim, and balance on a plank.

Learn how to form a line-up, distinguish the Pioneer signals on the horn and the drum, count off.

Learn three to five games of various kinds — table games, games of movement, and so forth.

Go on at least two one-day marches, know how to pack a rucksack, how to orient yourself by a compass, how to make a fire and cook on it, and so forth.

Learn two or three Pioneer songs and mass dances with your comrades.

11. *Pionerskaia Organizatsia Imeni V. I. Lenina,* a handbook for pedagogical schools (Moscow: Akademiia Pedagogicheskikh Nauk, 1950), p. 89.

12. *Uchitelskaia Gazeta,* July 31, 1958, published the full text of the "steps." The same reform also permits detachments to be formed outside the school, in apartment houses, and so forth. They must be part of the school brigade and a child can belong to only one detachment; parents are to help the new detachments.

13. For a discussion of this problem, see V. Yakovlev, "Stupeni Iunnogo Pionera," *Molodoi Kommunist,* September, 1958.

14. For a full list of rights and duties of a Komsomol member, see "Resoliutsii i Dokumenty XII syezda VLKSM," *Molodaia Gvardiia,* 1954.

15. N. S. Khrushchev, "Speech to the Thirteenth Komsomol Congress," *Molodaia Gvardiia,* April 13, 1958.

16. See I. Trifonov, *Studenti* (Moscow: Moskoskii Rabochii, 1956). This is also available in English translation from Foreign Languages Publishing House.

CHAPTER 18

This chapter was written by Gerald H. Read, with the assistance of notes contributed by J. Altena, C. Bergeson, R. Dunbar, E. Dyer, M. Edman, U. Fleege, L. Fox, G. Z. Gass, G. Goodwill, F. Horler,

L. Lindberg, A. Lowe, G. McConnell, C. Potter, J. Roth, S. St. John, I. Schlesinger, A. Stegall, K. Vickery, C. S. Williams, and F. Wirth.

1. V. I. Lenin, Address to the Third Congress of the Young Communist League, October 2, 1920.

2. F. Engels, *Anti-Dühring* (Moscow: Izdatelstvo Akademii Pedagogicheskikh Nauk RSFSR, 1957).

3. N. S. Khrushchev, "Ob Ukreplennii Sviazi Shkoly s Zhizniu i o Dalneishem Razvitii Sistemy Narodnogo Obrazovaniia v Strane," *Pravda*, September 21, 1958.

4. *Ibid.*

5. See Chapter 7, Note 14.

6. B. P. Yesipov and N. K. Goncharov, *Pedagogika* (Moscow: Uchpedgiz, 1950), p. 274.

7. Khrushchev, *op. cit.*

8. M. I. Kalinin, *On Communist Education, Selected Speeches and Articles* (Moscow: Foreign Languages Publishing House, 1953), p. 80.

9. Khrushchev, *op. cit.*

**SELECTED
BIBLIOGRAPHY**

Communism in Comparative Perspective

Barbu, Zavedei. *Democracy and Dictatorship*. New York: Grove Press, 1956. 275 pp.

Bereday, G. Z. F. "A Comparative Look at English, French and Soviet Education," *Current History*, vol. 35, no. 205, September, 1958.

Chauncey, H. "Some Comparative Checkpoints between American and Soviet Secondary Schools," *Comparative Education Review*, vol. 2, no. 3, February, 1959.

Conant, J. B. *The Citadel of Learning*. New Haven: Yale University Press, 1956. 79 pp.

Ebenstein, W. *Today's Isms*. Englewood Cliffs, N.J.: Prentice-Hall, Inc., 1954. 191 pp.

Ebon, M. *World Communism Today*. New York: Whittlesey House, 1948. 536 pp.

Eells, W. Crosby. *Communism in Education in Asia, Africa, and the Far Pacific*. Washington: American Council on Education, 1954. 246 pp.

Hans, N. *Comparative Education*. London: Routledge and Kegan Paul, 1951. 333 pp.

Kandel, I. L. *The New Era in Education*. Boston: Houghton Mifflin Company, 1955. 388 pp.

King, E. J. *Other Schools and Ours*. New York: Rinehart and Company, 1958. 234 pp.

The Soviet Union: Education

Alt, H. and E. *Russia's Children*. New York: Bookman Associates, 1959. 240 pp.

Anderson, C. Arnold. "Educational Dilemmas in the USSR," *The School Review*, vol. 67, no. 1, Spring, 1959.

Benton, W. *This Is the Challenge*. New York: Associated College Presses, 1958. 254 pp.

481

Bereday, G. Z. F. "American and Soviet Scientific Potential," *Social Problems,* vol. 4, no. 3, January, 1957.

Bereday, G. Z. F. "Changes in Soviet Educational Administration," *School and Society,* vol. 86, no. 2124, January 18, 1958.

Bereday, G. Z. F. "Recent Developments in the Soviet Schools, I, II," *Comparative Education Review,* vol. 1, nos. 1 and 2, June and October, 1957 (and bibliography therein).

Bereday, G. Z. F., and Pennar, Jaan (eds.). *The Politics of Soviet Education.* New York: Frederick A. Praeger, 1960. 218 pp.

Bereday, G. Z. F., and Rapacz, R. V. "Khrushchev's Proposals for Soviet Education," *Teachers College Record,* vol. 60, no. 3, December, 1958.

Black, C. E. (ed.). *The Transformation of Russian Society.* Cambridge: Harvard University Press, 1960.

Boiter, Albert. "Khrushchev's School Reforms," *Comparative Education Review,* vol. 2, no. 3, February, 1959.

Brickman, W. W. "The Training of Soviet School Teachers," *America,* vol. 49, no. 7, May 17, 1958.

Counts, G. S. *The Challenge of Soviet Education.* New York: McGraw-Hill Book Company, 1957. 330 pp.

Counts, G. S. *Khrushchev and the Central Committee Speak on Education.* Pittsburgh: The University of Pittsburgh Press, 1959. 80 pp.

Counts, G. S., and Lodge, N. *Country of the Blind.* Boston: Houghton Mifflin Company, 1949. 378 pp.

Counts, G. S., and Lodge, N. (trans.). *"I Want To Be Like Stalin."* New York: John Day Company, 1947. 150 pp.

Deineko, M. M. *Forty Years of Public Education in the USSR.* Moscow: Foreign Languages Publishing House, 1957.

DeWitt, N. "Basic Comparative Data on Soviet and American Education," *Comparative Education Review,* vol. 2, no. 1, June, 1958.

DeWitt, N. *Soviet Professional Manpower.* Washington: National Science Foundation, 1955. 400 pp.

DeWitt, N. "Soviet Science Education and Its Challenge," *Mathematics Teacher,* vol. 51, no. 2, February, 1958.

Dobinson, C. H. "English and Russian Education Contrasted," *Educational Forum,* vol. 22, no. 4, May, 1958.

Esipov, B. "The Problems of Curricula in Secondary Schools in the USSR," in G. Z. F. Bereday and J. A. Lauwerys (eds.), *The Secondary School Curriculum; The Year Book of Education, 1958.* New York: World Book Company, 1958.

Feldmesser, R. A. "Social Status and Access to Higher Education: A Comparison of the United States and the Soviet Union," *Harvard Educational Review,* vol. 87, no. 3, Spring, 1957.

Fisher, George. "Soviet and American Education; Mistaken Envy," *The Progressive,* vol. 22, no. 3, March, 1958.

Fisher, R. T. *The Pattern for Soviet Youth.* New York: Columbia University Press, 1959. 452 pp.

Froese, Leonhard. "Soviet Education from a German Perspective," *Educational Forum,* vol. 23, no. 2, January, 1959.

Grant, D. (ed.). "The Humanities in Soviet Higher Education," *University of Toronto Quarterly,* vol. 28, no. 1, October, 1958.

Havighurst, R. J. "Is Russia Really Outproducing Us in Scientists?," *School and Society,* vol. 86, no. 2131, April 26, 1958.

Havighurst, R. J. "Russian and American Education — Like and Unlike," *Educational Record,* vol. 40, no. 3, July, 1959.

Hechinger, F. M. *The Big Red Schoolhouse.* New York: Doubleday and Company, 1959. 240 pp.

Herzer, A. *Bolschewismus und Menschen-Bildung.* Hamburg: Gesellschaft der Freunde des vaterländischen Schul- und Erziehungswesens, 1951. 251 pp.

Hulicka, K. "Political Education in Soviet Schools," *Soviet Studies,* vol. 5, no. 2, October, 1953.

Johnson, W. H. E. *Russia's Educational Heritage.* Pittsburgh: Carnegie Press, 1950. 351 pp.

Johnson, W. H. E. "Teacher Education in the USSR and Eastern Europe," *Journal of Teacher Education,* vol. 7, no. 4, December, 1956.

Kalinin, M. I. *On Communist Education.* Moscow: Foreign Languages Publishing House, 1949. 479 pp.

King, B. *Russia Goes to School.* London: New Education Book Club, 1948. 185 pp.

Kline, G. L. "Education toward Literacy," *Current History,* vol. 35, no. 203, July, 1958.

Kline, G. L. "Russia Five Years after Stalin: Education," *The New Leader,* vol. 41, no. 24, June 16, 1958.

Kline, G. L. "Russia's Lagging School System," *The New Leader,* vol. 42, no. 11, March 16, 1959.

Kline, G. L. (ed.). *Soviet Education.* New York: Columbia University Press, 1957. 192 pp.

Korol, A. C. *Soviet Education for Science and Technology.* New York: John Wiley & Sons, 1957. 513 pp.

Korol, A. G. "Contrasts in Education: The Soviet Union versus the United States," in P. M. Halverson, *Frontiers of Secondary Education.* New York: Syracuse University Press, 1958.

Krupskaya, N. K. *N. K. Krupskaya on Education.* Moscow: Foreign Languages Publishing House, 1957. 193 pp.

Lazarévitch, I. and N. *L'École Soviétique.* Paris: Îles d'Or, 1954. 208 pp.

Leonhard, W. *Child of the Revolution.* Chicago: Henry Regnery Company, 1958. 447 pp.

Levine, D. *Soviet Education Today.* New York: John de Graff, Inc., 1959. 170 pp.

Levine, Irving R. "Trouble in Soviet Schools," *The New Leader,* vol. 42, no. 23, June 8, 1959.

Lilge, F. *Anton Semyonovitch Makarenko: An Analysis of His Educational Ideas in the Context of Soviet Society.* Berkeley: University of California Press, 1958. 52 pp.

Lilge, F. "Impressions of Soviet Education," *International Review of Education,* vol. 5, no. 1, 1959.

Litchfield, E. H. *Report on Higher Education in the Soviet Union.* Pittsburgh: University of Pittsburgh Press, 1958.

McAndrew, Andrew. "Are Soviet Schools Better Than Ours?," *Reporter,* vol. 18, no. 4, February 20, 1958.

Makarenko, A. S. *A Book for Parents.* Moscow: Foreign Languages Publishing House, 1954. 411 pp.

Makarenko, A. S. *Learning to Live.* Moscow: Foreign Languages Publishing House, 1951. 3 vols.

Makarenko, A. S. *The Road to Life.* Moscow: Foreign Languages Publishing House, 1953. 650 pp.

Medlin, W. K. "Soviet Pedagogical Academy and the New School Plans," *Comparative Education Review,* vol. 2, no. 2, October, 1958.

Meek, D. L. (ed.). *Soviet Youth.* London: Routledge and Kegan Paul, 1957. 251 pp.

Ploss, S. I. "Political Education in the Post-War Komsomol," *The American Slavic and East European Review,* vol. 15, no. 4, December, 1956.

Read, Gerald H. "The Big Reform in Soviet Education," *Phi Delta Kappan,* vol. 40, no. 5, February, 1959.

Roucek, J. S. "Juvenile Delinquency and Crime in the Soviet Bloc," *Comparative Education Review,* vol. 3, no. 3, February, 1960.

Shore, M. J. *Soviet Education.* New York: Philosophical Library, 1947. 346 pp.

Smirnov, A. A. "Les Réussites Scolaires et les Problèmes de la Psychologie," *International Review of Education,* vol. 3, no. 3, 1957.

Soviet Education. New York: International Arts and Sciences Press. (Translations of Soviet magazines.)

Timoshenko, S. P. *Engineering Education in Russia.* New York: McGraw-Hill Book Company, 1959.

U.S. Office of Education. "Education in the USSR," *Bulletin No. 14.* Washington: Government Printing Office, 1957. 226 pp.

U.S. Office of Education. *Soviet Commitment to Education.* Washington: Government Printing Office, 1959. 135 pp.

Vigdorova, F. *Diary of a School Teacher.* Moscow: Foreign Languages Publishing House, 1954.

Volpicelli, L. *L'Évolution de la Pédagogie Soviétique.* Neuchâtel: Delachaux et Niestle, 1954. 235 pp.

Volpicelli, L., (ed.). "La Scuola e la Pedagogia Sovietica," *I Problemi della Pedagogia*, vol. 2, no. 45, July–October, 1956.

Vucivich, A. *The Soviet Academy of Sciences.* Stanford, California: Stanford University Press, 1956. 157 pp.

Widmayer, R. "The Evolution of Soviet Educational Policy," *Harvard Educational Review*, vol. 24, no. 3, Summer, 1954.

Wiloch, J. T. "New Models in Soviet Education," *Comparative Education Review*, vol. 3, no. 2, October, 1959.

Yelyutin, V. *Higher Education in the USSR.* New York: International Arts and Sciences Press. 55 pp.

Soviet Union: General

Bauer, R. A., Inkeles, A., and Kluckhohn, C. *How the Soviet System Works.* Cambridge: Harvard University Press, 1956. 274 pp.

Bauer, R. A. *The New Man in Soviet Psychology.* Cambridge: Harvard University Press, 1952. 229 pp.

Bauer, R. A. *Nine Soviet Portraits.* New York: John Wiley & Sons, 1955. 190 pp.

Belfrage, S. *A Room in Moscow.* New York: Reynal and Company, 1959. 190 pp.

Brzezinski, Z. *The Permanent Purge.* Cambridge: Harvard University Press, 1956. 256 pp.

Cartier-Bresson, H. *People of Moscow* (photographs). New York: Simon and Schuster, 1955. 163 pp.

Current Digest of the Soviet Press. Washington: Joint Committee on Slavic Studies,

Dallin, D. J. *The Changing World of Soviet Russia.* New Haven: Yale University Press, 1956. 422 pp.

Djilas, M. *The New Class.* New York: Frederick A. Praeger, 1957. 214 pp.

Fainsod, M. *How Russia Is Ruled.* Cambridge: Harvard University Press, 1953. 575 pp.

Feldmesser, R. "The Persistence of Status Advantage in Soviet Russia," *American Journal of Sociology*, vol. 59, no. 1, July, 1953.

Goodfriend, A. *If You Were Born in Russia* (photographs). New York: Farrar, Straus, and Cudahy, 1950. 192 pp.

Hazard, J. N. *The Soviet System of Government.* Chicago: University of Chicago Press, 1957. 256 pp.

Inkeles, A. *Public Opinion in Soviet Russia.* Cambridge: Harvard University Press, 1950. 379 pp.

Inkeles, A. "Social Stratification and Mobility in the Soviet Union," *American Sociological Review,* vol. 15, no. 4, August, 1950.

Koestler, A., *et al. The God That Failed.* New York: Harper & Brothers, 1950. 273 pp.

Laqueur, W. Z., and Lichtheim, G. *The Soviet Cultural Scene 1956–1957.* New York: Frederick A. Praeger, 1958.

Maynard, Sir John. *Russia in Flux.* New York: The Macmillan Company, 1951. 546 pp.

Miller, Murray Lincoln (project co-ordinator). *Living in the Soviet Union Today* (film-strip series). Chicago: Society for Visual Education, Inc., 1959.

Moore, B. A. *Soviet Politics: The Dilemma of Power.* Cambridge: Harvard University Press, 1950. 503 pp.

Moore, B. A. *Terror and Progress: USSR.* Cambridge: Harvard University Press, 1954. 261 pp.

Moorehead, A. *The Russian Revolution.* New York: Harper & Brothers, 1958. 301 pp.

Roberts, H. L. *Russia and America, Dangers and Prospects.* New York: Harper & Brothers, 1956. 251 pp.

Rostow, W. W. *The Dynamics of Soviet Society.* New York: W. W. Norton and Company, 1953. 282 pp.

Schwarz, S. M. *The Jews in the Soviet Union.* Syracuse: Syracuse University Press, 1951. 380 pp.

Schwarz, S. M. *Labor in Soviet Russia.* New York: Frederick A. Praeger, 1952. 364 pp.

Seton-Watson, H. "The Soviet Ruling Class," *Problems of Communism,* vol. 5, no. 3, May–June, 1956.

Simmons, E. J. (ed.). *Continuity and Change in Russian and Soviet Thought.* Cambridge: Harvard University Press, 1955. 563 pp.

Simmons, E. J. (ed.). *Through the Glass of Soviet Literature.* New York: Columbia University Press, 1953.

Spinka, M. *The Church in Soviet Russia.* New York: Oxford University Press, 1956. 179 pp.

Wetter, G. A. *Dialectical Materialism.* New York: Frederick A. Praeger, 1958. 609 pp.

Wolfe, Bertram D. *Khrushchev and Stalin's Ghost.* New York: Frederick A. Praeger, 1957. 322 pp.

Wolfe, Bertram D. *Six Keys to the Soviet System*. Boston: Beacon Press, 1956. 258 pp.

SOVIET UNION: NOVELS

Dudintsev, Vladimir. *Not by Bread Alone*. New York: E. P. Dutton and Company, 1957. 512 pp.

Gusenko, Igor. *The Fall of the Titan*. New York: W. W. Norton and Company, 1954. 629 pp.

Koestler, Arthur. *Darkness at Noon*. New York: Modern Library, 1941. 267 pp.

Orwell, George. *Animal Farm*. New York: Harcourt, Brace and Company, 1946. 118 pp.

Orwell, George. *1984*. New York: Harcourt, Brace and Company, 1949. 314 pp.

Pasternak, Boris. *Doctor Zhivago*. New York: Pantheon Books, 1958. 558 pp.

Trifonov, Yuri. *Students*. Moscow: Foreign Languages Publishing House, 1953. 498 pp.

OTHER COUNTRIES

Alexander, R. J. *Communism in Latin America*. New Brunswick: Rutgers University Press, 1957. 449 pp.

Black, C. E. (ed.). *Challenge in Eastern Europe*. New Brunswick: Rutgers University Press, 1954. 276 pp.

Cretzianu, A. *Captive Rumania*. New York: Frederick A. Praeger, 1956. 424 pp.

Dobosiewicz, S. *Our Progress in Education*. Warsaw: Polonia, 1955. 46 pp.

Einaudi, M. *Communism in Western Europe*. Ithaca: Cornell University Press, 1951. 239 pp.

Juhasz, W. *Blueprint for a Red Generation*. New York: Mid-European Studies Center, 1952. 101 pp.

Kautsky, John H. *Moscow and the Communist Party of India*. Cambridge: Technology Press, 1956. 220 pp.

Kracauer, J., and Berkman, P. L. *Satellite Mentality*. New York: Frederick A. Praeger, 1956. 194 pp.

Milosz, C. *The Captive Mind*. New York: Alfred A. Knopf, 1953. 215 pp.

Rossi, A. *A Communist Party in Action*. New Haven: Yale University Press, 1949. 301 pp.

Schmidt, D. A. *Anatomy of a Satellite*. Boston: Little, Brown and Company, 1952. 512 pp.

Schneider, R. M. *Communism in Guatemala, 1944–1954*. New York: Frederick A. Praeger, 1959. 320 pp.

Schwartz, B. I. *Chinese Communism and the Rise of Mao*. Cambridge: Harvard University Press, 1951. 258 pp.

Seton-Watson, H. *East European Revolution*. New York: Frederick A. Praeger, 1951. 406 pp.

Simon, B. *Education in the New Poland*. London: Lawrence Wishart, 1954. 63 pp.

Swearinger, R., and Langer, P. *Red Flag over Japan*. Cambridge: Harvard University Press, 1952. 276 pp.

Ulam, A. *Titoism and the Cominform*. Cambridge: Harvard University Press, 1952. 243 pp.

Wolff, R. L. *The Balkans in Our Time*. Cambridge: Harvard University Press, 1956. 618 pp.

PICTURE CREDITS

INSERT ONE

Page 1. Robert Brown
Page 2. Robert Brown
Lorene Fox
Robert Brown
Page 3. Ruth Dunbar
Ruth Dunbar
Page 4. Ruth Dunbar
Ruth Dunbar
Lorene Fox
Page 5. Ruth Dunbar
Robert Brown
Page 6. Urban Fleege
Ruth Dunbar
Page 7. Ruth Dunbar
Chester Williams
Ruth Dunbar
Page 8. Julian Roth
Urban Fleege

INSERT TWO

Page 1. Murray Lincoln Miller
Page 2. Lorene Fox
Ruth Dunbar
Ruth Dunbar
Page 3. Murray Lincoln Miller
Van Sprang from
Black Star
Page 4. Robert Brown
Robert Brown
Page 5. Chester Williams
Robert Brown
Urban Fleege

Page 6. Julian Roth
Urban Fleege
John Tenny
Page 7. Ruth Dunbar
Robert Brown
Page 8. Ruth Dunbar
Murray Lincoln Miller

INSERT THREE

Page 1. John Tenny
Page 2. John Tenny
John Tenny
Page 3. Julian Roth
Florence Rosenfeld
Page 4. Robert Brown
Page 5. George Bereday
Julian Roth
Julian Roth
Page 6. Ruth Dunbar
Ruth Dunbar
Ruth Dunbar
Page 7. Czechopress from
Black Star
Wide World Photos
Edo Koenig from
Black Star
Page 8. Ruth Dunbar
Lorene Fox

INSERT FOUR

Page 1. Florence Rosenfeld
Page 2. Wide World Photos
Wide World Photos

489

Pressens from
Black Star

Page 3. Robert Brown
Chester Williams

Page 4. Robert Brown

Page 5. Chester Williams
Robert Brown
George Bereday

Page 6. Robert Brown
Julian Roth
Robert Brown

Page 7. Julian Roth
Julian Roth
Florence Heisler

Page 8. Robert Brown
Robert Brown

INDEX

Abacus, 172
Ability grouping, 361–62, 363
Abstract art, 370
Abstracts, 332
Academic Union of Professors, 48
Academy of Pedagogical Sciences, 7, 73, 101, 110, 190, 213, 229, 321–334, 347; activities and publications of, 328–34; aims of, 324; Institute of Artistic Education, 147, 204, 327; Institute of Defectology, 328, 339, 345, 353–56; Institute of Methods of Teaching, 183, 213, 215, 218, 228, 326–27; Institute of the Nationality Schools, 229, 327; Institute of Physical Education and School Hygiene, 166, 203, 327–28; Institute of Psychology, 149, 182, 325–26, 355, 417, 438; Institute of the Theory and History of Pedagogy, 149, 244, 249, 324–25, 326, 380, 427; organization of, 324–28; origin and membership of, 82, 321–24; research institutes of, 324–28
Academy of Sciences, 31, 32, 289–90, 332
Academy of the Social Sciences, 84
Administration, 100–102, 109–15, 138; of higher education, 272–73; kindergarten, 158–59; managing details of, 129–30; and parents' committees, 134–37; relations of, with staff and students,

130–34; and school plans, 128–29; secondary-school, 189; of special education, 338–39; training for, 115–26
Admission, to boarding school, 207, 208; to evening and correspondence courses, 276; to higher educational institutions, 53, 83, 253, 274, 278, 290–91; to institutes, 285; to Komsomol, 396; to medical academies, 287–88; to pedagogical institutes, 296; to Pioneers, 393–94; to preschools, 144; to primary school, 184; to special schools, 365, 366, 368
Adult education, 9, 100
Aesthetic education, 147–49, 327
Afanasenko, E. K., 90
Agricultural training, 103, 104
Agricultural work, 194, 264, 269
Agriculture, Ministry of, 273
Aims of Soviet education, 53–54, 98–99, 141, 159–62, 271, 298, 301, 340, 351, 423
Aksakov, Ivan, 40
Alalia, 355
Albania, 77, 105
Alexander I, 35–37
Alexander II, 41–45
Alexander III, 45–46
Alexandroff, Nikolai, 265
Alexis, Tsar, 27
Algebra, 171, 198, 214
All My Sons (Miller), 404
All-Union Exhibition of Children's Technical Ingenuity, 374

491